ROCKETS AND REVOLUTION

ROCKETS AND REVOLUTION

A Cultural History of Early Spaceflight

MICHAEL G. SMITH

University of Nebraska Press

Lincoln & London

© 2014 by Michael G. Smith

A portion of chapter 6 previously appeared as "Cosmic Plots in Early Soviet Culture: Flights of Fancy to the Moon and Mars," *Canadian-American Slavic Studies* 47 (2013): 170–99. Published by Brill Publishing.

The front cover image—a portion of K. F. Iuon's *New Planet* (1921)—was also featured on the front cover of Richard Stites's *Revolutionary Dreams: Utopian Vision and Experimental Life in the Russian Revolution* (New York: Oxford University Press, 1989). This pathbreaking book, which has inspired my own approach here, is now in its twenty-fifth year of publication.

Library of Congress Cataloging-in-Publication Data
Smith, Michael G., 1960–
Rockets and revolution: a cultural history of early spaceflight / Michael G. Smith.
pages   cm
Includes bibliographical references and index.
ISBN 978-0-8032-5522-7 (hardback: permanent paper)—
ISBN 978-0-8032-8654-2 (epub)—ISBN 978-0-8032-8655-9
(mobi)—ISBN 978-0-8032-8656-6 (pdf) 1. Astronautics—
History. 2. Astronautics and state. 3. Astronautics—Social
aspects. I. Title.
TL788.5.S5835 2014   629.4'10904—dc23   2014024760

Set in Minion Pro by Renni Johnson.

For our sister, Roberta Maria Smith (1949–2007)

Contents

Illustrations

Tables

ROCKETS AND REVOLUTION

Introduction

Have some fun,

Shooting the heavens by rocket.

Chart your own course,

Take a spin along its parabola.

—VLADIMIR MAIAKOVSKII

The exploration of outer space, one of the more dramatic and complex technical achievements of our time, owes much of its success to a scientific paradigm of relatively distant origins: Sir Isaac Newton's third law of motion, "to every action there is always opposed an equal reaction."[1] This simple precept from the seventeenth century, once it was applied to the rocket engine of the twentieth, helped to launch America's Apollo missions to the moon. The conquest of space was not some grand "paradigm shift," some momentous "spaceflight revolution" of our times.[2] It was the result of forces and trends already long at work in our world: in modern astronomy and physics, in artillery ballistics and chemical engineering, in all the many experiments with heavier-than-air flight.

By 1924 Albert Einstein's theories of relativity represented the true new wave in science and were accorded significant debate in the academic and popular press. But Einstein's theories were difficult and obscure. A Newtonian universe made more sense to the average readers of modern science and to the rocketry enthusiasts among them, especially in Russia. One popular Soviet text from 1941 still taught the simple truth that our planet was round, that "up is always up above our heads wherever we are on earth, either in the USSR, or even somewhere in America."[3] The early Russian pioneers appreciated Newton more than Einstein. Theirs was still a mechanical age. Their hopes for rockets and space travel were fueled by his trusted celestial mechanics and differential equations, already over two hundred years old. Any future step toward rocket power first meant a step "backward to Newton" and to the truth of his famous rocket-powered carriage (whose image was widely disseminated in Russia). For his "genius" had been to discover the law of attraction (gravity) that binds us to the earth and the law of force (reaction) that allows us to escape from it.[4] The Russian pioneers understood that there was something uniquely modern about rocket power, something that set the human form itself into motion: enveloped in its machine, liberated by its own power of wonder and reason, placed on a trajectory into outer space. In truth the pioneers of rocketry and spaceflight theory worked between two historical eras: calculating from traditional Newtonian mechanics, if breaking out of its absolute, fixed universe; and moving into the freer, mobile depths of Einstein's relative, curved space.

Rocket propulsion straddled these two worlds, Newton's solar system and Einstein's spherical universe, always pointing upward and forward. Rockets were simple and elegant in design, a streamlined alternative to the rather cumbersome new technologies powering our lives: from steam and combustion to diesel and turbine. The wheel needed land, the steam wheel needed water, and the airplane propeller needed the air. The rocket operated through all three but most efficiently in the vacuum of outer space, without any supporting medium except its own. Its thrust was altogether self-generated and continuous, dependent only upon its own design and mass and upon the chemical and mechanical processes that we human beings had mastered to sustain them. In a moment of rare candor America's premier rocket experimenter, Robert H. Goddard, author of the pioneering *A Method of Reaching Extreme Altitudes* (1920), put it best when he defined the unique character of liquid fuel rockets as "the release of power *from within themselves*." Robert Esnault-Pelterie, one of his rivals in the new field of rocket science, then called "astronautics," honored the rocket as a "self-propelled fuse," the perfect expression of human motion and achievement.[5]

These rocket pioneers translated Newton's calculus into applied geometry, into the very trajectories and parabolas upon which they imagined people moving through space. The scientific mingled with the existential. The modern mind was geometrical, proclaimed Henri Bergson in *Creative Evolution* (1907), read widely in Europe, the Americas, and Russia.[6] "The lines we see traced through matter are just the paths on which we are called to move." The material world was but an ocean "in which we are immersed," he wrote. We are always in flux, masters of the "movement that generates the curve," the curve that is also a "line," a "wave," a "vortex" of human action.[7] Bergson announced the mystic force of an "élan vital," or vital spirit, within us. "All the living hold together," he wrote, calling forth his Newtonian images, "and all yield to the same tremendous push." The task of humanity was to perceive the world of objects in their synthetic wholeness, to divine how "the smallest grain of dust is bound up with our entire solar system." Against "that undivided movement of descent which is materiality itself," human beings were born to act. We were born to give way to that "single impulsion," to fulfill the "overwhelming charge able to beat down every resistance and clear the most formidable obstacles, even death."[8]

The powder fuel fireworks rocket, not yet the liquid fuel space rocket, was one of Bergson's central metaphors for the movement of the human will and intellect through history. Human life was like a rocket, *"creative action which unmakes itself . . .* like the fiery path torn by the last rocket of a fireworks display through the black cinders of the spent rockets that are falling dead."[9] People similarly raced forward into the future, collapsing present into past, at the dynamic interface between life and death. Bergson transformed Newton's rather static model of natural attraction and repulsion into a dynamic model of human "ascent" and material "descent." He called the "ascending movement" an "impetus" and a "leap," a "recoil" and "thrust," corresponding to "an inner work of ripening or creating." Or as he wrote, "Matter . . . is weighted with geometry; and matter, the reality which *descends*, endures only by its connection with that which *ascends*. But life and consciousness are this very ascension."[10] "Creative evolution" was not some horizontal, two-dimensional timeline in space. It was a vertical, three-dimensional curve ascending through history. The human form created itself, sui generis, like the rocket's movement upward.

These values were by no means unique to Bergson. They were already at the heart of the European experience, at one with its "self-consciousness," as René Descartes might have said. *Cogito ergo sum.* Or remember G. W. F. Hegel, who in his lectures on the philosophy of history celebrated the Age of Enlightenment, when "thinking becomes the principle, the thinking proceeding from itself."[11] Human sovereignty came to mean political self-rule, self-regulating markets, and self-evident rights—the modern ideal of "self-determination," be it Karl Marx's "class" or Woodrow Wilson's "nation" or Vladimir Lenin's "party." Friedrich Nietzsche called it our "will to power," embodied in his gravity-defying Zarathustra. Sigmund Freud called it our "sex drive," instinctive in each of us. As Marshall Berman explored in his study of modernity, writers as diverse as Johann Wolfgang von Goethe and Nikolai Chernyshevskii also spoke of the modern spirit as a "self-heightening, self-awakening, self-liberation." The modern world "pours us all into a maelstrom of perpetual disintegration and renewal, of struggle and contradiction, of ambiguity and anguish." To be modern is to be part of a universe in which, as Marx said, in a premonition of the rocket, "all that is solid melts into air."[12] Berman's fields of study were literary criticism and political theory, not modern science; his grounds were city streets and skyscrapers, not rockets. But his expressions and images, again and again, referred to modernity as a mutual striving and hurtling, a propelling and thrusting forward, a plunge into a constantly changing and challenging future. These are the verbal constructs that describe the rocket, that trace a parabolic line through historical time. They express the equations and theorems of modern mathematics and physics. They are the existential moments captured by modern writers in their traumatic story lines, by painters in their abstract designs. They are the very narrative arcs by which we moderns have defined ourselves.

The dramatic technological innovations at the turn of the twentieth century emboldened this ethic of self-creation. Rocket power followed the "automobile" and the "flying machine" as mechanical extensions of the human form, mechanizations of our bodies and cultures. Europeans and Americans crafted a whole new symbolic world to make sense of these invented things, especially the airplane, in a "passion for wings" ascending into the air and into our dreams.[13] At times, in the precise angles and curves of applied geometry, the scientific and the existential mingled with the occult. Some of the leading rocket enthusiasts and pioneers shared a sense of gnostic purpose, as if crafting a whole new structure of space and time and motion, a bridge by which they might escape from a cursed and broken Earth. Their spatial trajectories, as parabolas and hyperbolas, prefigured a teleology at the heart of the European consciousness: moving from ignorance to knowledge, from corruption to salvation. These pioneers were the "sun-snarers," according to H. G. Wells—the "fire-worshippers," as G. E. Langemak termed them. Goddard's own father called him an "angel shooter," as if under the spell of his own rocket creations, entranced by the sky and sun toward which they raced.[14] A few of the rocket pioneers and enthusiasts were even more dedicated. Max Valier, Hermann Oberth, and Jack Parsons actively promoted and participated in occult practices, as if rocketry, mixing chemistry and experiment, was a kind of new magic in motion.

Space exploration had its conflicted origins too. Amid the controversies raised by the publication of Hermann Oberth's book *The Rocket into Planetary Space* (1923), Goddard already predicted "something in the nature of a race" for rocketry.[15] This was nothing so very new. Europe and America had joined such contests before: the race for Africa, for empire, for the North and South Poles, for big battleship navies, eventually for Paris or Berlin. Aviators were already racing for distance, speed, and altitude records. The rocket pioneers worked within these strategic terrestrial and aeronautical paradigms, simply calling for another kind of race: one toward space. The distinction may seem trivial, but this was not yet a race *to* space, a competition to get into space first. Rather, it was more of a race to define the terms and technologies of space travel, to create a brand-new model of rocket science and astronautics, all in a competition *toward* outer space.[16]

Russia enters the story in a dramatic way, a humbling way perhaps for most American audiences. In this race it enjoyed a remarkable series of initial firsts: the first theorist of spaceflight; the first popular monograph on space travel; the first public agency to promote interplanetary travel; the first media images of rockets reaching into space by reaction power and parabolic line; the first world exhibition on spaceflight; the first international language dedicated to spaceflight; the first encyclopedia of spaceflight; the first state institute and conference devoted to "reactive" (jet and rocket) propulsion; and the first theoretical tract on "cosmonautics." These initiatives combined to give Russia what one enthusiast called international primacy in the new field of "reactive astronautics."[17] The USSR was leading the way to rocket science. We have not yet even mentioned *Sputnik*, not to speak of the many other Russian space firsts that followed from it.

The Russian Revolution of 1917 played a critical role in these advantages. Its logic of crisis and resolution presumed a radical break in time, as if everything was now possible. Its intense political and economic development also drove the country's commitment to science and technology. To survive in a fiercely competitive world, impoverished Russia had to match the best achievements of the West. The imperative to race with it was always a function of a partly real, partly perceived sense of inferiority. To borrow a phrase from Louis Althusser, who borrowed it from Leon Trotskii, Russia "was at the same time *the most backward and the most advanced nation*," fraught with severe contradictions but also with unique opportunities.[18] Soviet Russia occupied a backward space on Earth but, thanks to the Russian Revolution, it had moved farther ahead of the historical curve. Its predicament was to catch up, not so much in time as in space, the real physical spaces of machines and military forces, factories and industrial techniques. The very pace of technological change, its interplay between obsolescence and innovation, meant that the backward USSR might be able to outstrip ("catch and surpass") the leading West. Aeronautics and astronautics were all about "tempos." As one Soviet calculus had it, "what today is a world record by tomorrow is already obsolete." Rocket power and space travel offered Russia symbols of advancement as well as measures of geopolitical advantage. Just as it had leaped past the bourgeois to the proletarian revolution, so it might also leap from railroads to rocketry.[19]

Over the span of three tumultuous decades—first around 1914, again in 1924, and once more about 1934—rocketry and space travel became serious topics of public debate. With the new Soviet regime especially, the technocratic strain in Marxist-Leninist ideology added value to both ends and means: the whole universe as an arena of human action and progress, the rocket as machine par excellence. Technology was the premier mark of competitive advantage and strategic power. But ideology also dictated the certainty of war with the capitalist states of Europe and the United States. This theme of class warfare predisposed the regime to see the universe as a site of inevitable conflict and the rocket as a mighty weapon in its arsenal. Aleksandr Beliaev was already fighting the Cold War between Russia and America in his novel *The Struggle in Space* (1928).[20]

At its origins the race toward space was governed by Russia's attraction to, and repulsion from, much that was American, a function of Althusser's historical predicament. In contrast, Walter McDougall's Pulitzer-winning monograph, *Between the Heavens and the Earth*, has argued that the United States first borrowed something of the technocratic and statist impulses from its archrival, the USSR, after the stunning launch of *Sputnik* in 1957. *Sputnik* was the consummate "saltation" in American government policy and national character, forcing it to become something less of a democracy, more of a military-industrial dictatorship, this in order to better compete in the Cold War "race to space."[21] But that is only one in a pair of mirror images. Yes, Americans looked eastward to the Russians, true. But Russians looked westward to the Americans as well. They recognized the values of technocracy, and borrowed them first, from the American experience. McDougall's "saltation" was a turn around more than a turn toward. It was a turn back to ourselves, to the model of technocratic efficiency that the Soviets already imagined us to be.

The history of Russian and American competition in rocketry and space exploration is in this sense a history of language barriers.

The Russians broached their language barrier first. They were reading about us (in the 1920s and 1930s) long before we were reading about them. For them this was a long-term advantage, to be engaged in a race toward space that the other side hardly valued at all. Few Americans and Europeans read or spoke Russian; little reliable news came out of the country soon after the revolution. As a result, the West understood Russia poorly at best. "The image of pre-Sputnik Russia," one historian has written, "was that it was populated with heavy-bearded Moujikas [peasants] and with scientists possessing no unique scientific or technological know-how."[22] Americans saw little threat in Soviet Russia. They broached their language barrier much later, after *Sputnik*, during the classic eras of the race to space and moon race and arms race in the 1960s and 1970s.

Both interventions are fraught with mistranslations and misunderstandings. Both remain incomplete. Besides McDougall's, we have some fine models of "comparative history."[23] Building on their notable achievements, my research methods for this work have been to read widely: including periodicals, scientific tracts, poetry, literature, and political essays. This book is more a free history of ideas than a strict history of science; more a broad history of popular culture than a study of "science and technology." Science without the culture does not make much sense. By the turn of the century they were invading each other's realms. This work could have easily become reductive, focused on what were rather peripheral and obscure issues in their day. But the sources themselves constantly offered correctives, drawing the topic out into wider and deeper contexts: how the rocket was a product of worldwide innovations in science and industry; how it was intimately connected to issues of war and peace, life and death; how it was a metaphor for humanity's ascending place in the cosmos.

The rocket appeared in scientific designs and public discourses at a time when a whole variety of new machines served as "metaphors and analogues for changing structures of life and thought." Writers and artists took the X-ray as a metaphor for their own power to understand inner truths. They saw the airplane as a symbol of overcoming space and time.[24] As I explore here, they also saw the rocket as just such a machine metaphor, a window onto such enduring mysteries as the origins of life and the existence of other worlds. Rocketry's lines of motion, its circles and ellipses, its parabolas and hyperbolas, were narrative arcs, integrating two related discourses: the first on interplanetary travel (the conquest of space) and the second on human immortality (the conquest of time). They were fables about the human past and future, about our capacity to create the artificial envelope of the rocket fuselage in order to pierce the natural envelopes of the atmosphere and gravity and even immortality.

The rocket's parabola, that far sloping line reaching from Earth into outer space, is the central theme of this book. It was one of the great fictions of the modern era. The planets and most comets, after all, fly in elliptical or hyperbolic orbits. The parabola is a rare trajectory for any heavenly body.[25] Yet for space enthusiasts and publicists it was a powerful symbol. It represented escape velocity, the curve at which humanity freed itself from Earth's gravity, at the crucial velocity of 6.95 miles, or 11.2 kilometers, per second. Here was a symbol of humanity's self-created reach for infinity and eternity: the parabola's focal point (perigee) at the center of the earth; its farthest point (apogee) nothing more than the rocket itself, racing along through the vacuum of space. It became the perfect arrow, that human saltation, or "leap," through space and time: the German *vorstoss* or the French *saut* or the Russian *pryzhok*. It was also an image widely featured in the twentieth-century's historical timelines, as if humanity was now moving both upward and forward, a culminating point as much for the capitalist West as for the communist East. The parabolic arc was a reflection of both a visionary technology (rocket power) and a transformational biology (evolutionary theory). It appealed to space as a forum for human action, involving a new optics (spectroscopy) and even a new linguistics ("interplanetary communication").

The Russian Revolution and its legacies at once humble, complicate, and enlighten the history. The triumphs of Cold War rhetoric, the pomp and circumstance of the race to space, too often exaggerate both Russia's and America's dizzying successes and dramatic failures. Big events and personalities crowd out the nuances of historical fact. We need instead, through the prism of the Russian Revolution, to maximize the historical, to reach back in a broader interpretive reading of genesis and structure. What counts are less the grand facts and persons, more the relations and contexts between them. What counts are not so much priorities and lineages as plural origins and contexts. What counts are not countries pitted against each other, more the translation of scientific and technical values between them.

Recent glasnost and post-Soviet memoirs play a corroborative role here. The new archival discoveries and revelations have been useful. But my central arguments come straight out of published literature long available in the United States and the USSR. This book could have been written fifty years ago.[26] That it was not owes much to the capacity of science, at least as a public phenomenon and historical exercise, sometimes to obscure as much as to illuminate. The translation and reception of its values has been far from perfect. Russian books and articles have revealed, for example, the depths and dimensions of Russian achievement previously held in secret. Yet they were in large part compromised by the Soviet victory culture after *Sputnik* or by the setback of failing to reach the moon. They were tied to a cycle of rhetoric and polemic in the American-Russian rivalry of the Cold War. They posed as valid and objective historical accounts. They told truths. But they were half-truths.

Only a comparative, global history will do, one that integrates the Russian, the European, and the American contributions to rocketry and spaceflight theories in their mutual influence and interplay. As just such an approach, this book offers a study of the universal and of the particular: rocket science and the Russian Revolution. Nothing was perhaps more universal in the interwar years, or has been since, than rocket science. It empowered the liquid fuel rocket as a means of traveling into interplanetary space and its twin, the ballistic missile, as a measure of superpower status and intercontinental reach. These were the technologies that could not be contained or monopolized, at least among the great powers. Their character was essentially the same, based on the universal truths of modern physics. Yet rocket science also had its basis in the particular, in the national values and histories of the new rocket states. It took on varied forms, pursued different objectives, embodied distinct values.

Nothing was more particular, more determined by a specific place and time, than the Russian Revolution of 1917, that momentous event locked together by a chain of causes and effects, actions and reactions. Yet the Russian Revolution also made its appeals to the universal: to the totality of Marxist dialectical materialism through history and across the globe. This book meets at the confluence of these several universals and particulars.

Priority does count. It counted for the rocket pioneers and enthusiasts, for their political patrons, and for their reading publics. This was not so much a question of who would get to space first but who accomplished what first. Before the actual achievements of space travel, the retrospective counted most. Who was the true "father" of rocket science? Who invented the basics of spaceflight theory? Who launched the first successful liquid fuel, continuous exhaust rocket? Russian and American and European writers disputed these questions. They were part and parcel of this contentious race toward space, this universal moment of "multiples," of nearly simultaneous discoveries and inventions in rocketry and spaceflight theory. As the three rocket pioneers—Konstantin Tsiolkovskii, Robert Goddard, and Hermann Oberth—discovered each other's names and works, they retreated ever more into the assurances of their own priority. Each believed that he alone was the founder of modern rocketry, his innovations the brilliant result of individual enterprise and national character. In a simple act of division, these three men separated the national from the global. But we can safely rule out extraordinary genius. None of these thinkers was self-made. No one ever really is. The wide and narrow dimensions of the topic, the universal and the particular, teach us that questions of priority were also questions of perspective—not any one perspective, except perhaps at this moment of achievement or that, but of all perspectives fit together, like a jigsaw puzzle, or more abstractly, like a multidimensional game of chess, re-created from the last moves to the first. The history of the first space age must become a history of perspectives, of universals through particulars, of the whole through its parts.

France, for example, offers us one of the essential perspectives, somewhat lost in the historiography. Its writers set a pace of futuristic thinking about humanity's role in the cosmos. First among them was the influential publicist Camille Flammarion, more poet than scientist, though recognized as both. He took European and American readers to space, an imagined Newtonian tour of the solar system, long before twentieth-century technology ever did. His science was astronomy, not physics. His technologies were telescopes and spectroscopes, not rockets. He also established the body of scientific evidence on the "plurality thesis": against the "smallness" and inhospitality of Earth, but a "speck of dust," Flammarion posited the "vastness" and "unity" and "infinity" of the universe, a great "ocean" bursting with life, prosperity, and abundance. His works were self-consciously bold, beginning with his multi-edition *The Plurality of Inhabited Worlds* (1862), stirring the popular imagination about the future with literary inventions from the past, all at the exciting boundaries of modern science.[27]

The American and Russian competition for rocketry and space travel was predicted, coincidentally enough, in several of the first and most popular science-fiction treatments: works by the Frenchmen Jules Verne, Georges Le Faure, and Henri de Graffigny. When these writers imagined the race toward space, they looked not so much to France but farther West and farther East. They imagined the Americans and Russians getting there first. Jules Verne's *From the Earth to the Moon* (1865) sent the Americans to space first, under the patronage of Impey Barbican and the Baltimore Gun Club. They were the practical engineers and cannon makers, representing human action as both a life-giving and life-destroying force. Much of the story was dedicated to long soliloquies on artillery themes: ballistics, trajectories, and chemical mixtures. Yet old Europe, in the character of Michel Ardan, offered the Americans more scientific means and ends: all the precise calculations of air resistance, gravitational pulls, and propulsive force. A pacifist and humanist, Ardan reconfigured the cannon for peace, turning it into more of a rocket, a "cylindro-conical" shell, to fly by Newton's laws beyond the planet. He was also a visionary. The earth was not a prison but a platform. Human history was not a closed circle of eternal returns but an outward, ever-ascending, and opening spiral, a trajectory pointing to the living heavens. Ardan was the master mathematician who calculated the differential equations of mass and velocity, what Verne later called the parabolic and hyperbolic "open curves" reaching into the infinities of outer space. The spacecraft, in sum, was a new Earth, a "fiery meteor" racing through "the oceans of space."[28]

From the Earth to the Moon followed upon Verne's own recent science fiction successes, with stories of balloon travels and journeys to the planet's core, amid a continuing European interest in the possibilities of inhabited worlds beyond Earth. He was at one with a long and hallowed literary tradition of "fantastic" and "extraordinary voyages," from the ancient Greeks to the present, one of whose favorite settings was the ethereal "ocean" of interplanetary space. As the most extraordinary of "extraordinary voyages," space travel became a quintessential kind of science fiction. It was an expression of human activity and exploration, a way into the future or into new territories, always beyond ourselves, sometimes coming back too.[29] Verne understood the power of sensational "space" news stories, such as the infamous "Moon Hoax" of 1835, to grip readers and sell newspapers.[30] With many elite European readers of his day, Verne also appreciated the modern view of the universe embedded in Alexander von Humboldt's influential *Cosmos* (1845). Humboldt had offered an elegant, scientific survey of "the sidereal and terrestrial phenomena of the cosmos in their empirical relations," one "embracing all created things in the regions of space and in the Earth." But it was also eminently readable and cinematic, figuratively journeying from outer space down to our planet and back again: "from the remotest nebulae and from the revolving double stars, we have descended to the minutest organisms of animal creation." Earth became, for Humboldt, a wonderful "cosmical island," a jewel within the greater cosmic "ornament" and "order" of the universe."[31]

This space setting, part imagined and part real, became a powerful metaphor by the twentieth century, an indispensable means for both science and fiction. It was the site for new theories on the origins of life on Earth, the "biosphere." It was a place of imagination and discovery, the field upon which the liquid fuel rocket was meant to move. For the Russians the "ethereal ocean" represented multiple meanings. The United States and outer space became for them the same kind of place, the same object of longing. One was discovered; the other was yet to be. One was far across the Atlantic Ocean; the other was the last great ocean of discovery. Both were sites of technological innovation and challenge, of order and chaos, mysteries that unlocked the way forward through history. In a bold act of historical telescoping, Russians peered out upon the planet and into outer space, bringing both distance and the future up close. Historical progress and the planets now seemed within easy reach. Russia's peripheral vision, admiring the West from its geographical and politico-economic edge, became a double vision, seeing its own future and fulfillment both on the planet and beyond it.

The Russians, according to the French, went even farther into outer space than the Americans, as was the case for Georges Le Faure and Henri de Graffigny's *The Extraordinary Adventures of a Russian Savant* (1888–96). Its initial setting was the exotic Russia of Orthodox cupolas and unwashed peasant masses. Mikhail Vasilievich Osipov, professor of astronomy, member of the Russian Academy of Sciences and of the "Aerial Navigation Society," led its expeditions to the moon and the planets beyond. "You may be surprised to know, dear sir," said Osipov to one of his French protégés, "that Russia is no longer a country of savages" but of the most advanced science. And he went on to prove it. Flammarion wrote the preface to the work, lending it the mark of his academic authority, applauding its scientific foundations built on astronomy, its survey of a living universe full of splendor and wonder.[32] Threaded with the melodrama of extreme travels and alien encounters, the trips were also based on smart scientific facts and a host of amazing techniques: solar energy drives, chemical food pastes, pressurized space suits, parachutes, fuel cells for light-based telecommunications, solar sails, light-metal spaceships, flying saucers, and space balloons. Most impressive was an interplanetary, cigar-shaped spacecraft (called the *Molniia*, for "lightning strike"), something like a rocket, which used an internal tube to engage and expel the debris of an asteroid, propelling itself by way of reactive force. A Russian invention, it reached the greatest speeds, up to eighty-five kilometers (fifty-three miles) a second.

With these pioneering French works, science fiction—what the English called "scientific romance," what the Russians called "scientific fantasy"—became a series of conversations between the writers themselves, between the writers and scientists, and between journalists and their reading publics. Theirs were dialogues across national boundaries and over several generations. They set standards of imitation and innovation, some parts borrowed, other parts new. This was also a kind of literary concordance of popular science, an archive of scientific personalities, facts, and possibilities that belonged to all of humanity. These items were cross-referenced between national presses, tucked into small news stories, what the journal *Science* grudgingly called "newspaper science"—a phenomenon soon enshrined in the beloved Sunday supplement. The turn of the century literally saw the appearance of a new "global mass culture that was obsessed with technological conquest and scientific alteration of space," as Anindita Banerjee has phrased it. It followed upon the rise of a worldwide industrial and commercial economy, markets joined by sea lanes and railroads, by communication lines and worldwide media networks (newspapers and magazines).[33]

European and American audiences were primed for more and more stories about interplanetary travel, "cosmic romances," stories bridging fiction and fact. That bridge, so well refined by Verne, was what made the stories believable. Readers wanted not to suspend belief but to anticipate it. Science fiction was a gauge of the popular attraction to the real. It made the seemingly impossible become real, "the improbable seem true."[34] The common presumption of the day was that science fiction was fast becoming science fact, that modern people first fancied and imagined new worlds of science and technology before they actually created them. As Robert Goddard put it most dramatically, in the conclusion to his graduation speech at South High School in Worcester, Massachusetts, on 24 June 1904: "The dream of yesterday is the hope of today and the reality of tomorrow." Or as the magazine *Amazing Stories* later advertised: "Extravagant Fiction Today . . . Cold Fact Tomorrow."[35] Here was the great conceit (and cliché) of most of the pioneers and enthusiasts of the space age. At the margins of the new mass media of the twentieth century, through science fiction and popular science, scientists and engineers were turning their truths into a modern kind of alchemy. It was as if time no longer mattered, as if writers conjured up facts from fictions, as if the rocket pioneers drafted their engineering designs from pulp novels, as if the breakthroughs of the modern world were somehow the miraculous inventions of the imaginative mind alone. But these writers and their readers, especially the rocketry pioneers among them, were a bit too consumed by the cycle of scientific and technological innovation. They forgot that the science and invention came first. They mistook the historical cycle for a narrative arc, with their own wondrous imaginings as a genesis point.

The conceits were not without some merit. The turn of the twentieth century was a revolutionary moment, at least in the self-perceptions of many who lived through it, who were beholding a new scientific "community of knowledge." This was a way of doing science that crossed boundaries: between the empirical and the fictional, between the elite and the democratic, between the intellectual and the commercial, between this nation or that. The great novelty of the age, its true "innovation" (*novum*), was science itself.[36] It celebrated how scientists and engineers created new ideas and things; how science writers, through either fact or fiction, reported and extrapolated from them; how readers of popular science and science fiction anticipated every new word and promise, be it ultimately true or false; how politicians interpreted and applied the new science and technology to governance. All of these venues helped people to imagine new historical possibilities, even radical alternatives to the present. Science was more than a way to knowledge or a kind of literature. It was a field of action upon which seemingly everyone could participate: the scientists and engineers who made some of it come true, the writers who reproduced or preordained it, the readers who consumed it, the politicians who made it their own. Modern science put people into motion and kept them moving, like the rocket.

PART ONE

The Surveillance of Outer Space
and the Russian Empire

1

Envisioning the Biological Universe

By the late nineteenth century interplanetary travel was still a matter of imaginative visions more than of any actual machines. It was about grand lines of ascent rather than plotted trajectories. In these ways it shared some traits with revolution. Rocket science lined its arrows upward into space the way revolution lined its arrows forward through time. They both appreciated leaps and bounds. This marriage between rockets and revolution also returns us to the very origins of the term *revolution* in modern usage, to the astronomical innovations of Nicolaus Copernicus and Johannes Kepler, Galileo Galilei and Isaac Newton. Their work displaced our planet from the center of the universe, transforming it into one part of the greater sum of celestial mechanics, one of many possible worlds. But their work also put the earth into motion. In some of its earliest scientific and political contexts, as in the case of Copernicus's classic *On the Revolutions of the Heavenly Bodies, revolution* meant either the ordered trajectories of the heavenly bodies or the similarly ordered pattern of bodies politic. To the modern mind planets and people move according to the predictable laws of nature, joining the natural with the social, bound to "Newton's concept of absolute space and time," to the tension of "action and reaction" near and far.[1]

Leo Tolstoi expressed the insight at the conclusion of *War and Peace* (1869), offering a Copernican revolution for historiography, displacing the notion of an absolute hero along with the fiction of a stationary earth. Newton's laws, he proposed, applied to human history as much as to the steam engine. The proper material of history writing was not any one king or conqueror, any one abstraction of power or progress, but the complex of coincident forces and circumstances. History happened within the dense relations between people, positioned within space and through time, balanced however precariously between "freedom and necessity." Free will was a human force like the natural force of gravity, holding people together and moving history in relative freedom, just as gravity held the planets together and moved them by the laws of attraction.[2]

At the turn of the twentieth century, supported by the recent technical advances in telescopes and spectroscopes, along with the new field of astrophysics (the study of the chemical and physical properties of the planets), the Copernican Revolution and Newtonian universe were just becoming fully present to a mass readership.[3] They were the intellectual foundations for a new planetary consciousness. The mechanical heavens and Earth joined within a well-ordered creation, guided by movements both traceable and sure. Yet the cyclical was also giving way to the linear, ancient revolutions to modern evolution, simple movement to complex progress. Within these contexts the academic and popular media began to debate the possibilities of alien life and space travel. This discourse was by no means neat or fixed. Commentators often confused images of cyclical evolution and linear progress, historical pessimism with revolutionary optimism. But through all of this the media consensus held that human beings were in some measure an integral and conscious part of the wider cosmos.

Narrative Arcs of Nature and Culture

Comets remained something of an exception in these scientific frameworks. To be sure, they were part of the elliptical revolutions of the planets and stars. They were at one with the cosmology that placed the earth within the dome of skies and heavens, mapping "the vault of the clouds and the stellar vault as parallel curves," as "flattened arches bending down to the horizon."[4] But comets also strayed dramatically at all angles from the regular orbital planes of the planets. They flew above and beyond, "the Comet like a Rocket to be shot out of the Sun." Their lines of motion seemed to taunt us just as the vaulted lines of the stars seemed to imprison us. Publicists had traditionally assigned deep political meanings to comets, portents of divine intervention in the rise and fall of solar systems, dynasties, and states. Even Isaac Newton and Edmund Halley judged "comets as harbingers of cataclysmic events and World reform," as overturnings of either the heavenly or terrestrial. Calling up the traditional view of comets as signs of impending doom, Thomas Malthus wrote that the French Revolution of 1789, "like a blazing comet, seems destined either to inspire with fresh life and vigour, or to scorch up and destroy the shrinking inhabitants of the Earth."[5]

Observers took in Halley's comet, and the associated "Great Daylight" comet of 1910, in much the same way, as a sign of coming catastrophe. Newspapers around the world (from London to Tokyo, New York to Moscow) reported scenarios of mass destruction, including death by poisoning and suffocation from the deadly potassium chloride gas of the comet's tail. The media frenzy peaked on 17 May, as Europe waited into the night for the earth to pass through the comet's wake. None of the worst ever happened, of course. Halley's comet was more a sign of land-bound events, namely the burgeoning global culture of popular science and media panic, fixed upon a phenomenon of worldwide dramatic scope from above, with many mainstream scientists joining the fray.[6]

Flammarion's popular novel *The End of the World* (1893) had fed the expectation of doom, in a captivating story about a "green-colored comet" come "from the depths of space" to boil the seas over their banks, bury millions of people alive, or suffocate them to death with poisonous fumes. Set in a twenty-fifth century of magnificent progress, in a sense mirroring Flammarion's own world, the pathos of the story was that humanity could not avoid political cataclysms of its own creation, the wars and revolutions of its past, any more than it could avoid natural cataclysms, the return of a comet too close to the earth. Readers of the French popular science magazine *I Know All* (*Je sais tout*) were treated to such scenarios: how even progressive political revolutions on the planet were eclipsed by the destructive powers of inscrutable cosmic revolutions.[7] One enterprising Russian writer, S. Bel'skii, borrowed from Flammarion's timeline in his own fantasy, *Under the Comet* (1910), to warn that all the hopes of European civilization, present and future, could not escape the comet's impact. In the ensuing panic and mass destruction "all of humanity would be scattered into its basest living parts, like grains of sand torn about by a storm." "The fate of humanity," after all, "follows the orbit of the Earth and of the stars." According to one testimony, many people came to believe these prophecies. During the partial eclipse of the sun in April 1912, visible in St. Petersburg and adjoining provinces, bystanders from every walk of life gathered on the streets as if on a "religious pilgrimage," enshrouded in darkness, witnesses to a "mystical" event: "doomsday."[8]

By the time of the Russian Revolutions of 1905 and 1917, the term *revolution* also suggested an event of singular transformative depth, not so much a catastrophe from above as an upturning of political power from below.[9] The new meanings spoke to the power of human agency through history, humanity made new, as its own kind of natural cause. For Russian Social Democrats, nature enabled culture; the laws of historical materialism were the necessary precondition for human action. Or as one revolutionary put it, paraphrasing Newton on the "parallelogram of historical forces": the "wheel of history" moved within and along the path of two parallel lines, right and left. The model presumed that for every action there was possible an equal and opposite reaction. This demanded a maximal program of revolutionary will and action: revolution against counterrevolution. People and parties needed to force historical change. For all the influence of G. W. F. Hegel's complex dialectic (thesis, antithesis, synthesis) upon Russian revolutionary thinkers, Newton's theories offered a simpler push and pull.[10]

Marxist historical determinism posed a scenario of movement and process, of expectation and result. The French Revolution offered Russians a classic trajectory. Its events were a distant horizon for Russian revolutionaries, more of mythic weight than of any tactical or strategic significance. The symbols did count, however, as in the case of the "solar myth" of the revolution, expressing the millenarian victory of light over dark, new over old, life over death. It had astronomical scope. It was pristine: part natural science and protoreligion, part Isaac Newton and Maximilien Robespierre. After the

ENVISIONING THE BIOLOGICAL UNIVERSE

revolution, according to the myth, "what emerges is empty space, a free horizon. . . . Homogenous and 'isotropic' like the space of the new celestial mechanics, open in all directions to the universal force of gravity."[11] The young Georgian radical I. V. Dzhugashvili (Stalin) tapped into the myth in 1905, when he wrote that "the Russian revolution is inevitable. It is as inevitable as the rising of the sun." This was just a few years after he had been looking up to the heavens by night, as a meteorological recorder and astronomical observer at the Tiflis Geophysical Observatory, meanwhile conspiring for the overthrow of the tsar by day. "We had to keep awake all night and make observations at stated intervals with the help of intricate instruments," remembered one of his comrades. "The work demanded great nervous concentration and patience."[12] Until his appointment as commissar of nationalities during the October Revolution of 1917, this was Stalin's first real job: as meteorologist and astronomer. The message from his future biographers was clear enough. He began his career as something of a scientist, so they claimed, with all the virtues of a patient watcher of the skies.

Stalin's choice of reading material to prepare for his job was telling. He had probably read Flammarion and other mainstream popular science texts, perhaps while watching the skies from his post at the observatory. We know that he read one of J. Norman Lockyer's old classics, *Astronomy* (1876), an international best seller, translated into German and French, Italian and Russian. Stalin could have purchased something much less challenging, one of the dozen or so lowbrow astronomy texts on the market. But he chose a scholarly treatment, his introduction to the truths and timelines of the "Cosmos." Lockyer's was a comprehensive and readable survey of recent findings: including the spectral studies of the sun and planets and stars; their magnitudes and positions and kinds; the facts of the solar system; the measurements of time and the predictability of eclipses and cosmic phenomena. Here was a prideful inventory of humanity's latest discoveries about the planet and its place in the universe around it.[13]

All of this new knowledge must have been intellectually thrilling to the young Stalin, only recently liberated from his rote studies and

ritual devotions in the Orthodox seminary. For many Social Democrats, propositions about alien worlds helped to shatter the authority
of the Russian Orthodox Church and Tsarist state. Popular astronomy meant progressive astronomy with a political-philosophical
edge. Romantic youth and political radicals shared a self-professed
"faith" in science and politics as the means and ends of transformative change. Stalin was joining the thousands of Russians interested
in this "leap" in human consciousness.[14]

All varieties of the political spectrum entertained this leap. The
progressive Auguste Comte entertained it with his positivist take
on contemporary astronomy, what he considered as the most modern of sciences and a convenient weapon against Christian theology
and the church. The astronomer Ormsby M. Mitchel entertained it
as well: with his lecture series and popular book *The Orbs of Heaven*
(1851), translated into an influential Russian edition. Mitchel took
his readers on a grand "journey" through the "blue ocean of space."
Earth was the planetary shore upon which humanity gazed out at
the planets, through which man "boldly wings his flight to the star-
lit vault."[15] The human being was, thanks to the latest science and
technology, already becoming something of a comet, a wanderer in
space. Like us, comets moved in willful ways. "They come up from
below the plane of the ecliptic, or plunge downwards towards the
sun from above, sweep swiftly round this their great centre, and with
incredible velocity wing their flight far into the fathomless regions
of space."[16] Astronomy, Mitchel taught, was essentially a science of
the revolutions of the planets and comets and stars, the mathematical computation of their orbits and motions through the "four beautiful curves" of circles, ellipses, parabolas, and hyperbolas. These
were not yet rocket trajectories, but they were already pathways for
human calculation and imagination about the great "island universes" and other worlds of the cosmos. The trend in human history was in fact pointed toward these plural worlds. The "onward,
steady, triumphant march of mind," was even "godlike" in applying its "highest energies" in the quest to "unfold the mysteries of
the stars." Human history took the shape of a "self-built pyramid"
pointed toward outer space.[17]

Like many of their colleagues in astronomy, Lockyer and Mitchel were appealing to a new *paradigm of magnification*. It was the perfect device for Flammarion's "plurality of worlds" thesis. The microscope and telescope offered science new perspectives on inner and outer spaces, on atoms and solar systems. Lockyer and his colleagues now placed a metaphysical scope upon the earth, transfixing this insignificant planet into something truly grand. It was but "a small planet traveling round a small star." The "whole solar system," wrote Lockyer, was "but a mere speck in the universe—an atom of sand on the shore, a drop in the infinite ocean of space." Yet as David Starr Jordan, president of Stanford University, later put it, that universe was "so finely put together, so delicately adjusted, so eternally interdependent, that the smallest of all its parts is as large as the largest."[18] F. S. Gruzdev's popular astronomy adapted such an approach for Russian audiences, if with a tone of excessive optimism. Although "just a speck of dust in comparison with the whole universe," we were well along the way to becoming "complete masters" of nature.[19]

Science was beginning to draw lines outward to an infinite panorama of planets and stars. They were joined together in a sequence of creation seemingly within human understanding and reach. More and more popular science and science fiction stories now took their readers toward the planets, with the common scene of Earth receding from view, Mars or Venus coming into focus on approach, whole new continents and landscapes seen for the first time from space. Human beings suddenly became "inhabitants of the terrestrial globe," wrote one Russian journalist. We became planetary beings, or "earthlings."[20] This new relativistic view shrank the human being and earth into mere specks of existence. But the space voyage ennobled as much as it humbled. Its parabolic itineraries set people on course, gave them depth perspective, a new field of vision. It magnified us as approaching travelers, diminished us as receding ones, always a function of accelerated movement. Humanity became a measure of the universe's distant spaces, of its existential orders of magnitude, carried along in a spacecraft, a new microcosm amid the macrocosm of outer space.

According to this paradigm, to magnify was to delimit and enlarge, all with one sweep of the scoping eye. Outer space was a function of optics before it was a function of rockets. The French artist Odilon Redon captured this truth in his sketch *The Eye, like a Strange Balloon, Moves toward Infinity* (1882), an eyeball balloon peering and rising toward the heavens. Innovative planetariums and observatories, such as Berlin's Urania (1888), literally screened the heavens, offering panoramic views of the actual sky as well as dramatic spectacles on the origin and evolution of the universe. Louis Bonnier turned our gaze earthward with his massive globe exhibit for the Paris World's Fair (1900), encased in a spiral ramp around which we human beings were meant to orbit and observe, as if from space. Charles Woodridge graced his "perfect" city (1902) with a massive parabolic dome, housing a hall of astronomy and observatory aligned to the planets and stars; celebrating Copernicus, father of the new sun-centered astronomy and "unity of space." All these spheres were artificial planets of a kind, emblematic of humanity's conquest over the elements. They were human-made terrestrial envelopes, precursors to the artificial envelopes of balloons and dirigibles that soon enabled us to overcome the natural envelopes of gravity and air.[21]

As the plurality thesis took greater hold among mainstream scientists, dissenters took exception. Most notably, Alfred North Wallace's *Man's Place in the Universe* (1903) asserted that the earth was rare. Our solar system was located at the center of the universe, ours the lone inhabited planet within it. The chances for life elsewhere, given Earth's unique circumstances and the delicacy of life itself, were small indeed.[22] From Russia the conservative Nikolai N. Strakhov had already launched such a critique some thirty years earlier. His thoughtful book *The World as One* (1873) argued against the "plurality of worlds," argued for this terrestrial "world as a whole," a singular, interdependent, structured world unto itself. Humanity took up the "central role" in all of nature. "The human being is the summit of all nature, the node of all existence," wrote Strakhov, "the principal essence and principle phenomenon and principle organ of all life." The human being, in other words, was the "thinking organism," the sum product of natural history.[23]

Strakhov refused to extrapolate from modern astronomy into metaphysical theories about the plurality of worlds and extrater-

ENVISIONING THE BIOLOGICAL UNIVERSE

restrial life. He refused to "discuss creatures about whom we have no exact knowledge and with whom we cannot enter into any relations."[24] That kind of speculation was but crass romanticism, in his estimation, like that of the spiritualists, who presumed to communicate with ghosts and aliens. "We fly away in thought to the happy inhabitants of the planets so as to take a rest from the very tedium and melancholy of our own earthly existence." We populate the planets with our own dreams, our own historical "utopias" (like the lost city of Atlantis), partly out of disappointment with our own selves, partly out of an innate quest for space and time horizons of our own making. These dreams were the rightful material of philosophers and writers but not yet of scientists—for science revealed but "one planet adorned with life, all the others empty and silent."[25]

In an interesting digression from Wallace, but altogether appropriate for his own context of a Tsarist Russia increasingly hobbled by populists and radicals, Strakhov made all of this political. Meditating on the plurality of worlds was not just the folly of utopian dreamers. It was also the scandal of the Russian revolutionary movement, the "political fanatics" who plotted to overturn established traditions and orders for their own abstract, alien ideals. Political revolution, like the intellectual revolution about inhabited planets beyond, was a perversion, a revolt against the very nature of life and history.[26] Strakhov the Slavophile, the fierce defender of the Tsarist political and cultural order, was prescient enough. He saw the subversive power of an idea: the play between life revolving upon other worlds and political revolutions here on Earth.

Timelines of Evolution and Revolution

Besides his status as one of the world's foremost astronomers, Lockyer was also a leading patron of scientific and social Darwinism. This was no coincidence. After all, Charles Darwin's theory of evolution, following Newton, confirmed a model universe governed by predetermined laws. Evolution was doing for history and time what gravitation had already done for motion and space.[27] Astronomy already had its own evolutionary scheme: the "nebular hypothesis" of Immanuel Kant and Pierre-Simon Laplace, still a favorite interpretation at the turn of the century, which held that our solar system first evolved out of the radiating heat and cooling contractions of a great gaseous cloud of stellar materials. This was the cosmic dust from which we all came and, rather bleakly, to which we would all return. Spectroscopic studies had found the essential elements of life throughout the solar system: in hydrogen and carbon, nitrogen and oxygen. Science presumed that if evolution was universal, given the proper chemical combinations, life elsewhere was eminently possible too, in one form or another.[28]

All of this implied, to one degree or another, that nature was its own creator, its own self-contained creation. Evolution made humanity, not any one or more acts of godly creation. Russian radicals, under the sway of the positivism and scientism of Auguste Comte and Herbert Spencer, received Darwinism as part of their new "religion of humanity." "Man is a worm" (*Chelovek-cherviak*) was their chant. They meant it quite literally, according to the model of "spontaneous generation," which held that the human being had descended through worms, if only to become a worm unto other men. Such reason and secularism raised a powerful barrage against the alleged superstitions and rituals of the Russian Orthodox Church. In his well-known memoir Semen Kanatchikov recalled his first contact with the theory of evolution as "the beginning of my apostasy," unnerving him "as if a piece of thin, cold steel was being thrust into [his brain]." He told the story of one propaganda lesson for workers: to fill a box with soil, apparently lifeless dirt. "Then put the box in a warm place for about two weeks, and you'll see that without fail worms or little insects will begin to appear there. . . . And then other creatures will begin to develop from the creatures, and so on. . . . And, in the course of four, five, maybe even ten thousand years, man himself will emerge."[29]

Developments in the natural sciences created a powerful field of secular enlightenment thought, a frame of reference linking the earth and heavens, the evolution of humanity with the evolution of the solar system, possibly even with an inhabited universe. The British atheist and social Darwinist William Winwood Reade was perhaps the most influential writer along these lines. His popular work

ENVISIONING THE BIOLOGICAL UNIVERSE

The Martyrdom of Man (1872) saw over a dozen English-language editions by 1900. In Reade's conception history was cyclical, based on the foundational principle of attraction and repulsion, "the primeval 'Pull and Push,' which lay at the basis of all Nature's operations." But history was also linear, thanks to us, turning the circles into more of a spiral. Reade traced human history from the time of the ancient empires and religions, culminating in the present age of European-inspired democracy. Drawing from the immense powers of "Science," we humans would eventually subdue all of "Nature," even come to predict our future, just as science predicted the routine orbits of the planets and the regular appearances of comets. Humans had the power to turn evolutionary forces from the passive to the active, from mundane circles to progressive lines. This meant turning natural into historical revolutions, overturning traditions and institutions. The revolutionary impulse came from within human history, however violent and costly in human lives, in the "martyrdom of man." Past tragedies such as the French Revolution or future tragedies such as the overthrow of institutional Christianity were necessary for progress.

Reade's survey of natural history, mixing Lockyer's astronomy and Darwin's evolutionary theory, was even more compelling. We humans had always been amphibians, he posited, living between water and land, land and air, organic life having first risen out of the "primeval sea" as "ambiguous specks of matter" formed from chemical reactions powered by the all-encompassing sun. We ultimately came from the ocean of space, borne out of the furnace of stars, according to the Kant-Laplace theory. It was to that great ocean of space that we were now to return, as navigators. Human beings were about to conquer the natural world, rise to new Promethean heights, even control the realms of air and space, master life and death, explore new worlds beyond. As Reade argued, in a stunning display of modern hubris: "Disease will be extirpated; the causes of decay will be removed; immortality will be invented. And then, the earth being small, mankind will migrate into space, and will cross the airless Saharas which separate planet from planet, and sun from sun. The earth will become a Holy Land which will be visited by pilgrims from all the quarters of the universe. Finally, men will master the forces of Nature; they will become themselves architects of systems, manufacturers of worlds. Man then will be perfect; he will then be a creator; he will therefore be what the vulgar worship as a god."[30]

Most philosophers engaged these questions with more modesty. Ernst Haeckel's works, widely published in the West and in Russia, defined terrestrial evolution as part of a grand ascending scale of cosmic evolution. His "monism" locked all matter and mind into one great self-generating and self-moving nature. The human being descended indirectly not just from the apes but ultimately from inorganic matter, from the "colloidal carbon and hydrogen atoms" of a still-young, cooling planet. Here was an eloquent and inspiring materialism and atheism, so appealing to European radicals and socialists. All reality was matter and energy in motion, mechanical in origin and design, subject to the observable and knowable natural laws of similarity and difference, attraction and repulsion, contraction and expansion, transformation and adaptation. The human spirit or "soul" was nothing more than the sensitive and conscious brain, a machine of physical and chemical components. Ideas were close approximations of real things in the real world. Haeckel's most famous quote, that "ontogeny recapitulates phylogeny," was for many of his followers more than a scientific factoid embodying the organism with evolution. It expressed a metaphysical meaning too: that the individual was necessary for the survival of the species; that human history was a knowing force within natural history; that our progress might even someday supersede chance mutation.[31]

The German naturalist writer Max Wilhelm Meyer helped to popularize Haeckel's ideas as a pan-vitalism. All of life, from its smallest atom to its greatest star system, was part of one great cosmic fabric and followed an eternal cycle of life and death, birth and rebirth. This was a tenacious model of natural history into the 1920s. Atoms were a "microscopic world," a "minute galaxy" of electron suns and planet parts. Stars and planets were like a "living organism." The "micro-cosmos" and "macro-cosmos" were mirrors of each other.[32] Worlds held together. Everything in the universe was bound together by the force of electronic or magnetic or gravitational attractions,

ENVISIONING THE BIOLOGICAL UNIVERSE

by "sympathies and antipathies." Even inorganic life was bound as one by a mysterious, even erotic, force of "universal love."[33] Meyer saw these worlds as overlapping, following tracks of both the mundane and miraculous. Even "a single daily revolution" of the earth contained the eternal truth of light and dark, birth and death, cosmos and chaos. Yet all of life was headed on a path toward higher perfection, toward more harmonious forms, toward "higher stages of evolution," for we humans were conscious of the infinite, of an "eternal uplifting."[34]

By the early years of the twentieth century these ideals translated well in Russia and America and places in between. As one Russian scientist put it, the laws of evolution applied equally to the origins of our solar system in cosmic "dust" as well as to the origins of life on our planet in its primordial swamps. The law of universal gravity transformed the chaos of matter in motion into the moving order of the cosmos, the coming together and centering of all matter at the great "cosmic dawn." Nature's laws applied universally to "an atom, a tree, a man or a star," wrote Horace Clark Richards of the University of Pennsylvania. The cosmos was a unity through multiplicity, a series of worlds within worlds, from atoms to organisms, from ecologies to cultures, from solar systems to star clusters.[35]

V. I. Lenin's infamous *Materialism and Empiriocriticism* (1909) owed much to these new trends in the sciences. It was more of a political polemic than philosophical tract, directed against the "empiriomonist" faction of Bolsheviks, gathered around Aleksandr Bogdanov, intellectuals who were attracted to English and German empiricism. Lenin derided them for holding that the human mind existed prior to matter—that human sensation created reality and that consciousness organized all experience, defined all scientific and social forms. For Lenin the human mind was secondary to matter. Its sensations and consciousness were but reflections and images of the real, objective world. In his own philosophy of dialectical materialism, he drew from the several classic works of Friedrich Engels. But he also found ballast in the natural sciences, in "Newton's principle, the equality of action and reaction," in celestial mechanics and in evolutionary biology. Natural science was "instinctively" materialist, a materialist monism that reflected the objective world. Science disclosed "objective law, causality and necessity in nature."[36] Among contemporary scientists Lenin singled out Haeckel for special praise. His "natural-scientific" monism was "an invincible weapon in the great struggle for emancipation of mankind." For Lenin, as for Haeckel, reality and consciousness were one, the mind a reflection of objective reality. Matter held no inner spirit to be divined. It was indivisible with man, a creature of nature and history who was obliged only to come to know their discrete laws and act upon them more perfectly.[37]

Along with his preference for progressive astronomy, Stalin appreciated the natural sciences for the "monist materialism" and dialectical methods at their core. He most valued the work of thinkers such as Ernst Haeckel, Hermann von Helmholtz, and Max Wilhelm Meyer. Remarkably, instead of Charles Darwin, he favored the ideas of Jean-Baptiste Lamarck, revealing his preference for quick and progressive transformations in nature. Darwin had defined evolution as a blind process of natural selection, chance mutation, and the long struggle for existence. Lamarck instead saw evolution as a process of powerful environmental influences that drove the "inheritance of acquired traits." Russian academics were caught in the creative tension between the two.[38] For Stalin, Darwin was far too passive. He had to side with Lamarck. As he wrote, "Evolution prepares for revolution and creates the ground for it . . . minor qualitative changes sooner or later lead to major, qualitative changes." Darwinism was essentially "evolutionary and quantitative." Lamarck spoke directly to the revolutionary and qualitative change. Like many other Russian intellectuals of his day, he found Lamarck's views much more dignifying of human action in history: the idea that the progressive human manipulation of nature and culture might actively engage its own selected paths of evolution, its own kind of ascending self-evolution.[39]

Publicists in the United States likewise began positioning arrows of human progress forward and upward. From the pages of the Hearst newspapers, Arthur Brisbane promoted a "cosmic wisdom" for the masses. "We are like a swarm of human beings cast away on some desert island," he wrote. Humanity was but one point of life, one outpost in an inhabited universe. We humans occupied a fragile moment in time too, still young and unformed on the ladder of evolutionary and universal development, plagued by poverty and inequality, corruption and criminality, disease and brutality. But better lives awaited us: industrial and technological growth, fuller equality between peoples and sexes, the gradual conquest of outer space and the edges of the universe, contact with beings far more intelligent and developed than us. The distant hope of the future, Brisbane proclaimed, was in all of us becoming astronomers, joined to the heavens by sense and sight and shape, speaking to the Martians, as he envisioned, in the universal language of geometry.[40] He gave expression to a new global consciousness, one that counted history forward by millennia. He weighed the fragility of our human life, the potential for meteorological destruction and planetary apocalypse, against the probability of human immortality, the strong chance that we are "indestructible specks of cosmic intelligence, lighting up and animating one material body after another—never destroyed."[41]

Imagined Wars of the Worlds

In all of these ways, be they academic or political, modern science set the universe in motion, along a path of progressive development. But not without risk. The universe became a site of harmony and disharmony, hope and despair, cosmos and chaos. Life took on all the natural benefits and dangers attendant to any other living world orbiting any other star. Popular astronomy and science fiction also had their darker side, an underlying fear of apocalypse. Just as we began to look to the universe for life and enlightenment, we came to find it as a possible source of death and destruction. Predictions of impending disaster for Earth, sooner or later, came in steady waves to the Russian reading publics, either as science fact or science fiction.

Nineteenth-century science itself entertained the logic of rise and fall. The "first" law of thermodynamics, codified early on by Nicolas Sadi Carnot and others, held that the sum of energy was never lost but was ever constant. Energy was indestructible, always conserved. By midcentury, thanks in part to the work of Hermann von Helmholtz and William Thompson (Lord Kelvin), the "second" law of thermodynamics held rather bleakly that the higher powers of energy always fell lower. Energy degraded and dissipated. Intensity became entropy. Following the logic of the nebular hypothesis, the sun was bound to die, cloaking the planet in a sea of ice.[42] To the German naturalist writers and their Russian interpreters as well, space was the mother of all our life, but that life was not eternal. Meyer prefaced his book *The End of the World* (1902) with a dramatic image of the last humans huddled around the world's last tree, cowering before a blanket of cold and ice that have come from the depths of dark space. He offered some consolation: our atoms would eventually congeal into novel forms to create a new solar system. "The end and the beginning of the world are two extremes that touch each other." Wilhelm Bölsche also prophesied a future cosmic ice death from a dying sun. "Is not the Earth finally doomed? Is it not written in the stars that . . . the ice dragon eat its death meal of life?" The only solution was for humanity to continue to master ever more demanding and fulfilling technologies, to domesticate the planet and to reach for flight and refuge in cosmic space beyond.[43]

Science fiction writers set all of these ideas to their plotlines. Flammarion entertained the "parabolic curve of life," a "geometric curve" of progress. Yet in his pessimistic view the curve was not forever upward. It moved from nadir to "apogee" and back again. Or as he wrote, "The geometric curve which represents this progress of the race, falls as it rises: starting from zero, from the primitive nebulous cosmos, ascending through the ages of planetary and human history to its lofty summit, to descend thereafter into a night that knows no morrow."[44] This image of a closing circle, reaching between the curves of human progress and regress, had already been made popular by Edward Bellamy. As he wrote in his science fiction novel *Looking Backward* (1888), "Tending upward and sunward from the aphelion of barbarism, the race attained the perihelion of civilization only to plunge downward once more to its nether goal in the regions of chaos." Jules Verne wrote of it, too, in one of his last stories, *The Eternal Adam*, about the far future and the discovery of a lost civilization, once magnificent and now in dust: the archaeological ruin of Verne's own Europe.[45] For these writers progress was only temporary, bound to eternal recurrences, to the rises and falls of civilizations.

ENVISIONING THE BIOLOGICAL UNIVERSE

H. G. Wells's classic *War of the Worlds* exploded onto this scene in 1897, beginning a succession of Russian-language editions by the following year, one of the most popular and reproduced pieces of science fiction into the twentieth century. Wells mixed together the currents of evolutionary theory and the plurality of inhabited worlds, discovering a fragile planet in a forbidding cosmos. The invasion, with all of its scenes of destruction and chaos, was plausible. It was also panoramic. The power of the narrative was in its visual effects, looking down upon Earth from Mars, "only 3,500,000 of miles sunward." The story shrank suffering human beings, as if they were tiny creatures under the pin of a microscope, defenseless against the giant blood-sucking Martians. And they came from outer space. Earth was no longer the "secure abiding-place for Man."[46] Wells had drawn an arrow down to us. These scenes of destruction were total, the English countryside and cityscapes reduced to ruin. This was a war of machines, the perfect Martian metal of flying cylinders and torpedo fighters, heat rays and poison gas. The Martians had of course perfected space travel, something like rocket propulsion, their crafts becoming "missiles" or "falling stars," leaving in their wake a "jet of fire," as "flaming gases rushed out of a gun." Only chance mutation saved humanity in the form of Earth's own "microorganisms," which felled the Martians to their death cries, "*ulla, ulla*."[47] Physiology trumped technology.

The Belgian writer J. H. Rosny (the elder) also helped to invent this ghastly genre. His story *The Death of the Earth* (1910) depicted the end of the world, the human species slowly extinguished by climactic disaster over the course of a hundred thousand years. The main character, Targ, was one of the "last men," watching the earth become "as uninhabitable for humanity as Jupiter or Saturn." Evolution was upended to favor the mineral world, the reign of the "ferromagnetics," new metallic life forms that fed on the iron (hemoglobin) in human blood. Human beings had achieved miracles of technology, in airplanes and motorcars, in drilling and tractor machines, in atomic energy and population engineering. By graceful turns Targ even mastered the depths and heights of his world, mining into subterranean caverns in search of water, flying in beautiful "arcs" and "parabolas" over desolate landscapes. All was in vain, however, against the evolutionary life cycle and the degeneration of humanity.[48]

These kinds of stories reflected concerns about the growing arms race at the turn of the century. Wells predicted Europe's own coming aerial wars with even more realism and technical expertise in his two novels, *War in the Air* (1908) and *The World Set Free* (1914). With the very first appearance of Zeppelin dirigibles in 1900 and airplanes in 1908, war was bound to spread into the air, with the direst of consequences. Whole armies would be blanketed by, whole cities destroyed by, a "rain of bombs and shells."[49] But he was hardly the first or the last to raise the specter of the "coming war" in creative fiction. Such novels, featuring outer space adventures, were common enough at the turn of the century, often in works by the same author.[50] They pitted Britain and France against Germany or the United States against Britain. They foresaw new technologies of destruction: fire-bombs, radioactive and biological and chemical weapons, electric power and ray guns, antigravity ships and aircraft. War from the air was sure to bring new breadths and depths of devastation.[51]

Russia and America figured in this genre in interesting ways. Russia was often the object of American or British military intervention, the reactionary Tsardom dispatched by the West's forces of justice and freedom. America saved the world from Martian aggression (or one of several Latin or Yellow or Black or Slavic "perils") at least twice: in Kurd Lasswitz's *Two Planets* (1897) as a force of last resort; and in Garrett P. Serviss's *Edison's Conquest of Mars* (1898), in which old Europe looked finally to young America, and the genius of Thomas A. Edison, to repel the invaders and beat them back to Mars using the power of antigravity spaceships and atomic death rays.[52]

The "future war" genre came to Russia most directly through France, namely Albert Robida's trilogy about coming life, beginning with *The Twentieth Century* (1883). Illustrator and travel writer, storyteller and satirist, Robida prognosticated on all manner of future technologies, including synthetic foods and control of the weather and climate, transatlantic tunnels and pneumatic trains, aerial ships and live television, even the culminating "conquest of interplanetary space." He was a master of cinematic voyages into the future,

ENVISIONING THE BIOLOGICAL UNIVERSE

people always in motion on wonderful new technologies. But he was also known for his visions of the coming wars of the twentieth century, total and catastrophic battles of germ warfare, poison gas, and aerial bombardments. Russia did not fare well in Robida's scenario, undone by its own "Nihilist Party," whose terrorism and massive bombs led to a series of freak tectonic shifts, floods, and near-total destruction. The vast country was replaced by a few oases of inhabited Russian towns amid the great "Moscovian Sea."[53]

Russia had its coming-war fiction too, often punctuated with an imaginary triumphalism never borne out in reality. In A. Belomor's *The Fateful War* (1889), thanks to its quick, light cruisers and mobile troops, the Russian navy seized the Bosporus and Dardanelles, occupied Venice and Genoa, defended Vladivostok, and established a new naval base at the Arctic Ocean, "Aleksandria," from which it spread its hegemony over the Northern Hemisphere and the world. Sergei Sharapov's *Within a Half Century* (1902) was even more optimistic. After a brief war with Austria, Russia declared a new pan-Slavic state, with its capital at "Tsariagrad" (formerly Istanbul), even converting Roman-Catholic Poland to Eastern Orthodoxy.[54] Yet the future did not always turn out so well, even for the Russians. Vladimir Semenov's series *The Queen of the World* (1908) and *Kings of the Air* (1909) played upon Wells's stories of war and destruction from the air. His version started out well enough, the world united by electricity, radio, and aviation, speaking a new international argot, "airspeak," with all the technological foundations of a new global democracy. In time, however, air pirates and revolutionaries preyed on a weak and vulnerable world, imperiling humanity's gains. The new and destructive technologies of war overwhelmed us.[55]

Another such science fiction story started out well enough too, featuring Kondratii Vasilevich Neveselii, who mastered the power of electromagnetic energy to negate gravity and propel his "great invention," a "cigar-shaped" craft that could speed up to 500 kilometers (311 miles) per hour and reach high altitudes. His dream was to erase state boundaries, unite the world, and establish a regime of socialist equality and prosperity for all, women included. Alas, his inventions were stolen by a German schemer, who terrorized the world with aerial piracy, death rays, and aerial bombs. An editorial caveat warned readers that this tale was not "pure fantasy" but a "thing of the future."[56] Indeed, when war finally came in the summer of 1914, the Russian reading public received it as confirmation of all the worst possibilities, as if in a novel by H. G. Wells. "Reality has drawn nearer to recent fantasies," wrote one author. We had become our own Martians. The road map of the next war, he predicted, would be found in science fiction, whose nightmares of long-distance bombs and gas attacks, aerial and undersea war, all contained a "grain of truth." In the first winter months of the war, beginning in January 1915, one popular literary journal even serialized Wells's *War in the Air* again, this amid actual news reports of real aerial combat and bombardments by planes and dirigibles.[57]

One of the most compelling and comprehensive historical treatments, manifestly nonfiction, was Jan Gotlib Bloch's massive multi-volume series, first published in Russia as *The Future War* (1898). Mixing the new sensibilities of interplanetary space and military competition, Bloch compared the rising panic over the new arms race to the bombardment of cosmic dust from outer space. Both were bearing down upon Europe with unseen mysterious force. Cosmic dust was like the smokeless gunpowder and long-range firepower newly deployed on Europe's battlefields, turning the traditional warfare of smoke and noise into surprise attacks and sudden death, brought on by the "invisible shafts of death" and the "death-dealing missiles" of modern war. Bloch's concerns may seem trivial nowadays; he was most worried about the modern rifle, machine guns, and artillery. These were formidable and deadly devices in their day, especially in ever larger armies. Technology was changing the conduct of war in dramatic ways, as, for example, Bloch's illustration, straight out of Robida, of an imaginary winged, propeller-driven, heavier-than-air flying machine, an awkward-looking thing wielding guns and "aerial torpedoes."[58]

The power of Bloch's work was in its perspective: looking forward in time, looking westward from the edges of backward Russia, collating and weighing the many English and French and German sources on the subject of the arms race, estimating their superior might and advantage in the global race for power. His appeals to pacifism were matched by a profound anxiety over Russia's inability to compete. Bloch's focus on technology certainly made for stunning predictive power in 1904, when in the Russo-Japanese War the Japanese rather easily defeated the Russians. An Asian power, deemed racially inferior by European standards, had broken part of Europe using its own technological means. Race did not count; machines did. Technology trumped phylogeny.

Russia had to contend with its own civil war and revolution in 1905, one perfectly attuned to the astronomical cycle of chaos and cosmos. Publicists entertained these images during the worst days of street violence. Anti-regime journals and magazines in St. Petersburg and Moscow imagined, from the deep perspective of outer space, the vast continent of Russia awash in blood, as if some higher beings on the moon or Mars were watching the barbaric events unfold, a falling comet the portent of doom in the background. In some of the deadliest months of the revolution, January and December 1905, Russia's poets and writers put these images into words. Maksim Gorkii posed the struggle in terms of evil overcome by good, darkness by light, death by immortality, the "troubling chaos of an anxious, unhappy life" surpassed by that "joyful star, the flame guiding us to the future." Valerii Briusov framed the unfolding bloodshed and nightmarish violence "before the world upon the canvas of the universe."[59]

Briusov's images are especially remarkable in this context. He was one of a loose coalition of Symbolist writers (among them Viacheslav Ivanov, Andrei Bely, and Aleksandr Blok), who were best known for their mystical verses and prose. The Symbolists often fixed their words upon the heavens, partly inspired by medieval cosmology and astrology, partly taken with the discoveries of modern astronomy, but always with a spiritual and meditative gaze. They projected human desires of fear and longing, love gained and love lost, on the moon and sun, planets and stars. Reality was a veil to be pierced, through the portals of myths or numbers, shapes or signs. Or as Ivanov wrote, "The ascending, spiraling line, the elation of impulse and overcoming, is dear to us as a symbol of our finest self-affirmation."[60]

Yet Briusov seemed overwhelmed by "solar chaos," by the cosmic lights that illuminate our oceans and mountains and minds.[61]

Fig. 1. Planet Earth, with a bloodied Russian continent in the foreground
and a comet in the background to illustrate the cosmic context of the
Russian Revolution of 1905. I. Bodianskii's drawing from the inside
cover of the magazine *Zarnitsy* 4 (1906).

His gaze was squarely upon us. Several of his short stories, collected
in *Earth's Axis* (1907), conceived of civilization in planetary, apocalyptic terms. He wrote of whole societies gone mad with disease
and obsession, quite literally through orgies of death and destruction. Most terrifying was his stage play on humanity's future, *Earth*.
First conceived in 1890, Briusov represented the piece as his study of

the "other," of our own humanity from the eyes of the distant, alien future. Set within a domed, underground city of perfect geometric shapes, of wheels and turbines, aqueducts and fountains, the story played upon the contrasts of light and dark, life and death, ascent and descent. Civilization was breaking up. The city's water supply was running out. The great machines that sustained it with artificial air and fire and water were failing, no one remembering their true technique and operation. Only elaborate and ever more meaningless elite rituals remained. One party sought salvation in decadence, to cleanse and liberate the city through terror and murder; its slogan was "Love for Death." Another party sought salvation in the "infinite heavens" to make way to the surface and sky, to fulfill our destiny as "heaven-dwellers"; its slogan was "To the Sun." The second party succeeded, ascending through the layers of the city, opening the dome's great cupola to the air, only to suffocate and perish, fulfilling the bloodletting dreams of its rivals.[62] The radical playwright, Leonid Andreev, captured this dynamic in the script for his play *To the Stars* (1906). The piece studied the generational and ideological gaps between parents, the "star counters" obsessed with the passive contemplation of the cosmic depths of space, and children, revolutionaries driven to violent and immediate change. Sergei Nikolaevich, the father astronomer, ultimately bridged the two, with cosmic soliloquies on life and death, eternity and mortality. "The path to the stars," he claimed, "is always laced with blood." Russia's dueling generations, so the moral went, needed to unite in a common act of revolutionary sacrifice.[63]

Aleksandr Bogdanov's novel of communist society on Mars, *Red Star* (1908), was written in this raw context. Russians were being bombarded by extraordinary stories from the West, by Wells's science fiction, or by any of the other popular space romances of the day as well as by dramatic stories of revolution and reaction at home. The story had its poignant moments, as when the Russian revolutionary Leonid was stolen off to Mars and he and his space comrades looked back upon our broken, bloodied continents, weighing humanity's urge for self-destruction. It was an image straight out of the Russian Revolution of 1905. But Bogdanov largely turned our gaze outward, as if humanity was watching the Martians, not the Martians us. Bogdanov's Earth and Mars were a study of the law of universal evolution, at work in two different places, at two different times: our planet still struggling with the vestiges of capitalism; a Martian planet struggling with the achievements of communism. The power of the work was in its rich play on the forces of attraction and repulsion between the planets, as between the West and East. At one point Leonid compared superior Mars and the advanced West to an inferior Earth and backward Russia, specifically "the logical discipline and experience of scientific reasoning" of the French as opposed to the "Asiatic" backwardness of Russians. "I stood on the border between them," said Leonid, "like a split second of the present between past and future."[64] In the part-imagined, part-real landscapes of outer space, Russian readers found a morality tale about their own planetary predicament.

By the first decade of the twentieth century Russia was a constituent part of the new media and literary cultures of the West, often with a sense of delay and sometimes diffidence. Russians participated in the age of science, too, and were joined to its complex and dynamic mosaic of correlations. They received the new astronomy and the new biology with various parts of optimism and pessimism. For them, as for Americans or French or Germans, outer space was a canvas upon which they drew their hopes and fears. The narrative arcs of transcendence were sometimes lovely, at other times foreboding. But we all shared the same vertical horizons. Russia's gaze was privileged in a way, being at the edge of the West, more open to the vast spaces between and above.

2

Mystical Economies of Earth and Space

Modern astronomy was no mere visual tableau upon which the planets and stars moved with predictable speed and regularity. Outer space was also becoming a living canvas, a field upon which cells and beings might migrate, through which live signals might travel, into which we humans might answer back. In the mid-nineteenth century H. E. Richter had proposed that the universe was filled with living things, "cosmozoa," germs that sailed upon the ether and its planetary bodies.[1] Leading scientists such as William Thompson and Svante Arrhenius further developed the "panspermia" thesis, widely disseminated in Russia, that life first came to Earth as organic spores in a state of frozen animation. Life was seeded here by either meteors or cosmic dust. Following the logic of the Kant-Laplace hypothesis, Arrhenius argued that the "pressure of radiation" throughout the universe offered a surface upon which the electrical charges of cosmic dust might travel, including microscopic bacterial spores. Even more interesting, Arrhenius argued that these interstellar and interplanetary "traveling germs" were actually launched from planetary surfaces by the power of "electrostatic repulsion," descending back by catching onto larger particles via the "action of attraction." Nature offered humanity its own model of space rocket launch and return.[2] Arrhenius also added a rather upbeat note to the bleak life-and-death cycles of the nebular hypothesis and new thermodynamics. Worlds had the capacity to regenerate, to "continue forever and undiminished."[3]

Max Wilhelm Meyer and Wilhelm Bölsche, whose translated works sold well throughout Europe, North America, and Russia, helped to disseminate the thesis. Bölsche speculated that "certain spores of the simplest living matter" may perhaps have "immigrated and settled on the cooled globe" of our planet. The universe was in motion as a great sea of life. "The milky way of the heavens," so he wrote, "stands opposite to the milky way of life," the oceans on Earth.[4] Here were echoes of that grand metaphor that has so often inspired the rhetoric of the space age. As people of the land and air, we humans stand between two oceans: the "ocean of space" upon which we might sail as bold navigators, from whence we originally came, to which we must ascend, just as we once left the oceans of water for land.

These kinds of ideas found their adaptation in Russia through the work of the librarian and philosopher N. F. Fedorov, as laid out in his *Philosophy of the Common Task* (1906–13), a foundation marker in the historiography of "Russian cosmism" and spaceflight theories. The aesthetic Fedorov was well read in the natural sciences, which he valued as radical forces for equality and democracy. Astronomy, he knew, based on spectroscopic analysis, was discovering the common basis of all universal matter; it was even compelling all of humanity to a new "consciousness of planet Earth," a living and breathing planet, one of many worlds beyond our own. The new technologies at the infrastructure of global trade and commerce were also promising. Fedorov was impressed by the dawn of the aerial age, seeing "aerostats" as a means to elevate and educate common people, to inspire them to "courage and inventiveness," to compel them to launch out upon "the paths to celestial space." He was also sensitive to the plight of the poor, to the suffering imposed upon humanity by the perils of nature and history, so long as we remained captives to their "blind forces." He championed social justice and civic peace.[5]

But Fedorov was foremost a man of deep and devoted Orthodox spirituality. He wrote in gospel terms, all of his published writings a meditation upon Romans 8:8–39, on humans conformed to Jesus the Son in honor of God the Father. As Christ conquered sin in the world, humanity should "conquer" nature in all its forms. His work bore the singular weight of his religious convictions, centered upon the fulfillment of Jesus Christ's Easter promise, turning humanity's "sense of sorrow" and "universal grief" into the joy of a new birth. Fulfillment meant transforming the Christian gospel of divine salvation into a vast market exchange between humble work and human resurrection. This was a central precept of his writings. His "project," or "common task," was intensely physical, a true labor of love. He proposed that modern people could become new messiahs, honoring the one Father and their many fathers. This meant uniting into great work armies to subdue the arbitrary forces of nature; turning all the earth into one great museum of human achievement; resurrecting dead bodies and engineering human immortality. And yes, even colonizing outer space in order to accommodate these reborn populations. This was Reade's socialist utopia all over again, if now sacred rather than profane.[6] One of Fedorov's followers, the avant-garde artist V. N. Chekrygin, later painted the dream in his *Resurrection* (1918), humanity busily at work reviving the dead.[7]

Gravity, for Fedorov, was more than a natural law. It was a creative metaphor for the burdens of human nature, our horizontal humanity. Gravity weighed us down, imprisoned us within our worldly desires for trivial things, for the fleeting pleasures of food and sleep and sex. We humans were tied to the planet just as it was tied to the sun and other stars. "We are not Earth's masters but its serfs," he warned.[8] Humanity was to find its ultimate fulfillment beyond these gravities: in outer space, in the discovery of fraternal worlds, in the transformation of our very physical beings, as a new kind of atomic matter, more spirit than flesh, fully at home in the apparent emptiness of interplanetary space. Physical pleasures were to give way to higher purposes. In an act of supreme "self-creation" (*samosozdanie*) horizontal humanity at rest was to become vertical humanity in motion, the human person as common builder, helper, seeker, and transformer, a partner in creation with the Father "God-Creator."[9] Humanity was thus to conquer the heavens, to perfect astronomy as the highest form of practical science.

More medieval than modern, Fedorov raised Copernicus over Newton. Copernican astronomy was to become the mother of all sciences, joining mechanics and physics, chemistry and biology, into a new roadmap to the heavens. Technologies such as the mechanical "electrocraft" or the organic "etherozoa" were to help transform human beings into "heaven dwellers," cosmic beings fully at home in ethereal space. Earth itself was to become a moving spaceship, a cosmic brain controlling the universe's many parts.[10] Fedorov's was an arc of transcendence par excellence, its trajectory spaceward, his unique answer to all the debates about Richter's cosmozoa and Arrhenius's panspermia seeding the heavens. He would now actively seed the heavens with humanity just as the heavens once passively seeded Earth with organic life. We were the ethereal seeds that counted.

Russia was no mere setting, no mute backdrop, for Fedorov's writings. It was an essential vehicle for humanity's salvation. The Russian Orthodox cupola tower, he liked to say, was itself symbolic of the human being raised toward the heavens, people upright in motion. The Russian popular "choral ring dance" was symbolic of the Copernican system of planets and stars. All of them together—human forms, church towers and cupolas, ring dances, planetary and astral rings—were emblematic of God's vast creation, the living "cathedral" of beauty and wonder bridging Earth and space.[11]

The unique character of the Russian landed state and its people, as rolling forests and plains, as a setting for wanderers and explorers, was a model for humanity's salvation. It was a new Rome, a sacred space that defied the West's materialism of "market-civic life" and raised its own moralism of invention and exploration, its "participation in cosmic life." The only hope of the world was for the pristine Russian village community to become the basis for a new universal human home. Russia's reach between Europe and Asia, its mastery of such a vast "free expanse" of lands, was the perfect foundation for the inevitable conquest of the "free expanse of celestial space." Just as Russia was a bridge between the far corners of the earth, so too would it become the bridge to the far corners of the solar system and galaxies beyond. Its people would translate their values of courage and exploration from the one place to the other. Outer space was a kind of new Siberia, "a new sphere of action for heroic exploits," a place of "new small estates" and "new worlds."[12]

Fedorov's students were dedicated, often obsessively so, to his ideals and memory. Leading writers and poets of the day found his ideas provocative and appealing, a "salvation myth" in Russian national culture. He has become, in several important studies from American academia, a mainstay of Russian intellectual and cultural life, leaving "Fedorovian" legacies far beyond his modest person and career. He seems to have influenced such eminent thinkers as Fedor Dostoevskii, Vladimir Solov'ev, Leo Tolstoi, Anatoli Lunacharskii, and Boris Pasternak.[13] In Soviet Russia, with such luminaries as Konstantin Tsiolkovskii and V. I. Vernadskii, he became the "founding father of the Russian philosophy of Cosmism," a movement in New Age spiritualism joining religious, philosophical, and scientific themes in a project for the total transformation of nature and culture.[14]

Yet these later historical lines of Fedorovism and cosmism are problematic. They tend to read Fedorov backward, not from within the unique idiom of his own writings but from a more secular and worldly future, just as perhaps many of his readers did. They privilege Russian personalities and movements as great chains of thought and innovation, masking the influences that helped to shape them from abroad. They reflect in part Fedorov's own Orthodox and Russian exceptionalism, his breathtaking xenophobia and intolerance of the Catholic and Protestant West and Muslim East. Russian cosmism is itself overdetermined, more a creation after the fact, its advocates stitching together a cohesive movement and school from myriad personalities and influences where none really existed at the time.[15] Several leading historians have offered an alternative approach, locating Fedorov as one crucial piece within the larger puzzle of modern "Prometheanism," the movement to transform nature and humanity by will and reason, technology and human action.[16]

Terrestrial Matter and Mortality

Fedorov no doubt was an original, a "brilliant autodidact" (*samorod*), as Nikolai Berdiaev called him. But his ideas enjoyed no monopoly. They were very much part of a broader world of contexts and influences. Take, for example, the "Copernicanism" and domed museum of Charles Woodridge. They were unmistakably Fedorovian. Or take the issues of human resurrection and immortality, cosmic travel and "spaceship earth"—centerpieces of Fedorov's philosophy. Flammarion confronted them, too, in *The End of the World*, whose fictional Archbishop of Paris decided the question in favor of the chemical and biological resurrection of the body, this thanks to the wonders of modern science. These values and images were currencies in wide literary circulation, as Northrop Frye has argued: this "total dream of man . . . of a human mind which is at the circumference and not the center of its reality"; this belief that "nature is now inside the mind of an infinite man who builds his cities out of the Milky Way."[17] As Fedorov's own students recognized, the American philosopher and mystic Prentice Mulford also celebrated these ideals of spiritual renaissance and physical immortality. They honored him with several translations.[18] Like Fedorov, Mulford was a zealot for the renovating power of the human spirit. Our reservoirs of reason and science, will and faith, might even create the grounds for a "reconstruction of the physical body," for "immortality in the flesh" and "perpetual youth," what he called the "body thus ever renewing, beautifying, freshening and strengthening." Like Fedorov, Mulford celebrated the planetary scope of natural evolution, the inventions of human technology, the coming human conquest of aviation, and the eternal ideal of ascent. "All things in this planet," he wrote, "are ever moving forward to greater refinement, greater powers, and greater possibilities."[19]

Fedorov's followers recognized that their quest for human resurrection and immortality had its grounds in modern science, which was transforming the impossible into the real, the fantastic dream of eternal life into the very real possibilities of cryogenic preservation and "revitalization." The Russian physicist and biologist P. I. Bakhmet'ev was their hero. His experiments with cryogenic "anabiosis," which were received with significant public acclaim in Russia, froze a variety of cold-blooded animals (insects, butterflies, and fish) and eventually some small warm-blooded animals (bats and rabbits) to temperatures hovering just below 0 degrees Celsius but not below -10 degrees. It was a very delicate process. Using a special refrigerator and thermometer of his own design to calibrate temperature, he was able to keep them in a state of suspended animation for up to eight months, by which they had "stopped living, but had not died." Their bodily fluids and hearts slightly frozen, he gradually warmed and resuscitated them to normal body temperatures, although they did not live long afterward. His practical objective was to apply these discoveries to improve agriculture by storing bees over the winter to save on their consumption of honey or to improve human health, treating tuberculosis patients through anabiosis.[20]

These discoveries and potentials came at a most exciting time in the young science of "cryogenics." By 1892 James Dewar had invented the process and machinery to liquefy oxygen and store it in quantity using the famous Dewar vacuum flask, essentially a thermos, at temperatures below -185 degrees Celsius. He did the same for liquid hydrogen by 1898, ultimately creating the very techniques that future rocket pioneers adapted for use in their propellant mixtures for liquid fuel rocket engines. But Dewar's discoveries had even more significant and immediate results for space travel theories. Scientists soon discovered Dewar's applications to cryogenic anabiosis. In one famous experiment they kept the formidable spirillum of *Cholera asiatica* and spores of *Bacillus anthracis* alive at temperatures hovering at -185 degrees for twenty hours, this "without losing any of their vital properties." These simple (and dangerous) forms of life were now known to survive at such extremely cold temperatures. All of this helped to prove that Arrhenius and Bakhmet'ev were right. The germs of life might very well be able to survive journeys through the vacuum cold of outer space. Animal life, and perhaps even human beings someday, might also be kept alive in such a state of suspended animation. Russians received these scientific theories with interest, recognizing similar laboratory experiments that proved that the simplest organisms could indeed survive the harsh conditions and dangerous rays of outer space.[21] Here were signal discoveries to enable humanity's someday journey to the stars.

In a 1904 essay Bakhmet'ev transformed his experimental physiology into his own literary fantasy, the vision of a perfect city for the promotion of the natural sciences. Andrew Carnegie was the initial benefactor, leaving four hundred million dollars to the cause, the establishment of an International Institute for the Natural Sciences, located in the Alps near the towering Mont Blanc. Here, in Bakhmet'ev's dream, a Central Scholar's Soviet was to manage an academic phalanstery of a kind, where scientists would be completely free to pursue theoretical and applied knowledge. But it was more than just an institution. It was a whole new "architecture" for scientific and cultural progress, a "cathedral of science" where its "immortals" would carry on the sacred calling of geniuses such as Newton and Helmholtz. Science was slated to discover the real possibilities of telepathy, projecting human thoughts over distances. It was to take its proper place as a civic religion, a monism that broke down the "artificial wall between the organic and inorganic realms." Science was to confirm what Bakhmet'ev called the "Great Intellect," or "Great Spirit," that inhabited every living atom, the great "Integral" that expressed all the "infinite number of differentials" throughout the universe.[22]

Bakhmet'ev's life and work, with all the dramatic promise of his laboratory methods, was cut short in 1913. He died of malaria during a lecture circuit along the lower Volga River. The Russian media mourned his death as a loss for world science and celebrated his work as a mark of Russian national achievement. Fedorov's followers were especially praiseworthy. To them Bakhmet'ev seemed to have proved in actual fact what their teacher had only claimed in philosophical fancy. With his notion of a "living inertia," Bakhmet'ev had literally redefined the conventional meanings of life and death. He had proven in practice that a living organism could inhabit a kind of temporary death. He had proposed in theory, along with a number of European scientists, that dead matter (such as crystals and various chemical substances) exhibited some of the primary signs of life. He had hinted at the real possibilities of someday creating synthetic life.[23] To the Russophile Fedorovians he had thereby created the building blocks for a "new Earth" and "new Heaven," turning tired human beings into "Children of the Sun," as one of his admirers put it. Thanks in part to Bakhmet'ev, the poet A. Gornostaev wrote:

> Matter, Nature and the Grave
> Have all come to naught.
> The Heavens have opened . . .
> The radiant force of an ever-cleansing Light
> Illuminates All.[24]

Yet Bakhmet'ev was part of a wider scientific trend. From Paris, Charles Eduard Brown-Séquard had already coined the term *rejuvenation* (*rajeunissement*) in 1889, after finding that once he had injected himself with the testicular fluids of dogs and guinea pigs, his physical and mental health revitalized. Brown-Séquard's method, what he called "organotherapy," soon became a fashion in Europe and the United States: the use of glandular secretions and tissue transplants (of the testicles, ovaries, spleen, and brain) as cures for all manner of diseases, maladies, exhaustion, and old age.[25] Modern science was making progress toward its ultimate goal: the conquest of mortal time. News also spread about a series of stunning laboratory experiments that shook our presumptions about the very boundaries between life and death. From Russia, building upon some of Brown-Séquard's other experiments, A. A. Kuliabko's tests proved that the death of the body did not always mean the death of its parts. He was able to keep an isolated heart beating (at first of small animals and eventually a human heart) in a nutrient solution for up to one week. A number of other scientists maintained embryonic cells and fruit flies alive in test-tube conditions well beyond their normal life expectancy. Most notable were the investigations of Alexis Carrel, of the Rockefeller Institute for Medical Research in New York City, who held the world record for keeping the heart cells of a chicken embryo alive in a laboratory test tube (since 1912), floating in a solution of chicken blood plasma. The record eventually turned out to be false. But for many years academia and the media gave credence to Carrel, in part because he was a Nobel Prize laureate, in part because he also eventually became successful at keeping animal and even human organs alive in specialized laboratory mediums and containers for days and even weeks on end.[26]

Readers received the newspaper and magazine articles about these innovators as dramatic medical "breakthroughs," like the rabies vaccine or the X-ray, new techniques that promised real results, better and longer lives. In Russia, P. Iu. Shmidt, a zoologist and ichthyologist, helped disseminate many of these new achievements of modern science in a number of popular works. He also framed science within a popular philosophy of vitalism: humanity's quest for immortality, that "secret fiery hope of the poor mortal human being," that deep desire to "prolong" our "sad, momentary split-second of life" within the "abyss" of time and the utter "vastness" of the universe. Shmidt teased readers that science, not religion or the occult, now promised some measure of achievement, perhaps not immortality but surely a longer and richer life; some conquest over entropy; some mastery over the forces of life-giving energy.[27]

Among the most famous "rejuvenators" was the Russian, Il'ia Mechnikov, second in name recognition only to the great I. P. Pavlov. Both scientists were renowned for their award-winning discoveries. Pavlov won the Nobel Prize in Medicine in 1904 for his research experiments in physiology and neurology: how the functions of the digestive system were closely related to the nervous system; how a scientist could manipulate an environmental stimulus to transform a basic reflex into a conditional reflex; how humans might someday master their very selves through behavioral conditioning. Mechnikov was a similar media sensation in his day, winning the Nobel Prize in 1908 for his discoveries of the bacteria-fighting qualities of white blood corpuscles and who also laid claim to his own authority about aging and rejuvenation.[28] He was also a philosopher of vitalism and optimism, a "brilliant scholar and thinker who enjoyed a surprising wealth of scientific fantasies and scientific ideas," as one of his students later wrote. He believed that he had found, in the body's immune system, the font of an organism's life drive, its creative will to survive.[29] As a member of the Pasteur Institute in Paris, Mechnikov proposed several new techniques to improve health and prolong human life, concluding that the bacilli of lactic acids, especially in yogurt, were the most influential. Diet and exercise helped too. The Russian media celebrated his ideas; Russians flocked to his "cures." This was, after all, a most dramatic and vulnerable moment. Publicists (both academic and popular) had begun to spread fears of racial and national "degeneration" and "neurasthenia," the social and demographic decay brought on by all the competing seductions of modern life, including the revolutionary alternatives in politics and all the "moral stresses of an upended social order." Russians, like industrial age Europeans and Americans, were becoming an exhausted and prematurely aging population. The result was a new cult of physical health, stressing such prophylactic measures as Mechnikov's diet, deep breathing exercises, physical hygiene, restorative baths, and gymnastics.[30]

But Mechnikov also made quite clear that the human body was meant to perish, to grow old and die. He only ever meant to prolong the quality and quantity of that life, to avoid the strains of pathological death, and to prepare the human being for our inevitable "natural death." In this sense Mechnikov was at one with the increasingly mainstream "Darwinian" view that death was a natural and necessary function of evolution and natural selection, an adaptation that sustained life by recreating it anew and better in generation after generation.[31] Fedorov's followers, as a result, paid Mechnikov little heed. Although quite an accomplished and dynamic philosopher in his own right, he took no stock in flighty questions of immortality. His stands were anathema to the Fedorovian ethic. The accomplished professor of anatomy and physiology V. V. Zav'ialov expressed this intransigence in a dramatic public essay linking immortality and space travel. Death and gravity, he argued, were not inevitable and inescapable. Each of us held an inherent "instinct for life" and a constant "struggle against aging and death." Science was discovering life's origins and processes, he noted, with the hope that someday we might even be able to reverse the "process." Drawing an analogy from the new technique of cinematography, we might very well learn how to "turn back time," running the reel of life backward, and thereby seize control over the very flow of time.[32]

Interplanetary Communication and Alien Life

Propositions about the tenacity of life implied that we human beings were gradually becoming the masters of space and time, creators of a radically new civilization that demanded nothing less than a whole new language. The academic and public media became fascinated with the promises of what *Scientific American* called "interplanetary communication" (*mezhplanetnye soobshcheniia* in the Russian media), a linguistic model of futuristic science and technology, half-real and half-imagined. The term had its origins at the intersection of two modern European inventions, the hot air balloon and the long-distance telegraph. By the middle of the nineteenth century the balloon had already defined the threshold of human reach. Science understood that there were altitudes beyond which such craft could not rise and within which the human body would not survive. We had only begun to breach the limits of the vertical. Yet the long-distance telegraph virtually obliterated horizontal distance. Humanity extended its reach, at least in terms of a simple Morse code, across national and even continental borders. If we would not be rising to other planetary worlds by balloon, perhaps we might be able to communicate with them by long-distance signals such as the telegraph. To speak to alien planets was to travel there, in a form, or at least to build the first such bridge for eventual flight.

Thus, with the potential of "interplanetary communication," outer space became a site of linguistics before it became a site for rockets. Through the nineteenth century scientists set out finally to confirm the "plurality of worlds" and "biological universe" by way of human signals to the planets: through huge geometrical figures or mirrors or fires (sometimes from the great landmass of Siberia) or through the new inventions of the telegraph and eventually the wireless radio.[33] Sir Francis Galton, renowned Darwinist and one of the founders of the eugenics movement, claimed to find signs of life on Mars, hoping that we might send an interplanetary Morse code of light flares back. By the early twentieth century the inventor Nikola Tesla suggested a telecommunications bridge to Mars, part of his greater "utopian" dream of harnessing electricity and energy to subdue nature: to eliminate poverty, control the weather, and build a new global community. The Italian inventor Guglielmo Marconi, too, proposed sending signals to Mars by way of his wireless telegraph.[34] The irony for Russia was that by 1900 it had only half of Germany's telegraph lines and a third of England's. It had not successfully invested in telegraphs here on Earth, not to speak of wireless technology, but it still eagerly joined the debate about sending signs through interplanetary space.[35]

Most dramatically of all, astronomer Percival Lowell's pseudoscience claimed to actually see, to the disinterest or skepticism of leading astronomers yet to the delight of the newspapers, an architecture of engineered "canals" on Mars. These he took to be signs of an intelligent life, desperately in need of irrigation on an arid, declining planet; made habitable by the massive engineered projects of an advanced technological civilization, far above humanity's low evolutionary state. Building from Camille Flammarion's studies, and beginning in earnest with the "opposition" of 1894 (when Mars and the sun were on opposite sides of the earth and thereby more clearly visible from our sky), Lowell framed these discoveries within the best means that science had to offer. He had a Harvard education, one of the world's best telescopes and observatories at his Flagstaff, Arizona location, along with all of the achievements of Darwinian evolutionary biology. Lowell tapped into an existing scientific paradigm about the rise and fall of planets (and civilizations), drawing clear analogies to Earth. We were fated to rise and fall, just like poor Mars.[36]

The astronomers William Campbell and Edward Barnard were, among others, forthrightly critical of Lowell's methods and claims. But the cumulative effect of his many press reports over the years was to raise his authority and relevance. In Russia, as elsewhere, academia and the elite media received Lowell with mixed reviews. His findings were provocative but inconclusive. The question was therefore open to entertaining and optimistic speculation. New data were exploding on the scene year after year, from telescopic observations to possible radio signals. More and more news items promoted the existence of a Martian civilization.[37] Capitalizing on Galton's project and on Lowell's visions, the Polish science writer and storyteller Wladislaw Uminski took the controversy into historical fiction, a story about building a gigantic machine to send light signals to Mars.[38]

Lowell's "discoveries" only heightened the quest to find some common language, some terrestrial means to communicate with Mars. We were already searching for a common tongue, an international language for Earth. N. F. Fedorov, for example, recognized that English was a widespread and powerful new means of international communication, a true "language of commerce." But for him its very strengths on the global market were its weaknesses. It had become flat and cheap. Its words had lost their true meanings, their comprehensibility and solidarity between people. English was essentially a "dead" language, he claimed. Fedorov called instead for the rediscovery of our common, ancient "original language" (*praiazyk*), a "philological resurrection" to complement his common task of bodily resurrection.[39]

A number of other international languages, first and foremost Esperanto, also came into vogue at this time. The world's best science and popular science journals—from *Nature* and *Scientific American* to *Popular Science* and *I Know All*—broached the question. If machines such as the telegraph and wireless, dirigible and airplane, were uniting people as never before, along with new world trade and media markets, then humanity needed a cultural and linguistic medium to match. An "interplanetary" language, a new way of speaking and writing, was not such a great leap beyond. The Russian science fiction writer A. G. Liakide proposed French as the new language of global interaction and a corresponding mathematical and geometrical language of signals for Mars.[40]

The search for a universal language in order to speak to alien worlds was a perfect play upon the Tower of Babel myth: to reach for the heavens by way of a common tongue. Several projects reached the news media. Some proposed mathematical signs and formulas for interplanetary communication. If physical and chemical laws were truly universal laws, surely the rules of mathematics were universal too. Others called for geometric shapes, even human stick figures. It was as if having divined the straight forms of the Martian canals, we were now obliged to draw the same kinds of straight lines back. We Earthlings had only to craft them; surely the Martians would understand. One of Lowell's Flagstaff assistants, and a recognized astronomer in his own right, W. H. Pickering of Harvard University, proposed a ten-million-dollar scheme to signal Mars by way of a huge array of mirrors, flashing reflections of sunlight Mars's way, hoping for some similar signal back.[41]

The work of interplanetary communications was easier, of course, in fiction. In our imaginations we traveled to the planets and found civilizations there, other earths really, even crafting cultures and languages for them. In *Across the Zodiac* Percy Greg had invented an ingenious version of the Martian language, "constructed deliberately on set principles, with a view to the greatest possible simplicity and the least possible taxation of the memory." It was a language of the simplest rules without exception, composed of short, staccato vowel and consonant combinations that followed strict logical forms. Verbal tenses were governed by a set of twelve vowels, six for men and six for women (Greg's Mars was patriarchal). The masculine verbal tenses for *to be* were, in their singular and plural forms, structured around simple vowel oppositions. Other tenses and noun declinations were governed by simple consonant markers, always expressing a predictable action or condition. All nouns, furthermore, closely mirrored their related verbal roots by sound and look. Words that signified similar meanings were sounded and spelled the same.[42] Greg's simplified Martian set a trend in the literature for years to come, whether by influence or coincidence. Kurd Lasswitz adopted it for the Martians in his popular novel *Two Planets* (1897). *Earth* became *Ba*; *Mars* became *Nu*. "Earthlings in the field" meant *Bati li war*; "A spaceship to Mars" was *Vel li nu*.[43] Here was the same preference for quick, telegraphic vowel and consonant combinations, almost like an interplanetary Morse code. Such projects peaked during the years of the Russian Revolution as radical artists and anarchists presumed to speak for the whole planet to the wider cosmos.

French and Russian commentators dutifully reported on most of these schemes, sometimes with excitement and hope but at other times with a healthy, critical doubt. One writer noted that even if we humans succeeded in building giant displays or telegraphic and solar signals, "then what?" (*chto dal'she*). There was no guarantee that the Martians would understand us or care. Why even signal them in the first place, argued another, for if they were anything like us humans, we might just as well be inviting them to conquer us by some horribly disastrous interplanetary war? A third asked poignantly, presaging Enrico Fermi's well-known remarks from some fifty years later: if speculators were so certain that the Martians had created an advanced civilization, where were they? Where were the aliens that so many were talking about? "Why have they not visited us yet?"[44]

Several of Europe's newsworthy spiritualists, out to commune with the human dead and alien life forms in perfect "interplanetary communication," had a simple answer to the query. The Martians had no need to visit us because we had already visited them. Hélène Smith, the Swiss psychic known for her colorful séances with Hindu spirits, claimed to have visited Mars in her trances after 1892, her human voice speaking for the disembodied guides and translators who took her on these journeys. She eventually communed with Martian beings of various sorts, famously speaking their languages, transcribing their phonetic and hieroglyphic scripts, drawing landscapes and portraits of Martian scenes. It turns out that she was a fabulous impersonator, adept at imitating a kind of Hindi and various kinds of French-like "Martian," filled with sonorous, chant-like vowels. These were the judgments of Theodore Flournoy, a professor of psychology at the University of Geneva, who studied Smith's trances and even participated in them. These were also the conclusions of several leading linguists of the day, including Ferdinand de Saussure, who were fascinated with her artificial language, which they discovered was bound by its own curious set of rules and representations.[45]

Charles Leadbeater, another spiritualist and occultist, also claimed to have visited Mars, in the shape of his alternate spirit being and astral traveler. To international curiosity, Leadbeater's *The Inner Life* (1911) drew a detailed Lowellian map of Martian geography and civilization. The planet was, in his cosmic scheme, a true utopia. The weather held steady at a constant 70 degrees Fahrenheit with blue skies, little if ever threat of rain or snow. In such arid conditions Martians lived mostly at the equator, where a system of canals captured the melting ice from the planet's poles in order to cultivate huge swaths of verdant fields. Martians also looked a lot like Scandinavians, with blue eyes and blond hair, if shorter and rounder, this to adapt better to the planet's gravity and atmosphere. They prospered under a welfare state, enjoying all the benefits of advanced science and technology (electricity, telephones, mechanized labor, an international language, and interplanetary travel) and rather free sexual mores (polygamy). All of this must have made for captivating reading in Russia, to whose readers Leadbeater's Mars probably sounded a lot like the West or at least their imagined parts of it.[46]

Outer space now became the site for some of Europe's favorite utopias. Andrew Blair's *Annals of the Twenty-Ninth Century* (1874) joined travel to the planets with the vision of a one-world state. Marie Corelli's *The Romance of Two Worlds* (1886) found serenity on a tour of the solar system by way of angelic and spiritual forces, powered by electricity. Wladislaw S. Lach-Szyrma's popular stories featured "Aleriel," a winged being from Venus who traveled to Earth and the other planets spreading good and fighting evil. Along the way we learn of advanced civilizations throughout the solar system, enlightened societies of labor equality and advanced technology, such as antigravity "ether cars" and streamlined cigar boats, great canal systems and floating cities. All of this was proof of "an integral unity of design, and yet an infinite variety of manifestations of the wisdom and power of the Divine Creator of the Universe."[47] The fictional Aleriel pretended to be a factual reporter, recommending that we humans answer the visual signs of the Martian canals with our own signals for "interplanetary space," be they geometric or human stick forms. Best of all was a great cross of electrically lighted ships anchored in Lake Michigan, this to celebrate Christianity, the discovery of America, and the great Chicago Exhibition of 1893. Humans were to honor Columbus's discovery of the Western Hemisphere by finding a new window to our neighboring planet.[48]

Russian Science Fiction and Outer Space

Russian publishers tapped into the emerging market demand for science fiction but with Russian color, characters, and pride—sometimes even with a revolutionary tinge, an accent on social equality and justice. Their first stories either sent us to Mars or brought Martians down to us. A. G. Liakide's *Upon the Ocean of Stars* (1892) took a traditional expedition through the solar system on a great birdlike craft, finding backward beings on Mercury, Venus, and the moon but a highly advanced civilization on Mars. There his Russian explorer found a people with light-blue skin and dark-green hair, peaceful vegetarians all. According to the presumptions of the day, Martians had surpassed human progress on Earth: building the infamous canals to adapt to their dry environment; living in clean, orderly, electrified cities under a Marxian socialism. The government owned the means of production as well as managed labor and supply and demand, all without the evils of commodity exchange and the price system, all for the benefits of a society of full equality and justice.[49] This was quite a radical utopia for late-imperial Russia but not the first to pass the tsar's censors, hidden under a veil of Western science fiction. One of Albert Daiber's stories did too; it was about a German expedition that discovered a Martian civilization of peace and order, economic equality and prosperity.[50]

L. B. Afanas'ev's thoughtful *Journey to Mars* (1901) gave the Mars craze and Tesla's Martian signals something more of a twist. Now a Russian hero, Nikolai Aleksandrovich Krasnov applied his mathematical genius to discover a means to travel to Mars. He was a "genuine Newton," a truly Russian "Edison"; his ship was named the *Galileo*. His unique power was the "Integral," the formula driving his differential equations and providing the electrical "counterforce" to power the ascending curves of his spacecraft. Cylindrical and conical in shape, made of a light metal, outfitted with liquid shock absorbers and solar energy cells, the craft set off for Mars after what was probably Russia's first fictional countdown, dramatically listing the hours, then the minutes, then the seconds, to launch. It held a crew of five: two other Russian mathematicians, a German professor stowaway, and a lovely English lady, Mary Edwards, a millionaire widow and love interest. The long journey had its moments of Russian-English romance and Russian-German enmity. But much of the time was spent pondering and even writing a poetry of mathematics, plotting the spacecraft's trajectories and corrections, their "burns" and atmospheric brakes to the planets.[51]

P. P. Infant'ev's *On Another Planet* (1902) was based, appropriately enough, on a series of actual news stories out of the United States and Europe about Tesla's signals from Mars and Lowell's advanced civilization and elaborate canals. Its main character, François Roche, was a follower of Flammarion. Set in an isolated observatory in the Alps, atop Mont Blanc, he communicated with the Martians through acous-

MYSTICAL ECONOMIES OF EARTH AND SPACE

tical tubes and telescopes, even venturing to the planet by a strange process of hypnosis and transfiguration. Infant'ev's first lesson was about evolution and the "struggle for existence." Martian forms were monstrous and hideous. They were creatures like toads, with bird-like heads and webbed feet, one-eyed and one-eared, well adapted to conditions on Mars. Conveniently, they also spoke fluent French and Russian. These flourishes served as entertaining background for the crux of the story: technology. Mars's advanced civilization included synthetic foods and robotic servants, flying machines and under-water cities, the infamous canals and hydroelectric stations, solar energy and climactic controls, telephones and televisions, and even "psychic-scopes" for extrasensory perception. These were all ratio-nal Martian adaptations to the planet's harsh conditions. They had taken control over evolution, an achievement inscribed at the ornate palace of the Central Statistical Bureau, located at the Lake of the Sun, really an "all-world exhibit" of museums and laboratories cel-ebrating the Martians' greatest technological and cultural achieve-ments. Their ultimate Fedorovian dream, as of yet only expressed poetically, was to master not only planetary but also cosmic space, to turn Mars itself into a planetary spacecraft, a "wandering comet" to escape a dying sun and reach whole new solar systems.[52]

V. Bariatinskii's more playful story "Letters from Mars" (1904) poked fun at the whole new genre of Mars stories, featuring an exotic, gold-skinned Martian with eyes for a human nose, a nose for human eyes. Shipwrecked at St. Petersburg, "Criks," as he called himself, spoke English, a language that he had learned on Mars thanks to an earlier space traveler who had come from our planet by balloon to teach the Martians not only our tongue but also how to play cricket, drink whiskey, and eat red meat.[53]

Also bridging West and East and these ideals of interplanetary life and "communication" was the prolific writer Vera Ivanovna Kry-zhanovskaia (1861–1924), author of a set of exotic novels that often joined romance and spiritualist themes with space travel. Fedorov's Orthodox economy of labor and love met its match in Kryzhanov-skaia's occult stories. Kryzhanovskaia was also known by a pseud-onym, J. W. Rochester, the name she gave to her alter ego, the spiritual medium who allegedly spoke through her as the reincarnated spirit of the English earl of Rochester, John Wilmot (1647–80), infamous poet and essayist, rake and libertine. The pen name was a perfect choice for Kryzhanovskaia, who occupied a strategic place amid the growing reading market for the erotic and esoteric during Russia's "Silver Age," part of the "fashionable occultism" of the day. It was a fashion that even poorly literate readers could join, whose cheap, mass-circulation newspapers and booklets taught rational scientific truths (against the official theology), often colored by the mystical and magical.[54]

Kryzhanovskaia's fiction found a ready audience among Russian elite and middlebrow readers consumed with European and American texts promoting mesmerism and galvanism, alchemy and immortality. What with the new discoveries and applications of radium and electricity, X-rays and radio waves, the supernatural and the scientific seemed to be joining all the more closely. A professor at Harvard University called wireless telegraphy the next step to telepathy: "The nerves of the whole world are, so to speak, being bound together." Well-known scientific authorities, from William James to Camille Flammarion to Sir Oliver Lodge, searched for scientific proofs of the supernatural and attempted to open a spiritualist discourse with the dead.[55] Flammarion's writings, addressing telepathy and reincarnation, were especially popular in Russia. Critics and fans alike called him the "prophet of a religion of science." His *Stories of Infinity* (1873), about spirit beings who traveled in space and visited alien worlds, was likely a powerful influence on Kryzhanovskaia. She published in this established subgenre of "mystical science fiction," made up of works that appealed to apparitions, reincarnation, extrasensory perception, and all manner of the paranormal. Angelic spirits often inhabited these works, spirits who traveled through time and across space, representing a higher existence as against a corrupted Earth.[56] This was interplanetary communication of a kind, too, a discourse with alien life beyond the mortal bonds of our own world. In imaginative ways it projected humanity upon the sensuous reefs of ethereal space.

Originally a spiritualist, Kryzhanovskaia led séances among St. Petersburg's high society, whose members were fascinated with psychic bridges between the living and the dead. She soon gravitated to the more doctrinal "theosophy," a small but influential movement founded by E. P. Blavatskaia (aka Madame Blavatsky) and her American friend Col. Henry Steele Olcott. Born in Russia as Helen Petrovna in 1831, Blavatskaia became a global sensation by the time of her death in 1891, having traveled and established a movement spanning North America, Europe, and South Asia. She was succeeded by her dynamic pupil Annie Besant; their works were widely available in various Russian translations. With its blend of monism and pantheism, Aryan and Hindu spiritualism, theosophy defined the universe as the site of one creation, one matter, one reason. The theosophists' ultimate goal was to rise toward the perfection and immortality of a "Universal Brotherhood," under the guidance of the "Eternal and Universal Life" force. The path was framed by all manner of occult practices (hypnotism, clairvoyance, Kabbala) and the laws of reincarnation and karma. Built into every atom (inorganic and organic) was the evolutionary principle, the path of spiritual perfection. Spirit ruled the cosmos; matter weighed it down. Both were united in cycles of ascent and descent, good and evil, life and death.[57]

For theosophists such as Kryzhanovskaia all was not lost with death, for each person was sure to trod a spiral of rebirth and improvement (or not), bound by the moral law that "every act must work out its full results." None of this was crass supernaturalism, so Besant cautioned, but took its veracity from modern science, from Newton's very own laws of nature: "By every action we modify the present and mold the future."[58] Although their processes and results differed, both science and occultism sought to navigate between the known and unknown, to uncover the mysteries of the cosmos and of human immortality. They also helped to disseminate the notion of the plurality of worlds. As Besant taught, "All the universe is pulsating with life . . . our little planet is but as a tiny speck of sand in the Sahara," but "one among countless myriads of worlds."[59]

Kryzhanovskaia wove these claims into the very fabric of her science fiction stories. *On a Neighboring Planet* (1903) sent characters to Mars, *On Another World* (1911) to Venus. Both were aristocratic utopias graced with advances such as interplanetary spacecraft, telecommunications, and eugenics. "Space and time, my friend, are relative terms," said one all-knowing Martian to the homesick hero, Ardea, who from his small-minded human perspective looked back to Earth, that "huge, pale emerald" sailing through space. From his Brahmin teachers Ardea learned that humanity—if in different evolutionary forms—was scattered throughout the solar system, guided by the caste of high priests, united by a common physical, chemical, and biological nature (including the laws of "attraction-repulsion" and "multiplication"). An eternal father god, the merciful master of light over dark, ruled over all.[60] The heroine, Psikheia, discovered a Venus of harmony and love, governed by a theology of cosmic creation, with a "Creator God" making whole planets and solar systems out of the "malleable grayish matter of the zooether," the living firmament of cosmic space. Earth, on the other hand, was a "stench pool" of vice and murder, egoism and license, a point of corruption against the universe's higher points of perfection. Terrestrial political revolutions were an especially poignant symptom of chaos, insults against the orderly revolutions of the planets beyond.[61]

With most marketable success in her five-part cycle *The Magi* (1901–16), Kryzhanovskaia's band of immortals traveled by telepathic powers and spaceships to other continents, spirit worlds, planets, and star systems, there to wage dramatic struggles between evil and good. Dr. Ralph Morgan, reincarnated as one of the leading magi, Supremati, made his way to these points beyond, spreading truth and goodness, saving dying worlds. Earth was beyond repair, trapped in the "miasma" of a poisoned culture and nature. In a stunning apocalyptic scene, something Kryzhanovskaia compared to the supernova of a star, our planet imploded in a fit of earthquakes and eruptions, reduced to a cloud of atomic matter, now to begin the life cycle once again. Only the last scraps of good humanity were saved, along with the better material artifacts of human science and art, transported by a massive "flotilla" of spacecraft to a new planetary home. At least some of us found salvation in the stars. As one of the magi noted while peering out at the Milky Way, "Worlds swarm about there, like specks of dust in sunlight; yet on each of these atoms of space are born, live, and die whole generations of humanity."[62]

MYSTICAL ECONOMIES OF EARTH AND SPACE

Kryzhanovskaia's writings were not high art. She wrote light fiction for casual readers, but her oeuvre was all the more significant because of its popularity. She found her niche, her audience, in the fantasies of flights to planets and places beyond a mortal Earth. Her stories were not elaborate. They lacked technological sophistication, centered mostly upon the basic insights of modern astronomy and the natural sciences. Her spacecraft were rather simple but sometimes hinted at the shape of a rocket. Ardea traveled to Mars on a "cigar"-shaped machine, a "long, narrow, shining metal casing," powered by the vibrating waves of attraction and repulsion that united the whole universe. Kryzhanovskaia even outfitted it with sealed compartments and metallic space suits. The same oblong "shell" appeared again in *The Magi* series, made of a "phosphorescent crystal," what Kryzhanovskaia also called an artificial "satellite" (*sputnik*), a "falling star" speeding away from Earth.[63]

This kind of craft was already a staple in both newspaper science and science fiction of the day, based on the famous Winan Cigar Steamer, designed as a cylindrical-conical sea vessel with "parabolic spindles" at each end. The steamer's efficient center of gravity and streamlining meant stability and speed through the water.[64] Yet in its very geometric shape, its variety of lines and curves, the cigar ship also prefigured the rocket, embodying its parabolic trajectories and curves into outer space. The craft ultimately transformed the deep heavens of the medieval and early-modern mind-set, a cage of divine creation and destruction, into the outer space of modern cosmology, the place where humanity itself might become inhabitant and master. For Kryzhanovskaia, as for Fedorov, the spacecraft plied the new routes of human spiritual commerce in the ether.

In a widely disseminated speech before London's Royal Institution, H. G. Wells gave perfect expression to all of these ideals when he celebrated humanity's "great will to live struggling out of the intertidal slime, struggling from shape to shape and from power to power, crawling and then walking confidently upon the land, struggling generation after generation to master the air." Human beings were insatiable, reaching for the far horizons of breadth and height. It was "a process of diffusion and aeration," an upward "scale" and "long ascent." It was a "rising curve" that would surely "rise yet more steeply and swiftly." It was a journey that would climax in a beneficent "world state" and cosmic existence, when future human beings "shall stand upon the earth as one stands upon a footstool, and shall laugh and reach out their hands amidst the stars."[65] Modern life was itself like a "shooting star," agreed one Russian commentator, instantly streaking across space, captivating humanity with surprise and wonder, illuminating the paradoxes of our backwardness and progress.[66] It was as if global lines of latitude and longitude had become unhinged, sprung into outer space, forming new contours and new pathways for human exploration and exchange.

3

The Mechanics of Interplanetary Travel

All of these diverse contexts and personalities bring us to Konstantin E. Tsiolkovskii, the founder of modern rocketry and spaceflight theories. One of the leading interpretations counts him among N. F. Fedorov's best students and disciples, a point also suggested by some of Tsiolkovskii's own writings. At the age of sixteen, so he remembered, he lived three years of joyful poverty: roaming Moscow's streets, living in hovels, spending his days in the library reading Fedorov's stacks of chosen books. But Fedorov's Orthodox religious ideals may not have been so definitive or all-encompassing. Tsiolkovskii, after all, hovered somewhere between agnosticism and deism. The most he admitted was that the great librarian provided him with library books more than ideas, this at a time when he was consumed with the study of mathematics and pure science.[1] Tsiolkovskii followed his own intellectual pathways, believing in science as his method, matter as his ground of observation, and the universe as his field of inquiry. He trusted things and the laws of physics and mechanics that ultimately made sense of things. As he admitted in his autobiography, he owed the most to Isaac Newton. He was a committed materialist, a patron of the "old Newtonian mechanics." He had, in other words, graduated from Fedorov's elementary school of Copernican religiosity.[2]

The overarching theme in Soviet historiography has also held that Tsiolkovskii received little recognition and reward in the late imperial era, when he first began his theoretical works. As one of his biographers put it, amid the "period of failure and depression" before the October Revolution, "the efforts of the inventor came to nothing." More recently, Russian historians have spoken of Tsiolkovskii's "second creative birth" after 1917.[3] These were myths that Tsiolkovskii helped to propagate too. Those closest to him remember a deep "pessimism" in his countenance, his sense of victimhood, his identity as a "sufferer for science."[4] He often despaired of his physical ailments, his several family tragedies, his professional failures. His personal correspondence was often filled with self-pity, frustration, and regret, speaking of a "life of sadness and difficulty." He wrote about constantly working and struggling just for a "piece of bread" and how life had given him a "bundle of sorrows."[5]

On this issue of his isolation in the late imperial period, quite the opposite is true. From the beginning of his career Tsiolkovskii published in some of the empire's best popular, technical, and scientific journals, including pieces on mechanics and fluid dynamics, on stellar astronomy and aerodynamics, including studies of a heavier-than-air apparatus.[6] He was a member of the Russian Physical-Chemical Society and a guest speaker before the Russian Academy of Sciences. He was best known for a topic that captivated him for the rest of his life: the all-metal dirigible, first published in a brochure of 1892.[7] The project helped make him well known, if not always well regarded, in Russia's rising aviation circles. One engineer, for example, judged that because the plan was pure theory, without any realistic drafts or models, it was still "premature." Tsiolkovskii, like his beloved all-metal dirigible, was a thing before its time.[8]

Little ever came of these insights and contacts. This was the result of the arrogance and prejudices of the academic communities and official government circles of St. Petersburg and Moscow. They looked askance at this "self-taught" and "self-generated" man (*samouchek* and *samorod*), without any advanced degrees or credentialed posts. For some of them Tsiolkovskii was a "fantasist," "maniac," and "crank." He conversely believed that official science spurned him, that it was too small-minded and "passive," that it was smitten with European and especially German science.[9] In part his isolation was his own doing. He was an eccentric: introverted and reclusive. Whenever he traveled beyond his home in Kaluga, he made hasty trips, always returning as soon as possible to his daily routines, to the serenity of his workshop, to admiring friends and the familiar scenes of his neighborhood, where he loved to ride his bike, sail his small boat, and fly his kites. He was also a prodigy but a provincial one. He never mastered any language other than Russian. He rarely used notes or citations in his own published works, and when he did, he referred to European and American thinkers by name, not to their specific works. He often read about them in Russian encyclopedias or newspapers, with the likely pretense that their ideas were already his, already somehow Russia's.

The Tsiolkovskii Rocket Equation

Tsiolkovskii made some of his earliest musings about space theory around 1878, with notebook sketches on the solar system and the effects of zero gravity on human physiology, compiled into a surviving manuscript, "Free Space" (1883). In it he also conceived of the advantage of reactive power, this to move a craft at "any desired curve and in accord with any law of velocity."[10] But he turned all of these ideas into "fantasy" tales, a kind of science fiction, well before he refined them as scientific fact. *On the Moon* (1893) and *Dreams of Earth and Sky* (1897) were simple and lighthearted stories, easy to follow, painted with flashes of humor and self-parody.[11] Both works brought the physics of outer space and the planets down to Earth, within the everyday walls of homes and schools. These were enlightening classroom lessons really, framed as casual astronomy or physics lectures. Tsiolkovskii brought to them the same pedagogical and preachy style that he brought to his elementary and middle-school lesson plans over the forty-one years of his teaching career. He was always the teacher, just as he posed several times for group or lone photographs, appearing somewhat distant with his spectacles, properly attired in suit and tie.[12]

On the Moon gently introduced readers to the wonders of the moon's gravity, in which an average person would be able to lift incredible weights, acquire the strength of Hercules, and move about "by leaps and bounds," making "somersaults in space." Tsiolkovskii lectured on the positions and rotations of the planets relative to the sun and Earth, on the basics of astronomy and lunar physics, on the moon's weak gravitational pull and its fluctuating temperatures.[13] In *Dreams of Earth and Sky* he found his literary voice, a new pace and confidence. We see the same preoccupation with free flight into zero gravity, his characters sweeping over the earth as if in "an imaginary fairy-tale world." But there was also a new sense of depth and scale, of relative proportions. Tsiolkovskii compared the human person to the earth, to the solar system, to the Milky Way galaxy, to the plurality of galaxies in the infinite universe. According to the paradigm of magnification, the human being writ large as observer became the human being writ small, like a grain of dust within the "grandeur of the Universe." He turned the human being into a kind of moving planet all its own, flying by its own exploratory orbits, without up or down, other planets advancing or receding from our own movable horizon.[14]

Neither of these two stories ever mentioned rockets or reactive devices. Tsiolkovskii's tales were truly flights of fancy. Long, involved dream sequences took his explorers into outer space as if by magic. When he discussed the mechanism to escape gravity in *Dreams of Earth and Sky*, he imagined either a fast-moving train located at the equator, acquiring speeds of up to eight kilometers (five miles) a second by way of centrifugal force, or Verne's cannon shell, which he cleverly outfitted with an even larger cannon and with an internal liquid cushion to protect the crew. All of these methods were very much in vogue at the time. Flammarion's novels *Lumen* and *Uranie* sent their characters to space by telepathy. In his popular survey *On the Moon* Father Théophile Moreux used telepathy to take his readers on a scientific adventure to the moon. First in fiction and later as possible science, the French writer Henri de Graffigny promoted an interplanetary rocket shot into space by way of the centrifugal motion of a great circular catapult.[15]

Verne's cannon shell remained the most popular means to space. Georges Melies's classic film *Voyage to the Moon* (1902) used it, resurrecting many of Verne's humorous and sarcastic twists for cinema, a wacky parody of the eccentric scientists and their craft, filled with traditional burlesque routines and new movie tricks. Yet Melies also conceived of his space crew as cosmic sailors upon the solar system,

THE MECHANICS OF INTERPLANETARY TRAVEL

Fig. 2. "Earthlight," showing Earth and cascading comet from the first human encampment on the moon. A drawing from Georges Melies's movie *Voyage to the Moon* (1902). Credit: Collection Cinémathèque Française, Bibliothèque du Film (Paris).

landing as explorers on the moon, all this highlighted against a streaking comet and Earth itself in the distance.[16] Jerzy Zulawski's space trilogy, beginning with *On the Silver Planet* (1903), used Verne-like cannons and projectile guns to reach the moon in a bullet-shaped craft launched from Earth along a "giant parabola." Packed initially with credible scientific and technical facts, including space walks and lunar expeditions, the story moved at a brisk pace. It followed the exploits of the main character, Jan Koretskii, as he mines the moon's resources, he and his descendants painfully adapting to its severe conditions, waxing poetically for home. A philosopher by training, Zulawski wove positivist science, philosophical idealism, and mythology into his complex plotlines. The series sold well in Russia, better than any of Tsiolkovskii's science fiction, perhaps for its accent on exotic adventure and thoughtful storytelling.[17]

Like these authors, Tsiolkovskii was initially taken with ends rather than means, with fanciful ideas rather than applied science. What intervened to compel his more practical interests in the rocket? Several works, by his admission, were decisive. A. P. Fedorov's *New Principle of Aerial Flight* (1896) was perhaps the most influential. It proposed a whole "new approach" to the problems of aerial flight then being intensely debated and tested throughout Europe and the Americas. Fedorov, a young student at the St. Petersburg Electro-Technical Institute, was bold and original. Why even bother at all with the atmosphere as a "support medium," as most specialists were arguing? His insight was to suggest provocatively that "from a mechanical point of view, the principles of bird flight and rocket flight are one and the same." The only difference was that birds propelled themselves by the force of the compression of air, rockets by the force of compressed (expelled) fuel, of which he proposed a gas forced out of a metal or aluminum tube. Fedorov's influence was dramatic, as Tsiolkovskii and those close to him testified time and again. They consistently anchored Tsiolkovskii's priority moment in 1896, the very year he read the book, enough to compare A. P. Fedorov's influence upon Tsiolkovskii (and his discovery of the space rocket) to the "falling apple upon Newton's discovery of gravity," the marriage of pure accident and creative genius.[18]

Tsiolkovskii was also deeply influenced by I. V. Meshcherskii's *Dynamics of a Point of Variable Mass* (1897), his thesis at the University of St. Petersburg. Before this work Newton's second law of motion had defined the rudimentary equations of mechanics but largely assumed no change of mass. Meshcherskii built variable mass into his whole approach, presuming a body whose mass changed by either natural forces acting upon it or by artificial means. His examples were varied: icebergs forming and breaking up as they drifted the oceans, meteors falling upon the orbiting earth, and rockets exhausting their own mass as they flew through the skies. He derived the mathematical equations to plot the dynamics of these varied objects of variable mass.[19] His model equations offered Tsiolkovskii, the prodigy and polymath, a natural bridge between celestial mechanics and interplanetary travel. For he knew with Meshcherskii that any

THE MECHANICS OF INTERPLANETARY TRAVEL

interplanetary craft would operate in outer space by way of the very same celestial laws as any planet or body in the solar system. Before Meshcherskii and Tsiolkovskii outer space was a realm of three-dimensional ethereal space, of the height, width, and depth of the planets and the sun, of the cosmic dust and star systems beyond. But now their work added a fourth dimension to space: human motion and time. They conquered it, at least mathematically, in the form of the human-made machine, the rocket.

Tsiolkovskii's most important work in the field of rocketry and spaceflight theory, "The Exploration of Universal Space by Reactive Devices" (1903), published in the scholarly journal *Science Review* when he was all of forty-six years old, integrated and elaborated upon the findings of these two works, giving A. P. Fedorov's ideas the mathematical foundations derived from I. V. Meshcherskii's differential proofs, all calculated by Tsiolkovskii's own hand. The essay established his indisputable priority as a founder of rocket science. It was the first work of its kind to define precisely the nature of liquid fuel rocket power, its launch capacities and its operation in the vacuum of outer space. Positioning himself rather awkwardly between Verne's famous cannonball and the "far distant nebulous future," he proposed a novel and sure way to outer space: "a reactive device, that is a kind of rocket, but one of enormous dimensions and specially designed," taking the form of an "elongated metallic chamber." By controlled explosions its "condensed flaming gases" were to "race out through the flare pipes with a tremendous relative velocity," forcing the rocket to "soar upwards," steered by the human mind and hand in control of its ascending pathways. For optimal performance Tsiolkovskii recommended the advantages of liquid oxygen and liquid hydrogen as propellants of "excellent" efficiency. He suggested regenerative cooling to disperse the extreme heat of the flaming gases.[20]

At the center of the essay, however, was what became known as "Tsiolkovskii's rocket equation," the mathematical model that defined the relationship between the rocket's exhaust velocity and mass ratio. As he wrote, "The increment in rocket velocity is proportional to the speed of the ejected explosion products." Tsiolkovskii expressed the formula symbolically:

$$v = v_1 ln(1 + \frac{m_2}{m_1})$$

The symbol V means the velocity of the rocket. V_1 is the relative exhaust velocity of the exploding gases and ln the natural logarithm. M_1 is the mass of the rocket without the propellant. M_2 is the mass of the propellant. Therefore, the rocket's velocity is dependent upon the ratio of its initial mass (of fuel and structure and cargo) and final mass (without the fuel) and the exhaust velocity of the very fuel propelling the rocket. The more efficiently the fuel ejected, the greater its reactive force and exhaust velocity; therefore, the faster and farther the rocket will move. In turn Tsiolkovskii discussed the actual signal velocities necessary for the rocket to overcome gravity and air resistance, even the gravitational forces of the moon and planets and asteroids. These were all rather tentative lines of "vertical ascent." But they were all powered by the rocket's own accelerating force, the very condition necessary to eventually fulfill that grander human design: to "trace out the cosmic curves of motion of a rocket in celestial space."[21]

The basic principles underlying this work were not original to Tsiolkovskii. He honestly admitted as much in the essay: "The idea is not new." Perhaps most famously, we know from retrospect that the German engineer Hans Ganswindt had introduced his own design for a reactive-style "interplanetary ship" (*Weltenfahrzeug*) in 1891, one that used dynamite charges to propel itself in a kind of bouncing and reaction effect through space. Like Tsiolkovskii, Ganswindt was also fascinated with new designs for dirigible, airplanes, and rockets.[22] Georges Le Faure and Henri de Graffigny's *The Extraordinary Adventures of a Russian Savant* (1888–96) entertained a rocket-like spacecraft (the *Molniia*). So did L. B. Afanas'ev's *Journey to Mars* (1901), whose mathematician hero applied Newtonian calculus and the power of the "Integral" to master reactive force. Tsiolkovskii probably read and was inspired by both stories.

There was an even more stunning coincidence in 1903, when the French commentator A. Le Mée upstaged Tsiolkovskii with a short

THE MECHANICS OF INTERPLANETARY TRAVEL

essay arguing for the theoretical and mechanical, the physiological and biological, possibilities of "interplanetary communication." Signals to a nearby planet were a distinct possibility with wireless telegraphy. So were spaceships of a kind. Le Mée recognized that Jules Verne's cannon was still the likeliest means to outer space, this to achieve the proper "takeoff velocity." But he also argued that the force of its blast would reduce any human passengers to "gruel." To avoid this, he advised the construction of a kind of bullet craft, applying gradual acceleration using a "step," or "staged," method. This was essentially a rocket, whose propulsive force came "from within," by unleashing the power of compressed air or some other explosive material.[23] Tsiolkovskii's and Le Mée's articles both highlight the spring of 1903 as a rather remarkable moment of simultaneous insight and lost opportunity. Through these two enterprising thinkers Russia and France were speaking in the same nascent idiom of rocket science. Le Mée's piece even circulated across continents, through an international print network of shared reviews and translations. But for unknown reasons Tsiolkovskii's article was not translated or reported. Perhaps this was because of the difficulties of comprehending his calculus, the differential equations at the heart of rocket science. They would have posed too great a hurdle for even the best French-Russian translator. Tsiolkovskii's piece was for the average reader an untranslatable tour de force.[24]

There was yet another coincidence of approaches that just preceded Tsiolkovskii's article. The electrical engineer and popular science writer John Munro took his readers on *A Trip to Venus* (1897) in a liquid fuel rocket. Like Tsiolkovskii, he had turned from pure science to science fiction in order to better reach the public with his novel ideas. His calculations were certain, predicting an initial velocity of five miles (eight kilometers) a second for his craft to reach space. It was a "rocket," an "aerial locomotive" of some twelve stages, driven by its own "self movement," meaning "the recoil of the rushing fumes will impel the car onwards." He described these rockets as new "falling stars" and artificial planets of human design, the basis for a whole "new field of research" that would "revolutionise" transportation and industry.[25] Munro's story also expressed some of the mystical currents at play in European and American science writing. He raised a gnostic quest to "quit the earth," this realm of the "lower life," a "hell" where "life itself hangs on a blind mischance." We were not forever bound to this corrupt planet Earth and its fixed laws of gravity. In the cosmos we would find proofs of universal evolution, fulfill our dreams of order and harmony and beauty. Munro drew this mystical philosophy of ascent in the shape of a Venusian flower, formed "like a serpent or the side of a wave . . . the most beautiful curve we know." Here was a perfect parabola reaching into space. In artistic terms it was the "line of beauty," a "symbol of the continuous unfolding of things; the graceful progress of development . . . the path of evolution."[26]

These were some of the very same approaches that in a flash of theoretical brilliance Tsiolkovskii had already proven mathematically, with deliberate scope and detailed proofs. In no way do any of these sources detract from his achievement. They only spotlight it all the more. Tsiolkovskii's famous essay was quite a coup for this provincial schoolteacher, published in *Science Review* (1894–1903), a leading intellectual journal in the radical tradition of "critical realism." It also helps to prove one of his claims that he had always been a revolutionary, always a populist in search of truth and justice. Under the direction of M. M. Filippov, *Science Review* was dedicated to the natural and human sciences: reaching from botany to astronomy, from linguistics to anthropology. As a talented mathematician and biographer of Isaac Newton, Filippov would have immediately grasped the relevance of Tsiolkovskii's work. Also underwriting *Science Review* was a current of militant Darwinism and scientific socialism, publishing essays by Vera Zasulich, Georgii Plekhanov, and V. I. Ulianov (Lenin).[27]

This was exalted company for the reserved Tsiolkovskii. Yet his article elicited no significant public commentary; the second installment never appeared. This was largely the result of the government's censorship of the journal and its closure after Filippov's mysterious death on 12 June 1903, perhaps from natural causes or an accidental poisoning. Rumor had it for many years afterward that he died in an explosion while testing his "Filippov's Rays," long-distance streams

THE MECHANICS OF INTERPLANETARY TRAVEL

of lethal electricity, a weapon of such massive destructive power that it was meant to end war for all time. Although the whole episode remains a puzzle, Filippov's sudden death blocked Tsiolkovskii's cause.[28] He had single-handedly invented the basic formulas and trajectories of modern rocket science. Yet his 1903 essay, filled with complicated differential equations, languished for many years in relative obscurity, little read and poorly understood. He remained best known for his fictional works and the occasional scientific or engineering article: a creative thinker of modest means.

Aviation Pathways to the Planets

Grander historical events also overtook Tsiolkovskii. Recognition had to wait. The years after his article saw Russia's collapse into the Russo-Japanese War, the events of the 1905 revolution, and several more years of government crackdowns. Europe and America, meanwhile, continued to make leaps and bounds in scientific and technological progress. Their scientists and inventors were preoccupied with the conquest of distance. By 1908 X-rays were seeing through things, electric grids were powering whole regions, the wireless was sending signals across the world, cinematography was projecting images from place to place. Science was also promising, at least through press reports, to relay sounds and images at a distance (television), to direct thoughts without sound through space (telepathy), or to rapidly send mail and cargo and even people across continents and oceans (by pneumatic tube). Nothing expressed the West's mastery of distance, its power of projection, better than aviation. The successful flights of Wilbur Wright at Le Mans, France, and Orville Wright at Fort Myers, Virginia, in the late summer of 1908 proved the realities of heaver-than-air flight once and for all. The achievement came in that pivotal year when Henry Ford's Model T went on the assembly line, when Theodore Roosevelt sent the "Great White Fleet" around the world, when Admiral Robert Perry set off for the North Pole. This was the moment when, as Thomas Edison said, "anything, everything, is possible." Or as another American commentator put it, "History has shown time after time that it is not safe to set limits to what science can accomplish." Progress, in the form of the "complete mastery of aerial navigation," better engines and airplanes for faster and higher and farther flight, was assured.[29]

The French aviation pioneer Robert Esnault-Pelterie certainly thought so. Famous for designing one of the world's first all-metal monoplanes (along with an innovative air-cooled, seven-cylinder axial engine and the world's first piloting control stick), he now offered his own predictions on the airplane of the future, this for the French popular science journal *I Know All*. Tucked away in its pages was a drawing of his futuristic craft, with a sleek fuselage and glider-type wings, without a propeller of any kind, powered only by a stream of jet exhaust at the tail. Here was a remarkable and true first, an original blueprint for Esnault-Pelterie's coming reaction craft, his rocket for interplanetary flight.[30] Esnault-Pelterie may have owed some of his inspiration to the work of René Lorin, who had already proposed a "reaction" motor for airplanes in 1907, something like an artillery projectile applying the forces of explosion and exhaust. He went on to propose and patent early ramjet engines.[31] Yet we also owe Esnault-Pelterie his due as an innovator and visionary. The French aviation pioneer Ferdinand Ferber counted him as such: one of those rare "supermen of the future" who were transforming the flying machine into a "dirigible" rocket, creating new machines "to vanquish the immensities" of outer space.[32]

This was a demanding moment for the Russian public. Aviation was a new reality, but it was not quite Russia's. The United States had set the foundation. France had begun to reinvent the engineering and industry. Russia had less to offer. K. E. Veigelin's early popular history, for example, was completely dominated by European and American achievements, Russia relegated to a short and disappointing appendix. Yet the pages of Russian newspapers and magazines soon began to report the country's aviation achievements, from the feats of its first aviators to the launching of its massive "airplane-dreadnaught."[33] Most revealing was the story of one of the country's first pilots, the engineer and aviator L. M. Matsievich, who was killed in September 1910 at only thirty-three years old in an aviation accident in the Crimea. The outpouring of grief joined all of Russian society—from the grand princes to the prime min-

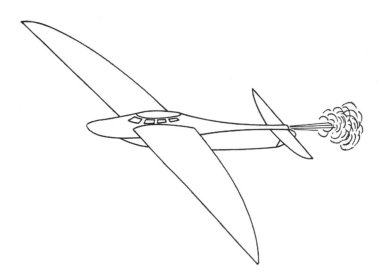

Fig. 3. Robert Esnault-Pelterie's liquid fuel reaction airplane (1908), the first such image in the news media that I have been able to identify. From the popular science magazine *Je sais tout* 4, no. 42, 15 July 1908, 725.

ister (P. A. Stolypin), from high school students to factory workers. Besides his tragic sacrifice, so the eulogies went, Matsievich was special because he was "ours," a truly Russian hero. He was also a "type of new man," one who was "victorious over the chaos [*stikhiia*] of the elements and space and time."[34]

In the imagery and metaphors of the time, Matsievich was not only one of Russia's first aviators. He was also its first astronaut. What mattered for him, as for his admirers, was not speed but distance, even the "reach for the stars."[35] Russian writers were in agreement about his significance: he was a living symbol of ascent, even to outer space. Leonid Andreev dedicated his story "Flight" to Matsievich's sacrifice—a dense psychological study of his willful fortitude. His fictional character Iurii Mikhailovich Pushkarev (the "cannoneer") embodied all of Matsievich's manly virtues, especially the courage to "cheat death" and gravity, to aim for the "boundlessness of space," to reach "ever higher," in looping arcs and lines, like a "loud-whistling rocket dashing straight upwards," like a "strange human star, speeding away from earth to heaven."[36] Another maverick pilot, the poet V. V. Kamenskii, expressed the same sentiment in a poetic sketch on flight, shaped in the form of a pyramid, peaking in the pilot's own "I" at the vanishing point in the sky, at the edge of space. A group of teenage girls represented this very image in their funeral wreath to the heroic aviator Matsievich. "The white swan flew up to the heavens," so went their remembrance, "and in the darkness the white swan disappeared."[37]

As aviation became more and more real to the educated public, Russians rediscovered Tsiolkovskii's various aviation dreams. Reality was literally displacing fiction. As one aviation commentator put it, what with the "relentless march of technology—the impossible and fantastic are becoming the possible and real."[38] The young engineer Aleksandr Gorokhov, a student at the St. Petersburg Technical Institute, observed that humanity was reaching for greater and greater speed and power in its aerial machines, something like a law of cultural progress. Humanity was destined to conquer the varieties of motion on land and in the air. The human being had become a master of natural forces, an "intelligent creator." In 1911, likely inspired by Esnault-Pelterie's magazine drawing, Gorokhov predicted that the method of "direct reaction" by way of air-breathing gas propulsion was the next wave in the human conquest of space and time. The all-metal rocket, not the wood and fabric airplane, was the end-all of aeronautics.[39]

At this dramatic moment, thanks to Russia's rising aviation "craze," a number of enterprising popular science journalists helped to turn Tsiolkovskii into a veritable newspaper sensation and Russian national hero. America might have its Wright Brothers; France might have its Robert Farman and Louis Bleriot. But Russia had Tsiolkovskii, the truly visionary inventor of a whole new principle of terrestrial and interplanetary flight. B. N. Vorob'ev, editor of *Herald of Aeronautics*, now republished Tsiolkovskii's original work, "The Exploration of Cosmic Space by Reactive Devices," made whole with the second part of the article, revised for a more popular audience and disseminated in a variety of public and professional forums. Tsiolkovskii literally gave shape to his rocket theories, offering the first drawing of his "reactive vehicle," a simple cigar-shaped dirigible "rocket" expelling its propellants via a straight and slender exhaust nozzle. He also found a new confidence, repeating that standard cliché of the age—"What is impossible today becomes possible tomorrow"— about turning dreams into realities, fictions into real facts, as if it all represented a chapter from his own autobiography. But what made the book truly remarkable was Tsiolkovskii's "parabola," the trajectory, or "vertical roadway," into outer space. It expressed the revolutionary escape velocity of just over eleven kilometers (about seven miles) a second, what he described poetically as the rocket "in the form of a fine vertical dash racing upwards and away."[40]

This parabola was as much an intellectual-cultural as a scientific-technical equation: freeing the human being from Earth's gravity, opening the way to other worlds. The science publicist V. V. Riumin celebrated how Tsiolkovskii's rocket turned us into true "automobilists of outer space." The great "autodidact" (*samorod*) Tsiolkovskii had drafted the proper course for the most perfect "automobile" (*samokhod*), the rocket: "There, ever higher and higher, to outer space!"[41] In an age still possessed with the deep pessimism and even despair of the second law of thermodynamics, with the law of energy turning to entropy, Tsiolkovskii had turned this dark thermodynamics into a more inspiring kinematics. Now, under his pen, the thermodynamics of rocket combustion transformed into the kinetic energy of launch velocities, transposing the human form against the planet and toward the stars. He confidently discredited "the gloomy views of scientists about the inevitable end of all living beings on earth and its cooling off due to the loss of the heat of the sun." "The better part of humanity will never perish but will move from sun to sun as each one dies out in succession." He called this idea the "infinitude of mankind," its perfectly rational and achievable reach for infinity and immortality.[42]

Validation, and controversy, also came from abroad. On 14 February 1912 Robert Esnault-Pelterie, delivered a paper in St. Petersburg, a guest of the Imperial All-Russian Aerial Club; the lecture was modestly entitled "Considerations on the Results of the Indefinite Lightening of Engines." This was his first public foray into rocket mechanics, how their exhaust velocity "lightened" their engines, presented later that year in revised form to the French Academy of Physics.[43] Russian audiences would surely have taken Esnault-Pelterie's words on faith. France had become, by 1912, the leading nation in aviation progress. Esnault-Pelterie was a star, second perhaps only to the Wright brothers and Bleriot in terms of notoriety and fame. Now he turned to the next step in aviation, his paper celebrating "the Rocket" as the sole machine capable of realizing fiction's dream of "traveling from planet to planet." A series of impressive mathematical formulas and planetary trajectories confirmed the propellant forces necessary to accelerate the rocket beyond Earth's gravity: an escape velocity of just over eleven kilometers a second, what he called the "critical velocity of liberation," enough to take human beings "to infinity." His conclusion: only atomic power (radium) would suffice to provide the propulsive force for such extreme velocities. Esnault-Pelterie also considered the physiological effects of spaceflight, artificial atmospheres and zero gravity, and heat and energy sources from the sun. None of these challenges were insurmountable. His itinerary was bold: the moon, Mars, and on to Venus. Humanity was destined, in his concluding words, to become a new "Halley's comet," to reach its "fantastic" velocities into interplanetary space.[44]

These propositions remained something of a continuing controversy over subsequent years. Whom exactly did they influence and how? Robert H. Goddard, America's future rocket scientist, probably read them in the summer or fall of 1913 as he was convalescing from tuberculosis in his Worcester, Massachusetts, home. True enough, Goddard had been thinking of rocket motors and spaceflight for some years, as attested by his notebooks from 1908–9 and by his experimental work at Princeton University in 1912–13. But Esnault-Pelterie's 1912 paper was very likely the catalyst that spurred Goddard to present his work publicly: as a patent, through lectures, and in published form.[45] From Italy, too, the young military and aviation engineer Giulio Costanzi drew from Esnault-Pelterie's work to postulate the new science of exhaust velocities and mass ratios for an accelerating rocket, what he called the "first auto-meteor" for "interplanetary space." Modern science and technology were ready for space travel, to open a new "Promethean age" and fulfill this "ultimate human dream." All that was needed, wrote Costanzi, was a "tenacious willpower" to turn "words and formulas" into reality.[46]

THE MECHANICS OF INTERPLANETARY TRAVEL

For some Russians Esnault-Pelterie remained a focus of interest, the true pioneer. His rocket calculations set a standard. The French would soon chart a journey from Earth to Mars, wrote K. E. Veigelin, while we Russians were still making our way "from Petersburg to Moscow." It was the French, wrote N. Tolstoi, who were allowing humanity to "step over the boundaries" between fantasy and reality with their project for a navigable "spacecraft." Henri de Graffigny himself soon proclaimed to Russian audiences that the "tasks of aviation have been resolved." All that remained was to take human conquest beyond the atmosphere and into space, a utopianism born of success with the airplane. All that interplanetary travel needed was to apply the sciences of physics and orbital mechanics to the task, in the manner of Esnault-Pelterie. Space travel was simply a matter of engineering the right machine—be it by cannon or rocket or giant centrifuge—matching human-made horsepower against the force of gravity. Just a few decades after his best-selling science fiction novels with Le Faure, Graffigny was predicting real human travel to the moon or Venus or Mars.[47]

Tsiolkovskii answered all of these claims with a smart volume, the first complete edition of his 1903 essay and succeeding articles, countering or correcting Esnault-Pelterie's propositions in detail. He also offered another drawing of his space rocket, now a bulky dirigible with a small aft pocket of a living and control module but mostly illustrating his principle of reactive motion, the serpentine flow of gases coiling through the rocket chamber to send it upward.[48] Soon after Esnault-Pelterie's visit, the physicist Ia. I. Perel'man also began to champion Tsiolkovskii's cause. Perel'man was the author of a popular physics primer, *Practical Physics* (1913). Much like Richard Proctor in England or Father Théophile Moreux in France, he was a patron of the mathematical sciences and of the new astronomy, mentor to a whole generation of science enthusiasts.[49] On 20 November he delivered a lecture, "Interplanetary Voyages," before a large audience of the Russian Society of Astronomy Enthusiasts in St. Petersburg. Perelman's talk inhabited a strange middle world between science fiction and fact, between possibility and technology. He essentially debated the approaches of the French Verne against the Russian Tsiolkovskii, the cannon versus the rocket, landing squarely in favor of the "Tsiolkovskii principle," the advantages of the liquid-fueled rocket in breaking free of gravity. In the ensuing debate that evening the astronomer G. A. Tikhov raised the possibilities of life beyond Earth, a topic that had inspired his recent telescopic observations of Mars, upon which he claimed to have discovered vegetation.[50]

By the outbreak of the First World War, Perel'man's book-length *Interplanetary Voyages* (1915) was already in print, based partly upon his lecture. It was the world's first comprehensive, popular monograph to discuss the possibilities of human spaceflight to the planets and beyond. Tsiolkovskii's pioneering work had convinced Perel'man that rocketry was the next great technology to serve humanity's last vast frontier, outer space. Space travel, he proposed, was the "utopia" of the twentieth century, with all manner of new physiological, social, and cultural forms to follow. Humanity had conquered the land, the seas, the skies. All that remained was cosmic space. Although often couched in fantastic terms, Perel'man's work was more a study of physics and astronomy than of rocketry and spaceflight. There were several analogues to it, reaching back to Camille Flammarion's classics and more recently to the work of Bruno Bürgel and Felix Linke in Germany and Edmond Perrier in France.[51]

But Perel'man went farther. He was Russia's new Flammarion and Tsiolkovskii combined, displaying that rare ability to master several challenging disciplines at once and to offer readers simple, practical, and entertaining lessons about them. His accent was not just on observing outer space and the planets but on charting a human path toward them. Isaac Newton's famous "mountain" was Perel'man's point of departure, a thought experiment from *Principia Mathematica* (1687) that imagined a cannon, standing upon a mountain high above Earth's atmosphere, shooting shells horizontally back to Earth. Depending on the explosive charges and speeds of the shells—all confirming his universal laws of motion—they also fell into circular or elliptical orbits. Perel'man now proposed that humanity need only design the proper rocket velocity to break beyond Newtonian circles and ellipses, to reach that "open curve" of the parabola.[52]

What with all of the new scientific theories and discoveries, complex spacecraft now began to appear more often in the literature,

МЕЖДУПЛАНѢТНЫЯ ПУТЕШЕСТВІЯ

Возможны ли междупланетныя путешеств'я? Можетъ ли человѣчество надѣяться, что когда-нибудь, въ далекомъ будущемъ, осуществится мечта о перелетахъ на другіе планетные міры, черезъ холодныя пустыни мірового пространства,—или человѣку суждено навсегда остаться плѣнникомъ земного шара?

На эту тему въ концѣ ноября прочитанъ былъ Я. И. Перельманомъ докладъ въ Русскомъ Обществѣ Любителей Міровѣдѣнія. Приводимъ вкратцѣ сущность этого доклада, собравшаго многочисленную аудиторію.

Успѣхи воздухоплаванія нисколько не приблизили, да и не могутъ приблизить разрѣшенія вопроса о межпланетныхъ путешествіяхъ.

Съ точки зрѣнія механики, между движеніемъ аэроплана и, напримѣръ, парохода или паровоза нѣтъ большой разницы: колеса паровоза отталкиваются отъ рельсовъ, винтъ парохода — отъ воды, а пропеллеръ аэроплана отталкивается отъ воздуха. Но въ міровомъ пространствѣ нѣтъ воздуха, нѣтъ вообще никакой среды, на которую могъ бы опираться движущійся снарядъ. Поэтому, чтобы осуществить межпланетныя путешествія, техника должна разрѣшить совершенно особую задачу — передвигаться, не имѣя никакой опоры въ окружающей средѣ.

Можетъ ли современная наука указать путь къ разрѣшенію этой задачи? И не намѣчается ли уже теперь, въ наше время,—напримѣръ, хотя бы въ фантазіяхъ романистовъ — форма осуществленія этой мечты?

Извѣстно, какъ разрѣшила эту проблему смѣлая фантазія Жюля Верна: романистъ посадилъ въ огромное пушечное ядро пассажировъ, зарядилъ этимъ ядромъ исполинскую пушку и выстрѣломъ отправилъ своихъ героевъ на Луну...

Весьма любопытно обсудить, что въ этомъ проектѣ Жюля Верна, такъ заманчиво представленномъ въ романѣ «Вокругъ Луны»,—что въ немъ исполнимо и что является неосуществимой мечтой. Читатели Жюля Верна обыкновенно думаютъ, что фантастична здѣсь самая возможность переброситъ ядро съ Земли на Луну; все остальное не вызываетъ уже у нихъ сомнѣній. Но это не такъ.

Жюль Вернъ, авторъ романа «Вокругъ Луны».

Идея отправить ядро на Луну—нисколько не утопична. Легко вычислить, что всякій предметъ, покидающій земную поверхность со скоростью болѣе 8-ми верстъ въ секунду, никогда уже не упадетъ на землю. Наши современныя пушки обладаютъ силою верженія въ десять разъ меньшей. Но это уже вопросъ техническій. Завтра химики могутъ напасть на соединеніе, обладающее взрывчатой силой вдесятеро большей, чѣмъ пироксилинъ — и тогда ничто не помѣшаетъ намъ наполнить мировое пространство пушечными ядрами, посылать ихъ на Луну, на Марсъ и т. д. Если бы напряженіе тяжести на земномъ шарѣ было всего въ десять разъ слабѣе, нежели теперь, то мы бы уже и сегодня могли отправлять ядра и пули на иныя планеты.

Больше сомнѣній внушаетъ идея посадить въ такое ядро пассажировъ: они едва ли могли бы остаться въ живыхъ послѣ выстрѣла. Мистеръ Барбикенъ — одинъ изъ трехъ Жюль-Верновыхъ пассажировъ—вполнѣ основательно предупреждалъ своихъ товарищей, что моментъ, когда ядро полетитъ, будетъ для нихъ совершенно такъ же опасенъ, какъ если бы они находились не внутри ядра, а впереди его. Напрасно Жюль Вернъ думалъ, что обезопаситъ своихъ героевъ, если снабдить ядро водяными или пружинными буферами: расчетъ показываетъ, что никакими ухищреніями немыслимо ослабить ударъ настолько, чтобы сдѣлать его безопаснымъ для жизни пассажировъ. Въ теченіе нѣсколькихъ сотыхъ долей секунды скорость пассажировъ должна возрасти отъ нуля до пятнадцати верстъ! Такое быстрое нарастаніе скорости выразится въ томъ, что пассажиры будутъ съ неимовѣрной силой придавливаться къ полу своей каюты; они словно станутъ въ нѣсколько десятковъ тысячъ разъ тяжелѣе и, конечно, должны быть раздавлены своимъ собственнымъ вѣсомъ.

Чтобы избѣжать такого быстраго нарастанія скорости, необходимо удлинить путь ядра въ каналѣ орудія. Разсчетъ показываетъ, однако, что только 600-верстная пушка можетъ отправить пассажировъ въ путь живыми,—да и то, если мы сможемъ удалить атмосферу, черезъ которую столь быстро

Fig. 4. Tsiolkovskii's dirigible rocket (at right) on a flight path to the moon, the first such image of a genuine liquid fuel space rocket that I have found in the news media. Jules Verne's portrait is at center. From the popular science magazine *Priroda i liudi* 8 (1914): 126.

including those with novel electrical and chemical energies. "Antigravity matter" was by far the favorite means of escaping gravity. Writers had been appealing to it ever since George Tucker's *A Voyage to the Moon* (1827) and "lunarium." Kurd Lasswitz's *On Two Planets* (1897) used "Stellit" and "Repulsor." H. G. Wells's *The First Men in the Moon* (1901) used "Cavorite." Aleksandr Bogdanov's *Red Star* (1908) used "minus matter." Antigravity energy made perfect sense as a function of Newton's laws. It was nothing more than a simple and efficient means of reaction energy, a way to conquer the universal law of attraction (gravity) by way of the universal law of repulsion. To this extent all the antigravity spacecraft in science fiction were reaction devices of a kind.

Bogdanov described his craft, the "etheroneph," as a rocket: a space gondola built of light aluminum and reinforced glass, propelled into interplanetary space by the reactive power of atomic energy, much like a "recoiling rifle." We do not know for sure if he had ever read Tsiolkovskii's science fiction or rocket theories. But Bogdanov's egg-shaped craft looked a lot like one of Tsiolkovskii's dirigible rockets. His terms and descriptions all suggest an influence or at least a common set of interests: in Newton's laws and calculus, in the law of kinetic energy, in zero gravity environments, in the "Ethereal Ocean" of space and the "Universe as a single, all-inclusive and self-determining Whole."[53] With Tsiolkovskii and our other pioneers, Bogdanov laid a claim to the rocket spaceship as the perfect measure of our better humanity, our interplanetary future.

Russia's Promethean Moment

None of our rocketry pioneers had a monopoly on spaceflight and cosmic themes. News of Perel'man's 20 November 1913 lecture, for example, was tucked between the myriad stories of the day, amid reports about the fast pace of both Europe's and Russia's aviation achievements and about the strange antics of Russia's futurist writers and poets. On the very same evening as Perel'man's talk, not very far away in dowtown St. Petersburg, Vladimir Maiakovskii and his band of Cubo-Futurists, some with arrows and anchors tattooed on their cheeks, others dressed in dazzling contrasts of colors, oranges and blacks, took the stage of the Troitskii Theater to shock the public with declamations and neologisms, abstract sound poetry and trans-rational language (*zaum*).[54] Their theatrics were part of an age of scandalous exhibitions, avant-garde artists confronting the public with radically new creations. Their venue turned toward the opera with the production of Aleksei Kruchenykh's *Victory over the Sun* (1913), graced by Kazimir Malevich's famous props, by which the pilot heroes of the future conquered the power of the sun. The futurists shared just such a passion for projection, as did Russia's spaceflight enthusiasts— for words "beyond reason" (*zaum*) and for flights of fancy "beyond the atmosphere" (*zaatmosfera*). Kruchenykh's famous sound poem "The Heights (A Universal Language)" is a case in point. Patterned after the words of the Russian Orthodox *Creed*, the verses alternate between high and low vowels, illustrating the heights and depths of existence, humanity's power of language and its reach for the infinite and eternal. Velemir Khlebnikov's poems were even more cosmic, studies in what he called a "star language": composed of sounds and letters encompassing small worlds of meaning—as, for example, *L*—the sound of liberation and flight; and including a material alphabet in which letters would have colors and energies all their own, in which consonants would be made of metal and vowels of glass.[55]

Kazimir Malevich eventually dated his artistic movement, "Suprematism," from 1913, what he termed his "self-birth."[56] Malevich's famous *Black Square* (dramatically placed in the position of a religious icon, in the upper ceiling corner of the room) was first in a series of Suprematist studies to come, at first plays upon the new non-Euclidean geometry, in time studies of Einstein's relativism, non-objective art expressing "currents" of energy.[57] Suprematist compositions floated in abstract space, experiments with new forms and projections, beholding straight lines and rectangles, struts and levers. Some of Malevich's own writings and sketches in these early years ascended into interplanetary space. He imagined human beings launched "enormous distances" upon the "crossroads" of the "heavens." He wrote of a "'take-off' from the Earth" and of a "striving toward space." He redrew *Black Square* as small crosses and planes (airplanes), flying at angles in a white vacuum, expressing his "feeling of universal space." These were symbols of what he later called

Fig. 5. Kazimir Malevich's *Supremus No. 56* (1916), representing humanity's
geometric reach for space, with parabola in upper right.
Credit: Scala / Art Resource, New York.

the creative and upward "movement of thought" and that he sometimes contrasted with the streak of a comet descending. He painted
one of his most cosmic of studies at this time, as Charlotte Douglas
has remarked of *Supremus No. 56*, with "its sensation of space and
flying" and its "hints at technology and celestial bodies." He also
paid homage to N. F. Fedorov, writing: "We must prepare ourselves
by prayer to embrace the sky. And those who will prepare themselves will be led out from the ashes of earthly sin towards the sky
and will be resurrected."[58]

Like the Symbolist poets before them, Maiakovskii and his avant-garde companions were drawn to the depths of the cosmos and stars as a measure of the complexities of human life, a mark of their romantic longings for other worlds. His own poems, from the beginning to the end of his writing career, were a running dialogue with the celestial bodies—sometimes lyrical and lovely, at other times satirical and vulgar; here conversing, there haranguing.[59] With the educated public, the avant-garde was also reading a wide variety of "cosmic" philosophies: from Charles Hinton's *The Fourth Dimension* (1904) to Henri Bergson's *Creative Evolution* (1907) to P. D. Uspenskii's *Tertium organum* (1911). These were all manifestos on the power of the human mind to shape new realities. Hinton's work was all about freeing us from our confining geometric spaces, from our terrestrial sense of dimension and direction. He represented this freedom as a triangle moving dynamically at the edge of the globe, pointed upward to the fourth dimension, a mystical realm of consciousness. Uspenskii built on these insights to actually investigate this psychic dimension, what he called a "spatial sensation of time"—something like a parabola, "the tracing of the movement in space of a three-dimensional body in a direction not confined within that space." This was a "cosmic consciousness" beyond our small grasp of matter and motion, up or down, left or right. It was a perspective from the heights—from a mountaintop or a balloon or even from outer space. It was a consciousness of the "living universe" and its "celestial harmonies," as he put it, of our potential for perfection and "personal immortality."[60]

The Russian futurists were further influenced by the cosmic metaphors of the Italian poet Filippo Tommaso Marinetti. By 1909 his original futurist movement was affirming the power of the machine to raise humanity to new heights of beauty and perfection. Body and mind needed to fuse with metal and motor in order to subdue gravity and fly beyond the planet. This was part pagan myth of Promethean glory, part Christian ideal of sacrifice and divinity.[61] These values also enjoyed some currency in Central Europe, where a band of writers and artists associated with Paul Scheerbart delved into cosmic themes. Best known for his theories of glass-colored architecture, Scheerbart also wrote fantasy stories bridging his visions of perpetual motion apparatuses, flying machines, spiraling towers, and interstellar life. One of his drafts imagined a "mobile architecture": circular buildings of steel and glass whose towers interconnected and whose parts moved up or down and rotated, much like a solar system all its own.[62] His followers Bruno Taut and Wenzel Hablik translated these visions into images of translucent flying cities and illuminated kaleidoscopic heavens, worlds illuminated by the pure crystal light of the sun and moon.[63]

The ideas of the Canadian psychiatrist Richard Maurice Bucke enjoyed a wide appeal among the Russian futurists. His book *Cosmic Consciousness* (1901) taught that humanity was on the verge of a philosophical and psychological breakthrough, in part provoked by the new technologies of "aerial navigation," which he expected to create a dramatic "material, economic, and social revolution," including the abolition of individual property and all its "riches and poverty."[64] Bucke had instituted novel techniques, such as rejuvenating physical and social therapies, for the treatment of the mentally ill. His cares soon turned to all of humanity, crafting his own grand historical philosophy of human social and spiritual evolution. An intense friendship with the poet Walt Whitman and an emotional awakening of his own in 1872 gave him spiritual depth and purpose. Whitman was one in a long line of superior, godly, human types—figures such as the Buddha, Dante Alighieri, and Francis Bacon. They personified Bucke's perfect "cosmic consciousness." They were morally pure, without sin or shame, consumed with a "sense of immortality" and a "consciousness of eternal life." They were extraordinary humans, the progenitors of a whole "new race" of beings who would one day meld into "THE WHOLE." This was but another way of expressing God, the "universe," as "a vast, grandiose, terrible, multiform yet uniform evolution," "entirely immaterial, entirely spiritual and entirely alive."[65]

For Bucke, as for many of the Russian intellectuals and artists who read him, Walt Whitman represented this cosmic consciousness in poetry and life. Most Russians discovered Whitman rather late, just around the time of the 1905 revolution, first in the odd magazine or journal piece, later in several book-length translations. His poems reached across political and ideological, artistic and disciplinary grounds—as much to the painter Il'ia Repin as to the revolutionary Iosif Stalin.[66] In Whitman's poetry, through Konstantin Bal'mont's fluid translations, Americans and Russians both celebrated the human role in natural evolution, terrestrial and cosmic.

> A vast similitude interlocks all,
> All spheres, grown, ungrown, small, large, suns, moons, planets,
> All distances of place however wide,
> All distances of time, all inanimate forms,
> All souls, all living bodies, though they be ever so different, or in
> different worlds,
> All gaseous, watery, vegetable, mineral processes, the fishes, the brutes,
> All nations, colors, barbarisms, civilizations, languages,
> All identities that have existed or may exist on this globe, or any globe,
> All lives and deaths, all of the past, present, future,
> This vast similitude spans them, and always has spann'd,
> And shall forever span them and compactly hold and enclose them.

> Smykaiut' vse obshirnyia podob'ia,
> Vse sfery, chto vzrosli i ne vzrosli, miry bol'shie, malye, smykaiut'
> vse solntsa, luny, i planety,
> Vse razstoian'ia mest', khotia v' obshirnykh',
> Vse razstoian'ia vremeni, vse formy, v' kotorykh' dukha net',
> Vse dushi, vse zhivushchiia tela, khotia b' oni vsegda razlichnyi
> byli v mirakh razlichnykh',
> Vse to, chto proiskhodit' v' glazakh, vlag', rasten'iakh', mineral-
> akh', mezhdu ryb', sredi zverei,
> Smykaet' vse narody, vse kraski, varvarizmy, iazyki,
> Vse tozhdestva, kakiia tol'ko byli, il' mogut' voznikat' na etom' share,
> Vse zhizni, smerti, vse, chto bylo v' proshlom', chto v' nastoiash-
> chem', v' budushchem' idet',
> Obshchirnyia podobiia skrepliaiut', vsegda skrepliali vse, i budet'
> vechno
> Skrepliat', smykat', derzhat' vse plotno, tsel'no.[67]

Bal'mont's reception of Whitman also followed closely upon one of his leading interpreters in the West, John Addington Symonds. To Symonds, as to Bal'mont, Whitman was the poet of "the imperturbable optimism and unrestricted faith" in a "Cosmic Enthusiasm." He encompassed all the earth and all its forms, a giant of a man like Buddha or Socrates. "He is circumambient air. . . . He is the globe itself, all seas, lands, forests, climates, storms, snows, sunshines, rains of universal earth. He is all nations, cities, languages, religions, arts, creeds, thoughts, emotions," wrote Symonds in his best Whitman style. "He is an immense tree . . . stretching its roots deep down into the bowels of the world, and unfolding its magic boughs through all the spaces of the heavens." Bal'mont, Russia's premier interpreter of Walt Whitman, lifted these very words as his own. With such thrilling hyperbole and adulation, America and Russia each celebrated the poet as their native son, as the voice of the cosmic future that they were bound to share. Konstantin Chukovskii's later translations and appreciations went a step too far, it seems. Tsarist censors banned and destroyed his volume *Walt Whitman: Poet of the Coming Democracy* (1913) for giving him too American, too revolutionary, an edge.[68]

Yet as Russia's artistic and intellectual elite discovered Walt Whitman in these years, they were also rediscovering notes and rhythms from one of their own, none other than N. F. Fedorov. After all, Whitman's poems celebrated free and creative spaces: the seas and shores and natural wonders of the American lands; the diversity and integrity of the earth as a planet; the "eternal spaces" of the living universe beyond. These notes played through many of his poems and most dramatically in his essay "Democratic Vistas" (1871). In it he measured imperfect humanity against the manifold "physical kosmos." The essay spoke of a nagging "ennui" but still held out hope for a "new Earth and a new man," for a newly planted and tended garden, "all-surrounding and kosmical." Ultimately, America was to become "a new creation, with needed orbic works launch'd forth, to revolve in free and lawful circuits—to move, self-poised, through the ether, and shine like heaven's own suns!"[69] Whitman's cosmic verses matched Fedorov's cosmic theology so well. Both turned the horizontal, terrestrial human at rest into the vertical, ascending human in motion.

Not all artists and writers bought into these models. Literary "Acmeism," founded at this very time by Lev Gumilev, Anna Akhmatova, and Osip Mandelshtam, took the opposite track. To Symbolism's extravagant cosmism and futurism's flights of fancy, Mandelshtam offered the poetry of Dantean descent, a reverence for tradition and fate, tombs and cathedrals, stone and ground. As he wrote in 1912: "I abhor the light / Of indifferent stars." He preferred the "arrow of living thought" to the "tower's pointed height."[70] He scolded all those spiritualists who sought out higher abstract mysteries of the fourth dimension. He called for a self-conscious "piety," admonishing us to take joy in the "three dimensions of space." "The fine arrow of the Gothic bell tower is angry, because the whole idea is to stab the sky, to reproach it for being empty," he wrote. Acmeism promised no great arcs of transcendence within time. Mandelshtam took no stock in the ethic of ascent. "We do not fly; we ascend only such towers as we ourselves are able to build." Air and space offered no quick and total salvation. "Acmeism is for those who, seized by the spirit of building, do not meekly renounce their gravity, but joyfully accept it in order to arouse and make use of the forces architecturally dormant in it."[71]

These kinds of critiques were the exception. The wider trend was for utopian ascent. Fedor Sologub's trilogy, *The Created Legend* (1907–14), crafted a fantasy world around the main character, Georgii Trirodov, retired professor of chemistry, both engineer and alchemist. He communicated telepathically across time and space, transformed matter and energy, shrank bodies, built spaceships, and even revived the dead. From his tower laboratory he mixed chemical potions and incanted his spells, playing part Fedorov, part Tsiolkovskii, part wizard. As Trirodov said to one of his romantic conquests, he was one of those rare mortals "inclined to dreams and utopias, who passionately desire to transform fantasy into reality."[72] Like Tsiolkovskii, Trirodov defied gravity with his mathematical calculations and mechanical inventions. Trirodov's spaceship was no rocket, more a domed space station (masquerading in his estate garden as a greenhouse), filled with lush plants and its own self-sustaining atmosphere, made of an indestructible crystalline blue glass and steel girders, powered by none other than the antigravity matter Cavorite, as discovered by H. G. Wells. This imagery of the spacecraft as a planet or comet all its own, racing through space to plotted destinations, was becoming more and more popular. Trirodov set his "sphere" into motion, effortlessly rising like a "small planet," giving it "a rotational motion of a specific speed," pre-calculated to propel it into orbit or for travel to the moon and space beyond. For both Tsiolkovskii and Sologub the rocket spacecraft was always a minor means to a greater end, cosmic liberation of a kind, to something greater and bolder in ourselves.[73]

One faction of futurists, the "Centrifuge," Nikolai Aseev and Boris Pasternak two of its prominent members, discovered a novel kind of action-reaction in "rotation-reaction," with poetic images of humanity in its machines scattering, spiraling away from Earth to the far parts of the universe. They turned the mechanical turbine into a revolving centrifuge, a machine to destroy the dead weights of the past and ascend into cosmic space: "Above the world to nest / . . . The whistling circleflight."[74] Later joined by the poet Khlebnikov, the group echoed Fedorov's call for the world unity of free thinkers and scientists, to conquer terrestrial and cosmic space for the "militant vanguard of the inventor / explorers" against the old cliques of "investor / exploiters." Turning Wells's Martian victory cry "ulla, ulla" on its head, "Alloo, Alloo," the poets saw themselves as new Martians of a kind, aliens from the future, come to escape from "Planet Earth's" small globe into the freedom of "outer space."[75]

In all these terms Russians were preoccupied with the conquest of air and space and with the conquest of life and death. The union between human flight and human immortality was more than symbolic, what with the airplane's ascent into the heavens above the mortal earth. It made practical sense. The airplane literally shortened distance, saved days and weeks of travel time, extended and enriched our lives. Like the railroad before, it was a quantum leap in human engineering, a conquest of distance that was also a kind of time travel. Space travel, as extreme flight, meant an exponential conquest of time, even over death. Bogdanov wrote of this in his poem

"A Martian Stranded on Earth," looking forward to the day "when space, yes, and time have been conquered by man / And the elements and death are but words." Khlebnikov saw the relationship in purest terms, writing in one of his letters that "if gravity is so all-powerful, then aeronautics and relative immortality are closely connected."[76] The pioneer inventors and engineers were often joined by a common presumption that space exploration would indeed open the gates of human immortality. Technology was giving way to eschatology.[77]

In an interesting historical coincidence Tsiolkovskii and his enthusiasts were futurists of a kind, at work in their "laboratories of dreams"; and the futurists, in their own manner, were cosmists of a kind. Both schools shared the thrill of provoking the public to think and imagine in new ways. Over time both came to share the very same stage, lecturing to eager audiences at the State Polytechnic Museum in downtown Moscow. The poet and polymath Khlebnikov even became something of a second Tsiolkovskii. Like him, Khlebnikov roamed the streets of Russia's city streets as a young man, destitute but overjoyed with life, immersed in books and calculations, obsessed with the heavens and the stars. Like Tsiolkovskii, Khlebnikov was taken with Newton's laws of nature, with the laws of thermodynamics and earth science, with the order of the planets. Like him, he counted. Khlebnikov literally counted the number 317 and its multiples, which he considered a measure of the waves of human history, of the rise and fall of nations and cultures. Tsiolkovskii and Khlebnikov also shared an aversion to foreign fashion. A dedicated Slavophile and defender of the Russian language, Khlebnikov berated all admirers of the Italian futurist Marinetti when he visited Russia in early 1914. Just as Tsiolkovskii and Perel'man set out to upstage and overshadow Esnault-Pelterie, Khlebnikov demanded that Russian scientists begin to make some of their own "hammerblows in this forge of the New Age," begin to create "heroic exploits" of their own, take "first place."[78]

The spaceflight enthusiasts and futurists also shared the metaphor of escape, the thrilling possibility of leaping into outer space right along with the mass readers of popular science and science fiction. Highbrow found common cause with the lowbrow in a strange new democracy of expectation. People from all walks of life were fascinated with the possibilities of life on other worlds and with the human quest to get there.[79] Russia was seized with Promethean tasks, with extraordinary voyages, with the new scope and depth and pace of modern life, with debates on space travel and immortality. Tsiolkovskii, for one, turned his thoughts to the remaking of "planet Earth," captivated by the powers of human intelligence and technology to clear away nature's obstacles. He compared his projects to reach beyond gravity and the atmosphere with his related projects to tunnel to the planet's core, to invent a true submarine, to discover a new continent, indeed even to "improve life and to cure disease."[80] The Russian science fiction writer I. N. Potapenko devoted a short story to the marriage between American technical prowess and Russian inventive genius. Set in the year 2912, the story celebrated the West's mastery of efficient transatlantic passenger flight (with homage to Henry Ford and John D. Rockefeller) and the East's discovery of the means to transplant human organs and prolong human life (with homage to Il'ia Mechnikov). No matter that speedy air travel and bodily rejuvenation ended up with all kinds of humorous complications: American generosity clashing with Russian bureaucracy. Readers likely got the point, that human progress demanded the double mastery of higher space and future time.[81]

The Russian press echoed these themes—for the "human genius" and technologies that scaled mountains and subdued deserts; spanned oceans by steamers; crossed continents by railroad and flew across the world with planes. Technology followed paths of evolutionary development yet sometimes made "revolutionary leaps" in quality, in space and scope, turning utopia into reality. Periods of seeming inertia and adaptation were always framed by periods of rupture and innovation. The globe was becoming one place, one country. Yet it also meant that "the discovery of some new America was simply no longer in the cards for any would-be Columbus out there." All that awaited us was to "dash into the new frontier of infinite outer space."[82] The Symbolist poet and science enthusiast Valerii Briusov expressed this Prometheanism in a poem, "The Young Earth" (1913), calling on humanity to master the globe, rebuild it with rivers encased in granite, with tunnels between the poles, with "towers upon towers." But he also demanded something more, according to the tenor of the times:

Rule over the movements of the planets,—
By a streak into universal space,
Send out light signals
To unknown worlds.[83]

Radical political thinkers tapped into the trend. As the intellectual N. N. Koshkarev wrote, "The Promethean fire has, for a second time, been stolen from the heavens." The dawning of an age of "cosmic sensibility" and of "collective altruism" was at hand. Soon we would control the secrets of matter, wield complete "power over nature," even create a new science of immortality. Soon humanity would "master the world, disseminate their kind to distant outer space, vanquish whole planetary systems." Nikolai Bukharin later built the logic into his survey of Marxist "historical materialism," marrying Darwin to Marx, natural to social evolution, adapting biological forms to the human technologies and ideologies that surpassed them. As part of the struggle for existence, the human being intervened in nature, like Goethe's "Prometheus," with modern science and its own machines, all to conquer space and time.[84]

Russians aimed their utopias upward. Sergei Solomin's short story "Tomorrow" (1912) aimed for the atmosphere, set in a future of world peace, with a global market, the brotherhood of nations, an international language, and aviation technologies. Humanity was creating a "heaven on earth."[85] B. Krasnogorskii's *Upon the Ether's Waves* (1913) and *Islands of the Ethereal Ocean* (1914) aimed beyond. The stories featured an ingenious Russian flying saucer, the "Victor of Space" (*Pobeditel' prostranstva*). Launched from St. Petersburg's Field of Mars by balloon, the craft rose elegantly to the heights. The first expedition to Venus ended in failure, the spaceship caught in a meteor storm not far from the moon, though it did land safely back at Lake Ladoga. The craft itself performed magnificently, the first volume offering a host of exact calculations and designs relevant to the astronomy, mechanics, and physics of spaceflight. The ship was a massive disc-shaped parabolic mirror of light metal. It revolved around a central control and living module fixed to it by an axle. For space propulsion it used the reaction power of liquid oxygen and hydrogen, reaching speeds of up to 250 kilometers (155 miles) per second. It also drew energy from the sun's rays and from planetary gravity, tacking its way through the solar system. The story continued in the second volume with a more adventurous battle between the Russians and Germans, the former seizing victory to explore a "Stone Age" Venus filled with prehistoric dinosaurs.[86]

Several writers extrapolated on the projection power of the cinema. When Sergei Gorodetskii imagined his version of a more perfect, future society, he filled it with highly evolved human beings, streamlined in body and demeanor and dress. They lived in a great global, domed city of glass and steel. They were consumed by space travel, by ascent to the "vacuum of space," by the power "to fly upwards by vertical lines." But they were also entranced by the "geo-scope," a machine that screened historical truths, past and present, onto the sky for all to see. Gorodetskii's imagined futurists achieved full transparency, pierced the envelopes of gravity and the spans of distance and time. Another leading rocketry pioneer, N. A. Rynin, recognized cinema as a revolutionary new medium with the power to unify the world by way of shared images on the movie screen, to project human vision through space and time. This was one of the boasts of the day: that moving pictures and eventually television would conquer humanity's final frontiers, turning every absence into a presence. Rynin appreciated the power of human signification and depth perception, the function of space as a tableau upon which to fix the human imagination and technique, turning matter into energy and energy into pictures. He recognized the kinematics of both rocket flight and cinematography.[87]

None of these were purely "Russian" insights. They were already becoming stock themes in the popular literature of the day. All the amazing technological transformations on Earth and in space recalled Kurd Lasswitz's "Retrospective," past-televisions of a kind that read the light rays moving through space; or Friedrich Wilhelm Mader's "paleoscope," an invention that could see past history by way of the light emissions from Earth as reflected in the stars. They recalled Hugo Gernsback's classic short story "Ralph 124C 41+" (1911), packed with the dazzling inventions of computerized translation by machine, videophone communication, undersea tunnels, solar energy, and space travel. They recalled Bernard Kellerman's best-selling novel *The Tunnel* (1913), the story of the engineering coup of the century, a transatlantic tunnel from the United States to Europe.[88] The Russian Marcus Karenin, one of H. G. Wells's characters in *The World Set Free* (1914), sounded just like Tsiolkovskii when he proclaimed, from the redemptive East, amid a world destroyed by human avarice and violence, that technology might yet transform outer space into a "great window opened." Wrote Wells: "This round planet is no longer chained to us like the ball of a galley slave. . . . In a little while men who will know how to bear the strange gravitations, the altered pressures, the attenuated, the unfamiliar gases and all the fearful strangenesses of space will be venturing out from this earth . . . our spirit will reach out."[89]

Humanity had reached a pinnacle of discovery and conquest. Following the lead of the great master Jules Verne, who paired his lunar voyages with voyages to the North Pole, Europe's premier writers of space fiction plotted their own ways to the planet's edges and to outer space. Both destinations tested the limits of the human stamina and imagination. Both were sure to sell for young readers and old.[90] The French popular science writer Max de Nansouty celebrated our remaking of the natural environment with electricity and automobiles, chemical and civil engineering, with dirigibles that promised the "conquest of space," with wireless telegraphy that promised "interstellar" communication.[91] The inventor Hudson Maxim, in a dramatic speech before the American Chemical Society, went even further. Conscious technological evolution, he said, was surpassing awkward natural evolution. Modern mechanical achievements were truly cosmic, an architecture for the ages. Humanity had "hewn highways through the granite hills and web-worked the world with the iron rail." It had even "sounded the deeps of the eternal skies." It had seen through telescopes "the fortune and fate of a million worlds." It was poised to conquer all of space and time.[92]

Americans helped to set the trend, at least initially, in science fiction. Arthur Train and Robert Williams Wood introduced us to the rocket in their space adventures *The Man Who Rocked the Earth* (1915) and *The Moon Maker* (1916), the later work translated into an influential Russian edition. Train wrote the book, but Wood, a famous professor of experimental physics at Johns Hopkins University, conceived the plot and all scientific and technical elements.[93] The story was about the enigmatic "Pax," fiction's first real rocket scientist, inventor of the "Flying Ring," an airship and spacecraft that "rose from the earth rocket fashion," maintaining "automatic stability" by several gyroscopes that "kept the Ring on an even keel."[94] The hero, Benjamin Hooker, professor of applied physics at Harvard University, saved the world by learning how to fly it, powered by the "disintegrating rays" of atomic matter (uranium), giving the rocket the reactive propulsion and velocity to escape gravity and reach speeds of twenty miles (thirty-two kilometers) per second on the way to the moon, even approaching the speed of light. Or as the narrator put it, "Then it darted up, up and almost out of sight, leaving a fading streak behind it like that of a shooting star."[95] The tale had its playful moments, offering something of a satire, poking fun at all the media frenzy about the "space flyer" and the "Columbus of the Universe." Lighthearted passages recall some of Tsiolkovskii's own, about space travelers floating in zero gravity or jumping in leaps and bounds through lunar gravity. As Professor Hooker taught his wife, Rhoda, with a gentle push through weightlessness, "action and reaction—to use the words of one I. Newton—are equal and opposite in their effects." Rhoda thereby became something of a human rocket, looking back through interplanetary space upon a rising "crescent earth."[96]

But the story did not end there. In 1915, the very year of Train and Woods's rocket-propelled Flying Ring, the young physicist Robert H. Goddard delivered a scholarly lecture on a similar theme, "New Methods of Reaching High Altitudes," at the Physics Colloquium of the Worcester Polytechnic Institute. He discussed the theoretical work and calculations that he had already completed at Princeton University in 1912 and 1913 and the experimental work that he had just begun at Clark University, on the potential of sending a rocket into the vacuum of space, given the proper mass ratio and the proper efficiency of the fuel. A small whirlwind of local press coverage followed, including rumors about his fantastic invention and the possibility of reaching into outer space. One reporter even called it a "veritable new science."[97] At least for some American readers, then, "rocket science" was born in this busy year of 1915, as both fiction and fact.

To what extent did Tsiolkovskii and his collaborators give all of these trends and developments a uniquely national, Russian spin? Perhaps it was in their intensity, in their passion of commitment. Perhaps, too, it was in their apparent power to see into the future, to embrace and predict it, as Bogdanov tried to do in *Red Star*. Within a few short years the Russian Revolution of 1917 confirmed and justified their deepest hopes. But even this bent for the revolutionary was not wholly Russian. It was as much American too, this prognostication about coming revolutionary change, as natural in the prairie universities of the American Midwest as in the workers' ghettoes or intellectual circles of Tsarist Russia. In an address to the Indiana University chapter of Sigma Xi and the Liberal Lecture League of Indianapolis, in December 1913, M. E. Haggerty proposed that revolutions were a normal and healthy "part of our modern world." Science and democracy were the two great revolutionary forces of the present, the means and the ends of human progress. They were bound to join forces to overthrow the old orders of superstition and injustice, if peacefully in the West and more violently in the East. Kaiser Wilhelm and Nicholas II were marked men. Revolutions were acts of human will and creation, much like the nature of rocket power. "The fires of significant revolution" burn from within until they can longer be contained, exploding "as the breaking forth of a long suppressed flame."[98] Rocket power was a metaphor for revolutionary transformation, in time and space, setting humans in motion through parabolas of flight toward the planets and stars. Numbers plotted their trajectories. Trajectories pointed the way to the moon and planets. The rocket would take us there.

PART TWO

The Mastery of Time and the
Bolshevik Revolution

4

Lyrical Cosmism of the Russian Revolution

The Bolshevik regime opened new vistas for rocketry. By 1918, well before any of the more dramatic news came out of the United States and Germany, Russian publicists were already raising the People's Will terrorist Nikolai Kibalchich as a rocket pioneer worthy of Bolshevism. Awaiting execution in St. Petersburg for his part in the assassination of Tsar Aleksandr II in 1881, Kibalchich had sketched a basic device for reaction-powered flight in the atmosphere. He had more famously helped to establish a secret underground laboratory to make explosives for political murder, sanctioned by the Executive Committee of the People's Will. Kibalchich's act helped to transform the terrorism of the nineteenth century into the cosmism of the twentieth. Terror was adaptable, or at least its explosives were, to the conquest of interplanetary space.[1]

Against the mainstream opinions of his day, which sought to model human flight upon bird flight, Kibalchich advocated the engineered design of actual machines. His "rocket," as N. A. Rynin described it in a prominent magazine display, was a bulky flying machine, attached precariously by thin rods to the deck of a square ship. Had it ever been launched, the exploding gases would surely have engulfed the whole apparatus. Yet his project became a last will and testament, drafted just before his execution. For he had been "immersed in calculations," wrote one of his jailers, as if counting on immortality. Kibalchich had sacrificed his life for a higher good, socialism, under whose regime the rocket might just empower humanity to someday leave the dying earth for the distant realms of space.[2] The

Soviet regime raised a generation of young Communists upon the notion that this founder of the Russian revolutionary movement was also a founder of rocketry and interplanetary travel. Tsiolkovskii's leading publicists, following Rynin's lead, were almost always sure to bow to Kibalchich as the first "Bolshevik" rocketeer and to herald him as "the true father of space navigation."[3]

Such leaps of the imagination were not at all unique to Tsarist Russia. In an interesting irony of fiction following fact, the popular English writer and socialist sympathizer George Griffith wrote just such a nihilist-terrorist into his pair of conspiracy novels, *The Angel of the Revolution* (1893) and *Olga Romanoff* (1894). The series began with an impoverished engineering student perfecting his heavier-than-air flying machine, which worked something like a rocket, by the "spontaneous" explosion of "two liquefied gases" in a dramatically simplified engine of few moving parts. Half–aerostat dirigible, half–propeller-driven airplane, it solved "that fatal ratio of weight to power" that had so bedeviled aerial inventors. "The dream had become the reality. . . . He had accomplished the greatest triumph in the history of human discovery. He had revolutionised the world, and ere long he would make war impossible." The young man donated his invention to the mysterious "Brotherhood of Freedom," a band of nihilists and terrorists, led by the conspiratorial "Chief" and the "Executive of the Inner Circle," intent on overthrowing the tsar of Russia by violent force and establishing a worldwide regime of peace and justice. Griffith later took some of his characters into outer space with the same fascination for revolutionary technologies. By the power of the "R force" (for "Repulsion"), his *Aeronef* launched his explorers by a "magnificent curve," sending them "rushing upward like a meteor through the clouds" on a wondrous journey to the planets near and far, this to achieve a kind of second birth and a sense of unity with the cosmos.[4]

Russian writers celebrated this archetypal revolutionary engineer in fiction. Andrei Bely wrote him into his surrealist novel *Petersburg* (1913), in the character of Nikolai Ableukhov, the terrorist enamored of perfect geometric lines and total order. Ableukhov carried around the infamous ticking time bomb in a sardine can to destroy the old and establish the new. Sergei Mstislavskii, the leftist Socialist Revolutionary and one-time chronicler of the Russian Revolution of 1917, wrote the archetype into his novel *Partiontsy* (1933), converting it into both revolutionary terrorist and dreamer of space travel. What was once to explode by projection "shell" against the body of the tsar was now to explode by way of a flying "shell" into interplanetary space. In both instances Kibalchich's technical expertise served as a "signal," a stimulus to both worldwide revolution and global technological achievement. Their common source was Newtonian mechanics, to be sure, but also the Kantian and Bergsonian moral imperative: the universal "duty" for order and justice, an imperative that was "its own law" and "its own judge," driven from within.[5]

Apocalypse from Outer Space

Perhaps even stranger than these fictions was the real person of N. A. Morozov. As a member of the Executive Committee of the People's Will and author of the manifesto *The Terrorist Struggle* (1880), with Kibalchich he had helped to justify and plan the assassination of the tsar, literally writing the book on revolutionary terrorism.[6] But through the subsequent twenty-five years of his imprisonment (1881–1905), Morozov largely gave up politics for science. He wrote dozens of scientific tracts on mathematics and physics, chemistry and astronomy. After he was freed, he published a book on integral and differential calculus, translated and edited Wells's science fiction, popularized Einstein's theory of relativity, and became a patron of balloons, dirigibles, and airplanes. He also published his classic work, *The Revelation in Thunder and Storm: Birth of the Apocalypse*, complete with a lecture circuit, in which he set out to explain the Book of Revelation not as revealed truth but as a piece of science fiction, based on the natural events happening in the skies when it was written. From his prison cell he had projected himself back to ancient times, reading religious texts and looking up to his own skies, aligning several constellations and a solar eclipse with the stories of the Four Horsemen of the Apocalypse, replacing supernatural symbolism with the predictable signs of the natural heavens. These were topics, the promotion of modern astronomy and the debunking of religion as superstition and myth, to which he dedicated the rest of his life.[7]

In several other works, both prose and poetry, Morozov celebrated alien life and interplanetary travel, even the possibility of rising "ever higher and higher" (*vse vyshe i vyshe*) into the weightlessness of outer space, albeit by a rather bulky craft of cylinders and turbines. There, much like Tsiolkovskii, he pondered the "pale-blue crescent" of Earth, one among a "million far islands of the universal ocean." The Marxist Morozov entertained a mystical "new religion" of "panpsychism": that we human beings are but "feeling atoms," part of an eternal spiral of physical, chemical, and evolutionary adaptations.[8] Morozov's popular book of poetry *Star Songs* (1910) landed him in prison again for a year, this time as a cause célèbre: accused of conspiring against Tsarist authority, insulting the Russian Orthodox Church, and provoking the populace to rebellion. Morozov admitted that the poems were only peripherally about the stars and were really more about an ethical "striving toward the stars," about humanity's struggles to reach out of the depths of oppression and injustice for higher values. The book became a best seller, a model of revolutionary imagery about the longing for freedom and equality. Written from the darkness of his earlier prison cells, as he dreamed of seeing the sun and stars again, the poems read more like the romantic verses of the Symbolists, with a political edge. Reprinted in two celebratory volumes by 1921, the verses helped inspire a whole new generation of intellectuals to similar themes, a veritable "cosmism" of the Russian Revolution.[9]

The revolution actually inspired a strange mix of cosmic images, ranging between dread and hope, calamity and liberation. For critics such as H. G. Wells it was a "debacle," a "torrential catastrophe." T. Konstantin Oesterreich, professor of philosophy at the University of Tübingen, compared the Russian Revolution to the corresponding revolution in physics: the first a descent into barbarism and "wholesale terrorism," all for the conquest of power; the second a leap into relativity, promising the dissolution of the elements and the conquest of matter and energy. As he wrote in dramatic tones: "The red flush of a setting sun already casts its dying reflection over the whole body of knowledge of the modern world. All is changed." French conservatives, gathered around *La revue universelle*, similarly threaded their news reports about the misdeeds and abominations in Soviet Russia with philosophical critiques of Einstein's relativity, as if the whole world were becoming undone.[10] One American observer was more optimistic. In a widely distributed essay the eminent astronomer W. W. Campbell drew analogies from his own field to teach a curious civics lesson. The movements of human history, he argued, followed lines of motion much like the planets of our solar system: "direct" motion forward to progress and "retrograde" motion into decay and stagnation, both against the humbling canvas of the deep stars. To be sure, the difficult years of the First World War had culminated in a series of "disturbances," "radical transformations" and "revolutions," including the Russian. Yet however anarchic and destructive they seemed to be, these events nevertheless represented the human drive and "impulse" for progress, "onward and upward to greater things."[11]

It was clearly a poignant, conflicted moment for Russia, fraught with war and rebellion, economic dislocation, hunger and disease. Yet out of all this chaos arose the first symbolic representations marking the great break of the Russian Revolution of 1917. As the revolution unfolded in Petrograd in February, one astronomer painted a dynamic portrait of the universe beyond, one in "eternal and unceasing motion, always moving and evolving and transforming." Magnificent comets sped through it against the foreground of small planet Earth, we the "bits and pieces of organisms just dawdling" upon it.[12] For its makers the revolution was an event of extraterrestrial proportions, so The News (Izvestiia) put it, the "starlight radiance" of communism "giving light to the thorny paths of history." For its sympathizers, such as Andrei Bely, revolution was like a "subterranean quake, smashing everything . . . a hurricane, sweeping aside forms." Most of all, its spiritual ethos was like a "comet flying toward us from beyond the limits of reality," a parabolic "reflection in the heavens of what is going on in the heart," the "broadening of a point of a star into the flying disk of the comet."[13]

Russia's revolution presaged the victory of worldwide communism, a turn of truly dramatic proportions. "There must either be complete disintegration, hell broth, further brutalization and disorder, *abso-*

lute chaos, or else communism," read one ideological primer. Communism was the new cosmism and the proletariat, guided by Lenin and the Russian Communist Party, the "TRUE SAVIOR OF MANKIND."[14] Cosmic communism took the form of mass spectacles, street theater, political art and propaganda, poetic verses and painting. They were filled with images of rising red suns, brilliant red stars, or giant globes held aloft by workers and peasants. They accentuated the cosmic collective: discordant voices joining into one symphonic chorus, colossal images of Promethean workers or of hammers and sickles, poems to the coming "world commune." The Proletarian Culture movement (*Proletkul't*), tens of thousands strong and at its peak in the civil war years, sponsored much of this dramatic imagery, from the masses and for the masses, in metaphors celebrating the machine and factory.[15] Lenin personified this new mentality. He became a new "sun," his face often adorning the front covers of books and magazines, looking down upon Earth from the depths of the heavens, as if it were a whole new sign of the zodiac. Maiakovskii codified such imagery in his epic poem "Vladimir Il'ich Lenin" (1924), whose protagonist, the "sun-faced" liberator, became the "sun" of a new dawn, a whole new era in world history. The poet Vasilii Kazin wrote:

> Amidst the sluggish stars,
> We denigrate our race,
> By calling a man simply Il'ich,
> And but a lowly star the worthy name of Saturn.

One propaganda poster framed Lenin's tomb as a kind of ziggurat or rocket rising to the heavens, a comet cascading in the background. Or as Anatoli Lunacharskii wrote on the fourth anniversary of Lenin's death, "His guiding star still shines brightly in our skies."[16]

The Russian geologist A. E. Fersman expressed the tensions of the times in a series of compelling essays. After years of bloodshed Europe, and especially Russia, was exhausted and anxious, suffering a "tormented consciousness," with so many millions dead and crippled, so much valuable property lost. Capitalist Europe and the United States had invented new means of death and destruction in the great world war yet had also left legacies of science and invention that offered the makings of a whole new world, a "fantastic" and "fabulous" world of human achievement and prosperity. Scientists had the rare capacity, much like the raw power of the working class, to break the bonds of the nation-state and use their talents and knowledge to conquer space, time, and matter. They would tame the Saharan desert, reach the limits of aeronautical speed and distance, exploit the energy of the wind and sun. Soviet Russia, he argued, now stood between these two worlds, both physically and temporally. Fersman's solution, easy for a geologist, was to count history not by human time but by geological and even cosmic time. The Russian Revolution had placed human consciousness into these new "orbits."[17] The geochemist B. P. Veinberg set just such a program down in science fiction, in a parable about the utopian future of humanity, its pathway from "egoism" to "altruism." Veinberg envisioned a "Committee for the Improvement of Planet Earth" that, thanks to American and English discoveries, adapted solar energy into mechanical power, transformed the oceans into productive land, and converted all the earth into a climate-controlled ecological system, governed by rational science and a world language. The future meant exploring the planet's core to depths of 120 kilometers (74 miles), traveling to the moon, and even communicating with Mars by way of an "Association for Interplanetary Communications."[18]

These kinds of ubiquitous images, in picture and in word, announced the birth of a new era of freedom and justice on a world and even universal scale. Hyperbole seemed the perfect fit in these desperate and hopeful times. The regime gave its festivals a spiritual veil. One of the perfect emblems of this moment was K. F. Iuon's painting *New Planet* (1921), soon housed in Moscow's premier Tretiakovskii Gallery. In stunning colors the canvas depicted human beings confronting the birth of a new planet, some arising in joy, others falling in despair. But what planet was this? Iuon gave the impression that this was a red earth, its continents convulsed by subterranean shifts and cosmic rays, like the rebirth of some lost Atlantis. With Iuon's biographers N. I. Bukharin praised his "cosmic" ideal, a perfect sign of the new Soviet person's "fiery zeal" (*pafos*) to discover whole "new worlds."[19]

Fig. 6. K. F. Iuon's *New Planet* (1921), an allegory on the birth
of the communist and the death of the capitalist worlds.
Credit: Scala / Art Resource, New York.

The poet Nikolai Aseev rewrote Iuon's canvas as prose, in a short
story set in a dark future of underground cities and interplanetary
war. Here was N. F. Fedorov's vibrant future of a peaceful and godly
solar "chorus" gone astray. In Aseev's compact and gripping scenario
Mars declared war upon Earth: the "heavy interplanetary howitzers"
of the "bloody red Martians," like "hissing and glowing meteors, cut
through the darkness and raced along in their zigzag line toward
Earth." Humanity's desperate response was to fight back, thanks to
the invention of the "great Lotsman," who created an energy weapon
of such power as to shake our planet from its orbit, to become a roving battleship, a "miraculous shell, flying by a parabolic rendezvous"
to subdue Mars. The battle waged, this roving planet Earth, by its
own force of invention and "terrestrial will," cinematically shook
Mars loose from its own orbit, sending it careening off into space
and sure destruction.[20]

N. I. Mukhanov's *The Flaming Abyss* (1924) replayed these scenes
in lush detail in an imaginary war between Mars and Earth in the

LYRICAL COSMISM OF THE RUSSIAN REVOLUTION

year 2423, a brutal "war of the worlds." It was a "hellish nightmare" that reduced parts of both planets to ashes and provoked civil war and revolution on Mars. In the tradition of Russian philosophizing, Mukhanov threaded the narrative with discourses on the epic struggles between energy and entropy, chaos and harmony, good and evil. The story was filled with many of the stock items of a European cosmic romance: Martian spies conspiring on Earth; our exiles in the underground caverns of Mars; new planetary languages of logic and efficiency; the Atlantis myth; anabiosis and organ transplants; interplanetary spaceships that flew "like asteroids," outfitted with antigravity elements, force fields, and elastic motion. Yet the editors at the publishing firm of P. P. Soikin took care to note that none of this, in the day of K. E. Tsiolkovskii, was pure imagination. "The most fantastic dreams of the utopians are turning into reality," they wrote. We stood before "unlimited possibilities." True to these forms, the tale ended with humanity overpowering Mars with an "inertia machine," one with the power to shift whole planets and comets from their orbits as well as shape cosmic evolution to human designs.[21]

None of these apocalyptic images were unique to Soviet Russia. They were already staples of European science fiction. Théo Varlet and Octave Joncquel's set of "planetary novels," for example, offered vivid scenes of Mars attacking Earth, recounting how the Martians flew trajectories along the orbits of the planets on their pilgrimage to the sun. In the stories Earth and its resources became a "world condemned" under the rain of Martian bombs, the capitals of Europe reduced to ashes, Baku burned to the ground, and waves of revolutionary panic spread around the globe. All of humanity's scientific and technological progress, including its achievements in interplanetary communication, counted for nothing. In the end only the "solar fraternity" of Jupiter saved Earth from total defeat.[22]

Proletarian Cosmism in Poetry and Art

In Soviet Russia a leading group of proletarian poets expressed the idea of cosmic fraternalism in verse. They were a relatively small number of writers, spread out far and wide over the remains of the

Russian empire: in places such as Tambov and Samara, Tver and Saratov, Odessa and Tiflis, Ekaterinoslav and Vladivostok. But thanks to party patronage and the generous dissemination of their works (this at a time of severe print shortages), they enjoyed an influence and coverage well beyond their numbers and perhaps even talents. Their fierce independent streak was reflected in their public image as "self-taught" adepts (*samouchki*), as artists engaged in the valiant pursuit of "self-activity" (*samodeiatel'nost*), discovering the place of the individual within the collective, combating capitalism's alienations and deprivations, raising a powerful "cult" of humanity instead.[23] Although the proletarian poets organized into two associations— Moscow's " Forge" (*Kuznitsa*) and Petrograd's "Cosmist" (*Kosmist*)— their cosmism was really less a movement than a technique, a set of lyrical images meant to transport the reader beyond reality, to plumb the depths of the mystical, much as the Symbolist poets had done before the revolution, if now with more of a political edge. Aligned to the revolutionary events of 1917, the proletarian poets conversed in high-flowing images of titanic workers, Nietzsche's "supermen," who towered over the globe and who overcame its very gravity. They appealed to wondrous natural images on Earth (volcanoes, waterfalls, and mountains) and to distant astronomical images in outer space (the sun, planets, and galaxies) as points of reference to celebrate the revolution.[24]

The proletarians also engaged in a prideful dialogue with mechanized, developed America, promising that Russia would overwhelm its industrial and technological achievements. Their inspiration came from none other than Walt Whitman, whose poetry and essays were wildly popular at the time. His appeals to positive science and natural evolution, to humanity's role in the universe, fulfilled something of a religious need, especially for Russian young adults.[25] Aleksei Gastev even modeled his classic *Shockworker Poetry* (1918) upon Whitman's rhythmic cadences and cosmic references, machine metaphors and global scope. The poet and industrialist Gastev is perhaps best known for his admiration of men such as Henry Ford and F. W. Taylor, whose practical successes and technical efficiencies made them foundations for an "Americanism" in Soviet labor and culture. But before Ford and Taylor, there was Whitman.[26] So inspired, Gastev indulged in his own "planetarism": to build up the globe through the iron foundations and steel grids of factories, through metal and glass towers that reached to the "cupola" of the heavens. Encased in fabricated steel, half-human and half-machine, the planet was to become a "forge of the universe," on the move remapping orbits and remaking solar systems.[27]

Thus, even Russian cosmism, after a fashion, was a kind of Americanism. But the proletarian poets took Whitman's and Gastev's verses to new ends and heights. Events were racing toward the unification of the working class and the final victory of communism. In acts of poetic license the proletarians freed themselves and the revolution from the bonds of Earth. They ascended by rails and towers, wings and propellers, never rockets. But they nevertheless ascended into outer space. For M. P. Gerasimov ascent took on Bergsonian tones, spurred by the fire of human will and Bolshevik determination.

> Dressed by the winged dawn,
> We will boldly fly to the skies
> Like a fuming comet
> We will cut through the Milky Way.
>
> We the cosmic millions. . . .
>
> We will make our way to the Moon's craters
> Our victory flight will slice
> In the milky-light lagoons,
> The steel arrows of red rails. . . .
>
> We will build on the canals of Mars
> A Palace of World Freedom,
> Where there'll be a tower of Karl Marx
> Shining like a fiery geyser.[28]

In a remarkable manifesto of the new style Georgii Iakubovskii framed the cosmists as poets of "sun and steel," bards of the planet earth in a living universe. This was an aesthetics, he admitted, inspired by the stories of Nikolai Morozov and the poetry of Walt

Whitman. But it was also inspired by facts, by the achievements of the industrial machine and modern science, by the victory of the Bolshevik revolution in politics. It was built upon a "materialist monism," joining Ivan Pavlov's reflexology with Karl Marx's dialectics. By celebrating the human mastery over body and mind, politics and history, the cosmists envisioned the victory over the "realm of necessity" and the achievement of the new "realm of freedom." This meant a regime of free labor and a whole new "planetary architecture," a victory even over death and a drive for the true "fraternity of the cosmos."[29] These images also reached into official popular culture: in sanctioned skits, games, poetry readings, and songs for youngsters. They were filled with references to Lenin as the "sun of new days"; to the USSR as an "iron giant"; to the proletariat as both "global and universal"; to the Soviet quest for "treasures / on the earth / and among the stars."[30]

Poetic cosmism was not spared criticism. Opponents panned it as sentimental and shallow, weak in form and tone.[31] From official quarters *Proletkul't* leaders and literary authorities scolded the poets; Aleksandr Voronskii targeted their dreamy "pantheism" and "quietism," the misplaced love of the planets and sun over the actual proletariat, the search for a "holy Nirvana" in the "cosmic abyss."[32] One of the poet laureates of Bolshevism, Demian Bednyi, pilloried cosmism. As he satirized in one prominent verse:

Success is certain
On our interplanetary course.
Strong and true in union
With the celestial working class.

Leon Trotskii defined cosmism as a "flat romanticism."[33] These were weighty indictments, that such poetry was fantastic and escapist, far afield from the more important tasks of proletarian memory and state building. The independent poet Osip Mandelshtam gently mocked the cosmist urge to fly into the heavens. "They say the cause of revolution is hunger in the interplanetary spaces," he wrote. It was as if "one has to sow wheat in the ether." For Mandelshtam what mattered most was life, plantings and harvests in the soil, the solid and heavy actions of real human beings. The earth was not corrupt, and salvation was not in outer space. Gravity was not a prison. It was our most natural element.[34] In a stunning reproach to all the totalistic ideologies of positivism and materialism (from Hegel and Comte to Marx and Spencer) he cautioned that the nineteenth century's intellectual and cultural "essence" was "projection," the false artistry of drafting lines and arcs through space and time. To him this simply meant the power to plunder world history for selfish ideological purposes and, like an "immense mad projector," screen its new scientific methods across the "terrible . . . starless sky."[35] Georgii Florovsky, defender of Russian Orthodoxy, similarly derided the current fashion to dream of the "primordial cosmic potentialities of existence," that part Hegelian rationale, part Bergsonian impulse for the "'despotic ocean' of faceless all-unity."[36]

For all these critiques the wider artistic trend was still for cosmism. The futurists tapped into its themes. Vladimir Maiakovskii and Vsevolod Meierhold staged their play, *Mystery-Bouffe* (1918)—threaded with sometimes grandiose, sometimes parodied imagery about the cosmic scope of the revolution—around the devastation of the planet through fire and flood and its rebirth through revolution. In defense of the coming "Celestial Soviet," the authors surmised, "in another fifty years the air-borne battleships of the Commune may be rushing to the attack of distant planets." The revolution was full of such leaps, without bounds.

> This is our victory chorale.
> Let the whole universe sing!
> Thanks to the "Internationale,"
> Mankind beholds a new spring.[37]

Maiakovskii's poetry remained drawn to the planets and stars. His poem *150,000,000* split the world into two camps, Soviet Russia and capitalist America, calling upon the star systems and Milky Way to join the proletarian struggle. His words ascended to the heavens, but only after appealing to the power of the Model T Ford and Cadillac, Chicago's skyscrapers and Manhattan's Brooklyn Bridge. Maiakovskii proclaimed:

From aboard
a starship
brother to the Big Dipper
I shout out poems to the noise of the universe.
Soon!
Soon!
Soon!
To space!
Up close![38]

Rockets appeared in his works with some frequency now, less as rockets than as metaphors for sudden drama, for explosive power, for human beings and human history in motion. Take the overtly political lines, dedicated to Maksim Gorkii:

By deeds,
by blood,
by this very line,
never once for hire,—
I praise
roaring upwards like a Red rocket
the banner of October,
sworn to
and sung to,
beaten by bullets![39]

More true to character were his lines about himself in motion, like a rocket:

We've taken flight,
but still—not far enough.
If it is necessary
to bend arcs—
toward Mars
please,
allow me
to give
my small life.

Here was Maiakovskii once again flying into outer space upon human-made parabolas.[40] This was the poet at his best, his most optimistic. Universal space was one of his favorite metaphors, an ocean upon which he sailed, in the ship of his own self. But like all of his metaphors, it served as a curse as much as a blessing. It was movement that gave him life and hope, and it was movement that refused to give him peace and rest. As biographer Edward Brown wrote of Maiakovskii's path to suicide in 1930, "With mounting despair he wanders the emptiness of interstellar space."[41]

Artists expressed cosmism in sculpture and painting. One of the most influential works of the revolutionary period was Vladimir Tatlin's *Monument to the Third International*, premiering in Petrograd and Moscow in late 1920, part of the government's "Plan for Monumental Propaganda," the model only some twenty feet (six meters) high but aspiring to dwarf even the Eiffel Tower. Scholars have marked it as a perfect symbol of the revolution's marriage between Earth and cosmos. The critic Viktor Shklovskii called it a fitting memorial to a twentieth century christened for "iron," spiraling up and winding down, expressing the fury and vertigo of the present, "as beautiful as the wisest Martian" in a story from H. G. Wells. Its tenacious power, I will argue, rests on its varied material meanings. It was a clocklike architecture for a new world's fair, part Crystal Palace and part Columbian Exposition. It was a new Tower of Babel, dedicated to communist propaganda. It was a projector, meant to display movies and texts upon its own surfaces and the clouds. And it was a kind of rocket, its interior halls hermetically sealed, "like a thermos," as Nikolai Punin put it, its diagonal strut like a launch ramp at a tangent to its liberating spiral.[42] With Malevich's *Black Square*," Tatlin's "Tower" came to be recognized worldwide as an image of Russian revolutionary culture. Tatlin displayed a model at the International Exposition of Modern Industrial and Decorative Arts in Paris (1925), the birthplace of art deco, where the Tower appeared at the top of a grand staircase in the Soviet exhibit, framing a bust of Lenin, as if sculpture and leader were launching into space. The Soviets celebrated it into the 1930s and beyond as a kind of rocket, a "spiral" revolving into the heavens, representing the dialectical "ascent" of the proletarian class.[43]

Fig. 7. Vladimir Tatlin's model for his *Monument to the Third International* (1920), a Soviet spiral toward outer space. To be made of metal and glass, the telescopic structure was designed to rotate in time with the heavenly bodies: the cube (legislative halls) at bottom once a year; the pyramid (executive offices) at center once a month; and the cylinder and hemisphere (propaganda and communications rooms) at top once a day and hour. The banner reads, in an echo of the linguistic Tower of Babel, "Council of Workers' and Peasants' Deputies of Planet Earth." Originally in N. N. Punin, *Pamiatnik III Internatsionala* (Peterburg: Izo NKP, 1920). Credit: Bridgeman Art Library International.

For his part Malevich and his followers, now organized in the group the Affirmers of the New Art (*Unovis*, 1920–24), turned to more truly cosmic themes, sending their art off into outer space. Their objective was to reconceptualize and remake a new architecture for the whole world. Their shared symbol, a kind of logo, or patch, was his *Black Square*, as if a new medium to the cosmos; their password was the trans-rational "*U-el-el'-ul-el-te-ka*," a play on Wells's Martian dirge. Malevich's studies of these new architectures, his "architectons" (*arkhitektony*) and "planits" (*planity*), were meant "to clothe the earth in new forms and meanings," as one Unovis declaration put it. These were solids of squares and rectangles and circles that represented human feeling, invention, and "pure action." The geometric signals once meant for Mars became a new geometry of symbols meant for us.[44] El Lissitzkii's "Proun" compositions (short for *Proekt Unovisa*) were emblematic too. He described them as halfway between painting and architecture, cut loose from the page, along with the viewer detached from the bonds of the pictorial axis and gravity, set free in "cosmic" space. At first they were settled on the ground, as in his sketches for towns and bridges, but they eventually ascended into air and space, placing the viewer in motion, floating in fields of white or black without gravity or weight. His "Proun-Star" and "Two Squares" were without horizons, no parallel lines to converge, no axes, no up or down or fixed sides, "the vanishing point at infinity." He even gave them human shape, as in "The New Man," as dynamic as Tatlin's Tower, perhaps ascending toward or perhaps descending back from outer space, the perfect diagonal man.[45]

None of these studies were actual rockets. They were simpler geometric planes and forms, without any visible means of propulsion. But they still reached, in dramatic ways, to the very cosmic realms where rockets would take us in time. They expressed the abstract Suprematist value of "projection," the charge to advance new architectural grids for the future, a new world of vast scope and depth, to reconfigure the earth and interplanetary space for future humanity. They were part of the broader Soviet "project-mania" or "projectionism," the utopian obsession with all-encompassing human progress: casting light and knowledge onto the present, propelling

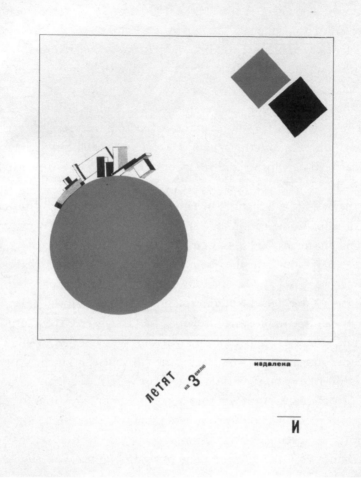

Fig. 8. El Lissitzkii's *They Fly on to Earth from Far Away and . . .* (1920), representing interplanetary travel, two extraterrestrial squares (*upper right*) approaching Earth, accentuated by the diagonal word for "they fly" (*lower center*), at a tangent to the globe. Originally in the children's book *Two Squares* (1920), published in Berlin (1922). Credit: © 2014 Artists Rights Society (ARS), New York. Digital image © The Museum of Modern Art / Licensed by Scala / Art Resource, New York.

Fig. 9. El Lissitzkii's *New Man* (1920), the human form as parabola or shooting star, retooled for outer space. From his designs for the stage play *Victory over the Sun*. Credit: © 2014 Artists Rights Society (ARS), New York. Tate, London / Art Resource, New York.

us forwards and upwards in time and space. In one of his ideological manifestos Malevich called these forms a "new Suprematist satellite" and "technological organism," something like a rocket in that they were "integrated" and whole, without clumsy moving parts. They were certainly launched on parabolic trajectories, designed to "move along an orbit shaping its new track," on a "straight line of circles" between the planets.[46]

Il'ia Chashnik's paintings put these forms decisively in motion as aerial and space machines (the *supremolet* and *planit*) approaching Mars. His "blueprints" and "plans" were meant for "ruling off the earth's expanse" and "charting those points and lines out of which the forms of Suprematism will ascend and slip into space."[47] Inspired by these aims, Aleksandr Rodchenko devised a whole new architecture for the atmosphere and outer space. If the Americans had invented the skyscraper, set like building blocks upon a cityscape both vertical and horizontal, revolutionary Russia ought to create a whole new edifice, an Egyptian pyramid inverted, "with only one end attached to the earth, the rest in space."[48] Georgii Krutikov's "Flying City" (1928) turned this pyramid into an elliptical "parabaloid" curving from the edge of Earth into orbital space, floating thanks to the power of atomic energy. It was to serve as clean and spacious apartment housing, reached by small teardrop spaceships. Viktor Kalmykov even visualized a "Saturn Ring City" to circle a space-age Earth, rockets flying about in outer space (1929).[49]

These stirrings for the cosmos, for the zero gravity and free movement of outer space, were not altogether unique to the Suprematists. French cubists and Italian and Dutch futurists, together with members of the Bauhaus group and innovative soloists such as Joan Miró, flirted with these themes as well, if with somewhat less an ideological scope and something more of a delay. They shared an appreciation for science and technology, for experimental technique, even at times for socialist revolution. Their maverick artistic and architectural forms were also a function of developments in the real world: the astronomical observations of the planetary circles and lines of the moon and Mars; or the ubiquitous images of rounded dirigibles, of angular and curved airplanes in flight.[50]

Nor was Russian revolutionary cosmism merely the province of elite poets and artists. It became a regular feature of public discourse, both high and low, far and wide. Newspapers in the Americas and Europe buzzed with reports about the possibilities of alien life. *Interplanetary communications* (*mezhplanetnye soobshcheniia*) became the catchword phrase, implying that humanity was not alone, that it was on the verge of contact with other worlds. This speculation was fueled by new discoveries about Mars, the dissemination of radio, the perfection of "super" telescopes, the discoveries of new stars and planets, and the coming of rocket power. Mars was probably inhabited. Radio signals sent there might one day be returned.[51] The rocket might even someday take us there. Humanity was marking all kinds of new sound and sight and motion pathways through outer space. In the wake of the First World War one publicist even felt the need to yell out to the heavens, from an infantile Earth to "an older and wiser" Mars, about our recent "struggle for democratic ideals."[52]

In Russia, with all its revolutionary upheaval, these kinds of authoritative news reports from abroad took on new and different meanings, more believable rings of truth. As Evgenii Zamiatin recollected, it was as if "today, the Apocalypse could be published as a daily newspaper; tomorrow we shall calmly buy a ticket for a journey by sleeper to Mars."[53] When the poet Nikolai Aseev imagined communication with Mars, he framed his words out of a news story, featuring Thomas Edison's voice, not Lenin's:

Listen!!!
This is Earth.
Edison speaking
A son of humanity answers you.[54]

When Valerii Briusov conceived a story on space travel, "The First Interplanetary Expedition" (1920–21), he wrote it in the form of a news release, with snippets from a diary, referencing the worldwide interest in the event, disseminated in scores of magazines and newspapers "in all languages." These were not simply devices to feign reality. They reflected a reality already at play in the news. To reach the full heights of realism, Briusov made his interplanetary expedition an

American one, this to give depth to the event, whose facts were otherwise "well known to every reader." The members—comrades Morley, Paris, and O'Rourke—were American Communists. Their work proceeded under the patronage of the "American State Astronomical Society" (ASAS), its name prominently displayed in Latin letters. Their spacecraft was a rocket, called the "eteronef" after Bogdanov.[55] In all of these ways, for all its sentimentalism and hyperbole, Russian cosmism had a rational, realistic tinge. It was a function of the world around it, from the facts of the Russian Revolution and civil war at home and from the reports about the possibilities of interplanetary communication from abroad. The fantastic seemed to be becoming ever more real, ever more possible.

Utopias of Russian Biocosmism

These passions for the cosmic were actually the centerpieces of a small faction of truly unique anarchist "biocosmists" in Soviet Russia. They entertained a universal civilization of true freedom and justice, based on the physical rejuvenation (and potential immortality) of the living, the precondition for a future of space travel and human evolution beyond our home planet. With the proletarian poets they shared images of the Russian Revolution as a struggle of titanic forces, as a radical break in time, as a Slavophile rising of the East against the West. But their conceit was also to see the revolution almost exclusively as a cosmic event, fulfilling their passion for a new biology of the abundant, infinite, and eternal.

Aleksandr Iaroslavskii's poems represented this intense and unapologetic style.[56] Amid the devastation of the civil war, he contrasted the rotting corpses of a corrupt planet with the certain hope of a new life in the pure vacuum of outer space. The Russian Revolution reached from Petrograd to Berlin and Paris, even to Venus and the stars, a cathartic event of total destruction and re-creation, against all the world's "machines and dollars," all its "servility and slavery." Russia's revolution would join the whole earth to the movements and lives of the planets. It would send out spaceships to the living worlds and "brothers" of the cosmos, forging a new "federation," a "union of planets." So he proclaimed: "We will tame the planet Earth / And will be warmed by Happiness / In the desert of the ice world."[57] Our globe, in other words, would become a "planetary ship," a "sailor upon the universe," set upon a course to "storm the sun." Earth, not Mars, was the real "Red planet." As he wrote:

—Hey, Mephistopholes,—
Click your castanettes,—
The cosmos is turning black to white!—
To the sun—stand at attention!—
Planets form into line!—
—Give way—to the Red Earth![58]

A more structured biocosmist project took shape among the pro-Soviet "Universalist" anarchists between 1917 and 1921. They were "borne out of the stormy explosion of the revolution," as their sometimes leader Aleksandr Agienko (aka "Sviatogor," meaning "sacred mount") put it, with the promise to break out of Earth's gravity and achieve eternal life in the heavens. Their platform was based on two simple principles: "immortalism and interplanetarism." Sviatogor and his comrades presented them to the Moscow public in a series of scintillating debates during the winter of 1921–22 (among the participants were the philosophers Nikolai Berdiaev and Sergei Bulgakov). They formed an association, the "Creatoriia of Biocosmists"—not crematoria to burn dead bodies but "creatoriia" to immortalize and resurrect them. They even aimed to establish "Immortality Councils" (Soviets) all over the country and the world. Russians read about the movement in the press and corresponded, one worker even modestly offering his own body for the first experiments in immortality.

The biocosmists despised every abstract "localism." They rejected the localism of "time," meaning human mortality and all the idealisms that accompanied it, as well as the localism of "space," meaning pride in one's race or homeland, really any urge for crass material achievement. Even proletarian internationalism, being a "planetary localism," was suspect. Only interplanetarism would do, this at a moment when humanity was conquering the air, with the conquest of interplanetary space sure to follow. The members launched an anarchistic assault on death (the ultimate authority, after all) and all its sorry manifestations in our lives: our selfish fear of it and our conceited instinct for survival; our reliance on mysticism and religion to make sense of it. They proposed, instead, to research and promote an achievable "individual immortality" as the basis for true collective solidarity. Only when each and every one of us was assured of our own physical immortality, along with the resurrection of our fallen relatives and comrades, could we hope to achieve social and political peace. These efforts, in turn, would pave the way for the conquest of the heavens by "cosmic navigation," or "cosmonautics" (*kosmoplavanie*), the first such reference to the term that I have been able to find in the literature. As the biocosmists argued, "Interplanetarism is the challenge of flying into cosmic space, becoming citizens of the cosmos, active participants in cosmic life, becoming wiser and willful rulers over the movements of cosmic bodies, fully able to regulate and transform and create new worlds."[59]

These values and visions may have sounded a lot like N. F. Fedorov's positions. But the biocosmists were openly contemptuous of him, implicitly in their attack on organized religion, explicitly in their open hostility toward Fedorov's mysticism and conservatism. The biocosmists parlayed a radical break with the past, even against Copernicus and the traditional thesis about the plurality of worlds. Humanity and Earth were not mere specks in a greater universe. They were bigger than the whole cosmos. They already encompassed it. Humanity was destined to subdue nature everywhere and always.[60] Granted, these visions were "fantastic," admitted the biocosmists, but not purely utopian. "Science and technology" guaranteed their success, as did the proletarian revolution, which had set in motion the very logic and "teleology" of human fulfillment that biocosmism promised to complete. Facts preceded the fantastic.

For Sviatogor some of those facts referred to Bakhmet'ev's "anabiosis," a proven means of prolonging and renovating human life, or to the experiments of N. P. Kravkov, one of Russia's leading biologists, who was able to maintain whole rabbit ears and human fingers "alive" in his special laboratory solutions and who tested the reinvigorating effects of hormonal injections. In Moscow the surgeon F. A. Andreev had also experimented with the application of an electrical current and adrenalin to revive failed hearts.[61] Sviatogor and the biocosmists delightfully celebrated all of these recent achievements. Fedorov's ideas were being surpassed by modern science. But Sviatogor drew most confidence about the scientific potential of "immortalism" from the West: namely, the work of Eugen Steinach in human "rejuvenation."[62] A professor of biology at the University of Vienna, Steinach was famous for his vaso-ligature operation, tying off the vas deferens to promote internal secretions of the male sexual glands. He had claimed it promoted healthier internal organs and the treatment of disease, with the most spectacular results (if later proven wrong) in restoring a lost youth and vigor to his elderly patients, now become "young old men." In time leading surgeons in New York City, London, and points beyond performed the operation on thousands of patients, including Sigmund Freud and William Butler Yeats. Newspapers and magazines in Europe and the Americas captured the imaginations of their readers with news of Steinach's results, this so soon after four years of a terrible and costly war in human lives. Mortality had never been so stark and real, the promise of continued youth never more appealing.[63] The "Steinach method" became all the rage in early Soviet Russia too. One editor even asserted that the two premier issues of the day, Steinach's rejuvenation and Einstein's relativity theory, deserved further study in tandem with Soviet materialist science, a means to finally conquer the oppressive burdens of time and space. Immortalism and interplanetarism were currencies of public exchange.[64]

With the biocosmists two other "cosmic" anarchists also stand out in these years, the brothers A. L. and V. L. Gordin, founders of an anarchist cell during 1917, the Union of the Oppressed Five. It was dedicated to five specific goals: the complete liberation of people from property, children from schools, society from the state, nations from empires, and women from men. The group's maximal program of "pan-Anarchism" aimed for a total renovation of culture and politics, religion and science, from below—"universal statelessness, cosmic anarchy," they called it. Of special note was their nihilistic approach to both religion and science, humanity's premier illusions. Science was an idol to the modern mind just as religion was to the traditional, merely substituting "abstract" ideals for the "supernatural," "Nature" for "God." Both were contemptuous conceits of the human imagination. Newton and Darwin did not speak to truth. Their so-called natural laws were only so much capitalist nonsense: mechanics no more than a clever design to build better manufacturing machines, evolution but a ruse to promote better livestock breeding. Modern science held people back from the truth, from their own process of self-discovery. As the brothers Gordin wrote, the universe "has neither beginning nor end, neither origin (cosmogony) nor cause, neither laws nor knout-like forces. The universe and every natural phenomenon is always 'itself' . . . spontaneous. In the universe as in every natural phenomenon there is nothing external, no coercive order, but rather *anarchy,* i.e., internal (immanent) order, independent and spontaneous."[65] The human being embodied the whole universe—in our existential "actions and affinities," in our "muscles" and "technics." These traits gave us the inborn human rights of "social experimentation, improvisation and invention," based on the movements of the human body and mind, what the brothers also called "the physiological, the only proper, natural and just dictatorship of free activity."[66]

V. L. (Vol'f Lvovich) Gordin eventually adapted these precepts into his philosophy of human "inventism," centered on his ultimate invention, the international language AO.[67] AO eventually became the world's first language for interplanetary travel among Moscow's anarchist-cosmists of the later 1920s. As Sviatogor and comrades were promoting a new biology of space travel, V. L. Gordin was advancing its new linguistics. Perfectly streamlined, Gordin's AO was based on vowel and consonant sound combinations for speaking and number and sign combinations for writing. V.L. even wrote sophisticated grammars and bilingual dictionaries with thousands of entries.

Table 1. Sound and sign designations in AO

	Vowels	Consonants
Speaking	a o e i u	b c d f l
Writing	x 0 + √ -	1 2 3 4 5

AO was a remarkable achievement in terms of its novelty and simplicity. Grammar was embedded in the sound system and alphabet. The various sounds, letters, and signs were symbolic representations that logically corresponded to nouns or adverbs or other parts of speech. "AO," for example, was written as "x0." The A and x signified the verb "action," the O and 0 signified a proper noun. AO literally meant "the action," or "the invention." True to the anarchist ethic, V.L.'s new language altogether dispensed with gender (signifying male oppression), as well as possessive cases and possessive pronouns and the genitive case (signifying property relations). Pronouns were sounded and written as such.

Table 2. Pronouns in AO

Me	You	They
bi	ci	di
1√	2√	3√

So, V.L.'s name was "beobi" (written as 1+01√) and literally meant "society" (be), "the" (o), "me" (bi). The overarching goal of AO was to achieve the greatest meaningful and logical "correspondence" between words and concepts and things as possible, essentially creating a classification scheme, a catalog of the human experience. V.L.'s five fundamental linguistic concepts are a case in point (table 3).

Table 3. The five fundamental linguistic concepts in AO

Time	Motion	Number	Matter	Energy
bao	cao	dao	fao	lao
1x0	2x0	3x0	4x0	5x0

Table 3 shows how V.L. established an exact correspondence between sounds and concepts. "Time" (bao) is what "I" (bi) first experience as an individual and ultimately, together with "you" (ci), transform into "motion" (cao) multiplied by "they" (di) in "number" (dao). Matter and energy were the actual bridges between the one and the many. AO offered a compact circle of logical meanings that its adepts believed would make perfect sense in outer space.

Although one of the most perfect the world has ever seen, V. L. Gordin's artificial language was isolated and obscure, lost within the sweep of the revolution and civil war. It also had several more successful rivals in Western Europe. "Esperanto" surged in popularity during the interwar years as an auxiliary, international language—a status conferred in the USSR through the government-backed Soviet Esperanto Union, which promoted Russian proletarian internationalism by way of labor unions and pen pals. A faction of French Anarcho-Esperantists, the World Non-Nationalist Association (*Sennacieco Asocio Tutmondo*)—directed by the charismatic Eugene Lanti and dedicated to a world without nations or boundaries—even rivaled V. L. Gordin's own anarchistic philosophy.[68] So did the ideals of the French anarcho-syndicalist Victor Coissac, who proposed an interplanetary language of mathematics and geometry for future space travel. In the traditions of French utopian socialism, Coissac founded a small egalitarian phalanstery outside of Tours between 1911 and 1935, dedicated to the ideal of the "Integral," his mathematical metaphor for a society of full equality, prosperity, and "goodwill." The pathway to this new "Eden" was by way of rationalism and modern science, understanding the universal laws and the plurality of worlds beyond our own. We lived in a self-motivating and self-calibrating universe, Coissac believed, moved by the physical forces of attraction and repulsion, of biological adaptation and transformation. Our destiny was to perfect evolution by way of mind and will, to survive the birth and death of planets and stars, to travel into outer space and begin to speak to other worlds.[69]

Granted, these were eccentric projects in their day. The closest the average reader came to such strange new languages was still science fiction, works such as Vivian Itin's *The Land of Gonguri* (1922), one of the first such works after the Russian Revolution. In the tradition of the cosmic romance Itin also crafted the makings of an alien, interplanetary language for his story, almost mimicking Gordin's AO. It was filled with quick consonant-vowel combinations, the primitive and strange declarative phrases such as "Ra, Tarage, Ogu" and personal names such as Paon and Onte, Sea and Neatna, Marg and Nolla. The novel offers yet another study of the "revolutionary" cosmic. The story of a condemned man, moving halfway between the mass mur-der of the First World War and his hypnotic dreams of a grand inter-planetary future, it married the infinitesimal earth to the infinity of the universe. Itin drew from his own experience as a Bolshevik com-batant in the civil war, serving on revolutionary tribunals that sent condemned to their deaths, all in the name of a higher justice. His poems between the years 1912 and 1920, inspired by the Symbolists and written in the cosmist style, expressed the same values: human-ity as reaching for angelic justice but falling back into bestial violence; the civil war as an arena of cosmic struggle (after Dante Alighieri, whom Itin admired); the sun as a source of irrevocable, purging fire.[70]

Itin's *The Land of Gonguri* was just such a fable, a morality tale about the war and revolution. Itin's "Gonguri" was a land of good order and abundance. Its engineers had mechanized production and distribution. They managed the economy by efficient plans and chemical engineering. They had overcome the power of gravity and so were able to move whole mountains and cities at will. All of soci-ety was one great machine. Gonguri's civic monuments expressed the catchwords of the day: "For the Transmutation of Matter" and "For the Victory over Gravity." The citizenry moved about by way of antigravity packs, offering each individual the "narcotic" high of aerial flight. This was also the ideal of society at large: the urge "upward," the quest "ever higher and higher."[71]

Itin's inventor, "Vezilet" (the "all-flier"), mastered interplanetary travel, setting off to discover and explore the cosmos. His space-craft, after Krasnogorskii, was named the *Victor of Space* (*Podeditel' prostranstva*). He and his crew experienced the "ecstasy of contem-plation" in the infinity of space. They saw their small planet recede from view and their smaller "I" magnified to become its own planet, engaged in its own new "struggle for existence," battling the elements on alien planets, sailing among the "reefs of interplanetary space."[72] Itin's story put in place all of the artistic pieces to imagine human-ity in these new worlds, the gifts of science as much as of fiction, in machines and environments of its own making. These kinds of ear-nest visions, fragments of Russian revolutionary culture, mapped a human pathway to outer space.

5

The Pioneers and the Spaceflight Imperative

With the inauguration of the New Economic Policy (NEP) after 1921, Russians joined utopian ventures with practical tasks. They finally had the opportunity to rebuild following seven years of war and revolution, a breathing space to consider once again the values of rocketry and spaceflight. Political empires had fallen. A whole new world of nation-states and economic markets surrounded them. Governments now appreciated the role of machines, especially flying machines, for war and peace. Aviation became a mark of prestige in the world. In Russia it had not proven decisive through the First World War or the civil war, but policy makers nonetheless understood, thanks to such works as N. A. Rynin's *Aerial Warfare* (1917), the coming military and political ramifications of airplane and dirigible attacks. Rynin offered some of the first vivid accounts of English and German aerial power: as if in a scene from a Wells novel, planes weaving through the heavy winds, the roar of the motors approaching then fading, terrifying the civilian population with their "waves" of "disturbing alarm."[1]

A number of similar works soon followed. René Lorin even raised the military possibilities of the jet or rocket as ballistic missile, an "aerial torpedo" able to reach deep into enemy territories and destroy urban areas at will. The American military scientist William Sherman predicted that the airplane would revolutionize warfare. "It is a thing *sui generis*," wrote Sherman, the perfect means to cover battlefields, blanket whole countries, even circumnavigate the globe. He also predicted new kinds of "missile weapons" for strategic bombing.

Here was offensive war on a radical new scale.[2] The pacifist writer Will Irwin expressed all of this in a rocket metaphor: the next war "will not be declared; it will burst. Upon the promptness and speed of the initial thrust may depend victory." The coming war, with the invention of newer and better aviation and artillery (with firebombs, poison gas, and germ warfare) would perfect the human capacity for "projection power." The airplane was already like a jet or rocket. In its reach and precision and "lifting capacity," it was a "self-propelling shell," a "bursting charge beyond the previous imagination."[3] Modern science would create such a "war by machinery," fashioning even unpiloted planes with wireless controls that would create a "wholesale version of the retail air-holocausts" of the First World War. Paris would turn "from a metropolis to a necropolis."[4]

None of these observers matched the cold logic and steely prose of the Italian colonel Giulio Douhet, whose *The Command of the Air* (1921) became the standard work on strategic air power. He envisioned a new way of mapping battlefronts: as killing fields from the air, radii of death, subject to aviation's harsh geometry of reach. The next war, he surmised, would allow opposing forces to "strike mortal blows into the heart of the enemy with lightning speed." Air power would engage all the "points in a circle having A for its center and a radius of hundreds of miles for its field of action." Cities such as London would be pummeled with surprise attacks, merciless bombing campaigns of hundreds of squadrons and thousands of bombers, with targets from anywhere between five hundred and two thousand "meters in diameter." This meant a capacity to strike at the "very heart" of an opponent, its capital, to "plunge the city itself into terror and confusion." It was all a matter of technical sophistication: higher altitudes, stronger and lighter metal frames, bigger and faster planes. It was also a matter of industrial capacity: more planes meant more bombs, more targets, more victims.[5]

These visions quickly filtered into the popular media. American and Russian magazines tended to follow the very same lines of prophecy and doom, to share the worst scenario of the future war: the marriage of aerial bombardment and poison gas, made all the more powerful by radio control for precise triangulated attacks. The future war, in all its mechanical fury, would engulf whole societies. It was bound to break out on the land, underground, in the air.[6] As one Soviet observer put it most ironically, the laws of war and the arms race recalled Newton's own third law of motion: "Every action provokes a corresponding reaction." A cycle of competition and escalation, matching a rival's technologies with those of one's own, was captivating Europe and America. The next war was sure to bring the horror of mass destruction. "Every citizen will become a soldier; every point on the map, the front."[7] Rynin painted a stark picture as well. "The future aerial war will be a real hell in the air." Hinting at the coming power of rockets, he warned: "Everything will move over to the space beyond the clouds."[8]

Douhet never spoke directly to the power of the long-range rocket. But his whole approach presumed its relevance and reach. His fellow military scientists in the Italian armed forces certainly thought so. They helped to lay the groundwork for the military and aviation applications of rocket power. One naval theorist, in an effort to confront the new realities of "distant offense," first raised the possibilities of "direct reaction propulsion": the "aerial torpedo" as "self-propelled explosive." Col. G. A. Crocco was already deliberating the advent of "super-aviation" and "super-artillery," terms that included rockets as short-range ballistic missiles. Their speed and altitude would make them invincible by all contemporary measures of military and civil air defense, fulfilling Douhet's wildest predictions and impressing Soviet analysts with their potential.[9]

Crocco's reference to super-artillery was actually a military challenge first raised by the German General Staff and its infamous "Paris Gun" of 1918. Deployed in the very last months of the war, it sent a warhead toward the edge of space, an altitude of 40 kilometers (25 miles), for a maximum ballistic range of 130 kilometers (81 miles). The cannon did minor damage relative to the wider war, killing about 256 and wounding some 620 others, the shell more menacing as a weapon of psychological terror. European civilization was in crisis and decline by 1918, so Oswald Spengler wrote in *The Decline of the West*, but the power of this "long-range weapon," in his words, whereby "the tense force of the gases of explosion are converted into

THE PIONEERS AND THE SPACEFLIGHT IMPERATIVE

YBP Library Services

SMITH, MICHAEL G., 1960-

ROCKETS AND REVOLUTION: A CULTURAL HISTORY OF
EARLY SPACEFLIGHT.
                                    Cloth   431 P.
LINCOLN: UNIV OF NEBRASKA PRESS, 2014

AUTH: PURDUE UNIVERSITY.

LCCN 2014024760
  ISBN 0803255225   **Library PO#** FIRM ORDERS

                                    List   34.95 USD
  8395 NATIONAL UNIVERSITY LIBRAR   **Disc**   14.0%
  App. Date   3/11/15   SETC   8214-08 **Net**   30.06 USD

SUBJ: 1. ASTRONAUTICS--HIST. 2. ASTRONAUTICS &
STATE.

CLASS TL788.5   DEWEY# 629.410904   LEVEL GEN-AC

YBP Library Services

SMITH, MICHAEL G., 1960-

ROCKETS AND REVOLUTION: A CULTURAL HISTORY OF
EARLY SPACEFLIGHT.
                                    Cloth   431 P.
LINCOLN: UNIV OF NEBRASKA PRESS, 2014

AUTH: PURDUE UNIVERSITY.

  LCCN 2014024760
  ISBN 0803255225   **Library PO#** FIRM ORDERS

                                    List   34.95 USD
  8395 NATIONAL UNIVERSITY LIBRAR   **Disc**   14.0%
  App. Date   3/11/15   SETC   8214-08 **Net**   30.06 USD

SUBJ: 1. ASTRONAUTICS--HIST. 2. ASTRONAUTICS &
STATE.

CLASS TL788.5   DEWEY# 629.410904   LEVEL GEN-AC

energy of motion," was emblematic of the tenacious and still-ascending "spirit of the Western technique." Spengler might as well have been describing the rocket, just as several Italian strategists suspected.[10]

When enthusiasts imagined the suborbital and orbital limits of rocket flight in chart form, they used the maximum altitude of the Paris Gun (sometimes mistakenly called "Big Bertha") as their baseline. It was the record to beat. The "shell of Bertha," for American and European audiences, was the height of human achievement, the highest object placed into the far heights of the air, well above the modest heights of balloons and airplanes. The editors of *Scientific American* illustrated all of this in a full-page chart on the earth's atmosphere and stratosphere (and its boundaries with outer space), dramatically accompanying an article and portrait featuring Robert H. Goddard. America's marker to the world, it became a mainstay in popular science literature for a decade.[11]

This chart of Earth's altitudes, reaching into the stratosphere and beyond, was already the beginning of a new sensibility about outer space, its radical conversion from a metaphysic to a map, a place not so much to be imagined as to be navigated and explored. It illustrated how conventional airplanes, even the shells of the Paris Gun, always hit the upper boundaries of the atmosphere, our envelope of air. They flew horizontally. But the magic of Goddard's rocket was to aim up, in a parabolic arc of vertical ascent, mirroring the magnificent descents of meteors falling to Earth. The French popular astronomer Father Théophile Moreux put it most bluntly when he wrote that a voyage to the moon, at the "parabolic velocity" of just over eleven kilometers per second, was now within the realm of the possible, given the proper calculations and technologies. Perhaps a world state might achieve this goal in the near future, in the interests of global peace, "with the same ease by which the Krauts bombarded Paris."[12] The Paris Gun was the father of the rocket.

All of these strategic considerations played a crucial role in Soviet Russia's state-sponsored aviation campaign of 1923. As Scott Palmer has discussed, the campaign encompassed initiatives both practical and symbolic, secret and public. The objective was to invest in air power and build fleets of planes, to inspire the country to great

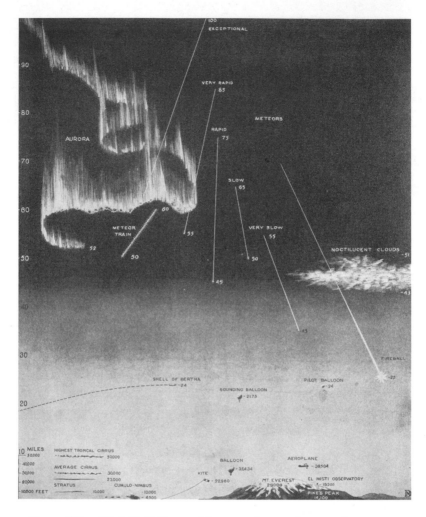

Fig. 10. "How High Up?" The earth's atmosphere and stratosphere, a new map for navigation, revealing the shell of the German Paris Gun in flight, the highest reaches (so far) of airplanes and balloons, and the new frontier for Robert Goddard's rockets. This picture was disseminated worldwide, first appearing in *Scientific American* (July 1926): 16. Credit: Reproduced with permission. © 2014 Scientific American, Inc. All rights reserved.

technological feats, to conquer ground and aerial "space." The secret initiatives had already begun with several hidden corollaries to the Rapallo Treaty (1922), essentially a German-Russian military pact that offered cooperation in the joint development of better tanks, chemical weapons, and airplanes. When Leon Trotskii (as commissar of the Red Army) and Soviet military officials launched the public campaign in March, their slogan was straight out of Douhet: "There is No Victory without Command of the Air." The essential task was to compete with the West. The Red Army had no choice but to occupy that new front of warfare, the "ocean" of air, with whole fleets of dirigibles, bombers, and fighters.[13]

With all the flourishes and hyperbole of Bolshevik propaganda, the campaign turned into a craze of sorts. The famous song "March of the Aviators" (*Avia Marsh*, 1920) expressed the aerial optimism of the moment. The songwriters had composed it during the battles of the civil war, amazed as they were at the bravery of the Red pilots flying such antiquated and unworthy airplanes into the fight, to their probable deaths. Russia's aerial optimism, it turns out, was often a function of its very own political and military backwardness.[14] The song touched on a variety of current tropes: turning dreams into realities, conquering time and place, transforming human flesh into moving metal. "We were born to make the fairy tale come true / To overcome space and distance." The lyrics set Russia's sights upon the envelope of the air, upward to "the flight of birds," outward to the "tranquility of our borders." The accent was on process, on the human being as a pilot, moving "ever higher, higher and higher."[15]

The accent was on ascent. The song's lyrics echoed Iakov Perel'man's and Nikolai Morozov's pleas for Russia to attain the terrestrial and cosmic heights. They recalled some of Gastev's lines too:

We go to the mountaintops, we take them!
Higher still, yet higher!
. . . We have no wings?
We will! They will be born in an explosion of burning wish.[16]

Several of the proletarian poets borrowed the phrasing in their own verses, to mean flight into the skies, or even as S. A. Obradovich put it, "To fly higher, higher, people, / To Mars, Orion, and Leo."[17] Russian observers took this all in, craving to be a part of these new worlds, racing even farther into the future with prognostications of wonders soon to come. Valerii Briusov expressed it best in a poem, as if "flying to America" was to fly into the future, "launched skyward by unseen lines," as if the world now inhabited every possibility. "Storm the heavens!" he wrote, "chart a course from earth / Into the starlight, on an interplanetary aero!"[18]

The Goddard Phenomenon

These rather fantastic visions were justified by the facts, such as they were. Robert Goddard's proposal to fly to the moon was just becoming known to the wider Russian public, if with something of a delay compared to most of the world. He had published his classic work *A Method of Reaching Extreme Altitudes* in the winter of 1919–20, a dense technical piece on the possibilities of rockets reaching to the upper atmosphere, to the stratosphere, and beyond. Like Tsiolkovskii and Esnault-Pelterie before him, but by his own original work, Goddard offered pages of proofs and differential equations on the feasibility of a powder fuel "step" rocket to reach into "extreme altitudes," even at velocities to "escape the earth's attraction." He figured the precise mass ratios and exhaust velocities for his new "theory of rocket action." He proved by experiment that the rocket operated in a vacuum, by its own propulsion, not in reaction against the air. Except for matters of air resistance and gravity, it was completely self-contained, "an apparatus that reacts against matter, this matter being carried by the apparatus in question." He offered a design for his new type of rocket, driven upward by the successive firing of its powdered-fuel cartridges. This was not yet a liquid fuel rocket of the Tsiolkovskii type. Goddard was not so bold. But it was a radical redesign for outer space.[19]

All of this, filled with Goddard's equations on the "Theory of the Motion with Direct Lift" or "Theory of Spring Impulse-Meter," must have been quite difficult for the lay American reader. This was aviation science become a kind of rocket science. Aviation had already become, thanks to the military imperatives of the First World War, much more of a formal engineering, dependent on the complex forces that now constituted the working airplane: the structure of its fuselage, the horsepower and lightness of its engine, the forms of its wings and ailerons. All were functions of precise calculations and rigorous designs. Goddard worked within this emerging paradigm but offered something more: a whole new engine with vertical power and supreme altitude. His modest objective was simply to raise "recording instruments" to high altitudes to study the weather, the nature of the upper atmosphere, and solar physics. None of this was terribly dramatic, except for the last few pages, almost an afterthought, outlining the possibilities of sending a rocket by a "'parabolic' velocity" (6.95 miles or 11.2 kilometers a second) to an "'infinite' altitude" in order to drift forever into the depths of space, or perhaps just go to the moon, so as to explode a signal flare upon it for observation from the earth. This was not really of any scientific value, Goddard recognized. But his rockets did have great potential for the future, he teased, given their speed and range. Perhaps most important, his new theory of space rockets "depend upon nothing that is really impossible."[20]

Like Tsiolkovskii's experience in 1903, Goddard's piece first appeared in a scholarly gray area, somewhere between obscurity and notoriety. The Smithsonian Institution, which published Goddard's essay, was one of the world's premier scientific organizations. Its *Annual Reports* and *Contributions to Knowledge* were forums for the best of American and international scholarship. To be featured there, in either the English original or in translation, was a mark of significant achievement. Among recent eminent studies were Otto Lilienthal's "Flying and Soaring" (1893), Henri de Graffigny's "Explorations of the Upper Atmosphere" (1897), and Guglielmo Marconi's "Wireless Telegraphy" (1901). Goddard enjoyed the Smithsonian's patronage, but given the dense mathematical nature of his work, it appeared in the supplementary series, *Miscellaneous Collections*, a place reserved for the arcane data of astronomical observations, meteorological findings, chemical tables, and such. His own study, for example, was bound in volume 71 of the *Collections*, along with an article listing detailed observations on "The Brightness of the Sky" and a piece, "New Species of Piper from Panama," on the tropical pepper plant, written from start to finish in Latin.[21]

Yet the Smithsonian management was also well attuned to the power of newspaper science. Its director and Goddard's erstwhile patron, secretary Charles G. Abbot, was a respected astronomer and science writer fascinated with interplanetary communication, what he called the chance "to talk freely with intelligences existing on another world." Perhaps, he even suggested, some new and more efficient method was on the horizon (the rocket) that might make interplanetary communication come true.[22] It took Abbot's Smithsonian press release on 11 January 1920 to get the country's attention, turning Goddard into an international sensation, the media dubbing him the "Moon man" and dramatizing his measured, precise calculations and claims as popular fantasy becoming fact. The *New York Times* helped to set this story line in motion with a leading article on 12 January. The piece reported that "Professor Goddard," sponsored by the Smithsonian Institution, had already "invented and tested" his new device, "a multiple charge and high efficiency rocket of an entirely new design." The newspaper's readers, for the first but not last time, now learned some of the basics of what they would eventually come to know as "rocket science." "The determining factor of the efficiency of a rocket is the velocity of ejection of the gases due to the explosion of the propelling material," so lectured the newspaper piece. After "a large number of experiments," Goddard had devised the necessary elements to shoot a rocket into outer space.[23]

These were strong words and promises in the day of Thomas Edison and Henry Ford, marrying confidence to expectation. Goddard fit the molds. Like Edison, he was a master inventor and was very protective of his scientific and technological creations, as his many patents confirm. Like Ford, he was a hopeful entrepreneur, methodically creating and testing his rocket parts, perhaps with an eye on eventual assembly lines and mass production. But Goddard was something more of a dreamer. We know that he loved science fiction, especially the apocalyptic power of H. G. Wells's *War of the Worlds*. Like Tsiolkovskii, if more modestly and less publicly, Goddard feared for the planet and saw our salvation in space. His unpublished essay of 1918

"The Last Migration" envisioned a dying sun and the death of civilization, for which humanity had no other alternative than to send its genetic material out into cosmic space to find a new home. This was "a problem which will someday face our race as the sun grows colder, even though, by dint of jet propulsion, we succeed in moving sunward." He also wrote, in mystical tones, about the eternal reproduction and reincarnation of the universe, if at "very great intervals."[24]

News reports about Goddard gave him proper due as both realist and fantasist. Hugo Gernsback described his powder fuel step rocket as a potential moon rocket driven "forward due to pure reaction." But he also listed it along with several other rather incredible proposals, including Jules Verne's cannon, Arthur Train's "Flying Ring," and Gernsback's own circular "Space Flyer." Goddard's rocket was also the inspiration for several short space travel films in 1920 and 1922, featuring the atomic-powered "Projectocar," bullet-shaped with telltale rocket exhaust. This impressive image found a ready audience in the United States and Europe, as historian Frank Winter has discussed. Take the newspaper cartoon that proposed sending all manner of "Red Radicals—Bolsheviki—I.W.W. Anarchists, etc.," straight up into outer space oblivion. Their fuel? Nothing more than their very own "vicious-vitriolic vituperations of hatred and contempt" for American capitalism, which via "continuous explosions projects the rocket forward with great force and velocity."[25] American readers were already marrying rockets to revolution.

Beyond the initial news wave Goddard's rocket had mixed effects in Europe. The secretary-general of the French Aerial Association, Georges Houard, met his proposals with diffidence, referring to Goddard as "an American scientist" who promised us the moon but lacked the necessary high-powered fuels and sophisticated craft to actually get us there.[26] France preferred Esnault-Pelterie's rocket and space travel theories, now republished after the war. One writer even turned them into fiction, celebrating his French "rocket" (la fusée), powered by atomic energy and launched to beat the Germans to Mars.[27]

For Soviet Russia, Goddard's proposals were altogether premature. The pace of the civil war eclipsed them. The first months of 1920 saw profound events unfold. The fortunes of the Soviet republic ebbed. Its cities were starving and in disarray as the Red Army battled the White Armies all around. The interventions of Allied military forces in Murmansk, the Caucasus, and Siberia were in full sway. War communism was harassing the countryside for its grain and resources. Goddard's dramatic entrance onto the world news circuit never really reached Russia with the same effect as elsewhere. The Latvian Russian rocket pioneer Fridrikh Arturovich Tsander did recall making something of a sensation in late 1920 at the Moscow Regional Conference of Inventors, where he offered a proposal for a rocket plane to space, replete with flight modes, human passengers, and a zero gravity environment.[28] Although open to dispute, Tsander claimed that at the conference he had met V. I. Lenin, who apparently received him warmly, offering his hand and pledging support, calling the "reaction engine" the best possible means for speedy transportation in the atmosphere and above, a "grandiose revolution in technology."[29] Lenin may even have had Tsander (or Kibalchich or Tsiolkovskii) in mind when, just a few years later, he commented that "fantasy" was "extraordinarily valuable" in having given birth to mathematics and differential and integral calculus. Even they would be impossible without it. To think it was exclusively the realm of poets was a "foolish prejudice."[30]

Yet Lenin's greeting to Tsander, if it ever happened, was only a passing moment, a reflection of his charms and talents as a politician. The handshake was about as firm as the support got. Lenin's national priorities were more modest: to improve the basic material culture of most Russians, to raise them out of backwardness and provide them with better hygiene, basic literacy, and education, framed by good roads, city services, and electric power grids. His utopia was practical, the "utopia of electrification," as H. G. Wells had put it. Wells must have certainly thought so during his visit to Soviet Russia in 1920, eyeing the devastated landscapes of the civil war. For one of his Russian hosts the visit even had the feel of a science fiction novel: as if Wells had come to Russia in just the same way as one of his own characters had gone to the moon.[31]

The general Soviet reading public first learned about Goddard and his proposed flight to the moon during the aerial "craze" in the

THE PIONEERS AND THE SPACEFLIGHT IMPERATIVE

winter of 1922–23. K. L. Baev, a young astronomer, Communist, and committed atheist, introduced this "'Columbus' of the cosmos" and his "interplanetary dirigible," though with a plug for Kibalchich and Tsiolkovskii as noble predecessors.[32] Or as another scholar wrote in the magazine of the Communist Youth League (*Komsomol*), the human conquest of the "ocean of air" gave hope and potential to the conquest of the ocean of "ether" beyond. Our coming to know the beauties and wonders of the atmosphere was but a prelude to mastering the mysteries of the stratosphere and interplanetary space. The airplane was inspiring the rocket.[33]

These public stirrings for the air and space were part of a remarkable moment that winter, notable for the founding in Moscow of the Bureau for the Study of Reactive Engines, which met in formal sessions over the course of several months. Details about the bureau are sketchy, based on the memoirs of Aleksandr Chizhevskii, a close friend and follower of Tsiolkovskii from a young age (they lived near each other in Kaluga). It convened under the patronage of L. K. Martens, chair of the Committee on Inventions of the Supreme Council of the National Economy. Representatives from the Revolutionary War Council and the Air Force Academy also attended, keen to discover the war-making potential of rockets. Several scholars surveyed the current achievements in rocket power, from Konstantin Tsiolkovskii to Robert Esnault-Pelterie to Robert Goddard, charging the USSR with the task of taking lead. Thus, the bureau served as a state inquiry into the possibilities of the liquid fuel rocket. Martens and the military held court for the scientific experts to testify. But nothing ever came of the proposals. Without Tsiolkovskii's or Tsander's participation, Chizhevskii alone was left to manage what he called a "fiasco" of failed efforts.[34]

Oberth and the German Pioneers

Yet Russians soon received a second and even more important confirmation of the possibilities of rocket flight: Hermann Oberth's classic *The Rocket in Planetary Space* (1923). Here was the first truly comprehensive treatment of what Oberth called "rocket theory." He provided detailed coverage of his "Model B" space rocket, of its liquid propulsion and fuel supply (either an alcohol and oxygen or hydrogen and oxygen mix), of its engine designs and multiple stages. He discussed mass ratios, exhaust velocities, and rocket trajectories in precise mathematical terms, highlighting the essential "cosmic velocity" of some eleven kilometers a second, this necessary to carry the rocket, perhaps humanity's most perfect "machine," beyond orbit. The body of the work was filled with just such calculations, no greater a mark of authority to European and Russian audiences. The scientific principles were sure, the technological possibilities within reach, for the "free flight of the rocket into ethereal space."[35]

Oberth also briefly discussed spacecraft and future space stations (with docking and living modules) and even the possibility of travel to the planets. Space was destined to become our future habitat. In this, as in his attention to liquid fuels, Oberth far surpassed Goddard's more modest published proposals. He surveyed the physical and physiological effects of acceleration, abnormal pressures, weightlessness, and deceleration, sometimes from experiments on his own body and mind. The sensation of weightlessness (apparently induced with topical anesthetics, underwater tests, and perhaps even a few narcotics) gave Oberth the power to "function with extreme intensity," with a heightened reasoning ability. "Time seemed to stand still," he wrote. Two minutes passed as if they were four hours. Clearly, weightlessness in space offered a whole new dimension of physical and mental experience to the human space traveler.[36]

In Germany, Oberth's book opened a spirited debate on the possibilities of the liquid fuel rocket and spaceflight. Mainstream academics had their doubts, cautioning that rockets would never be able to fly in the vacuum of space without any external medium, such as the air against which to propel. Perhaps following the lead of these German critics, even B. M. Lobach-Zhuchenko, a respected aviation engineer in Russia, falsely described the "reaction" of rocket propulsion as moving against "first the earth, then the air, which creates the movement of the rocket."[37] Others among Oberth's reviewers offered measures of enthusiasm and support.[38]

The effect of these debates was to grant a modest legitimacy for the new science. Oberth's mathematical proofs were tested and retested

THE PIONEERS AND THE SPACEFLIGHT IMPERATIVE

in open forums. His rivals set out to falsify his methods and conclusions, trying to prove them unfounded. In an effort to deny their validity, they instead came to employ his very terms, formalizing and verifying them in the course of debate. Even Hans Lorenz, a professor of mechanical engineering at the Danzig Technical College, following a series of published disputes before the Association of German Engineers and the Scientific Society for Aerial Flight, came around to accepting Oberth's calculus. It was indisputable.[39] In a dramatic addendum to his own book, Oberth also recognized Goddard's 1920 Smithsonian paper, which he had read "only after setting the type for this work," comparing their individual contributions in some detail. Befitting his rather humble character, with the same respect he later showed to Tsiolkovskii, Oberth bowed to Goddard's wealth of practical experience and institutional resources. But he also took care to note that he had "proceeded independently of Goddard" with his own original work reaching back to 1907.

Oberth's recognition of Goddard revealed the growing international dimensions of the idea of rocket flight into outer space. The decade from 1912 to 1923 had been one of roughly parallel discovery and development. From Italy, for example, Luigi Gusalli offered his own mass ratio and exhaust velocity calculations in 1923, based on the findings of Esnault-Pelterie and Goddard, whose "Method" was becoming world renowned. Gusalli had first read about Goddard from French and Italian popular science articles, boosting his own optimism about the ability of modern society, through its machines, to conquer the "navigation of space" with what he called a "vehicle train," or multistage rocket. Goddard had proven its feasibility. All that remained was really an issue of quantity, not quality, basically outfitting the rocket train with the proper amount of fuel. Perhaps the moon was really within human reach, Gusalli pondered. The 360,000 kilometers (224,000 miles) was but the distance "a rural mailman travels . . . on his legs over the course of twenty years." And the task of building the large "train" rocket was comparable to building five hundred planes or maybe one dreadnought.[40]

For official science in the West, Oberth's book was mostly a curiosity. The authoritative journal *Nature* recognized his achievement, his theoretical design and mathematical calculations, his improvement over Verne's cannon shell with a precisely described and powered self-propelled rocket. But the reviewer also noted that Oberth was at the fringes of science, there with those "certain types of individuals" who want to fly to the moon. He was at the fringes of time too, so far ahead of present possibilities that the dream of spaceflight was better suited to imaginary futures, to science fiction.[41]

In Soviet Russia, Oberth's book caused more of a sensation, press reports recognizing the amazing potential of rocket power. Rynin launched the public interest with a lecture, reprinted in *Izvestiia*, on the possibilities of interplanetary flight via rocket (powered by atomic or solar energy). Technology was forcing humanity higher and farther, upward and beyond. France and England, the United States and Japan, were already locked in a race: for squadron planes, for flights beyond the current time record (36 hours and 5 minutes), and for flights beyond the current distance record (4,650 kilometers or 2,889 miles). Rockets were the next logical turn. "The world has already become too crowded for humanity," he wrote. The coming frontier was space.[42]

Tsiolkovskii found the new publicity both exhilarating and alarming. Goddard's and Oberth's work had proven the truth of his ideas. But his original contributions were also being lost in all the new media interest. He simply could not compete with the print reports about rockets in the West. One of his supporters had to remind the readers of *Izvestiia* that Russia, thanks to Tsiolkovskii, was the leader in rocketry and spaceflight theories.[43] His stalwart publicists, Perel'man and Rynin, defended his priority. Riumin confirmed that Tsiolkovskii was somehow lost between the West's ignorance of the Russian language and Russia's own practical fixation on "utility" and short-term results. Still, he added, "you have written your name into world history and the annals of human thought, which shall repeat it with pride for generations to come."[44]

In turn Tsiolkovskii was not kind to Goddard, warning in a series of private letters that "his rocket will not rise even to 500 versts" (roughly the same in kilometers), and as for the moon, "that is a task difficult even for theory."[45] With the encouragement of Chizhevskii,

Tsiolkovskii reprinted his earlier 1903, 1911–12, and 1914 works on rocketry in combined, revised form, now with an accent not on the "interplanetary" or "ethereal" but on the "cosmic." The book, *The Rocket in Cosmic Space* (1924), was meant for one purpose really: to confirm his priority in the field as against recent American and German claims. The title, soon cited in a number of leading German works on rocketry and space travel, marked the true birth of the cosmic in spaceflight theory. Tsiolkovskii was its premier founder, an honor Hermann Oberth eventually recognized with his coining of the term *cosmonautics*. Another patron contributed the funds to have Tsiolkovskii's first portrait done, a photograph from 1924 to supplement the book, its subject attired at his most elegant and sure, with suit and cape and walking stick, the consummate academic.[46]

Oberth, true to his genuine modesty and good nature, eventually gave Tsiolkovskii his due. "You started the fire" (*Vy zazhgli svet*), he later wrote in honor of the master's seventy-second birthday, in 1929. Granted, for German audiences Oberth tended to boast more about himself, referring to "my invention of the rocket."[47] Goddard was less accommodating, unable to read Russian and ignoring Tsiolkovskii altogether. He and Oberth did share respectful letters. Goddard made no public declarations about his priority status. But he did let his distaste for Oberth be known in subdued ways through the popular science writer Mary Proctor. He eagerly read a draft of chapter 7 of her *Romance of the Moon* (1928), a work dedicated to recent advances in spaceflight studies. But he let stand the erroneous and misleading statement that Oberth had developed his rocket projects only "after correspondence with Professor Goddard."[48] America's premier rocket scientist was not about to let his pathbreaking work be undone.

Yet other developments from abroad fueled Soviet speculation about rocket power as the coming scientific and technological prize. In the summer of 1924 the brilliant Max Valier, inspired by Oberth's differential calculus and rocket designs, wrote his classic book *The Advance into Space: A Technical Possibility*.[49] Already an accomplished astronomy and popular science writer for leading newspapers and magazines, Valier adapted Oberth's rather dry explanations and calculations for a mass audience. More than any other of the pioneers, he crafted a whole new terminology to express Oberth's rocket theories. As we once imagined our science fiction aliens speaking to us in strange tongues from outer space, now Valier spoke to us in a strange new idiom from right here on Earth—with terms such as *rocket flight* and *spaceship* to describe the "rocket machine" and *spaceflight* and *cosmic pilot* to describe its inevitable achievements in space.[50] With equal parts reason and passion, Valier argued that past dreams of spaceflight were about to become new realities. This was all thanks to the recent work of Goddard and Oberth, founders of a whole new "science" of rocketry. They had calculated the necessary speed to reach beyond orbit. They had charted the "pathways," the trajectories and "velocity curves," to the planets. These were not straight lines but Valier's beloved Keplerian ellipses, if now human-made. We were about to break away from the "pull" of gravity, new Prometheans setting off by "cosmic parabolic velocity" into space, upon the "self-propelled" rocket, what Valier and others pictured as a rival to the comets, or as a human being shadowed by the rocket form.[51]

Valier's early space travel studies were followed by a number of remarkable German-language works on rocketry. Each confirmed the viability of rocketry and spaceflight, building on Oberth's and Valier's new terms with calculations and conditions all of their own. Walter Hohmann's *The Attainability of the Heavenly Bodies* (1925), based on the formulas first worked out by Tsiolkovskii and Oberth, was a tour de force of differential and integral calculus. He offered a study of the possible trajectories to orbit, to Mars, to Venus, and ultimately to the outer planets of the solar system—a whole series of well-proportioned launches, trips, burns, descents, landings, and returns. These paths of "free flight in space," he proved, were already marked by the authority of mathematics and physics, by the very movements of the planets and comets. Hohmann thereby transformed the dreamy "ascent parabola" of rocket flight into a series of modest but elegant "transit ellipses" to the planets, especially the "optimal tangential ellipse," the path tangent to the orbits of the departing and arriving planets, using their very gravitational fields and atmospheres for acceleration or braking. His front cover was beautifully decorated with a geometric, starlike human figure, astride the earth, reaching by three tangential points for the planets and even for the stars. As once European explorers had chased the observation of the transit of Venus across the sun, as Capt. James Cook did in 1769 during his Pacific voyage, now Hohmann transformed the explorer into a self-propelled cosmic traveler, actually taking a transit (by proper rocket trajectory and gravity assist) to the planet Venus itself, a future space colony for Earth.[52] These were bold proposals for their day, captivating both the popular media and professional circles. Just as Charles Lindbergh was crossing the Atlantic in his nonstop flight, the German Aero Clubs and Scientific Society for Aviation entertained Max Valier's lecture on the coming day when a German might very well cross the threshold of outer space.[53]

In 1926 the chemical engineer and science reporter Franz von Hoefft, with mechanical engineer Guido von Pirquet, joined forces to establish the Austrian Scientific Society for High Altitude Research, one of the first organized movements for the study of "rocket theory" and space travel in Western Europe. Hoefft came to entertain a meticulous orbital rendezvous plan: to build liquid fuel sounding rockets; then stratospheric rockets; then orbital rockets, space stations, and eventually "manned planetary rockets" for the exploration of outer space. These were his ascending "cosmic flight ways." One of them, he planned, would fulfill Goddard's scheme to send a small explosive charge to the surface of the moon, if now to reveal not American but Austrian and German prowess.[54] Pirquet charted his own ideal liquid fuel rocket trajectories to the planets near (Venus and Mars) and far (Jupiter and Saturn), with attending mass ratios and exhaust velocities, seeing the necessity for a variety of space stations as staging points for orbital engineering and "cosmonautical" flights. His interplanetary charts, based on the orbital mechanics of the solar system and the flight mechanics of human-made rockets, were literally "road maps to the planets," the rocket making its own free way through the orbits of the solar system.[55]

Following several of Oberth's approaches and suggestions, Hermann Noordung offered a comprehensive survey of rocketry and spaceflight in *The Problem of Space Travel* (1929). Tinged with the romantic, an appeal that humanity was now "free to be able to rise into the heavens," Noordung compared the terrestrial rocket to the meteor come from outer space, if now headed on its own "self-activated" course, an arrow pointed for "infinity." In mathematical terms he transformed the "cosmic velocities" of celestial mechanics into the "cosmic flight velocities" someday attainable by humanity. Noordung positioned the human being as a new free factor "in empty space."[56] Most remarkable was his space station, the "living wheel" moving in a geostationary orbit of Earth, an experimental laboratory for terrestrial and astronomical observations, for both military and civilian use. Noordung designed his station in intricate detail, powered by solar energy and a system of heat-producing mirrors. Shaped as a torus, with airlocks at the center for space walks, with tunnel spokes leading to living quarters and laboratories, its revolutions created the necessary centrifugal force and artificial gravity to become a planet all its own. He vividly described the new human existence there, an environment of lights and darks, sounds and silences, new gravities to escape the old. Noordung actually pictured people at work and rest in the very tubing of the station, a first in the graphic design. In time the "conquest of space" meant ultimately to save humanity's myriad achievements for eternity, against all the random and chance events that might imperil a fragile Earth. It meant releasing creative humanity in the rocket spaceship upon the new spaces and soils of the cosmos.[57]

The Society for the Study of Interplanetary Travel

The Soviet regime and Russian society reached something of a turning point within all of these competing contexts. The regime found its bearing by 1923–24. People were eager to be entertained again. The fascination with rocketry and interplanetary communications took on a center stage in political and cultural life. Enthusiasts gathered in the classrooms of the Air Force Academy at the "Petrine Palace" of the Red Army in north-central Moscow; at the Central Moscow Observatory on Bol'shaia Lubianka Street #13, just around the corner from the headquarters of the Soviet secret police; and in the downtown auditoriums of the State Polytechnic Museum and Moscow State University. The country's leading newspapers and journals propagated the new technology and frontier as worthy goals: *The Truth* (*Pravda*) for party and state elites; *Young Guard* (*Molodaia gvardiia*) for the Communist Youth League. Over the next decade Perel'man's *Interplanetary Voyages* was republished almost every other year, a running serial of the dizzying changes in the spaceflight theories of the day.

In the wake of news reports about Goddard's rockets and just as news of Oberth was breaking, Tsiolkovskii delivered several lectures at the Air Force Academy in August 1923, distinguished there as an "honorary professor," beloved by the young people in the classrooms, according to several accounts. They soon called themselves his "devotees" in the struggle to master the "secrets" of the oceans of air and space. His hosts were the students of the Aerial Navigation Section of the Military-Scientific Society, together with several rocket enthusiasts on the teaching staff: M. N. Kanishchev, who taught Aviation Technology using Tsiolkovskii's texts, along with V. P. Vetchinkin and B. M. Stechkin, both visiting lecturers and research engineers at the nearby Central Aero-Hydrodynamics Institute.[58]

In response the students even created an "interplanetary travel" and "reaction propulsion" study group at the academy in April 1924. Among them were M. G. Leiteizen, V. P. Kaperskii, and M. A. Rezunov, three young and idealistic first-year cadets. A photograph in the popular technology magazine *Science and Life* later captured them in their smart air force uniforms, poring over rocket designs and planning their high flights. Leiteizen was from a family of Bolshevik revolutionaries, friends of Lenin. Kaperskii and Rezunov were pilots. The three were eager for innovation, dedicated to rocketry as a legitimate new science and a viable new technology. They certainly must have been buoyed by the media's reports about the coming military technologies of the next war—their goal, to add reactive propulsion to the existing three-part academy curriculum (Aircraft Design, Airplane Engines, and Transport Networks) and to create a Reactive Engines Section in its Military-Scientific Society or perhaps even a rocket "scientific-research study group" attached to Moscow's higher education institutes.[59]

Yet in the end academy authorities were ill disposed to these ideas. They forbade jet and rocket issues in the curriculum as beyond the realm of "aviation technology." Rocket power was too far ahead of contemporary problems and challenges. Soviet Russia had not even yet built the rudiments of an air force.[60] Worse still, the rocket obsession distracted Leiteizen from his formal studies, which suffered by the summer of 1924, landing him on academic probation. Faculty mentors refused Kaperskii's and Rezunov's requests to complete their diploma projects on rocket engines. Rocket theory, in sum, was not yet a science.[61]

A profound conservatism among top Soviet officers and teachers also created something of a generation gap with their more enterprising students. Artillery experts tended to discount liquid fuel rockets as a chimera, disproving the possibilities of the "rocket shell" by lampooning Jules Verne's famous cannon shot into space. Rockets would not replace artillery on the battlefield any more than cannons would take a piloted projectile to the moon. Both were improbable by the standards of mathematical logic and common sense. To achieve the proper mass ratio and exhaust velocity, the shell would need a veritable train of "passenger wagons" and "over a thousand baggage cars filled with propulsive material." Such a multistage rocket was impossible and otherwise totally inhospitable to human flight. "It would appear difficult to fly away from earth," concluded one critic, "even in our fantasies."[62] The Soviet authorities were therefore unwilling to invest further time and resources. Support would have to come from some other quarter, in some other way.

Undaunted, the cadets retooled their efforts and went public, helping to establish the broader Society for the Study of Interplanetary Travel (hereafter referred to as the Society), the world's first national association for the propagation of rocketry and spaceflight studies.[63] Its patrons were a small but influential group of politicians and scientists interested in rocketry as the premier Western technology of the day. Among them were two leading administrators of the Supreme Council of the National Economy: Liudvig K. Martens, who had been a member of the now-defunct Bureau for the Study of Reactive Engines, and M. Ia. Lapirov-Skoblo, member of its Scientific-

Technical Department, a science editor for *Pravda*, and a director of government electrification and civil communications projects. A. K. Beliaev, astronomer and director of the central Moscow Observatory, provided an office and bookstore to the group.

The Society was led by a diverse and eccentric group of activists: G. M. Kramarov, a Communist publicist, veteran Bolshevik, and civil servant; V. Chernov, a master violinist with the Bol'shoi Theater; and the aviation and rocketry engineer F. A. Tsander. Joining them were several hundred students and civil servants, engineers and workers, who had become interested in rocketry and space travel, fed by the utopian leanings of popular astronomy and Bolshevik ideology as well as by the sensational news reports of the day. According to Chizhevskii, these were largely "nice people," well read and science minded, who were taken with Tsiolkovskii's designs for dirigibles and rockets, which were all the rage in Moscow, as he put it. Or in the words of one journalist who shared their passion, science and technology were the two "wings" that enabled the human being to fly, even possibly into outer space, which was now both theoretically and technologically feasible. "It seems as though there are no limits to the achievements of human reason," he wrote.[64] The logo the founders chose for their Society, similar to one for their planned journal, the *Rocket* (*Raketa*), pictured the USSR below, the rocket in flight above, a new human-made comet for outer space.

The work of the Society was buoyed by a mix of native and foreign sources. Its members were inspired by Russia's own cosmic thinkers and rocket pioneers. Their small library included Tsiolkovskii's founding works, some of Tsander's writings, Perel'man's first edition, and clippings of the major articles from Russia's first space craze between 1911 and 1915.[65] Their pride in Russia's original contributions also mixed with an anxiety not to fall behind the most recent promises of the new technology from the United States and Germany. Oberth's recently published book was the topic of discussions and lectures. But Goddard was the centerpiece of their attention. His was the technology to achieve. He was the person in the news, captivating audiences with the rumor, so often presented in the popular press as fact, that he planned to launch his rocket to the moon

Fig. 11. Seal of the Soviet Society for the Study of Interplanetary Travel—
Obshchestvo izucheniia mezhplanetnykh soobshchenii (OIMS)—from
1924, with its initials on the rocket, the USSR below, and cascading
stars above. Credit: Archive of the Russian Academy of Sciences (Moscow). This seal became an exemplar for others to come, such as that of
the Science Fiction League (1934), reprinted in John Cheng, *Astounding
Wonder* (Philadelphia: University of Pennsylvania Press, 2012), 231.

on the Fourth of July 1924.[66] Goddard was, among all the pioneers,
the only one ready or planning to turn theory into practice, to fulfill
what Chernov called America's "strict scientific logic" of invention
and progress. The Society prepared translations of his recent works,
including a popular piece, "The High Altitude Rocket" (*Monthly
Weather Review*, February 1924). Leiteizen wrote to him requesting collaboration. Goddard's respectful but evasive reply still sits

in the Society's archive, crisp white letterhead and envelope, hardly touched by time. "I shall be glad to cooperate in this work, in so far as it is possible." But he warned that he also had no concrete materials or findings yet about his "trial flight."[67]

In the interwar years Goddard was one of the significant public faces of Soviet "Americanism," the movement for the adoption of "Fordist" productivity, "Taylorist" efficiencies, and American industrial strength. True, Soviet communism was not rocket science. It was not even calculus. Lenin reduced it to a simple political mathematics: the sum of electricity "plus" (*plius*) Soviet power. Stalin in turn reduced Leninism to two alphabetical "characteristic traits": the combination of "a. Russian revolutionary momentum, and b. American efficiency." Yet by these he meant Lenin's impatience with "routine" and "conservatism"; his love of that "life force that awakens thought, surges ahead, breaks with the past, and offers new vistas of the future"; his appreciation for America's "untamable force" that admits no obstacles, forges ahead with "business-like persistence."[68] Stalin might as well have been describing Henry Ford and his Model T or Robert Goddard and his liquid fuel rocket.

Russia was moving forward in time by moving westward in orientation. America's achievements were a standard of measurement, a target of opportunity, and a political imperative. Or as Stalin quoted Lenin as having said in 1917: "Either we begin to catch and surpass the leading capitalist countries, or we perish." Stalin added a proviso of his own in 1931: "Yet we are still behind them by fifty to a hundred years. We must forge this distance within ten years." One journalist put it this way: air power in general and rocket power in particular were the golden standards of achievement, guarantees against the greatest enemies of all, against "cultural backwardness and political death."[69]

Rocketry became a fulcrum, a lever in Russia's struggle to overcome backwardness, to turn its very backwardness to its advantage and leap ahead of the West. These authoritative pronouncements for a Soviet Americanism married to a Stalinist pace worked their way into the new literary standards as well. The leading editor A. Voronskii defined the perfect Soviet literary hero as a "sort of Russian American who performs prodigies of economic and social reconstruction, solves the riddles of the cosmos with science," along with carrying on the militant struggle with self-sacrifice and stoicism.[70] For two of the most visible and successful of the spaceflight enthusiasts, Rynin and Lapirov-Skoblo, their love of rocketry and interplanetary communications was an outgrowth of their adulation for American technological prowess. In both cases this was a romance born out of personal experience. Rynin's travels from New York to San Francisco to New Orleans and points between revealed a "many-storied America" of "the most fantastic structures," a country made of metal and concrete, of "energy and enterprise," filled with cities that grew not "by days" but "by hours." Lapirov-Skoblo saw New York as the "gateway to a new country of incalculable wealth and fabulous exploitation." He had in mind the vast and dynamic grids of American life: its skyscrapers, advertisements, and electricity; its mosaic of peoples and networks of production. "Nowhere in the world is there such a scale of energy, relations, and movement."[71]

The Society translated this sense of urgency into its own public events of 1924. On 30 May, at its inaugural lecture in the great auditorium of the State Polytechnic Museum, Lapirov-Skoblo entertained the scientific possibilities of "Interplanetary Flights," a lecture he later published in two vanguard Communist Party forums. Gravity, he said, remained the only law of nature as yet unconquered. Newton's other law (the third), along with the coming advances of rocket propulsion, offered promise. Oberth was the amazing "scholar armed with mathematical analysis and the laws of celestial mechanics." But Goddard was building a moon rocket with the "colossal strength" of 11.2 kilometers a second, what Lapirov-Skoblo pictured in the form of an elegant parabolic trajectory reaching beyond the planet, the first such pictured line that I have been able to discover in the literature. Goddard was about to "open a bridge into space" that year on the Fourth of July and thereby inaugurate a "new epoch" for humanity.[72] The packed crowd sat in "absolute silence" from start to end, one audience member testified. What they probably did not know was that Lapirov-Skoblo had lifted significant portions of his talk straight out of the latest issue of *Popular Science Monthly*.[73] Such was

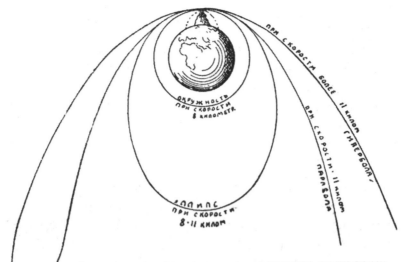

Пути ракет, выпущенных с различными скоростями.

Fig. 12. The Bolshevik parabola into outer space: Newton's "cannon" redrawn for Goddard's rockets and the Bolshevik Revolution, featuring the first parabola for space travel that I have been able to find in the news media. The picture is titled "Rocket Trajectories Launched by Different Speeds" and shows (*from right to left*): a hyperbola at a speed of 11 kilometers a second or more; a parabola at a speed of 11 kilometers a second (to leave the earth's orbit); an ellipse at a speed of 8 to 11 kilometers a second; and a circle at a speed of 8 kilometers a second (to orbit the earth). From M. Ia. Lapirov-Skoblo, "O puteshestviiakh v mezhplanetnye prostranstva," *Molodaia gvardiia* 5 (1924): 75.

his confidence in the veracity of the American press and in the certainty of American achievement.

The Society made an even bigger sensation, with more flair and spectacle, when it helped to organize F. A. Tsander's lectures and debates in early October, entitled "Flight to Other Worlds," held at the great auditorium of the Physics Institute at Moscow State University. It was cosponsored by two state organs—the Political Administration of the Military District and the Moscow Party School—again to standing-room only and overflow crowds (including members of the government). Tsander's lectures explained the revolutionary "turn [*perelom*] in Western Europe and America" toward the rocket; the "truth" behind Goddard's moon rocket, "the most powerful machine in the world"; and the possibilities of "liberating humanity from its Earth-bound captivity." His own design combined both airplane and rocket. It was to lift off horizontally, like any normal airplane, but once at the highest altitude, it would begin to expel a mixture of liquid fuels and liquid metals (drawn from the airplane's own parts), based on the rocket principle, to launch into outer space. He respectfully highlighted the "inefficiencies" and high costs of Tsiolkovskii's and Oberth's projects but framed and paralleled his own rocket plane and Goddard's rocket as the most feasible and promising of all.[74]

Tsander was gracious in his evaluations. Goddard's experimental work in 1920 and 1924, and the news stories associated with them, had clearly set a pace and rhetoric for much of the reporting to come: the noble experimenter, veils of secrecy, spectacular test launches, promises of the moon. Journalists soon added the extra drama of German and Russian competition in a race to match his technologies, in stories that mixed hard science, practical application, and appealing fantasy. In ensuing years Goddard remained a worthy topic of media interest. Referring to the "American inventor," magazines and journals and newspapers promoted his "steel shell" and "interplanetary ship" not as fantasies but as facts. He was perfecting the means for the "conquest of interplanetary space."[75] Goddard's "somersault" referred to the "half-loop" his rocket would make on reaching the moon's gravitational pull, when the exhaust would shift 180 degrees to ease its descent. This was as complex as 1920s-era lunar rendezvous ever got.[76]

In all of these contexts the Society had serious ambitions, with plans to build rockets and conduct research into human spaceflight. As chief of its scientific-research section and along lines that Tsiolkovskii had already proposed, Tsander raised a call for a stunning range of experimentation: in practical rocketry, its components and fuels; in its applications for military defense; in its implications for long-distance television (via satellite relays); and in the adaptation of plant and human biology for outer space. But this section hardly functioned at all. Propaganda and popular science were the focus of the Society's work, which sponsored dozens of lectures in 1924 and

1925 at clubs, schools, and factories throughout Moscow and beyond.[77] In the end the Society was short-lived, lasting only about a year. The reading public soon lost interest in its claims. The group's plans for a popular film and mass-circulation journal never materialized. Literary parodies in several newspapers undermined the group's standing and confidence. The Central Committee of the Communist Party refused to support the Society with funding. Most compelling was the decision of the Moscow City Council to disband the Society, judging its establishment as "premature" given an almost complete absence of scientific experts and proper facilities.[78]

One of the reasons for its demise may also have been Tsiolkovskii himself. He never publicly lobbied for the Society. He offered little more than kind words of support. He might even have helped to seal the fate of the rocketry movement with his misplaced project for an all-metal dirigible. It received wide publicity in the spring of 1925, with lectures and debates in May at the State Polytechnic Museum, site of the recent Society debates on interplanetary travel. The air force considered the merits of his project, purchasing a scale model from Tsiolkovskii and negotiating for more concrete designs and closer collaboration, even promising him a fully functional laboratory at the academy. But all Tsiolkovskii could give from Kaluga were scale models and "interesting ideas," in the words of one evaluation. He offered no "construction drafts" whatsoever, even expressing his own doubts about the whole enterprise, admitting that it was perhaps "beyond our present strengths." The air force rejected the project.[79]

The impracticality of Tsiolkovskii's metal dirigible must have soured the military and political establishments to the rather fantastic possibilities of rocketry and spaceflight. Tsiolkovskii's all-metal dirigible and interplanetary rocket were in a sense the same object. They were different designs and structures, made for different purposes, with dramatically different propulsion systems and engines. But they were essentially the same "envelope," the same symbolic thing: one meant to conquer the ocean of the air, the other meant to penetrate the ocean of space. The images of Tsiolkovskii's rocket, drawn by his own hand or drawn for him in publications, were basically "rocket dirigibles," or as they were also called, "interplanetary

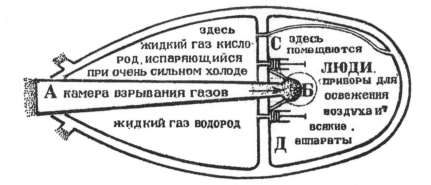

Fig. 13. Interior of the Tsiolkovskii dirigible rocket, with compartments
for liquid fuels and propellants as well as living quarters for space
travelers. From Valerii Iazvitskii, *Puteshestvie na
lunu i mars* (Moscow: Gosizdat, 1928), 33.

dirigibles," the all-metal dirigible equipped with the fuel tanks and
engines for spaceflight.[80] One cadre of aviation enthusiasts even proposed to build an all-metal interplanetary rocket dirigible in V. I.
Lenin's "sacred" memory:

> Upon the celestial planes, the starry heavens,
> We will create a new fable for the ages,
> We will forge it into solid, ringing steel
> And send it through interplanetary space.[81]

Such powerful liquid fuel rockets were fully compatible with Communist ideology, but they remained the stuff of dreams more than
actual machines.

6

Rocket Spaceships as Science Fictions

The classic rocket spaceship actually premiered in science fiction with Konstantin Tsiolkovskii's cosmic novel *Beyond the Earth* (1918), the first among his stories to send humanity to space in a liquid fuel, multistage rocket. Fulfilling a lifelong urge for public recognition, *Beyond the Earth* was also a parable about Tsiolkovskii, the Russian scientist "Ivanov" in the novel, sharing his nation's revolutionary brilliance with the geniuses of Europe and America: Galileo, Newton, Franklin, Helmholtz, and Laplace. Tsiolkovskii had in mind, perhaps smarting from the rivalry with Esnault-Pelterie, to lecture the French, who at first found his machine inconceivable. "It's a flying gun, with thin walls, and it emits gases instead of cannonballs," he explained, citing Jules Verne. "It's quite simple. I'm talking of a kind of rocket." For the assembled geniuses this was a moment of surprise, for Russians one of intense pride. "Ivanov was the great dreamer; yet he was also a man of vast erudition. Pre-eminently the thinker among them, he was the one who more often raised such strange questions."[1]

According to one of his biographers, Tsiolkovskii did not initially take the Russian Revolution well. The Bolsheviks came as something of a shock. "They seemed to him as if people from another planet, like Martians come to seize power on Earth," said one friend. His brief moment of arrest and imprisonment by the secret police in 1919, on false charges, probably contributed to this disfavor.[2] Appropriately enough, *Beyond the Earth* was his last major piece of science fiction. From then on he wrote for fact. Events unfolding here on the planet were compelling enough, it seems. The novel was definitive, no more perfect a statement of Tsiolkovskii's core beliefs, if something of a throwback to more innocent times. The story expressed his abiding interests in rocket propulsion, space habitability, and cosmic evolution. These were issues that captivated him to the end of his life.

Tsiolkovskii's story included detailed calculations of rocket velocities and trajectories; spacecraft designs; lessons on physics and astronomy; exciting descriptions of life in zero gravity, with space suits, ease of free labor, and mass production; recycled atmospheres and greenhouses for solar energy; discussions of the infinite universe and the plurality of worlds. He took the issue of free labor to new lengths, likely inspired by the Russian Revolution. His space colonies were now sites of true economic opportunity and justice. Tsiolkovskii's space explorers left their petty histories and class complexes behind. Their losses were relatively few: severe "depression," "apathy," and "boredom" brought on by the long-distance travels. But their rewards were many: abundant supplies of food and fresh fruits; troves of precious diamonds, emeralds, and gems; freedom from garments and disease and squalor.

These were all staples in the genre of the Western "cosmic romance." Yet Tsiolkovskii gave them his own unique plot spin. In all of his stories outer space was not a thoroughfare, a means to reach some exotic alien race or play out some entertaining space opera. Rather, space was a destination. The aliens were us. We became the space creatures writers once dreamed of in science fiction. Tsiolkovskii entertained a plotline of dissolution, as we first shed our possessions, then our clothes, then in time our own bodies, becoming androgynous beings, all spirit and no matter, what he variously called "genii," crystalline points of light and mind and love in ethereal space; "angels in human form"; or the "free children of the ether." In bold and colorful strokes Tsiolkovskii predicted a "Great Migration," the human colonization of space by new satellite moons and Saturn-like "living" rings of space stations, eventually by a whole new "independent planet, a satellite of the sun and a brother of the earth." Human beings were to tap in to solar energy, mine asteroids, create whole new "greenhouse" ecosystems in space, share labor and resources.

This was all part of our inevitable struggle for a "release from the chains of gravity," an expression of our "love for an eternal striving outwards to the sun" and the "boundless expanses of the cosmos."[3]

Literary Approaches to the Rocket

Tsiolkovskii's literary spotlights, both upon his rocket and himself, did not last for long. Evgenii Zamiatin's classic dystopian novel *We* (1921) soon overshadowed them as a powerful, many-dimensional work. Critics have expertly weighed it as a parody of the utopian Russian cosmists. Zamiatin's imagined totalitarian regime, the "United State," exhibited many of the flourishes of Gastev's *Proletkul't* writers and the proletarian poets, with their labor marches, formulaic lingo, and celebration of metal. He parodied the Taylorists too, with their obsession for social order: in the ranks of citizen numbers, the "Hour Tables" of uniform daily routines, the ticking metronome, and the fifty chews for every piece of food.[4] Zamiatin's ire was perhaps most focused upon Fedorov's cosmic visions. *We* prefigured a broken Earth, part barbaric and part modern, reaching for the vacuum, the purity and stellar perfection of outer space, all in Fedorov's terms. The defiant rebels, people beyond the "Great Wall," were remnants from a backward human evolutionary stage. They were Fedorov's horizontal men, beasts of big hair and big teeth that lived amid the roots and woods of nature unbowed. The citizens of the United State, perfect vertical men, already lived a space-like existence in their sleek, skyscraper, streamlined, hairless, transparent existence. In Zamiatin's future food and sex were reduced, by Fedorov's law, to mechanical motions, pure techniques void of freedom and pleasure.

Yet the parallels to Tsiolkovskii's work are even more compelling. After all, the United State was consumed with the building of a rocket ship, the *Integral*, which from the very first page of the novel was to "rise into the limitless space of the universe" by a fuming explosive force. Its goal: to discover alien life beyond Earth and to colonize the planets. The ship was a creation straight out of Tsiolkovskii, with an "invisible propeller and lumps of frozen air as fuel." It was a rocket, an "exquisite, oblong ellipsoid," a glass "body" framed by "transverse ribs" and "longitudinal stringers," powered by a "gigantic motor."[5]

The narrator of the story, D-503, was a mathematician-engineer, like Tsiolkovskii, who precisely calculated the speeds and trajectories of his rocket ship. But the *Integral* itself was also something of a main character, its very name a synonym for *We* or for *the United State* or for *D-503*. The *Integral* was the symbolic universal set against the story's many faceless differentials. It expressed the totality of all relations, the higher equation that mapped out the trajectory to outer space from the dynamics of all lesser motions. It expressed, too, the very shape of the domed city of the United State, defining the area under the curve of an arc, the equation that turned a simple line, by orders of magnitude, into an interplanetary parabola.[6]

The *Integral* and D-503 were the same person and thing. For *We* was a story built around the essential paradox of "humanized machines and mechanized humans," as Zamiatin named it. D-503 transformed the *Integral* into a kind of person, visualized himself as a kind of rocket. The *Integral* was brought to life, "spiritualized" and humanized, by the "flaming" fuel and the trajectories by which it plunged into space. Its designer, D-503, at first a loyal citizen of the United State and one within the ranks of machinelike citizen numbers, became something of a rocket himself, spiritualized by a flaming love for I-330, by a newfound creative imagination and a depth of feeling, moving along his own trajectories of individual will and action. The rocket was "a symbol of the thrust of the unconscious against the conscious, fire against steel and glass." It was a perfect model for the Newtonian universe of action and reaction, translated into Zamiatin's thermodynamics of energy and entropy, a "balance of thrust and containment, irrationality and rationality."[7]

The geometry of *We* both imprisoned and liberated. Its cities were made of squares and quadrangles, of cubes and straight lines. The most terrible shape of all was the oblong ellipse, the very form that defined the curved capital city of the United State, its bell-shaped rocket, and the torture bell that subdued its unruly citizens. They were all oblong glass structures promising order through terror. Yet the novel was conflicted. Freedom also meant lines of motion and depths of feeling, as when the rocket launched into space upon a "blue spiral line," as if on a quest into the depths of the soul.[8] Tucked away deep within Zamiatin's dark dystopia was the inviting utopia of space travel, the entropy of the calcified United State become the energy of the space rocket in motion. He took his characters to the void of outer space, where in "dead silence" the world was turned "upside down," the characters floating "bodiless" in zero gravity.[9] For a political rebel and self-proclaimed "heretic" such as Zamiatin, outer space remained his one concession to the lyricism of the cosmist poets. Like the Symbolists and futurists before him, he could not help but dream of the liberating possibilities of cosmic flight, of the power of the *Integral* itself, the sum of all the spaces beneath its graceful trajectory arc. The rocket was the perfect emblem for Zamiatin's own concept of revolution, as both lived experience and futuristic ideal. He once remembered the years of the Russian Revolution, for example, as if the country was ascending in some "hurtling missile," as if "we were all locked up together in a steel projectile and, cooped up in darkness, whistled through space, no one knew where."[10] He identified the permanent revolution with the rocket's trajectory, the open circle of the spiral, "the constant dialectic path which in a grandiose parabola sweeps the world into infinity."[11]

Zamiatin's *We*, appearing in an English translation in 1924, was not published in the USSR until 1989. Parodies of that sort did not pass censorship. The main literary administration, Glavlit, suppressed it, though clandestine manuscripts circulated for a few years. In a rare mention of the book one leading critic panned Zamiatin's story about the "great Integral," built to "conquer the whole universe and give it mathematically certain happiness."[12] Subtler parodies, with an accent on the fabulous and romantic, were more the rule, as, for example, Aleksei Tolstoi's *Aelita* (1923), one of the best-selling books of the 1920s and a coming classic of Soviet and Russian literature. Here was the story of a brainy inventor, Mstislav Sergeevich Los', who engineers a rocket ship journey to Mars; enticed by the siren songs of the Martian princess Aelita; accompanied by the gritty Red Army soldier Aleksei Ivanovich Gusev, a point of some comic and political relief. The work's status was all the more remarkable because Count Tolstoi, a White émigré who converted to the Soviet cause, first wrote and published it while in exile from Berlin, watching and assimilating the emerging strains of Soviet cosmism from the industrialized West, recently broken by the First World War.[13]

The story was a fable of sorts about Mars as the dying West, the decadent Weimar Germany where Tolstoi was then living, and about Earth as the rising and revolutionary East, the Soviet Russia where he yearned to be. The fictional Mars expedition, after all, finally returns to Earth by the end of the novel, no doubt a reflection of Tolstoi's own genuine love for Russia, even the Soviet kind. All of this, along with Gusev's earthy Russian-ness (in speech and behavior) and his own heartfelt longings for home, made the novel much more than personal. It was deeply patriotic and political as well. A number of episodes and images confirm this interpretation. America, for example, figured into the story in a passive way: at the sidelines, watching and waiting; or as simple setting, the landing site for the Soviet spaceship. The intrepid reporter Archibald Skiles could only observe events unfold, gaze upon the Russian rocket with admiration and incredulity, belittled by the "inexplicable expression of superiority" in Russians' eyes, faces both supremely self-confident and "madly determined." Russia's cities were dilapidated, its people exhausted, yet they were still determined to "fly into space." Only Russia had the power to realize such "an extraordinary and sensational project for interplanetary flight," to dare "approach the speed of light" and race through space and time "like a meteor." The craft touched down at the coastline of Lake Michigan, of all places, to the astonishment of America's holiday vacationers, at rest and play on a sunny Sunday afternoon. A favorite setting of science fiction and adventure stories, Lake Michigan meant Chicago, and Chicago meant the World's Fair of 1893, whose Columbian Exposition commemorated the discovery of America some four hundred years earlier. Soviet Russia now discovered it again, if from outer space.

Tolstoi's main character, Los', followed this thread of "Soviet" patriotism. He was only the second Russian scientist in fiction, after Tsiolkovskii's Ivanov, to launch into space in a classic rocket (on 18 August 1923, and in an interesting coincidence, ten years to the day before Stalin celebrated Russia's first Aviation Day), turning about in zero gravity, setting off to create or explore new worlds. As several commentators noted at the time, Los' was none other than the fictional equivalent of Tsiolkovskii himself. Informed readers would have seen the connection, what with all the media attention on Tsiolkovskii just before the First World War and soon after the Russian Revolution.[14] Los' was a character study of Tsiolkovskii, a uniquely Russian national type: the genius inventor who "went to school on copper pennies, on my own since I was twelve." He was the able engineer who routinely drafted "such an extraordinary and sensational project for interplanetary flight," who advertised the news of racing "through space for fifty million kilometers" without any fanfare at all. He was the dreamer who was "certain that in a few hundred years airships will be traversing starry spaces."[15] The name Los' may also have been a sound play (a syllabic reversal) upon Tsiolkovskii's own name; no doubt it was also a reference to the subtleties of its German meanings: to "hurry" or "fire off" (los) in a parabolic trajectory to space.

Thus *Aelita* offered salvation from the East, a clever reversal of Spengler's *The Decline of the West*, then the talk of Europe's capitals. Tolstoi did not denounce the book but co-opted and adapted it in nuanced ways, subtitling his initial story "The Decline of Mars" (*Zakat marsa*), this only a few issues after the host journal, *Red Virgin Soil* (*Krasnaia nov'*), had featured several full-length critiques of Spengler's work.[16] Spengler had, of course, forewarned of the decline of Western civilization but all the while exalting the power and purpose of "Faustian," mostly Germanic, civilization. One crucial element of this culture was its yearning and reach for the infinite, its "craving" for "endless space, its "pathos of distance." Spengler represented these "Faustian visions" by "the upthrust of Gothic architecture, the Viking's voyaging into unknown seas, the language of Columbus and Copernicus," the physics and calculus of Newton. As he wrote, "An insatiable hunger drives us ever further and further into the remote." Yet much of the book simultaneously degraded Russian national culture as stagnant, as flat as the steppe, enclosed by the onion-domed cupola that marked its monotonous stretches. Russia lacked the depth and breadth of infinite space. It was manifestly not Faustian.[17]

Tolstoi's *Aelita* turned the tables on Spengler, revealing Soviet Russia as the consummate Faustian culture, projecting it into outer space by the power of Russian national genius and its specific invention, the rocket. Russia, not Germany, took the leap for infinite space. Tolstoi's Los' looked and sounded a lot like Spengler's ultimate Faustian man, "the quiet engineer . . . who is the machine's master and destiny." And his rocket operated very much like Spengler's perfect "*machine*, as a small cosmos obeying the will of man alone." Together they fulfilled the Faustian imperative. "The intoxicated soul wills to fly above space and Time," Spengler wrote. "An ineffable longing tempts him to indefinable horizons. Man would free himself from the earth, rise into the infinite, leave the bonds of the body, and circle in the universe of space amongst the stars."[18] Tolstoi might very well have written this himself. Several of his lines sounded perfectly Spenglerian, as when he celebrated the interplanetary bridge between Earth and Mars, marked by the "sign of the parabola" that united them and that heralded the human conquest of space. Or when he spoke of the force of will and reason that empowered space travel, "like the arrow stretched by a bow and directed by a steady hand," which meant that "directed knowledge is limitless."[19]

The myth of Atlantis, built into the plot, developed this theme of Russian superiority. It was an allegory within an allegory, conflating the myth of Atlantis and the planet Mars: the lost civilization fallen on Earth only to rise again on our near planet. This was a myth, moreover, that had become more and more open to scientific study by the early years of the twentieth century (much like the planet Mars itself), the venerable object of oceanographers and geologists, who speculated that Atlantis really did once exist. In an act of defiance Tolstoi reduced one of the most powerful myths of the early twentieth century to naught. With a twist in his plot he dismissed the "image of past perfection" that was Atlantis (and Mars and Western Europe): the "dream world" of "supermen and super science."[20] Perfection and salvation lay, instead, in Soviet Russian communism.

The Mars and Goddard Crazes of 1924

In all of these ways *Aelita* was a complex melodrama of simple parts. Its interlocking plotlines were cinematic: short and compact yet dense with exotic Martian landscapes of blue vegetation and purple shad-

ROCKET SPACESHIPS AS SCIENCE FICTIONS

ows; man-eating cacti, lizards, and giant insects; strange hieroglyphics and mysterious ruins. At points Tolstoi seemed to be echoing H. G. Wells, what with the look and language of the Martians, outfitted with armor, flying machines, and fields of electrical energy. They even sang Wells's refrain, "*ulla, ulla*," as a sad lullaby and funeral dirge. *Aelita* probably reminded most casual readers of Edgar Rice Burroughs's *Princess of Mars* (1912), already available in Russian translation at this time.[21] Both stories shared a number of plot elements: the Lowellian setting of a failing planet; the exotic races and tribes; the mythic rise and fall of civilizations; the battles with ungainly spiders; the male hero in the role of savior of the beautiful princess. Both stories began and ended with their heroes longing for their space sirens.[22]

Tolstoi probably read Burroughs and may indeed have borrowed from him. But Burroughs himself, as several scholars have pointed out, likely borrowed his own characters and plotlines from several successful "Mars" works, namely Gustavus Pope's *Journey to Mars* and Edwin Lester Arnold's *Lieutenant Gullivar Jones*.[23] Tolstoi might also have borrowed several elements from Gustave Le Rouge's *The Prisoner of Mars* (1908), including the remnants of a once-advanced civilization, now fallen into magnificent underground ruins; interplanetary signals and spacecraft ("falling stars"); alien monsters (like giant webbed moles and flying vampires); and vegetation of crimson, gold, and purple. Like Los' and Gusev, Le Rouge's Robert Darvel also sought to possess Mars and the Martians, "to learn their language, to impose his ideas upon them, and perhaps to achieve dominion over them." He has a love interest too, the diminutive and enticing Eeeoys.[24]

Like its rivals, Tolstoi's novel incorporated realistic and believable views of the future, all drawn from the recent discoveries of modern science. He built his story, for example, around several casual references to the popular astronomy of the day. A nod to Marconi's Martian radio signals gave it all a ring of newspaper truth. He advanced Svante Arrhenius's "panspermia" thesis that organic life traveled through the universe in the folds of meteors or upon the pressure gradients of solar energy. "The dust of life," he wrote, "races through the universe."[25] He also designed his Martian civilization around the "scientific" Mars of Flammarion and Lowell. As its original cover illustrated, Los' and Gusev traveled to a Mars studded with the famous canals.

In all of these ways Tolstoi's novel was timely, a literary prelude to the famous "Mars craze" that built momentum as the two planets approached another "opposition" in 1924. Mars and Earth were coming into perfect view, a chance finally to test the possibility of alien life there. Newspaper accounts set a tempo of anticipation. Marconi's signals, Lowell's canals, and Goddard's rocket all remained popular topics. The world also witnessed a "flurry of mysterious radio impulses." Perhaps they were from the Martians themselves, wrote one American journalist. Surely they proved the "immensity of the eternal universe to which Earth is an insignificant part."[26] In Russia journalists and popular astronomers reported that radio stations were receiving rogue signals from the "Red Planet" or even that Mars had broken out of its orbit and was headed for a collision with Earth or that Russia itself was preparing the greatest signal of all: human passengers for space on a Tsiolkovskii rocket.[27]

Mars was a well-established market draw in science fiction. Sophus Michaelis's film script (1918) and book *A Ship to Heaven*, featuring a Lowellian Mars, reached audiences from Europe to the Americas and Soviet Russia. The Martians turned out to be, much like Percy Greg's predecessors, blond fruit-eating Scandinavians, living in world harmony and united by pacifism and a single "mutual language." In the novel the journey began with a massive two-year project to build a spherical spacecraft driven by radio waves. In the film version it turned into a dirigible-like propeller plane (the *Excelsior*), which took six months to reach Mars, moving ever "higher" to establish a "bridge between the planets." There the brave space pilot "Avanti Planetaros," dashing aviator in his leather cap and cloak, fell in love with a beautiful Martian maiden, Marya, bringing her and her peaceful Martian values back home to our planet. Mars taught Earth the ultimate lessons: that "space is the mother of all life, embracing all our globes"; that humanity ought to appreciate the "happiness of death," the necessary transformations along the evolutionary ladder toward a more perfect "spirit" being of love; that "love is the force you call God."[28]

From France J. H. Rosny's latest work, *The Navigators of Infinity* (1925), which circulated in a rough Russian translation, took a crew of human adventurers on a realistic space journey to Mars not in a rocket but in a transparent artificial-gravity ship, the *Stellarium*. The French hero Jacques Laverande, furnished with space suits and ray guns, explored a fascinating ecology and a variety of alien beings: strange flying jellyfish and other monstrosities; the organic "tripeds" (with vertical and rounded bodies, six eyes and three feet); and the threatening mineral "zoomorphs" (flat and horizontal creatures). Rosny was the very same author who in this new work, and as part of a circle of rocketry and spaceflight enthusiasts gathered around Robert Esnault-Pelterie, offered the term *astronautics* (*astronautique*) for the new field of rocket science, a term that perfectly described his fictional team of "tiny" Earth sailors upon the grand ocean of space.[29]

Mars as a utopia of political order and justice, founded on science and invention and collective effort, was a favorite setting in European and American science fiction through the 1920s. One story even had its "ideal state"—a perfect "social democracy" of eugenics, engineering, and technocracy—invent the "Goddard rocket" for space travel.[30] In one of the more bizarre episodes of Mars fever, this one in real life, Hugh Mansfield Robinson, with the collaboration of A. M. Low (a popular science writer and future president of the British Interplanetary Society), eventually reported from London that he had finally established wireless communication with the Martians. His first words to them, tapped in Morse code, were the promising "Love to Mars from Earth." The response back was disappointing: a "long series of undecipherable dots and dashes." Unfazed, Robinson claimed that he was able to translate the mess of signals but only because he had already traveled to Mars several years back by bodily transmutation, dissolving here and reappearing there within four minutes. The code back, it seems, was coming from the capital city of Mars, Ookalonga, and likely from Robinson's Martian girlfriend and interpreter, Gomaruru, with whom he had established intimate relations on his last visit. "It was an amazing experience," he reported. "The Martians have airships, cars and railways. They live underground in caves. They electrify their fruit trees."[31]

Russian audiences were besieged from Europe and America with images of alien life on Mars. Older foreign classics—by Le Faure and Graffigny, by Lasswitz and Zhulavskii, and by Train and Woods— were redone in new editions, even though they were all somewhat outdated. One critic, for example, cautioned that after so many years of Martian fiction, "our readers know more about Mars than Lasswitz" ever could. Russians also had their own native fantasies from which to draw: Bogdanov's *Red Star* and *Engineer Menni* were republished in popular editions.[32] Tolstoi's *Aelita* was adapted to the screen in Iakov Protozanov's classic silent *Aelita: Queen of Mars* (1924). Much like Tolstoi, Protozanov returned from the West to serve the new Russian regime after the revolution and civil war. And like the novel, the film "shrewdly combined . . . a scattering of exotic inventions and ill-disguised borrowings," as Ian Christie has put it.[33] Both the novel and the film were filled with all the market hooks that attracted readers to space adventure stories: centered on a handful of Russian revolutionaries on the battle-scarred fields of Mars, making their way between fierce barbarians and technological sophisticates. The film remained honest enough to the original, pitting Aelita and the revolutionaries against the reactionary Tuskub and his traditional order. One of the future leaders of the Soviet space program, Boris Chertok, remembered it with nostalgia. The signals that the Martians sent down to Earth—*"Ante, odeli, uta"*—made him "crazy about radio engineering," so he remembered.[34] One of the Moscow printing houses even published a serial brochure as a sequel to the film, entitled *Aelita on Earth*. Its plot disguised Aelita as a popular cabaret singer, the voluptuous Maria Orelli, come to Earth by interplanetary rocket to lead the proletarian fight against Tuskub and his capitalist alliance, the reactionary "Gold Union." Thus began a struggle for the mastery of our science, technology, and political power, filled with secret codes, X-ray vision, and amazing rocket planes. "Who masters knowledge on Earth," promised Aelita to the working class, "will win."[35]

Several more films and stories drew upon the attraction of Mars. An eleven-minute short, *Interplanetary Revolution*, one of the USSR's first animated films, used paper collage figures to carry the Communist revolution back to outer space and a canal-studded Mars, where the Red Army was victorious against Earth's fleeing capitalists, who had found refuge there. Launched into space on a Tsiolkovskii dirigible rocket, the proletarians literally conquered the stars and comets, doing battle against fleets of enemy spaceships until finally Lenin's face straddled the planets, a new star in the sky.[36] What with signals to and from Mars all the rage, one enterprising Soviet author penned a novella on the topic, about a pair of intrepid Russians who built a radio tower and created a mathematical code to send the first true interplanetary signals to Mars. The hero Krichagin became a "new Prometheus" for reaching across space and communing with the Martians, for having "thrown a bridge across the great abyss of dead space."[37]

G. Arel'skii's stories about Mars painted colorful portraits of the planet, seen from the powerful telescope at Professor Dagin's observatory, fulfilling many of the stereotypes about Mars in fact and fiction. Part astronomy lesson, part adventure tale, he drew a landscape of a technologically advanced planet, filled with great and dynamic cities and machines, even mastering interplanetary flights (to its two moons) and the power to steer its own orbit. The Martian language was a telltale system of staccato consonant and vowel combinations, with names like "Tsi-Go-Ti" and "Ro-Pa-Ge." Mars was also a planet beset by strange rituals and religions, all along the inevitable trajectory of decline and fall, stock items in the genre. When, for example, the adventure and science fiction magazine *The All-World Traveler* announced an amateur writing contest in 1928, the winner was M. V. Volkov's rather hackneyed story about first contact with Martians. From distant Vladivostok the author told a tale filled with echoes from the science fiction canon. Martians spoke a simplified, phonetic language of abbreviated consonant-vowel syllables. They had mastered science and technology far beyond Earth's, with atomic energy and synthetic foods. Yet Volkov also ended the story on a pessimistic note. Mars was dying, its people sick and in search of a new planetary home.[38] Through all of this Soviet science fiction of the 1920s shared in the sometimes romantic, sometime tragic plotlines of imagined interplanetary life.

This Mars craze also turned into something of a Goddard craze throughout 1924, centered around his rumored flight of a space rocket on the Fourth of July. Goddard's rocket was already an established feature of German science fiction. The popular science writer Bruno Bürgel had first adapted it to his popular novel *The Star of Africa* (1921), never referring to Goddard by name but with manifest correspondences between their rocket spaceships. Both used the explosive charges of reaction propulsion to fly in the vacuum of outer space. Both took necessary measures for the protection against meteorites. And both were the objects of a media blitz. Bürgel's "rocket car" (with wings) was Goddard's rocket writ large: a "steel bird," a "huge metallic projectile that fired itself into space," if with German national genius and interests at play.[39] Otto Willi Gail based his popular novels *The Shot into Infinity* (1925) and *The Stone from the Moon* (1926) more explicitly upon the scientific achievements of Robert H. Goddard and Hermann Oberth. Fiction in these cases also followed fact.[40] Gail's rockets combined the best of Goddard's and Oberth's multistage designs, if outfitted with the telltale airplane wings to allow it to glide back to Earth (and to make more sense to readers). Here were living and breathing machines, human-made comets that reached into the heavens by graceful parabolic curves, positioning humanity for a space future of prosperity and freedom.

For American audiences the Goddard rocket was the premier technology for space travel, thanks largely to Hugo Gernsback's trend-setting magazines, especially *Amazing Stories* (1926). As its masthead proclaimed, "Extravagant Fiction Today—Cold Fact Tomorrow." Gernsback's writers now expressly predicated their fantasy and "interplanetary" stories upon hard science. This approach was preferred by one of the genre's core audiences, mostly young male technicians, engineers, and scientists of various degrees. They demanded that their science fiction be grounded in real or possible technologies, with men like themselves leading the way.[41] What counted were real facts and knowledge: the physical and mechanical and astronomical. This meant actual science fiction written by the scientists themselves—as, for example, the Cambridge biologist Julian Huxley or the Harvard astronomer W. J. Luyten. It also meant featuring the latest scientific-

ROCKET SPACESHIPS AS SCIENCE FICTIONS

technological advances, especially Goddard's liquid fuel rocket, now dominating the front covers of Gernsback's magazines: as a real laboratory achievement, as the platform to colonize Mars, and as the means to discover far-off solar systems.[42] J. M. Walsh also patterned his Martian "Gaudien Base" after Hermann Noordung's space station and space suit designs. J. Lewis Burtt's "The Lemurian Documents" applied Hohmann's gravity assists to make its space adventures more believable, centered on a modern "Prometheus," a favorite character in many such stories, who defied gravity and Earth, who conquered the sun by "one tremendous burst of power," in a parabolic trajectory, "traveling outward at a tangent to my former orbit."[43]

The new "Soviet" style in science fiction honored Goddard's rocket as well. The Society for the Study of Interplanetary Travel, for example, gave Goddard pride of place in its draft movie script of 1924. The screenplay began with the lathe operator Stepan, a "strong and brave dreamer," reading the newspaper at home one evening while his wife sat beside him sewing. "In America," the script read, "it has been proposed to send a rocket to the moon on 4 July."[44] Several more short stories featured Goddard and the Americans. In one the rocket was that fantastic technology that "pushes itself"—originally Tsiolkovskii's idea, now realized in practice by the West. "The American Goddard launched such a rocket to the Moon," so the story went, "an achievement of which the Russians could only dream." In another piece the Americans also first achieved a moon landing in 1930, through the American Society for Interplanetary Travel, which even had its own Russian filial and "Soviet-style" acronym, *Mezhplaso*.[45] M. V. Volkov's amateur story summed up these plotlines with an American victory over the Soviets. A fanciful Robert Goddard character, colorfully renamed William Amori, launched his space rocket from a secret base in Texas. As a fictional "news report" confirmed, "the craft rose not by a vertical but by a spiral line."[46] Soviet writers regularly put American rockets into space first.

In perhaps the greatest compliment of all, Goddard fell prey to Mikhail Zoshchenko's literary satires, which in one cartoon image had the redoubtable inventor "sitting pretty" in his "cannon-ball cottage." Because Goddard never made it to the moon in his tiny rocket

Fig. 14. Robert Goddard in his rocket *Shell Cottage*. From M. Zoshchenko and N. Radlov, *Veselye proekty* (Leningrad: Krasnaia gazeta, 1928), 7.

shell, Zoshchenko lampooned that the Soviet housing authorities ought to purchase the patent. It was, after all, just the right size for a workers' apartment.[47] The poet Osip Mandelshtam, too, made fun of the Goddard craze.

> All that stuff about the moon,
> don't believe that nonsense about the moon,

ROCKET SPACESHIPS AS SCIENCE FICTIONS

it's all a fairy tale . . .
Oh no, the moon doesn't grow
even a single blade of grass.

In the wake of the craze readers of one popular adventure magazine were also treated to a satirical romp through the solar system, as if scolding them for their silly dreams of rockets flying through space, toward alien planets of the most absurd sort, the hapless crew flying homeward on a comet—with the help of the devil.[48] A darker Russian satire came in the form of Andrei Platonov's short story "The Lunar Bomb" (1926). Its hero, engineer Peter Kreitskopf, invented a marvelous interplanetary sphere, destination moon, with captivating radio messages about zero gravity and time standing still. Yet the story's subtexts were layers of loneliness and abandonment, set against billowing crematorium fumes and industrial deaths from the nearby "foundation pit." The ultimate backdrop was the vacuum of outer space, the lunar explorer imprisoned in his shell, a "cramped grave." "Ahead was but one deadly dream—lunar flight." Kreitskopf opened the hatch at the end "to find release from himself" in a "simple act of suicide."[49]

Other space travel stories accented the ideological, brimming with Soviet Russian confidence and pride, if still lighthearted and entertaining. One Soviet Pioneer troop reached into the future by way of a crystalline temporal gate to the year 1957. It found an Earth united by a planetary communism after the final victory of labor over capital; captivated with marvelous futuristic technologies such as musical radio-planes and energy rays; framed by perfect social and political relations; even graced with a rocket, a "high-powered projectile" that could reach "the muzzle velocity of a bullet."[50] S. L. Grave, a propagandist and lecturer in the workers' colleges, published his rocketry notes as *Flight to the Moon* (1926), the first such booklet for children, centered on a Tsiolkovskii rocket and a heroic all-Russian crew: two engineers, Maleev and Basharin, and their young Pioneer sidekick, Petya. Valerii Iazvitskii's *Flight to the Moon and Mars* (1928) offered an everyman's fable about Sasha Ershov and Petr Gura and their discoveries of weightlessness in space, hedgehogs on the moon and half-civilized ape-men on Mars. They were initially part of an American-Russian space team headed by the serious professor Dzhon Airs, American money financing Tsiolkovskii's classic rocket design. But for most of the story the two men stole away for adventures on their own. Iazvitskii added a serious afterword on the physics of rocketry, on orbital mechanics, and on Lowell's Mars.[51] These strange new scientific-technological truths were the foundations for his compelling scientific fiction.

Rockets and Relativity

Along with rockets popular science and science fiction also provided creative forums by which to introduce and debate Albert Einstein's new theories. His general theory of relativity (1916) had already made its way from European intellectual circles to Soviet Russia by 1921, mostly through awkward and stumbling reviews, eventually in a series of more authoritative translations and original monographs.[52] The 1920s were a most remarkable decade in this sense, introducing the successes of the long-distance airplane and the rocket, along with the Russian Revolution and relativity theory, all in one great sweep of historical change. Airplanes continued to inspire the ideal of overcoming gravity and mortality, space and time. One Russian journalist imagined the airplane of the future, something along the lines of the Junkers all-metal monoplane but even better. It would join all of the latest achievements in altitude and speed and distance, become a "time machine" of a kind, break through all known human and natural barriers with "astronomical" precision and scope. Charles Lindbergh remembered that he "became conscious of a relativity of time" while preparing for his momentous transatlantic flight. When he flew alone in his plane, especially over great cities or in dangerous flying conditions or at great speeds, he felt time stop. "I entered a core of timelessness in a turbulence of time."[53]

These experiences with flight gave credence to Einstein's principles, helping to bridge his new theory of relativity with the new technology of the rocket. Einstein himself, in an interview in April 1920, took issue with dreams of reaching beyond the speed of light. "Nonsense," he responded, "the velocity of light cannot be exceeded." Yet

ROCKET SPACESHIPS AS SCIENCE FICTIONS

he did not exclude the range of possibilities between the technology of the airplane and the cosmic speed of light, essentially travel by rocket, meaning the possibility of "a journey into the universe at an enormous yet limited velocity."[54] True enough, the many new publicists of "relativity" did not yet make room in their work for space rockets. When Einstein and his followers first crafted examples to illustrate the "relativity of simultaneity" (about how two events are never simultaneous in an absolute way if they are separated in space), they used the rather mainstream technologies from the turn of the century: "compartments" such as railroad trains and oceangoing ships, automobiles and airplanes, speeding bullets and falling elevators. When they discussed the principle of the time-space continuum and relativity (about how time slows down at higher speeds), they turned back to that great stand-by, Jules Verne's cannon shell, or any number of strange flying craft. The physicist Paul Langevin set the trend with his famous "twin paradox" in 1911, a thought experiment comparing one twin stationary on Earth and aging normally, with another speeding to the stars and aging less. He imagined the one twin as traveling through outer space on nothing less than Verne's old-fashioned cannon shell.[55]

A whole series of academic and popular discussions on these questions soon followed suit. For French readers of popular science Langevin's shell promised to fulfill the dream of both space and time travel, to grant humanity some greater share in infinity. It was the perfect example of "yesterday's utopia" become "tomorrow's reality." From Soviet Russia the geologist A. E. Fersman reached into interplanetary space on Langevin's shell, speeding at 250,000 kilometers a second, traversing two hundred years in two.[56] The astronomer Charles Lane Poor imagined himself in his own study, "sealed up and shot off into space," reaching similar speeds of up to 170,000 miles a second, whereby the tick of the clock in space might equal a whole year of "ordinary earthly time." His colleague Sir Arthur Eddington illustrated the principle of relativity and the time paradox using a fanciful "magic carpet" to travel through space. But he also gave eloquent testimony to what his colleagues and educated readers were coming to know about relativity theory and space travel:

that they positioned us human beings in multidimensional realms beyond ourselves. "We have found a strange foot-print on the shores of the unknown," wrote Eddington. "We have devised profound theories, one after another, to account for its origin. At last, we have succeeded in reconstructing the creature that made the foot-print. And Lo! it is our own."[57]

Two other public personages of note showed signs of interest in Langevin's shell. Auguste Piccard, a physicist and pioneer of stratospheric balloons, promised that humanity would soon master atomic energy, enough to fulfill Langevin's mythical space voyage: living and traveling half a lifetime by light-years in space while we aged some hundreds of thousand years back on Earth. Iosif Stalin too, so his nephew told the world, was impressed with Langevin's sheer faith in our capacity to use technology to manipulate the laws of evolution, perhaps even to someday become spirit beings (the "solar universe animal") traveling toward the speed of light. Here were the elements of Stalinist "transformism," as Douglas Weiner has defined it, whose "blind optimism" set nature apart for conquest and exploitation, raised the human being as master race over all other creatures and things, and elevated "the transformation of nature by society as the sine qua non of human self-perfection."[58]

What about the space rocket as a medium to prove relativity theory? There were theoretical grounds for a marriage between the two. Rockets and relativity shared a set of common operating assumptions and methods. Like Meshcherskii and Tsiolkovskii, Einstein conceived and proved a new kind of mathematics, a new way of calculating relative moments through space and time. Like them, Einstein conceived of outer space traversed by human motion. He was already imagining humanity in outer space, in motion with the earth and planets and stars. He was "looking at the movement of the earth from *outside*," as Zamiatin recognized. "Life today has lost its plane reality: it is projected, not along the old fixed points, but also the dynamic coordinates of Einstein, of revolution."[59]

The rocket was the perfect logo for relativity theory. It was never in the same place, and it was never the same (given the dynamics of its changing mass). The pilot and passenger on the rocket were never the same too, floating about the cabin in zero gravity, unhinged in four-dimensional space. Newton's science enabled thinkers such as Tsiolkovskii to conceive of rockets. But it was Einstein's universe in which they soon came to imagine rockets moving. Two pioneers ought to share the credit for joining rockets to relativity at this time. The Italian military scientist G. A. Crocco first postulated that a rocket spaceship, with the correct fuels and thrust, would realize Einstein's famous mobile compartment, only "without any of the cables or pulleys or point of leverage imagined by the illustrious mathematician. The traveler would find himself in the comfort of a fixed point of gravity," much like a new Earth. With the proper mass-to-fuel ratio and escape velocity, it was theoretically possible for human beings to achieve "extra-atmospheric navigation," to reach "into interplanetary space." A spaceship applying "reaction propulsion" could thereby become a "dirigible in space," able to make trajectories from "Earth to the Moon" or "Earth to Venus."[60] Russian rocket pioneer F. A. Tsander similarly wrote of the possible "slowing of life and possibility of returning to earth alive after millions of years, by flying at a velocity near the speed of light, according to Einstein's theory of relativity"—flying at such a velocity, no doubt, in one of Tsander's unique rockets, even if still hypothetical, traveling from planet to planet, star to star, ever nearing the speed of light, defying gravity and cheating death.[61]

Aleksei Tolstoi had, of course, already done all of this in fiction. *Aelita* surveyed Einstein's theories of relativity: that a spacecraft approaching the speed of light might actually slow time down while moving through the curvatures of space. The whole work was really a play upon time, the travelers speeding by rocket through a time warp in space, then regressing to an alien world. They reached a Lowellian Mars, populated by colorful primitive tribes, ruled by the remnants of Atlantis, though their technocratic society was falling into an advanced state of decay. Meanwhile, back on Earth the USSR was speedily rebuilding and transforming from a country broken by the civil war into a country already modernizing and developing along the lines of Stalin's "socialism in one country." In these ways *Aelita* heralded the Soviets as the premier conquerors of time, either by the measure of Einsteinian relativity in outer space or by the measure of the Bolshevik revolution here on Earth. Both revolutionary conquests, however rooted in the traditional structure of the cosmic romance, represented the new Soviet realm of freedom as a utopia of time.

By the summer of 1923 the rocket had become the archetypical machine of the new relativity for the American general public as well. One of the first animated films, *The Einstein Theory of Relativity*, which premiered in New York City in February 1923, featured the Goddard rocket as humanity's way to the stars. It was yet another in a series of "triumphs of human invention over the forces of nature," at one with the transcontinental railroad, steel suspension bridge, radio, and X-ray. Only it would take us beyond the earth. Granted, the film (and accompanying book) used mundane objects to illustrate Einstein's principles: speeding trains and bullets, falling elevators and basketballs. No matter that the rocket looked more like a giant cannon in outer space or that the film also entertained something like Jules Verne's cannon-launched moon "projectile." Here was a definitive turning point in the history of motion pictures and popular science. "The miracles of yesterday are the commonplaces of today," as one of the film titles put it. Viewers were entreated to "follow Einstein into starry space," to "dash away" at the mind-boggling speeds of 79,000 miles (127,000 kilometers) a second, piloted by a space-faring human being, witnessing before their very eyes the proof of relativity by rocket power, the shrinking of the earth and the approach of the near planets. Here were screened, in simple and comprehensible ways, all the complex theories of the two "professors," Albert Einstein and Robert Goddard, along with the novel approaches to relativity theory and rocket science.[62]

As one Russian engineer wrote at the time, space travel was an intellectual "revolution" equal to Einstein's relativity or even to the Russian Revolution. Both had conquered time, reduced thousands of years to rubble, sped up evolution, and like flight itself, had created the grounds for humanity's "unlimited future." Humanity was becoming the very "god" it had once created in mythology: "all-powerful, everywhere-existing, all-managing, all-seeing, all hear-

ROCKET SPACESHIPS AS SCIENCE FICTIONS

ing, eternal, immortal."[63] Albert Einstein, too, eventually came to recognize the Tsiolkovskii type of rocket as a means to humanize relativity theory, to recalibrate its equations as a real and promising technology. "The use of a reactive shell," he was quoted as saying, "is a most sensible idea, and at present the sole means to break free from the shackles of earthly gravity."[64] For Einstein, as for his publicists and promoters, the interplanetary rocket was becoming the symbolic medium by which humanity might not only understand but also then conquer the continuum of space and time, marry relativity with something approaching immortality.

We see the same themes in V. N. Muraviev's extraordinary book *The Conquest of Time* (1924): humanity entering a new stage of evolution, symbolized by the invention of the balloon during the era of the French Revolution and the invention of the airplane during the era of the Russian. Technical progress always accompanied political progress. Both were expanding over the whole earth, including nearly all of humanity, and reaching even into the cosmos. Humans were becoming more and more of a vertical presence. Muraviev's innovation was to vanquish the whole concept of "time" by projecting human will and reason upon terrestrial space. All of human history was marked by chaos, confusion, irrationality, and death. He asked for nothing less than a total universal transformation, a new Fedorovian architecture for an ordered cosmos. Muraviev's priority was to engage the economical, to unburden history and to free up human action. His ultimate goal was to promote a new consciousness, subsuming the personal within the collective (the cosmic "We"), creating a new spirit-based, immortal humanity.[65]

The German educational film *The Wonders of Creation* (1925), set two thousand years into the future, offered similar insights for European popular audiences. The movie was part historical and astronomical documentary, part cutting-edge animation, and part adventure drama in the cosmos. Filled with novel cinematic techniques and a most dynamic pace, it included a journey by a saucer-like spaceship to the moon (propelled by electrical energy), the earth alternately shrinking or rising in the distance. It traveled even farther, to what appeared to be a "Lowellian" Mars (though the canals turned out to be illusions) and to the planets near and far, highlighting the human evolutionary struggle to survive. Building momentum from the basics of Newtonian and Einsteinian physics, the film predicted that humans would eventually reach the speed of light and explore the infinity of the cosmos, this to avoid the inevitable end of our world, either by ice death or the collision of planets.[66]

The Russian biocosmist A. Iaroslavskii translated all of these trends into his science fiction adventure *Argonauts of the Universe* (1926), which took his heroes (Volodia Gorianskii and his wife, Elena Rodston) to the moon in a Kibalchich-Tsiolkovskii rocket ship, the *Victor* (*Pobeditel'*). Powered by atomic energy, it had the rather amazing capacity to "drive itself along by its own propulsive force." The rocket was really one of the heroes of the story, a "small independent planet," leaving a trail of exhaust "like the tail of a comet," along a trajectory of a "winding, curved line" toward the moon. Iaroslavskii's victories in outer space, remarkably, coincided with the victories of Lenin and the Bolshevik revolution back on Earth. The new citizens of the Soviet Russian world "commune" became "citizens of the universe" too, opening a "road to the stars." Their discoveries were nothing less than exhilarating. In space they literally turned into Langevin's famous shell, proving Einstein's principle of relativity: their twenty hours of traveling in space equal to three months on Earth. On the moon they divined the mysteries of the cosmos and attained a higher consciousness, discovering an ancient civilization of alien beings, masters over time and space. The aliens were in fact the original colonizers and civilizers of lost Atlantis and of the Egyptian, Aztec, and Incan empires. Fulfilling the imperatives of a new transformational biology, they had achieved a total victory over old age and death by way of anabiosis. They were also masters of a universal brotherhood between the planets and star systems, the living organism and "circulatory system" of the cosmos, a culture of total "love." Here was the old spiritualist and biocosmist dream of a whole new human existence come true, if refashioned for communism.[67]

         ROCKET SPACESHIPS AS SCIENCE FICTIONS

7

The Origins and Ends of Life on Earth

Academic science had its own narratives about cosmic origins and ends. In the United States and Europe scientists continued to debate Arrhenius's "panspermia" and possible life on Mars and Venus. Perhaps Earth's originals seeds of life came from there?[1] This thesis enjoyed a short-lived resurgence after the Russian Revolution, when the leading plant biologist, S. P. Kostychev, critically affirmed panspermia in *The Appearance of Life on Earth* (1921). Organic life on our world was far too complex to have developed on its own; living matter, he said, came from outer space. The cosmos was the ultimate source of life. Spontaneous generation and "self-created life" made little sense. Life evolved. Life mutated into new forms and kinds, but it did not evolve from death. Kostychev held that living matter most likely came from "spores" borne through frozen interplanetary and interstellar space by the power of cosmic rays. V. I. Vernadskii gave this hypothesis further legitimacy with a smart philosophical review, arguing that life never arose out of dead or "non-living matter." Life always originated from other life. It was "*Aeternum*," eternal. "Life is a cosmic phenomenon," he wrote, "not uniquely terrestrial. We now know that the planets are not divided but are joined by matter."[2] Or as one leading publicist put it in regard to Arrhenius's traveling germs: "Interplanetary flights are already happening all the time."[3]

Kostychev's were rather attractive notions so soon after the Bolshevik revolution, a moment of intense anticlericalism, with state-sponsored attacks on creationism and all the alleged superstitions and obscurantism of the Orthodox Church. The new secular world-view held to an early big bang theory about the origins of the universe. As one editorial phrased it, "The universe is infinite and eternal in space and time, but it also evolves." Kornei Chukovskii remembered hearing a pedestrian, half-literate cultural commissar, one of the many self-designated "expert readers of *Science and Life*," as he put it, expound on the tasks of educating the dark masses in modern science and astronomy, namely "the views of Kant and Laplace."[4] Velemir Khlebnikov even heard a series of evening lectures at the People's University of Astrakhan in 1918 on the topic. Life was probably brought here on falling meteors from outer space, he learned. The streaks of cascading stars were replacing the hand of God at work in nature and history. Marxist publicists, like the veterinary pathologist A. V. Nemilov, also held to the Arrhenius panspermia thesis. Perhaps it came on meteors, almost like a plague, on "celestial rocks that infected our earth with life." Thus, the "first living creatures" might indeed have "come to earth on such a primitive stone vessel, completing a vast journey through the interstellar ocean." Or perhaps they came upon the folds of light pressure, which meant that the sun was the great "sower of life" throughout the solar system. In either case life was without a beginning or end. The sun might someday go cold. Life here might therefore perish. But it was bound to revive again someday, somewhere, somehow.[5]

Panspermia was open to dispute. One alternate view was that our planet's biology had a chemical foundation. This "abiogenesis" hypothesis circulated widely after T. H. Huxley's propositions in an 1868 lecture, "On the Physical Basis of Life." The origins of life, he maintained, were not in some mythical spontaneous generation or vital life force but in the complex chemical reactions that created the original "protoplasm" of half-inorganic, half-organic matter. Louis Pasteur's experiments with sterilization confirmed the hypothesis: microbial life did not just magically appear in a controlled, sterilized sample of inorganic matter. But it was possible that organic life first formed in the earth's prehistoric "simple, primordial jelly" of chemicals, proteins, and amino acids, catalyzed by the energy of volcanoes or lightning or the sun.[6] By 1925 Henry Fairfield Osborn, president of the American Museum of Natural History, argued that "the change from the lifeless to the life world" was based on chemical actions and reactions, joining soil, water, and atmosphere with "electric energy and the Sun's heat."[7] Earth was an integral part of the living universe—not as a passive receptor of life come from beyond but as an active source of life-giving power from within.

Abiogenesis became a staple of Bolshevik ideology both before and after the Russian Revolution. Aleksandr Bogdanov provided a detailed excursus on it, life sui generis, in his popular novel *Red Star* (1908). Or as Nikolai Bukharin wrote, "Organic nature grew out of dead nature; living nature produced a form capable of thought." Human beings were not original; they were not part of some mystical, supernatural order. They were accidental, the by-products of a natural order that claimed them from inorganic matter, if now organized also as mind, as matter in its most developed and perfected form.[8] Tsiolkovskii, too, now refuted the theories of Arrhenius that life came from outer space or another planet. Instead, he proposed, life probably originated right here, in some "quiet, spacious, freshwater lake," thanks to just the right chemical solution energized by the power of the sun.[9]

The Soviet biologist Aleksandr Oparin gave definitive shape to the classic theory of abiogenesis, another Russian "first" in the history of science and astronautics, in *The Origin of Life* (1924). Based on a lecture he gave before the Russian Botanical Society on 3 May 1922, as a newly credentialed professor, later republished in dozens of Russian and foreign editions, it was more of an ideological manifesto than a set of scientific proofs. Oparin laid a sometimes sarcastic, at other times brash critique of all manner of theories about life's origins, from panspermia to mythical spontaneous generation. They only masqueraded as science. What truly mattered were chemical and biological facts. Arrhenius was wrong. Alien life, if it did exist, was hundreds of thousands of years away from Earth. The stars were too distant, the spaces between them too lethal, to sustain the interstellar and interplanetary migration of life. The various adherents of traditional spontaneous generation, from Paracelsus to J. B. von Helmont, were wrong too. Human beings could not be grown from sperm and blood. Mice could not be made from wheat kernels and human sweat. Bugs did not form spontaneously out of manure. There was no mysterious "vital force" at work in life. This was sophistry and superstition.

Outer space and spontaneous generation did count for Oparin. He worked from the model of the Kant-Laplace universe, the formation of our galaxy and solar system from the "original chaos" and "clouds" of stellar material. The earth itself was created out of them, out of one common genetic material. It remained at one with the planets, at one with the universe at large. Yet organic life here on Earth, he argued from his own biochemical studies, had its origins in evolution from inorganic nature: in the hydrocarbons and myriad chemical reactions and interactions forming from them, in the "fire," the energy that spills out from Earth into outer space. True, once begun in a cycle of conception and reproduction, life could not replicate this moment of natural creation. Yet life was wholly predicated upon death, upon simple chemistry. A dead Earth was the precondition for life. This was a scientific "spontaneous generation." Life was at one time, by the best hypotheses of modern chemistry and biology, generated spontaneously, self-created, in a process of chemical self-separation and individuation. It began as a humble kind of organic slime but with the power to grow and assimilate. Oparin parlayed his thesis about life's origins into a trajectory both upward and outward. Outer space belonged to the very life that we humans had already become on our home planet.[10]

By the late 1920s Western science began to advance Oparin's original insights in myriad ways. Evolution needed a point of origin, a creation myth all its own: chemical spontaneous generation. The image of the radium clock (whereby one hour equaled some 250 million years), created by the American Museum of Natural History and reproduced in both American and Russian media, perfectly illustrated Oparin's origins within the shape of a spiraling time wheel: how the earth first formed out of a gaseous cloud, gave birth to life out of its primal oceans, and set into motion the inevitable process of natural evolution. Part parabola, part spiral, the time wheel expressed unstoppable motion, forward progress.[11]

THE ORIGINS AND ENDS OF LIFE ON EARTH

The British Marxist J.B.S. Haldane developed these propositions, first in a rough sketch and later along more certain biochemical lines, for which he has shared title to the "Oparin-Haldane" theory of abiogenesis. His short but significant article in the *Rationalist Annual* (1929), later reprinted in more accessible paperback editions, was crafted in secularist and materialist tones. It was half a critique of traditional superstitions and the Christian theology of the soul and half a reasoned defense of the experimental method and scientific proofs. Haldane offered a study of the boundaries between inorganic and organic matter, speculating that the first organism formed as an anaerobic molecule, our "one ancestor," self-synthesizing and "self-contained" from a combination of water, carbon dioxide, ammonia, and the ultraviolet rays of the sun. We descended not from a monkey or a worm but from a common virus, back when the "whole sea was a vast chemical laboratory."[12]

Oparin and Haldane shared more than the scientific method. As Marxists, they also shared a common utopia. Oparin, for example, ended his work on an interesting, optimistic note: "That which we do not know today, we will know tomorrow." Abiogenesis was but a modest hypothesis, he noted, one that scores of other biologists, chemists, and physicists would need to verify by their own work. But it was a modest proposal with the grandest of implications. In time modern science would undoubtedly "destroy the last obstacles separating the living from the dead." There was no vast difference between the mineral and animal worlds. Rocks and plants, crystals and human beings, all shared the same basic elements and chemical compositions, if in varying forms and complexities. They even shared similar powers of metabolism and change, adaption and reproduction, part of the same struggle for existence. Modern science, in a conscious rationalism, external to nature and internal to man, would conquer the very creation of life itself.[13]

More and more scientists around the world, socialists and non-socialists alike, shared such a transformational biology. In a lecture to the National Physical Laboratory of Great Britain in 1923 Sir Oliver Lodge looked forward to the day when chemists and physicists might even replicate the origins of life in the laboratory, creating by artificial means "a highly complex assemblage of organic molecules." Humanity was bound at some point to conquer even nature's origins. "Mind dominates over matter," he said, "and the mind of man is not altogether of different order from the mind of the Creator."[14] Haldane also shared this transformational biology, without the Creator, which he discussed in a series of popular essays and science fiction stories devoted to such utopian tasks as the promotion of racial eugenics and population control, laboratory-produced babies, and the communal upbringing of children under full socialism.[15] But he took the utopia even further—into outer space. In Haldane's scenario of a secular "Last Judgment," set forty million years into the future, humanity is able to domesticate the whole planet by exploiting the energy of the ocean's tides, by the remaking of the continents, by engineering a society of individual happiness and fulfillment. The average life expectancy rises to some three thousand years old. And when in this future the earth becomes uninhabitable, an elite corps of humanity sets off for outer space by rocket ship, refashioning itself by means of artificial evolution for the light and heat, gravity and atmosphere, of Venus. There it becomes a near-perfect civilization, a "super-organism" with the power of extrasensory communication. Humanity "proves that its destiny is in eternity and infinity."[16] Haldane was, in sum, invested in man's potential for "improving human nature," for "taking his own evolution in hand," a process that would peak with human exploration and colonization of the near planets and even the planets of other stars. It was a process that would culminate, in terms worthy of Fedorov, with the "complete conscious control of every atom and every quantum of radiation in the universe."[17]

These were also ideals that informed the hopes and dreams of one of Oparin's and Haldane's most devoted promoters, the fellow socialist J. D. Bernal, pioneer in X-ray crystallography and professor of physics at the University of London. He too concluded, from his own scientific interpretation of abiogenesis, that life on Earth was "self-generating," "self-realizing," "self-producing," and ultimately "self-conditioning," even over death. "For *life does not die* or, more accurately, *life on Earth has not died.* If life itself came about by the working out of logical processes independent of my conscious will, this is no longer so. In the future it will become more and more a function of human understanding and human virtues."[18]

Bernal's provocative utopian essay *The World, the Flesh, and the Devil* (1929) foresaw humanity mastering evolution along Oparin's and Haldane's lines, if now in even more fantastic ways. We were bound to re-create matter from the bottom up, to engineer new chemical materials to house and feed the world. We were bound to refashion even ourselves, to dispense with our "useless parts" and to become more of a "mechanized humanity," with scopes for eyes and microphones for ears, able to project our visions and words and thoughts at greater and greater distances. And we were bound even to launch into outer space by way of the rocket. It was the vessel by which the human being, well on its way to achieving immortalism, would also achieve interplanetarism. It was the rational and efficient machine of "high velocities" and "sufficient acceleration," based on Tsiolkovskii's and Goddard's principles, enabling humanity to fully conquer the "simple curvature of space-time." It was nothing less than a human-made "comet, ejecting from its anterior end a stream of gas which, meeting and vapourizing any matter in its path, would sweep it to the sides and behind in a luminous trail." It was a perfect metaphor for what Bernal called the dynamic progress at work in the modern world, its parabolic "ever increasing acceleration of change." It would lead to a permanent human presence in space colonies, where zero gravity would offer half-organic, half-engineered inhabited globes, pulsing with solar-powered life and orbiting with Earth around the sun. In time humanity would "invade" and colonize even the stars.[19]

On these scores Russian ideologues and scholars shared much in common with some of the best minds of the West, especially those among them with an absolute confidence in Marxian socialism or Darwinian evolution. Together they found a common bearing and cause in life's sui generis origins on Earth and its possibilities of reaching by rocket beyond. From the University of Vienna, Desiderius Papp praised Haldane for turning humanity into a new Genesis and new Prometheus, with the power to create life itself, to "preside over his planet like a little divinity." The human race was destined to rise upright from apelike creatures, to build skyscrapers and fly by airplane, to "climb to dizzy heights." This was the trajectory of human evolution. Papp's future humanity crossed oceans and continents, headed off to the moon and near planets, all by rocket, the culminating technology of human history. For the prominent biologist Hermann Muller the best hope lay in the USSR: it would teach humanity to master our own selves through science and technology, becoming new "Davids" against the "brute Goliath of the suns and planets." With rocket and atomic energy we would find "an Archimedean lever which might move the very worlds." "Man should then be free of the earth . . . emancipated from the need of the sun's light and heat," more "spirit" than body.[20] Even the conservative Winston Churchill, backed by all the glamour of *Popular Mechanics Magazine*, gave these propositions a public airing. He celebrated the world's "enormous revolution in material things, in scientific techniques, in political institutions, in manners and customs," along with the "new prodigious speed of man." He recognized Soviet Russia's propensity to better harness these forces under state-managed control. He honored science as the source for it all, for humanity's quickening pace of "technical achievement" and its "schemes of cosmic magnitude." These included the new sciences of synthetics and eugenics, controlling matter and mind; and the new technologies of dirigible, planes, and yes, especially rockets in conquering extreme distances.[21]

Imagining the Solar System

The earth's place in the solar system clearly mattered. This was especially true given what scientists had been discovering about the impact of the solar climate on natural and human history. Sunspots, for example, had long been a topic of growing interest. By the 1920s, thanks in part to newly compiled sunspot charts, scientists were linking solar activity to weather patterns, to earthquakes and volcanic activity, to the abundance of "fur-bearing animals," to the prevalence of icebergs in the North Atlantic, and to the rise and fall of water levels in Lake Erie.[22] But sunspots seemed to have corresponding influences on human history as well—on our propensity for chronic diseases, on our crop harvests and even business cycles. The proofs on the scientific charts were compelling. The corresponding lines, waves up and down, illustrated the coincidences. The sun, it was manifest, shaped all parts of our lives. The French popular science writer Charles Nordmann put it most poetically when he wrote, "Men are but little marionettes whose every movement and every gesture are governed by light golden strings, the beams of the sun."[23]

Aleksandr Chizhevskii, a longtime student and supporter of K. E. Tsiolkovskii, brought these solar approaches to culture—revolutionary culture, that is. We belonged to nature as much as we belonged to ourselves, a view not uncommon for the day.[24] The streams of electrical and magnetic energy released by the sun, he argued, as ionizing anode and cathode rays, reached the earth with physical and social effects: population shifts and migrations; diseases and ecological disasters; and even sociopolitical crises and political revolutions. Chizhevskii discovered a set of what he called stunning "correlations," not quite causal relationships, between physical events on the sun and political events on Earth, including such dramatic moments as the French Revolutions (between 1789 and 1871) and the Russian Revolutions (between 1905 and 1917). He plotted a wave series of sunspot activity, each lasting about eleven years, against corresponding wave patterns of low to high "excitability" of the masses, fitted to "mass historical events." These were moments when the masses became highly vulnerable to authoritative leaders and ideas. As the waves of sunspot activity rose to their maximum, the masses became more and more vulnerable, as was the case in the Russian Revolutions of 1917. All of this confirmed, so he argued, the unmistakable "influence of cosmic factors" on the "universal historical process."[25]

Human history seemed to be locked within a pattern of eternal recurrence. One prominent theory at the time held that the cycles of sunspot activity were caused by the orbits of some of the planets, especially Jupiter, working their gravitational effects upon the sun, forcing sunspots to expand or shrink.[26] Chizhevskii's theories therefore implied that the very revolutions of the planets helped to cause political revolutions here on Earth. The cycles of the planets in outer space thus influenced the very cycles of our own political histories. Yet the linearity of historical progress was also implicit in his sequences, which revealed a rhythm of ever more global and ever more revolutionary events. This was all radical stuff, as one astronomer commented: that we humans lived under the "complete dependence" of the sun, that its cycles of eleven-year maximal flares offered a decisive "push" to the underlying and driving forces of the Marxian means and relations of production.[27] As a promoter of Tsiolkovskii's space rockets (they also shared the same publisher), Chizhevskii presumed that humanity was about to perfect the means to break out of these solar and planetary rhythms, to reach spaceward by rocket, to become new revolving planets of our own.

Chizhevskii's views were quite unorthodox, even for the rich and creative years of the revolution and early NEP. They tapped into an existing model of scientific determinism at play in the Russian intellectual tradition. Just as Ivan Pavlov had discovered the effects of the environment and its stimuli on dogs and humans (through behavioral conditioning), so now Chizhevskii presumed to discover the effects of outer space and the sun on all of human history. The two scientists even met in 1926, Chizhevskii searching out the great master for confirmation about the effects of ionized air upon the human reflex system. Pavlov, the consummate laboratory scientist and aloof genius, more or less ignored him.

Although he had two significant patrons in the government hierarchy—Commissar of Enlightenment Anatolii Lunacharskii and Commissar of Public Health N. A. Semashko—Chizhevskii's prognostications also set off a sharp debate in the Soviet press. Official ideology was at risk, with mighty complaints leveled against him for upending Marxist historical determinism. Critics accused him of being a "sun worshipper." They had a point. Chizhevskii moved in Russia's top literary circles after 1915, meeting and conversing with the writers Konstantin Tsiolkovskii, Leonid Andreev, Aleksandr Kuprin, Aleksei Tolstoi, Valerii Briusov, and Maksim Gorkii. They knew him as a sensitive and romantic poet, whose verses reflected his search for the scientific "synchronicity" between sun and Earth. He was as much artist as scientist. Yet critics panned his work as pseudoscience, claiming that he manipulated the data to fit his theory, ignoring some facts and distorting so many convenient variables (dates,

THE ORIGINS AND ENDS OF LIFE ON EARTH

events, solar variations) to promote his thesis.[28] One entertaining science fiction story poked fun at Chizhevskii, based on the plotline of a war between capitalism and communism: now that everyone knew that "Bolshevism arose from sunspots," all the crafty American capitalists had to do was eliminate the sunspots (by a blast of rockets aimed at the sun) in order to "destroy Bolshevism."[29]

Unbowed, Chizhevskii retooled his efforts, setting forth to prove scientifically the health benefits of the sun's ion waves for growing children and for diseased adults, a treatment that matched well with the current European fad for "heliotherapy." This was the term for Auguste Rollier's proposed cure for tuberculosis and other ailments, as well as for the promotion of better health, set in a "sunshine clinic" high in the French Alps.[30] For Russians besieged by backwardness and poverty, dysfunction and all manner of disease, the sun was more than just a metaphor for enlightenment. It was a cure. One creative lesson plan for children even imagined the coming civilization of "Sun City," a utopia of light and warmth against the darkness of dirt, infection, fleas, and assorted bugs.[31] The Ukrainian national leader and exile Volodomyr Vynnychenko devoted a science fiction novel, *The Solar Machine* (1928), to the theme; his novel introduced a visionary new technology: the "solar machine." When paired with the imaginary mineral "helionite," it had the capacity to produce cheap and plentiful "solar bread," meant to turn the human being from a "plundering, carnivorous animal" into a peaceful, civic being.[32]

Chizhevskii's reception in Europe and the United States was also mixed. He found sympathy among two prominent astronomers who also happened to be Roman Catholic priests. Father Théophile Moreux, director of the Observatory at Bourges (France), recognized that sunspot cycles and their powerful electromagnetic bursts very likely influenced human physiology and neurology. He had found some "remarkable coincidences" between them and periods of war and peace here on Earth, matching peaks of solar flares with the Franco-Prussian War of 1870 and the First World War of 1914.[33] Father J. S. Ricard, professor of astronomy and director of the University of Santa Clara's "Western Observatory," appreciated the "Russian

Professor's daring conclusions." He found Chizhevskii's theories as possible support for his own take on the sun's likely influence upon weather patterns. He had devoted a career, and his own newsletter, the *Sunspot*, to advancing the thesis that disturbances on the surface of the sun influenced our lows and highs, the fallings and risings of barometric pressure. These were, for the discerning Jesuit father, purely physical effects, the natural confines within which we humans made our otherwise free moral choices.[34]

Chizhevskii stirred most interest in 1926, when he delivered a paper (in absentia) to the annual conference of the American Meteorological Society in Philadelphia, summarizing his views and predicting a three-year wave of sunspot crises here on our planet. This was actually not a bad correspondence at all, if a bit delayed, given what was about to come: the Great Depression in the United States and the Stalin revolution in the USSR. Chizhevskii's correspondences, after all, did sometimes make sense and did sometimes hit their marks. Yet Harlan Stetson noted that they were always more provocative than conclusive, infrequent rather than universal, studious but not all that scientific. The sociologist Pitirim Sorokin also devoted considerable argument (in his classic survey *Contemporary Sociological Theories*) to denying these theories as unproven, a silly if modern-sounding astrology. The disbelieving audience of weathermen at the Philadelphia conference shared this commonsense conclusion. Chizhevskii had simply "gone too far."[35]

Russians were no strangers to these brands of determinism. A century of French and American travel accounts and popular histories had already taught several generations of readers the stereotype of a Russia imprisoned in its own extreme climate and geography. The cold and harsh winters, the short summers, the confining forests and expanses of steppe—all had turned Russians into strange human hybrids, half-indolent and half-frenetic, partly provincial and partly messianic.[36] Chizhevskii's genius was to go global, to find the ultimate determinism, an explanation for all of human nature and behavior in the stars, or at least one of them, the sun.

Americans were no strangers to such determinism, even of Chizhevskii's rather eccentric kind. He had an unlikely partner in

THE ORIGINS AND ENDS OF LIFE ON EARTH

one of America's elder statesmen, none other than Henry Adams, formerly professor of history at Harvard University and more recently president of the American Historical Association. By around 1910, well before Chizhevskii (whom he never met or read), Adams had discovered his own astronomical model of historical change, what he called the "Law of Phase in History," a mathematical calculation predicting that history would next break around 1917, when either America or Russia would experience some measure of either "disintegration" or "acceleration."[37] Like Chizhevskii, Adams flirted with the notion of cyclical history, what he compared to the comings and goings of comets, always predictable in their perihelion and aphelion. He recognized cycles of acceleration and disintegration, of concentration and dissolution, at work in human history—eternal returns such as the cycles of energy and entropy at work in the natural world. Humanity was bound to fall at times. Yet Adams ultimately sided with a finely calibrated notion of historical progress. "Man alone enjoys the supernatural power of consciously reversing nature's process, by raising her dissipated energies, including his own, to higher intensities." Human "thought" had the capacity to overcome even the second law of thermodynamics (on the degradation of energy into entropy), to seize full control over the flow of energy and arrest its dissolution. If human thought was like a comet, it was more characteristic of a comet's "sharp curve" and "excessive speed," marks of its parabola through outer space.

Henry Adams thereby proposed a radical cosmism, one worthy of William Winwood Reade and Richard Maurice Bucke or even of Nikolai Fedorov and Konstantin Tsiolkovskii. His "law of phases" meant that humanity was bound to experience revolutionary leaps, surges even "more astonishing than the explosion of rockets." These were leaps from quantity to quality, from old forms to new. He ultimately placed his hopes in acceleration, not degradation. Thanks to the "projection of mind in nature," humanity could force a change in history's "direction." For "if man should continue to set free the infinite forces of nature, and attain the control of cosmic forces on a cosmic scale, the consequences may be as surprising as the change of water to vapor, of the worm to the butterfly, of radium to electrons.

At a given volume and velocity, the forces that are concentrated on his head must act." In other words, Newton's third law of motion and the Tsiolkovskii equation applied to human history as much as to rocket science. The human form itself, as mind over matter, was like a rocket. Humanity alone was the bridge between Earth and cosmos, plotted mathematically.

According to Adams's "scientific" law of the phases of history, "the average motion of one phase is the square of that which precedes it." So, the "Mechanical Phase" in history lasted three hundred years, between 1600 and 1900. The "Electric Phase" lasted roughly seventeen, years from 1900 to 1917. The next "Ethereal Phase," logic dictated, would last only about four years, roughly to 1925. With some fine-tuning of the timeline, it might even last as far as 2025. It all added up to a logarithmic, exponential timeline, the vertical slope of a timeline graph, history as ever-rising parabola. And we were its physical and spiritual passengers.[38]

Adams's ascending line of historical progress, however eccentric it may have seemed to English-language readers before the First World War (he was not translated into Russian), took on something of a prophecy afterward. The war had stimulated aviation designs and techniques. In word and image publicists now found proof of Adams's historical parabola in the ever-rising achievements of airplanes, the speed and distance and altitude records that revealed indomitable evolution. Louis Houllevigue, popular science writer and professor at the University of Marseilles, plotted those records, just like Adams's parabola, as the ascending slope of an x-y graph, measuring the "dizzying progress" of aviation over the course of twenty years, especially its airspeed records—from Santos-Dumont's 41 kilometers (25 miles) per hour in 1906 to Florentin Bonnet's 448 kilometers (278 miles) per hour in 1924. Humanity was modestly approaching cosmic speeds, fulfilling Bergson's charge to struggle bravely against the forces of time, to ascend by astronautics even to outer space. Houllevigue measured scientific progress the same way, as a gently bending S curve on the same x-y plane, with Europe at the center of its most vertical ascent, a mark of its "most rapid progress" and advancement.[39]

THE ORIGINS AND ENDS OF LIFE ON EARTH

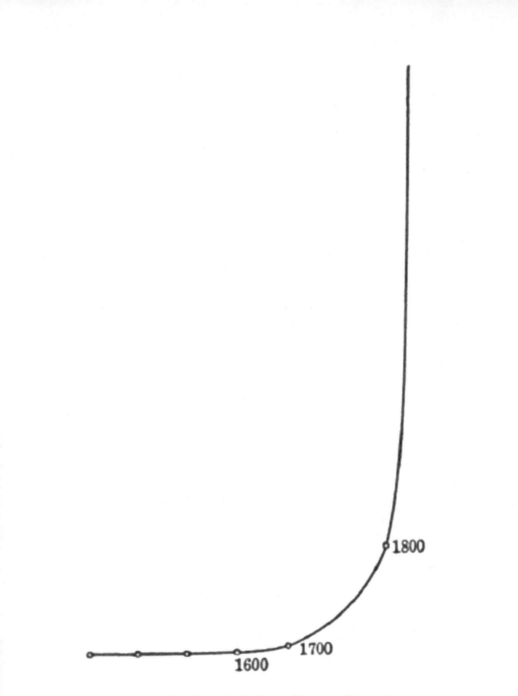

Fig. 15. Henry Adams's parabolic "Law of Progress." From Henry
Adams, *The Degradation of the Democratic Dogma*
(New York: Macmillan, 1920), 292.

We can also detect these principles of evolutionary ascent in art and graphic design, pictures that contrasted our humble evolutionary origins with our human mastery of the technologies of parabolic ascent. Take, for example, Aleksandr Rodchenko's cover for the avant-garde journal *LEF* in 1923, with an ape pointing its arrow upward toward a Russian biplane. Or take Hugo Gernsback's design for the title page of his new magazine, *Science Wonder Quarterly*, in 1930, showing a primitive caveman framing the bottom, the sloping arc of a space rocket framing the top of the page, with all of the achievements of natural evolution and historical progress in between. Or take Friedrich Mader's novel, *Distant Worlds* (1922), whose story and front cover prominently displayed both the chimpanzees who were part of the spaceflight crew and the comets streaming through the background of outer space.[40] The parabola reaching through outer space came to represent humanity's conquest over natural evolution itself.

Soviet-Russian commentators shared this sensibility about scientific-technological progress, with one caveat. The laws of Marxian historical determinism meant that communism would inherit the artifacts of material progress because politically it was headed "forward and upward," while capitalism was moving "backward and downward." Capitalism was like the disposable lower stage of a multistage rocket: spent.[41] But otherwise the law of constant human ascent applied. High-altitude airplanes and dirigibles were only the latest artifacts, after steam engines and railroads and the telegraph, proving the human capacity to subdue nature's limitations upon us, to maintain ever-improving forward progress. "Having now conquered the air and the force of gravity," said one popular science article, "we will come to master the realm of space itself. Forsaking the tight boundaries of the aerial ocean, the ships of the future will raise a free humanity to whole new worlds, to the stars, glistening in the bosom of the cosmos."[42]

Life and Death on the Planet

Soviet publicists and academics were attuned to these cosmic themes, if with something more of a pessimistic edge. Both Bogdanov's *Red Star* and Zamiatin's *We* had forewarned of the coming death of the

THE ORIGINS AND ENDS OF LIFE ON EARTH

sun and its planets. The Society for the Study of Interplanetary Travel held lectures and debates on the "fate of the earth," disaster by fire or by ice, featuring the rocket as humanity's best salvation.[43] F. Davydov, science and technology editor at *Izvestiia* and a rocketry enthusiast, once attributed a series of natural disasters to solar activity and cosmic dust: floods in Senegal, Nigeria, France, Germany, and Russia; unseasonably cold and wet summers in Leningrad and Moscow; the St. Lawrence Seaway and Guadalquivir River overflowing their banks; devastating typhoons in Formosa; killer tornadoes in Ohio.[44] Some in the European media blamed all of this on Mars, what with the approaching opposition in 1924. The Russian astronomer V. V. Sharonov saw in Mars nothing more than an older, dying version of Earth, a vision of our mortal future.[45]

These dire predictions were matched by threats of environmental catastrophe from within our planet itself. For several decades, ever since 1908, when Theodore Roosevelt had called the special Conference of Governors on Natural Resources at the White House, scientists and publicists had been warning of the forthcoming exhaustion of coal and oil resources worldwide. Earth was in peril from the Industrial Revolution. Only science could save us, by conserving resources and by tapping into solar and other new energies.[46] The First World War, spur to all kinds of intense industrial developments, had only worsened the problems. The West's most important "capital"—energy—was being depleted. Civilization, with all its recent mechanical achievements, was under threat.[47] For the new Soviet regime the problem took on class themes. Capitalism was robbing the globe of its natural wealth. Communism was being disinherited. The planet might soon be bare of key natural resources. B. P. Veinberg, the leading Russian authority on the issue, working from European and American models, focused his solutions upon the six "coals": the "red coal" of backbreaking animal and human labor; the "green coal" of plant life; the "blue coal" of water power; the "white coal" of air and wind power; the "black coal" of carbon resources (coal and gas and oil); and the "gold coal" of solar power. For Veinberg all human progress depended on our mechanical "power" to master and the planet's energy resources, especially those from the sun.[48]

V. P. Glushko, future builder of Soviet "Soiuz" rocket engines, joined the debate while he was a student at the Physics and Mathematics Faculty of Leningrad State University. As he wrote, humanity amounted to but a "small colony on a tiny planet lost in the limitless ocean" of the cosmos. Our long-term answer to the deficit of planetary energy was to travel beyond it by rocket, "to colonize celestial worlds, to organize their natural resources for the elders of earth." This would all begin, he predicted, with a "miniature artificial moon" to observe our own planet and those planets beyond.[49] Such apocalyptic fears, joined to utopian optimism, ran high in the West too. "Earth is doomed to extinction," wrote the engineer and rocket enthusiast Waldemar Kaempffert, from the *New York Times*. Rocketry was the only reasonable if still somewhat impractical means to escape, to colonize the friendlier planets and save humanity—"and let the Earth drift as it will an abandoned planetary wreck of its former self."[50]

Mainstream science, through the new discipline of geochemistry, also saw our own world as a fragile and mortal refuge. After a brief exile in France, V. I. Vernadskii returned to the USSR in 1926, the same year that saw the publication of the Russian version of his masterpiece *The Biosphere*. This term was already in wide circulation, inspired by the work of Edward Suess, the Austrian geologist whose *The Face of the Earth* (1883) had introduced "the biosphere," imagining the planet as if an alien being was approaching it "from outer space," peering through the veils of the clouds to discover the lacework detail of nature and culture on the thin envelope of a livable planet.[51] Vernadskii defined the earth in such integral terms: as a spherical world within the solar system, graced by its life-providing rocks, fauna, animals, humans, and atmospheres. Such was the "cosmic or common organism" of the biosphere. Vernadskii painted a canvas of the delicate colors and lines, shapes and forms, natures and cultures, which make our planet so unique. He, too, saw "the face of the Earth viewed from celestial space." He also imparted to the biosphere a unique spiritual force: that envelope or layer of plant and animal life, of atmosphere and ground, that captured the energy of the sun and gave life to an otherwise dead planet.[52] Human history was a chapter in the natural history of the living earth.

Vernadskii's devotion to eternal "life," to the intelligent design of "Creation," made him vulnerable to official Soviet ideological criticism, which labeled his writings as "vitalism," rent by religiosity and mysticism.[53] Yet he also entertained a Prometheanism that was consonant with Soviet values (and with Henry Adams's vision as well). "Man alone violates the established order," he wrote. We enjoy unique powers and promises. "It is man who ascends to the greatest heights of the stratosphere, unwittingly taking with him the forms of life that accompany his body or his products."[54] We were destined to venture into cosmic space, taking part of the biosphere with us. This approach mirrored what orthodox Marxists were also saying about humanity and nature. Some of Vernadskii's words, for example, were but an echo from Friedrich Engels: "Man alone has succeeded in impressing his stamp on nature, not only by shifting the plant and animal world from one place to another, but also by so altering the aspect and climate of his dwelling place, and even the plants and animals themselves, that the consequences of his activity can disappear only with the general extinction of the terrestrial globe." A. E. Fersman, one of Vernadskii's most successful students (and a famous Soviet academician), similarly wrote about the living earth as united with the chemical and mineral fabric of the "surrounding cosmos," about the human being as the "greatest of geochemical agents."[55]

M. Ia. Lapirov-Skoblo, patron of early Soviet rocketry, expressed this exaggerated humanism with a Trotskyite fervor, the power of Russian communism to inherit history's greatest achievements and to leap even farther forward, to "create a superman—a true tsar over nature and creator of a new and joyous life." Or as he phrased it in thrilling slogan form, "We shall grasp all! We shall master all! We shall rebuild all!"[56] A leading Soviet astronomer, V. A. Kostitsyn, elaborated on just what this meant. The human being would surely become the ultimate "creator and conqueror" by overcoming gravity and launching out into space by rocket at the parabolic speed of just over eleven kilometers per second. Following Oberth and Glushko, Kostitsyn also predicted that satellites would soon photograph and communicate with the earth and that probes would even explore the planets.[57]

Tsiolkovskii, too, began broaching these very same themes in his *Monism of the Universe* (1925), what he later considered as one of his most important theoretical contributions to science. To Vernadskii's micro-approach about planet Earth, he answered with a macro-theory about the material unity of the whole cosmos. Following Ernst Haeckel's materialism, Tsiolkovskii proposed that all matter in the universe was joined by natural evolution, part of a grand mechanical design. Yet he also affirmed that all atoms (inorganic and organic) were sensitive and alive. He painted a bold picture of the generation and evolution of life toward ultimate fulfillment and perfection, what he called "eternal joy of every atom."[58] As Michael Hagermeister has argued, this project demanded a coldhearted eugenics to cleanse humanity of its weak, all with the aim of perfecting the human race and preparing it for immortality in the pure and spiritual medium of outer space. That was our trajectory: to become whole new living planets orbiting around the sun. As Tsiolkovskii once wrote to Rynin about his book, "I want to comfort people about the unbroken and infinite chain of life and happiness." Or as he wrote in a letter to a children's engineering brigade in 1934, shortly before his death, "We are all matter, part of the immortal universe and therefore like it also eternal."[59]

This kind of metaphysical take on immortality was already part of a wider public conversation in the 1920s. Several of the world's leading scientists believed that an era of human longevity was at hand, largely based on the promises of Alexis Carrell's "immortal" cell. In Germany, Max Hartmann had also allegedly discovered a single-celled organism that could be kept alive indefinitely. Jerry Wodsedalek at the University of Idaho and C. M. Child of the University of Chicago were able to arrest and even reverse the aging process in insects and flatworms.[60] These experiments were fine enough for laboratory science, but what about reinvigorating and rejuvenating the actual living human body? Hormonal therapy was the key. Scientists in Germany and the United States predicted, for example, that insulin and other enzymes might prolong our lives up to even a thousand years. From Paris, Sergei Voronoff grafted parts of chimpanzee testicles onto his elderly male subjects, soon making exagger-

THE ORIGINS AND ENDS OF LIFE ON EARTH

ated claims: they were sickly and exhausted before, lively and restored afterward. No matter that the grafts probably failed after a few short days or that Voronoff's records lacked precision and rigor. The public was enthusiastic. Rejuvenation therapies offered the promise of longer and happier lives.[61]

This optimism reached into the prognostications of public health experts and sociologists. In his study *The Biology of Death* (1922) Raymond Pearl of Johns Hopkins University described a set of dramatic parabolic curves for the population growth of the world's developed countries. They all took the telltale shape of gently rising S curves, sloping slightly at first, then radically at the center, representing the effects on human populations of better science, better living conditions, better medicine. Like Henry Adams, he compared these curves to the very orbital lines that comets made in the heavens. Demographers, like astronomers, drew them from the insights of differential calculus. They represented the integral truths about orbital curves and "population orbits," that "life itself is inherently continuous," that death was not unconquerable and inevitable. For modern society to sustain them, it simply needed to master human biology and evolution from within, technology and the natural environment from without. Irving Fisher, professor of economics at Yale University, even proposed the "revolutionary" notion that we give up the whole idea of a "natural death" or "life limit," in place of the idea that "all death is accidental." The rationale was in the ever-accelerating trajectory of human history, which moved with the same "upward sweep" as the curves of higher life expectancy. We had learned to make tools, move with greater and greater speeds, kill our enemies at a distance, and invent all kinds of machines for life and labor. Medical discoveries and applications followed the same trends too, with vitamins, antiseptics, vaccines, hormone therapy, pharmaceuticals, and the latest "immortal cells." There seemed no limits to these cures for human mortality.[62]

A sure sign of its potential, this optimism even reached into actuary tables of the American insurance industry. Statistics proved that the conquest of disease and dirt by modern medicine and by public hygiene was lowering the mortality rate and instances of early death. The work of the Life Extension Institute and the Metropolitan Life Insurance Company was proving that longer life could turn a profit, in the form of healthier clients and longer premiums. Hornell Hart of Bryn Mawr announced a "parabolic law of progress," based on the "radical upward sweep of the curve" along "the plane of life expectancy." He foresaw "dramatic "accelerating increases in man's power to control his environment" and a parallel acceleration of the human life span by the year 2000, when most Americans would live to over one hundred years old and many of their children up to two hundred.[63]

Visions of Immortality in Outer Space

All of this publicity created quite a media stir in the USSR during the 1920s. After nearly a decade of war and revolution, deprivation and disease, the Russian reading publics were ready for some hope in life and longevity. Rejuvenation therapies were also appealing to the Bolshevik Party and state elites, given the exhausting scope and pace of their political work. The business of revolution and civil war, terror and communist-style governance was hard. Sociological studies of the day showed that even young people were suffering from nervous diseases and physical ailments—depression, ulcers, and high blood pressure—associated with their duties. Medical and hormonal remedies were essential to the life of the revolution.[64] In these contexts, given its simplicity and ease, Steinach's vaso-ligature operation spread throughout the country; many hundreds were performed in clinics and hospitals over these years. Voronoff's operation, given its complexity and the shortage of monkey glands, was much less in vogue, but most of his works were translated and celebrated for their application to the improvement of farm animal stocks and human beings. Both methods were part of the growing movement in Soviet eugenics.[65]

Soviet Russia also had its own native "rejuvenation" techniques from which to draw. N. P. Kravkov was one among the first Soviet recipients of the Lenin Prize, awarded for his work in the reanimation of limbs and in hormonal therapy. His testosterone injections—to improve the human physique and stamina—said one

THE ORIGINS AND ENDS OF LIFE ON EARTH

leading Soviet eugenicist, was a unique "Soviet" contribution to the science.[66] Bakhmet'ev's anabiosis remained an alluring topic through the 1920s. For young readers it was hailed as a fantasy becoming fact, with actual stories of bats or bees or domestic farm animals being revived after Bakhmet'ev's cryogenic hibernation. Science had finally answered sacred Scripture's false stories about reviving a dead Lazarus, reported one journalist.[67] By 1924, of course, all of these possibilities appeared against the backdrop of V. I. Lenin's dead body, resting in his public tomb. One definition of anabiosis, for example, was eerily reminiscent of the Kremlin's mausoleum scene: a condition in which the body "takes on the appearance of a corpse, though death has not yet taken hold. The organism is in a state of potential life, and with the coming of favorable conditions, life will return, the body will revive."[68] In these terms Lenin's very corpse, even if preserved in its dead flesh, must have become for informed readers an emblem for Soviet promises about the prolongation and rejuvenation and reanimation of life.

The USSR's commitment to these native sons continued all the way into the 1950s, for they were Bolshevik-style dreamers who were translating fantasy into reality.[69] The state also promoted a series of successors, innovators in the techniques of rejuvenation. Take the scientist Aleksei Zamkov, who prepared injections of "gravidan," made out of the urine of pregnant women, meant to restore youthful energy and cure diseases, a remedy for the exhausting pace of workers in factories and of peasants on collective farms (and based in part on the discoveries of Bernhard Zondek in the United States). Or note the amazing case of S. S. Briukhonenko, who worked on the reanimation of dogs' heads and came to test his methods on human body parts (like Alexis Carrell in the United States). *Pravda* hailed his work as promising us all the chance of a "second life."[70] Some of the Soviet cures came west, becoming health fads both in the USSR and the United States for a time. A. A. Bogomolets's longevity serum, made from an animal's blood, human cadaver spleen, and bone marrow, promised to cure diseases, heal wounds, and prolong life by stimulating connective tissues. Olga Lepeshinskaia's studies of the generation and regeneration of cells and her baking soda baths and enemas promised to achieve the same, possibly extending the human life span to 150 years. Both were ultimately proven meritless, though Bogomolets won the Lenin Prize, Lepeshinskaia the Stalin Prize, along the way.[71]

These developments built a momentum of expectation, a renewed confidence in the possibilities of improving human life. Some of Soviet Russia's leading scholars hinted in their public works that humanity was approaching a real conquest over death, that the future might very well hold a kind of immortality for us: partly the gift of medical science yet also partly the gift of space travel. Discerning fans of popular science found these very issues woven into the media forums of magazines and lecture circuits: reaching for immortality and reaching for the planets. Popular science was teaching the lesson that we humans were bound to pierce the envelopes of both eternity and infinity. Boris Pilniak perfectly united these themes in his novel dedicated to the Stalinist revolution in industry and its "great transformation" of nature, all by way of a new calculus and geometry of "parabolas, hyperbolas, ellipses." He magnified the story with appeals about the science of "human longevity" (Mechnikov and Steinach) and about communicating with Mars, sending rockets into space, and building "interplanetary stations." V. V. Valiusinskii set the themes into a captivating story about the "five immortals," recipients of a life-renewing brain transplant that enabled them to see a magnificent future world of antigravitational energy and aerial floating cities; airplanes, aerial saucers, and Tsiolkovskii's interplanetary "rocket aerons"; and even mass colonization and terra-forming of the moon.[72]

Voices of moderation did prevail against the media craze for the early rejuvenation therapies of the 1920s, critiquing them as exaggerated and unproven, countering that natural death was unavoidable and even necessary for human evolution. One well-known medical doctor and researcher, G.V. Shor, coined the term *thanatology* ("the science of death," originally from Il'ia Mechnikov) in order to transform pathology from the simple study and prevention of diseases into the more complex study of death in all of its traumatic, physiological, and social dimensions. The whole point of thanatology was to alleviate disease and avoid death as long as possible. All revitalization and rejuvenation techniques were only temporary. Death is the necessary "price" we human beings pay to achieve higher stages of evolution. "At a certain age, the human being must die." Such was the "golden rule" of life. The Marxist biologist A. V. Nemilov concurred. We are only ever immortal in our legacies: biologically in our children and culturally in our communities. Individual immortality and sexual rejuvenation were chimeras. "Everything that lives," he wrote, "must also die." We are like leaves on a large tree. "The leaves fall and decompose, but the tree remains. So it is that individual persons die, but the human race lives on." Or as he later argued, life is dialectical: its wheel only runs forward as a spiral of progress. The life of the individual gives way to the advancement of the species just as capitalism gives way to socialism.[73]

No matter how fantastic or unproven, the promises of human revitalization captivated reading publics as either academic science or news stories or even as imaginative fiction. Writers were especially keen on marrying the promises of rejuvenation to spaceflight. Bakhmet'ev's anabiosis was a favorite narrative hook for Soviet writers. Aleksei Tolstoi threaded it into one of his stories about the year 2024, a future of "complete rejuvenation" by way of chemical therapies, monkey glands, magnetism, and cryogenics, including urban electrification, underground cities, social freedoms, and aerial mastery.[74] The popular fiction writer A. Beliaev crafted a short story, "Neither Dead nor Alive," expressly dedicated to Bakhmet'ev, one more in a long line of genius "Russian inventors" (like Tsiolkovskii) whose discoveries were stolen by the West but later perfected by Soviet Russia through cryogenics, immortality, and space travel. The refrigeration engineer N. S. Komarov took Bakhmet'ev's ideal to even greater lengths with his story *Cold Town* (1927), set in the twenty-second century of insufferable high temperatures and drought, an era of a long global heat wave. His was a society of fantastic achievements: a fully "aerial" civilization, with television (the projection of words and images at a distance), psychic advertising, rail and refrigerated transport at 550 kilometers (342 miles) per hour, and cooling costumes. But the greatest achievement of all was inspired by Bakhmet'ev's extreme cold technologies. The American scientist Professor Wilson applied anabiosis to temporarily freeze human beings at various stages through their life to save on dwindling food resources. Most dramatically, the team of an American engineer, "Tom Hide" (*Tom Khad*), and Russian engineer Komov saved the day with their massive refrigeration units, this to enable a whole city of some ten million people, "Cold Town" (*Kolton*), to survive the global heat. "Instead of a symbol of darkness and death, cold became the foundation of humanity's greatest hopes in the struggle for existence." Refrigeration saved civilization.[75]

From Western Europe, Freidrich Freksa's *Druso: The Stolen World of Human Beings* (1931) entertained the plotline of a future Earth governed by a regime of eugenics and cryogenic anabiosis, eventually conquered by insect-aliens from the planet Druso, traveling through the universe as a spacecraft all its own. An alliance of reanimated humans, Nordic warriors, and remnants from the lost civilization of Atlantis finally defeats the bugs. Neil R. Jones's classic story "The Jameson Satellite" (1931) featured the enterprising Professor Jameson, launched into space by rocket to sleep in cold storage for forty million years, only to be awoken and re-outfitted with a new mechanical body (and his old brain) by the strange race of "Zoromes."[76]

Rejuvenation therapies were another favorite plot theme between West and East. Marie Corelli, author of an early occult space novel, *A Romance of Two Worlds* (1886), applied them in *The Young Diana* (1918), a popular story about the transformation of the aging Miss Diana May into a youthful goddess, a new Diana worthy of the stars. The creation of a Russian mad scientist (Feodor Demetrius), she was an "ethereal" spirit remade by electrical and solar energy, representing humanity's "own voluntary uplifting" and the final victory over the forces of "chaos" and darkness by the forces of "cosmos" and light. Or as Sally Hovey put it in her story, rejuvenation science expressed the powerful "surge within us . . . bearing us onward to progressively better things."[77] Noelle Roger's *The New Adam* (1924), which was published in both Russian and English translations, combined a series of endocrine grafts in the brain in order to reinvigorate and adapt the human being to the frenzied pace of modern technology.

THE ORIGINS AND ENDS OF LIFE ON EARTH

The "new Adam" achieves an "accelerated intelligence," inventing death rays, wireless telephones, globe-spanning airplanes, and even "fantastic flights through space."[78]

Russian writers published this kind of fashionable literature as well. Several early Soviet ideological utopias entertained these themes, set in future technocratic states of full prosperity and well-being, efficient city life, sophisticated global communications and clean energies. Each saw human beings master molecular biology and rejuvenation therapies to prolong human life spans to hundreds of years. Each saw humanity also conquer space. Iakov Okunev's *The Coming World* (1923) sent his time and space travelers two hundred years into the future, with an authoritative footnote and postscript that this was not pure fantasy but realistic possibility. In V. D. Nikol'skii's *In a Thousand Years* (1927) dirigible rockets fly over gridded cities of elevated superhighways. People are in constant motion, by wings and jet planes in the air, by rockets and orbital stations in outer space, new human-made comets racing through the heavens. The crowning achievement is an international space station, "a small planet" and new "satellite" (*sputnik*) of Earth. In Yan Larri's *Land of the Happy* (1931) people become "winged Icaruses," united in a grandiose project to build "starships" to conquer the moon and proceed to the "colonization of the planets." Spaceships trace "fiery paths" through the skies, like meteors. The hero builds a rocket craft in the designs of Tsiolkovskii, Goddard, and Oberth, with the ultimate aim of reaching human "immortality" in outer space.[79] Here were, in sum, the perfect literary models of Earth as a living planet and we the superior beings upon it, about to become a "rocket" planet all our own.

Perhaps most famously, Aldous Huxley's *Brave New World* (1932) entertained a future society of rejuvenation science and space travel. In his imaginative scenario a variety of hormone therapies (by chewing gum or injections) controlled human emotions, urges, and general health. Society manipulated the growth of laboratory embryos to define gender, talents, and intelligence. This endeavor included the breeding of superior "rocket-plane engineers," adapted to live and work in the "topsy-turvydom" of rocket flight. In the story the elite "alphas" (with names like Marx and Lenina), a caste of biologically engineered automatons governing a streamlined civilization of straight lines and calculus, fly "Red Rockets" into the heights. Huxley dramatically joined the reflex arc in the human body to the parabolic arc of the rocket in flight. Soviet censors even translated several chapters of the book, critiquing its eroticism and pessimism but recognizing its celebration of modern science.[80]

In the United States these rather strange approaches to science fiction mirrored, at least in the person of Charles A. Lindbergh, some of the potentials of science fact. Lindbergh envisioned his most significant flying experiences, from his first exhilarating flights to his nonstop transatlantic flight from New York to Paris, as studies in immortality. Flight offered what he called a "god's-eye view" of human life. In words reminiscent of Khlebnikov and Bogdanov, Lindbergh wrote that "aviation showed what miracles man could accomplish. If he could learn to fly on wings, which was once considered impossible, why could he not learn to live forever?"[81] This proposition inspired Lindbergh's two most significant professional collaborations in the 1930s: first with Robert Goddard and his rocket experiments; second with Alexis Carrell and his experimental medicine (cell animation and organ transplants). Rockets were not just a practical means of overcoming the limits of wings and propellers but a utopian means of achieving interplanetary and interstellar travel. Laboratory experiments with cell rejuvenation and repair meant eventually preserving human bodies, perhaps in frozen states, for future time. Together, rockets and rejuvenation constituted veritable "revolutions" in human history.[82]

"Think of ice-stiff human beings hurtling, like meteors, through space, unconscious yet alive," wrote Lindbergh, "products of earthly evolutionary epochs emigrating to universal vastness." With the mastery of science, humans could refine the human body and mind for immortality, this in order to colonize the planets and stars, to "become a universal creature piercing through space like a beam of light."[83] The singular human being, in union with the plural species, was like a rocket. "I tense with velocity, brace in turmoil," Lindbergh wrote, speeding through space and collapsing time. Thus, Lindbergh informed his practical work with Goddard and Carrell with a mystical worldview, an American cosmism that saw individual human mortality as part of a larger circle of species immortality, part of a "life stream" of "molecular and atomic replacement." As he philosophized, "I am life and I am matter, mortal and immortal. I am one and many—myself and humanity in flux . . . passing through the ether between satellites and stars." Space travel was at one with eternal life.[84] America, if only gradually and posthumously, eventually found its interplanetarism and immortalism, its Konstantin Tsiolkovskii, in the aviation hero Charles A. Lindbergh.

This rather exotic union of values, between the infinite and the eternal, took its most visible public shape in the USSR in 1927, the very same year that Lindbergh flew across the Atlantic, at the First World Exhibition of Interplanetary Machines and Apparatuses (yes, another Soviet first), held in Moscow to celebrate the tenth anniversary of the Bolshevik Revolution. The exhibition had its origins in Ukraine, just as Moscow's Society for the Study of Interplanetary Travel was retreating from the public scene. Several leading Kiev scientists had partnered with a small group of enthusiasts to promote spaceflight issues. They were gathered around A. I. Fedorov and G. A. Polevoi, in the Sector for the Popularization of the Problems of Cosmic Navigation, or "Star Flight," part of the all-union Association of Inventors for Inventors. In 1927, riding a wave of popular success, Fedorov and Polevoi brought their designs and exhibits to Moscow.[85] As unabashed cosmists and devotees of Nikolai Fedorov and Konstantin Tsiolkovskii, their motto raised a call "for interplanetary flights." The group ran the exhibition, with the funding and logistical support of the Moscow State Political-Education Office and with the help of young engineers from the Moscow Higher Technical School. Located on one of Moscow's most fashionable streets, at #68 Tverskaia, adjacent to a popular dining hall, the exhibition attracted large crowds, up to twelve thousand visitors in all, including members of Moscow's cultural elite (the poets Maiakovskii and Aseev), intellectuals and workers, and even the militia officers policing the site.[86]

The hall encompassed a number of small exhibits, filled with the models and diagrams of Tsiolkovskii, Ganswidt, Esnault-Pelterie, Goddard, Oberth, and Valier, among others. At its entrance a huge mural displayed human beings exploring a moon landscape, with the earth rising on the horizon; another showed the Martian canals amid Tolstoi's kaleidoscope of colors. Fedorov displayed his own space rocket, driven by electrochemical and atomic power to reach star speeds of twenty-five kilometers (sixteen miles) per second; Polevoi featured his own designs for space suits and space stations. The whole spirit of the exhibit presumed the total human conquest of nature, guided by the values of speed and ascent, the rocket as the fulfillment of trains and skyscrapers, reaching into outer space, a realm without height or distance, without even day and night.[87]

Although remarkably international, Fedorov's followers drew most of their inspiration from within: from native genius, from the font of Russian cosmism. Among the organizers was a core of firebrands who proposed to marry the revolutionary character of rocket power with a whole new language culture—none other than V. L. Gordin's international language AO. One of its speakers, Olga Viktorievna Kholoptseva, renamed herself "efofbi," aka "citizen of the universe" in the universal language of AO. The AO-ists were even given a stand at the exhibition. Tsiolkovskii, once again, had inspired them with his own sympathy for a common world language, the means to a truer "unity and brotherhood of all peoples."[88] They recognized him in turn with several noble titles: patron of "all-inventiveness," their own self-proclaimed movement to unite all "inventors of the whole earth" and reshape the human future. In strange echoes of Camille Flammarion's and Vera Kryzhanovskaia's spiritualism, he became "father of cosmopolism" and the number one "citizen of the universe," a "true fighter for monism."[89]

The exhibition was held at a precipitous moment. Esnault-Pelterie was active in France. The Americans had yet to prove their rockets in practice. The German rocket societies and pioneers were just beginning to form. Fedorov gave them space at the exhibition, all rivals for the moon's affections. In turn the Western media paid due attention to him. Fedorov, so one zany story went, was even planning a joint Russian-German trip to the moon, by way of Max Valier's giant rocket, something on the order of Tsander's project, applying Tsiolkovskii's vision of a greenhouse system for a renewable atmo-

THE ORIGINS AND ENDS OF LIFE ON EARTH

sphere and even involving the collaboration of a "Professor Robert H. Goddard of Clark University, Worcester, Mass." Goddard's "Moon machine" was finally in its construction phase, with a planned test flight for August 1927, the first in a series of such flights that, if successful, would turn the moon into a "terminus of a future line of aerobuses." The popular science writer Mary Proctor prominently reported the story. Said one professor from the United Kingdom in response to the whole strange scheme, with a perfect dose of traditional English common sense: "This foolish idea of shooting at the Moon, revived both in America and in Moscow, is an example of the absurd length to which vicious specialization will carry scientists working in thought-tight compartments."[90] British reason prevailed between the crazy projects of the West and East. Nevertheless, here was vivid proof that at least some of the great powers—the United States, Germany, and the USSR—were engaged in a race for rocket science.

PART THREE

The Rise of Rocket Science and the Soviet Union

8

The First Foundations of Astronautics

The Moscow First World Exhibition of Interplanetary Machines and Apparatuses, dedicated to the tenth anniversary of the Russian Revolution in 1927, closed a decade of remarkable approaches toward rocketry and spaceflight by Russian enthusiasts and the general public. But Russia could not maintain the momentum. Germany now eclipsed it. France set standards of achievement. America joined the competition in bold ways, often reported in the form of newspaper science. Goddard's prediction of a race for rockets was coming true.

At first the Germans appended rockets to cars. The automobile maker Fritz von Opel and popular science writer Max Valier began to test solid fuel rocket cars at the Avus Speedway in Berlin, reaching speeds of over 161 kilometers (100 miles) per hour with the Opel-Rak II in the spring of 1928. Their partnership virtually guaranteed newsworthiness, what with Opel's money and Valier's charisma. Valier had set out to turn what had been merely "spaceflight speculations" in the distant past or more advanced "rocket theory" under Hermann Oberth into a grand project of actual "rocket engineering." His slogan was "To actually do something is to realize its dream."[1] The primary objective was to introduce the rocket airplane, stunning the world with a transatlantic feat to equal Louis Bleriot's 1911 cross-channel flight. Valier relentlessly pursued this task, lobbying the Junkers firm for support and flooding the media with his proposals, centered on the dramatic images of his rocket: launched from Earth by a catapult ramp astride Berlin (filled with adoring, middle-class crowds); reaching for space, with a falling star in the background, two parabolas crossing in the night.[2]

Like a massive aerial bridge, it was meant to span Europe and America in one global leap. When the news became public, the credulous American ambassador sternly warned that any rockets flying over or landing at Manhattan would be under strict government controls, this to avoid any risks to American "life and property."[3] A *New York Times* editorial was kinder, predicting that in the near future, thanks to the rocket, "man vies with the meteors." One of its artists drew Valier's rocket plane into the famous *Scientific American* "stratosphere" chart: conquering Earth's orbit, with the arc of the Paris Gun ("Big Bertha") shell at lower center.[4]

The German Engineering of Spaceflight

In these contexts of rocket cars and transoceanic feats, the German spaceflight craze, a "popular fad" filled with "spectacular rocket stunts," peaked between 1928 and 1932. As Michael Neufeld has argued, it arose at the intersection of the Weimar infatuation with national pride, technological progress, and consumer culture.[5] Having lost the First World War, the Germans still had something to prove. They now upstaged their European and American rivals, not just with their Zeppelins and new all-metal Junker airplanes but with the rocket as well, helping to transform the world's obsession with horizontal speed into a craze for vertical flight.

A number of German inventors took up Valier's challenge with the first flights of rocket-powered airplanes. On 11 June 1928 Frederick Shtamer piloted his solid powder rocket glider, the flying "Duck," at the Wasserkuppe, Germany's national shrine to aviation in the Rhön Mountains. With the aid of an elastic band and catapult start, two engines flew the glider to some 1,500 meters (4,921 feet) in eighty seconds. From Osnabrück the experimenter Reinhold Tiling entered the media stage with his sleek, solid fuel rockets (made of aluminum and about two meters, or six feet, long), outfitted with unique vanes that unfolded into wings for a gentler glide back to land. In a much-publicized but never-confirmed flight on 15 April 1931, he claimed to reach 2,000-meter (6,562-foot) altitudes and over 1,126 kilometers

THE FIRST FOUNDATIONS OF ASTRONAUTICS

(700 miles) per hour speeds, though in a demonstration at Berlin's Templehof airport, one of his rockets nearly crashed into a crowd of spectators. From Austria, Fritz Schmiedl flew the first practical solid fuel mail rockets in early 1931, his "R-1" launching letters and post-cards just over 3 kilometers (2 miles) between the towns of Schöckel and Radegund (near Gratz). His special service (*Raketenflugpost Schmiedl*) soon introduced its own "flying rocket mail" stamps as well, imprinted with the alluring phrase "Flown by Test Rocket R-1."[6]

The premier amateur group in these years was the Society for Space Travel (hereafter Verein, from *Verein fur Raumschiffart*), active in Breslau and Berlin between 1927 and 1933.[7] The Verein mixed both the romantic and the real. It was, after all, a society for *space travel*, Oberth its inspiration. Members prominently displayed his various rocket models in exhibits at the central post office in downtown Berlin and at the entrance hall of one of their offices. Yet this was not some science fiction fantasy of impossible leaps. It was a practical and sequential project to build rocket motors and cars, rocket bicycles and sleds, rocket railroads and planes, and eventually pure rockets to launch human beings into the stratosphere, into Earth's orbit, and eventually to the moon.

The Verein's Rocket Flying Field (*Raketenflugplatz*), at Reinick-endorf just outside of Berlin, was its proving ground. Here its amateur engineers and technicians built the world's first successful test stands, launch gantries, concrete bunkers, and control rooms (not counting Goddard's modest Worcester site). Here they tested fuel mixtures and ignition techniques, fuel tank and engine designs for constant exhaust, stability and control measures, and even parachute returns. They had to craft metals light enough to reduce the mass of the rocket but also strong enough to endure the extreme cold of the liquid oxygen and hydrogen as well as the extreme heat of the exhaust. They experimented with regenerative cooling.

To sustained national and international acclaim, the Verein became the world's leading rocket society.[8] Among its notable achievements was the "Mirak" (minimum rocket), a project to build a rocket engine from its simplest parts, with test firings of ever-increasing times and thrusts between 1930 and 1931. From these initial probes the enterprising Johannes Winkler (an aircraft engineer at the Junkers company), joined by Rolf Engel, publicized the dramatic news of his 12 February and 14 March 1931 launchings at Dessau of Europe's first liquid fuel rocket, combining liquid oxygen and gasoline, to an altitude of over 600 meters (nearly 2,000 feet) and a 183-meter (600-foot) range.[9] The Verein's "Repulsor" test models were also successful, with about thirty launches of heavier liquid fuel rockets in 1931 and 1932 to 1.6-kilometer (1-mile) altitudes and nearly 5-kilometer (3-mile) distances. Thanks largely to the enterprising talents of Rudolf Nebel (a pilot and part-time engineer), the German military also began to watch and fund the group from its own new rocket base at Kummersdorf (1930), directed by Capt. Walter Dornberger and his superior, the colonel and professor Karl Becker. Visits were exchanged, some meager monies were passed to the Verein, and the military took note of several of its younger and more talented members, including Walter Reidel, Arthur Rudolph, and Wernher von Braun.[10]

Just as the Verein began to form, Oberth republished his magnum opus for a new postwar generation. Revised, lengthened, and retitled *Ways to Spaceflight* (1929), he offered an even more compelling set of proofs for his rocket theory, what he now figuratively called "cosmonautics" (*Kosmonautik*), the first such precise and formal use of the term in the scientific literature. It now entered the international scientific-technological lexicon.[11] Oberth thus helped to consolidate a whole new idiom of rocket science. The Americans and Russians soon followed suit with separate standard spaceflight terminologies of their own.[12]

Oberth's calculus remained largely unchanged. Only now he engaged in serious dialogue and critique with the recent works of his colleagues Valier and Hohmann, Hoeft and Noordung, and thanks to the translations and reviews of Aleksandr Shershevskii and Robert Lademann, even with the published works of Tsiolkovskii. Rocketry and spaceflight theories, he reaffirmed, were not fantasies. They were a true "science," tested and proven through its formal discursive practices. The rocket scientist was now becoming the rocket engineer (*Raketentechnik* or *Raketenkonstrukteur*). Humanity was about to "build machines" able to ascend beyond the atmosphere. We stood at the dawn of new era in human history, comparable to the revolutionary transformations brought on by the railroad and automobile.[13]

To his more precise mathematical work from 1923, Oberth now added a literary and even philosophical depth. He once again defined the crucial "parabolic velocity" of just over eleven kilometers per second necessary to leave orbit. But now he framed it within the rather elegant notion of "vertical ascent," with the rocket imagined as an arrow shot into space. "A body hurled away from the Earth at this velocity does not fall back; it describes a parabola whose second vertex lies at infinity."[14] He also envisioned a gradual approach to spaceflight, symbolized by his concept of "multiple-staged" rockets, which were to launch humanity by means of ever-progressing efficiencies, ensuring gradual achievement and progress, summarized as a "daring ladder to spaceflight." This ladder would eventually enable humanity to create a remarkable array of technologies: mail rockets, ballistic missiles, sounding rockets, stratospheric rockets, and rockets to orbit and even for interplanetary travel. This array was reflected in his models "A to E," applying various shapes, fuel combinations, and stages. They were to culminate with the building of an orbiting telescope, observation and communication satellites, solar arrays producing heat and energy for humanity, and inhabited space stations as miniature Earths.[15]

Oberth divided his work into two parts: the mathematical and the literary, highlighting the difficult calculations for the professional "specialist," leaving the rest for the public "layman." His democratic objective was to reach both audiences. But he also concluded on an elitist, technocratic note, rallying against Oswald Spengler's prophecy of doom and "decline" for Western civilization, affirming his faith that new cadres of specialists and experts would, through vast engineering feats extending into the biological sciences, vastly improve human life and social conditions.[16] Rockets were more than just machines; they were the means for the revitalization of the human race.

Oberth's classic has enjoyed a signal place in the history.[17] More than anything Tsiolkovskii or Esnault-Pelterie or Goddard ever wrote, it served as a catalyst for the influential German amateur groups out of which came, by one influence or another, the v-2 ballistic missile of the Second World War. In his wake the German enthusiasts celebrated rocketry with such slogans as "The Space Rocket Belongs to the Future" and "Upward into Space!" Or as Rudolf Nebel wrote in verse, "We want to fly higher, we want to fly farther, on such a rocket flight." Willy Ley boldly proposed that humanity's "reign" would soon spread to the near and far planets, opening a whole "new epoch in World History." Life in its chemical and biological facts was universal. Humanity was a favored race of higher beings, destined to master life elsewhere just as we had already mastered life here on Earth.[18] From the United States *Popular Mechanics* celebrated the Oberth rocket's amazing parabolic speeds. Thanks to it and to Goddard's contributions, humanity was immersed in a literal "race to explore space" and very well on the verge of its "conquest." The world was becoming "rocket-conscious." "Man's valiant struggle to conquer his universe seems now on the eve of another epic victory."[19]

In articles, brochures, and books Verein members and supporters also familiarized the reading market with the basics of rocket theory and interplanetary travel, what they honestly called the "rocket problem" (*Raketenproblem*). Valier and Ley now reconfigured their earlier works on space travel. What were once rather fanciful imaginings became more realistic possibilities.[20] Not simply a fad or craze, the movement proposed a most serious set of proofs, both mathematical and literal, to confirm the potentials of space travel. Several academic critics raised objections. But in the end the weight of argument fell in favor of the advocates of liquid fuel rocketry and space travel. Their works had a home in the Verein's journal, the *Rocket*, which was designed to both popularize and educate rocketry and spaceflight issues, filled with the radical new terms of "space travel" (*Raumschiffart*). But thanks to Verein publicists and sympathetic journalists, these issues went mainstream as well, disseminated into professional engineering magazines and academic journals.[21]

Aleksandr Shershevskii's book *The Rocket for Flights and Voyages* (1929) is a case in point; it was released by one of Germany's top publishers of engineering and aviation texts. A Russian expatriate and aviation writer (and expert in ballistics), Shershevskii devoted his mathematical talents to a precise study of the equations, ratios,

THE FIRST FOUNDATIONS OF ASTRONAUTICS

fuels, and trajectories of the liquid fuel rocket. Human expertise had transformed that very machine, he proposed, into a kind of "living metal," an invention without precedence in human history, the key to exploring outer space in the form of the "spaceship" reaching the parabolic velocity of some eleven kilometers a second. "By science to the stars" was Shershevskii's slogan. We stood, thanks to Newtonian calculus and modern engineering, on the cusp of the "cosmic era of mankind"—or as one Verein poem had it, in a mix of the realistic and futuristic:

Upon the fiery wings of the rocket,
The dreams of curious man
Will conquer, proudly and boldly,
Far away worlds.

The glorious work of the Human Spirit
Will master the supreme power of the Cosmos.[22]

These authors clearly entertained Oberth and the German rocketeers as a kind of culminating moment in the long and tortured history of rocket theories and experiments. Oberth himself had praised the worthiness of "the best German engineers and mechanics," now ready for the challenges of spaceflight. In his survey of rocket science Otto Willi Gail studiously praised German talent, naming Ganswindt as the "father of the Moon rocket," charging the German people to rise up and build Oberth's spaceships. As he warned, in a telling preview of the "race to space" after the Second World War, "the first nation to raise its flag in outer space will become the leading nation and will take command of the planet."[23]

But these enthusiasts also expressed a generosity of spirit, noting that they were participating in a moment of historical fulfillment and international scope, a true measure of human progress. They celebrated known Russia, French, and American achievements. Willy Ley recognized the ideas of Nikolai Kibalchich and the pioneering efforts of the Soviet Society for the Study of Interplanetary Travel. The aviation writer Robert Lademann named Tsiolkovskii as the true founder of rocket theory, this thanks to Tsiolkovskii's mathematical rigor and scientific proofs. After his and Esnault-Pelterie's theories, spaceflight merely awaited its rocket engineers and builders.[24] Shershevskii paid homage to Tsiolkovskii's priority in drafting the first true rocket theories as well as to Nikolai Morozov's science fiction and to a variety of Russian rocket pioneers. He also offered a strange mix of the rational and romantic, surveying Tsiolkovskii's certain rocket science, with all his mass ratios and exhaust velocities, yet also representing Tsiolkovskii's prophetic cosmic philosophy, how the human being was essentially as eternal and infinite as nature itself, how we were bound to become immortal "star wanderers."[25]

Most of all, the German rocket enthusiasts recognized Robert Goddard's unique union of theory and practice. He was the great experimenter. Of special note was his widely reported 17 July 1929 launch at Worcester, Massachusetts, marking Goddard's public priority in launching the world's first liquid fuel, constant-exhaust rocket. America, the Germans seemed to caution, was speeding ahead of Europe, was turning fiction decisively into fact. The *New York Times* certainly thought so, its reporters headlining Goddard's rocket, "sent through the air in an isolated part of Worcester this afternoon like a flaming meteor, with a roar heard two miles around." Here was the powerful metaphor of the rocket as "man-made meteor" and "falling star," now disseminated ever more widely in the U.S. media. From Russia, Aleksandr Rodnykh even compared Goddard's rocket launch on 17 July 1929 to the Wright brothers' first flight on 17 December 1903.[26]

The Verein's own work culminated in 1929 not so much with its rocket experiments but with the premier of Fritz Lang's feature film *The Woman in the Moon*, based on a story written by his wife and popular novelist, Thea Harbou. The book was a minor best seller (with twenty thousand copies sold), the story of a race into space between Germany and the United States, the German rocket scientist (Wolf Helius) securing his country's victory and humanity's destiny in the cosmos. The film's opening night, at the upscale Ufa-Palast am Zoo theater in Berlin, recalled the premier of *Aelita* only a few years earlier, this time the building bathed in light and dark, miniature rockets launching (if only by wires) from the ground into the shadows.[27] No simple moving picture, it cost over two million marks to produce, a testament to the popular demand for rocketry and space travel themes in mass entertainment. It was also a testament to Oberth's spaceship, as Lang had tasked Oberth with charting an imaginary trip from the heart of Germany to the surface of the moon, all based on strict scientific truths. The movie dramatized the world's first recorded countdown. It displayed a remarkably accurate moon rocket (Oberth's Model E), wheeled out of a huge hangar by railroad tractor. It offered scenes of humans in the zero gravity of space and upon realistic lunar landscapes. The movie's still shots became in quick time all around the world emblems of the real possibilities of spaceflight.[28]

As scientific consultant to the film, Oberth set out to build a prototype of a small stratospheric rocket to serve as a marketing prop, meant to be launched from a site at the Baltic coast to an altitude of sixty-four kilometers (forty miles). Among his eccentric band of assistants was the Russian émigré, Shershevskii, who was a constant source of rumor and news about the Soviet rocket movement, once even reporting that Tsiolkovskii had received 400,000 gold rubles to build a long-range rocket. As Oberth's translator, he also regularly corresponded with Tsiolkovskii in Kaluga about the progress and achievements of the Germans. In the fall of 1929, as the movie premier and his deadline for the rocket approached, Oberth bravely wrote to Tsiolkovskii that a working rocket was expected within weeks, though he was still not able to mix the fuels properly. "The road to the exploration of outer space by reactive apparatuses," he wrote with measured confidence, "seems open."[29] Alas, the movie rocket launch was not to be. The road did not open. The most Oberth achieved in terms of practical results was the successful test firing of his *Kegelduse* (cone) engine on 23 July 1930, after which he largely abandoned further practical experimentation.[30]

Rebuffed in practical rocketry, Oberth found some solace in his occult theories, an esoteric mix of cosmic monism and pan-psychism. Much like Tsiolkovskii, he believed that all matter everywhere in the universe was alive, never to die but only to be transformed and reincarnated into new life forms. Matter was imbued with soul and spirit, amazing capacities for extrasensory perception and the projection of feelings and thoughts. Humanity enjoyed vast stores of untapped talents and powers. Our destiny belonged to the eternity and infinity of outer space.[31] A number of German rocketry enthusiasts entertained such peculiar views. Valier was a patron of the "Glacial Cosmogony," or "Cosmic Ice," theory. Really a whole new way of conceiving astronomy and history, this was the belief that the universe was governed by a "cosmic polarity," the gravitational fire of stars and the colliding force of ice-bound meteors and planetoids. The universe was allegedly born out of this collision, forming the icy spaces of the ether and the icy masses of the Milky Way and planets. Their cyclical revolutions and periodic collisions (including our planet and its various moons) corresponded to grand historical and revolutionary events here on Earth, such as the "Great Flood," the rise and fall of the lost civilization of Atlantis, and the destiny of the next German Reich.[32] All of human history was dependent upon the movements of the cosmic ice.

Nebel was also taken with the "Hollow Earth" theory, that the globe was hollow and we were the inhabitants of its inner sphere, watching the skies and heavens not beyond into outer space but within, into the very center of an emptied planet. As the work of the Verein faded after 1932, Nebel even convinced several like-minded city leaders at Magdeburg to confirm the theory by launching rockets into the inner vacuum of the sphere and therefore to the other side of Earth. The media built up expectations for these flights through the summer of 1933, though they never took place.[33]

German writers tapped into these occult themes to sell their space adventures. Otto Willi Gail set the tone in his widely read novel for young readers *By Rocket to the Moon: The Story of Hans Hardt's Miraculous Flight* (1928), with vignettes either championing the Cosmic Ice theory on the moon or discovering an ice-bound space satellite from the lost civilization of Atlantis or featuring German-American and Russian-German rivalries in outer space. Yet Gail, a friend and supporter of the Verein, also centered his story on a technology "at the threshold of actual accomplishment": the Oberth rocket. He portrayed it as speeding off beyond orbit, making a "true gravitational curve in the form of a parabola," remaining "visible only as a dim point of light." Among the spectators "all eyes were fixed on the man-made comet sweeping across the sky." Alternately, the rocket became a new star, or even a miniature new planet, "soaring through space, an infinitesimal fragment of the Earth." We humans became space-craft too, as one of his characters suited up for a spacewalk, becoming a "Living Meteor" in transit.[34]

The Oberth rocket was a favorite in German fiction. Hans Dominik's popular books featured it, if in the simple form of "grenade-like" dirigibles. His tale *The Legacy of the Uranides* (1928) starts off with the civilized West defeating a barbaric East—a Communist, Russian-Manchurian state. The busy plot that follows is centered on a Western race for rockets, inspired by the brilliant German inventor Weland Gorm, who flies off in the end by German space rocket for the deep reaches of the cosmos.[35] Otfrid von Hanstein offered a more sophisticated approach, *World Rocket I* (1929), which sold well throughout Europe and the United States. The story follows several trodden paths: American-German engineering; scenes of the media frenzy for space travel; subplots confirming the myth of Atlantis and the Cosmic Ice theory. Yet at the center of it all is the "marvel" of Oberth's rocket. Or as von Hanstein wrote, "Streams of fire rushed out of the rocket. One explosion followed another . . . while a tiny dot disappeared faster than the speed of thought into everlasting space." With Oberth and Gail and Dominick, he also entertained the human being as rocket, in vivid studies of space walks, propelled by compressed gases just like the rocket craft. So we became our own "satellite" of Earth.[36]

These kinds of adventures kept the ideas of rocketry and space travel alive in the popular marketplace, often alongside news items about the Verein (and related groups). The romantic literally mingled with the real. Even the young Wernher von Braun excited readers with the immense power of the liquid fuel rocket, untangling its "mysteries," revealing them as proven scientific theories, as technical challenges now under practical experiment. With a brazen, youthful optimism he positioned the human reach for space as but the next and logical stage in the natural evolution of flight, if now to the highest altitudes.[37]

None of theses news items received the kind of attention Valier did, soon collaborating with Paul Heylandt, dazzling the public with their "Comet car." It was easily comprehensible as an automobile yet was also filled with mystery and danger, a strange hybrid machine combining a "blast furnace and refrigerator in one," mixing the propellants of liquid oxygen (kept at -183 Celsius) and gasoline (or benzene or methyl alcohol).[38] Valier's contributions to rocketry were more dramatic than any piece of fiction. He was killed on 17 May 1930 in an explosion of one of his liquid fuel cars, swallowed up by the flames and smoke, fatally hit by the metal shrapnel of its engine parts. Several members of the British Royal Aeronautical Society recounted the event: "A steel-blue flame, fifteen feet long, shot forth from the rocket tank, the car bounded forward and collapsed, and Valier, blown high into the air, fell in a crumpled heap that did not stir." For Americans and Russians alike, he became the "first martyr to the science of rocket propulsion."[39] More sacrifices were to come. Esnault-Pelterie lost parts of four fingers on his left hand, Oberth much of the vision in his left eye, after their own laboratory mishaps. Reinhold Tiling was killed at Osnabrück after a rocket explosion on 11 October 1933, along with his assistants Friedrich Kuhr and Fraulein Angelika Buddenböhmer. Having survived the explosion, they succumbed to the deadly fire.[40]

Jets and Rockets in Europe

The challenge for rocketry and spaceflight also came from the French, now focused on regaining something of their dominance in aviation and aeronautics from before the First World War, what Louis Breguet called their "first place" in these fields. Germany had proven its technological authority with new all-metal airplane designs. The United States had revived its own industrial prowess during the war. France had fallen behind. Its hope was to improve the efficiencies of the internal combustion engine, designing lighter, more fuel-efficient airplane motors to fly faster and farther, to expand the crucial "radii of action" joining Europe to Asia, Africa and the Americas. The evolution of the technology was dependent upon the advancement of the science.[41]

According to this logic, the traditional piston engine with screw propeller was exhausting its possibilities. What would come next? From Austria, Eugen Sänger experimented with liquid fuel rocket engines as the next true advance in aeronautics. Their initial application would likely be as takeoff assists for heavily loaded military airplanes. But his express purpose was to build an invincible supersonic and stratospheric rocket bomber, reaching for the highest speeds at the highest altitudes. Sänger's *Rocket Flight Engineering* (1934) was a serious study of the gas dynamics and internal efficiencies of rocket engines, of the aerodynamics of supersonic and rocket flight. He summarized it all by the power of the "integral," each moment of the differential equation integrated "along the horizontal path of the rocket's flight." Following Oberth's lead, the work was threaded by the universal language of calculus and by the confirmed findings of scientists such as Tsiolkovskii, Esnault-Pelterie, Oberth, Pirquet, Hohmann, and Noordung. Rocket theory already had a history and a set of founders—the "cosmonauts" (*kosmonauter*) and "cosmo-engineers" (*kosmotechniker*), as Sänger put it, the very scientists and engineers who were preparing the way for rocket flight.[42] Although he was a sober and serious academic, Sänger made quite clear that liquid fuel rockets were an altogether new kind of science and engineering, for flight into the highest altitudes, even at "extra-terrestrial speeds." He entertained his rocket flying over the curvature of the earth, into "outer space" (*Weltraum*) at a "field free from gravity and resistance," where humans would bring their own propulsion systems and atmospheres. He also foresaw a coming age filled with even more wonders, "special revolutionary discoveries" that would open up radically new opportunities and frontiers.[43]

From France, Maurice Roy published a related set of studies on the emerging science of jet motors, not liquid fuel rockets but air-breathing reaction engines for higher speeds and atmospheres, even the stratosphere.[44] Esnault-Pelterie renewed his charge for the rocket, adapting his original thoughts of 1912 in a paper presented on 8 June 1927 before the French Astronomical Society and a subsequent article in France's premier aeronautics journal, *L'Aérophile*, soon revised and extended in his book *L'Astronautique* (1930), a foundational text for the new science of "astronautics." All were meant for specialists, not the general public.[45] By now he was well informed about the work of Goddard and Oberth, Hohmann and Valier. He also began to cite some of Tsiolkovskii's works, if without full recognition of the Russian pioneer's priority. Aware and likely anxious of the burgeoning rivalries, Esnault-Pelterie was intent on securing his own position in the field, verifying that he had first begun to address the ideas as early as 1907–8, if now supplemented with new calculations and readings of his rivals. Tsiolkovskii, along with his spokesman Chizhevskii, were not at all pleased.[46]

The institutions of French popular and academic science rallied to Esnault-Pelterie's patrimony. They admitted that although the Germans and Americans might be surpassing French achievement, he had been the first pioneer to launch the new science of rocketry and space travel in 1912, transforming Verne's literary fiction into scientific fact. He was the alpha and omega, the first and last to publish the most pioneering and comprehensive pieces on astronautics.[47] Esnault-Pelterie and his publicists added their own flourishes, with detailed exposés on the intricacies and challenges of the new science, a utopian venture par excellence. Humanity discovered its most perfect machine-making and projection power in the rocket, the most direct and efficient transformation of matter into motion, without any medium but its own. Here was perfect "self-propulsion" that, once free of orbit at escape velocity, had the potential to travel at amazing speeds and distances, that human-made "Halley's comet" first introduced by Esnault-Pelterie in 1912. It would free humanity from being a "prisoner of our own planet." It would finally achieve Camille Flammarion's age-old dream of making the extraordinary voyage to more perfect civilizations beyond our own.[48]

In a fitting legacy to the work of Flammarion, Esnault-Pelterie also joined forces with his widow, Gabrielle, to form a Committee on Astronautics in the French Astronomical Society, with offices and observatory at #28 Rue Serpente in downtown Paris. They were backed by her financier and fellow science fiction enthusiast André Hirsch, along with a core of influential supporters, scientists, and engineers that included the physicist Paul Langevin. At the committee's inaugural meeting in 1927, Esnault-Pelterie had wanted to name the new science of rocketry and space travel "Sideration," meaning travel in the sidereal universe; Hirsch proposed "Cosmonautique" after Oberth. But the good sense and literary taste of science fiction writer J. H. Rosny prevailed. Rocket science became "Astronautique."[49] And one of the committee's first functions was to award the Prix Internationale d'Astronautique (the REP-Hirsch Prize): five thousand francs offered for the best published work on spaceflight theory or applications, encompassing astronomy and the natural sciences, ballistics and metallurgy, engineering and biology. Hermann Oberth turned out to be the first winner, on 5 June 1929, for his classic works on rocketry and space travel.

One of the coming winners of the prize, Ari Shternfel'd, was at the time busy working on his magnum opus about spaceflight. Born and raised in Poland, a student of the famed Jagiellonian University of Cracow, Shternfel'd eventually settled in France, where he studied engineering at the University of Nancy and the Sorbonne. Forgoing a stable career in engineering, by 1927 he was devoting his talents to the study of the new sciences of rocketry and space travel.[50] He became fascinated with the theories of K. E. Tsiolkovskii, with whom he exchanged letters, teaching himself Russian by translating one of Tsiolkovskii's books sentence by sentence. A socialist and atheist, he was also surrounded by Soviet sympathizers: his sister, Franka, and his future wife, Gustava Erlich, were members of the French Communist Party. In fact, his first publication on space travel was a promotional piece in the French Communist newspaper *L'Humanité* dedicated to Tsiolkovskii's theories and to Soviet Russia's pioneering rocketry work. In the tradition of the turn-of-the-century cosmic romance, Shternfel'd wrote that "the utopia of yesterday becomes the reality of today." Communism had essentially inherited one of the great clichés of the nineteenth century: "Only socialist society will open humanity's path to cosmic space."[51]

Shternfel'd's classic work *Introduction to Cosmonautics* (1933) was well received by French academic science, including the physicists Paul Langevin and Jean Perrin. Although it was never published in its French version, he submitted the whole manuscript to the Committee on Astronautics in December 1933, lecturing on parts of it before scholars of the French Academy of Science and at the Sorbonne. Hirsch and Esnault-Pelterie called him their own French "Oberth," awarding him a version of their prize in 1934.[52] The work was a tour de force of the theoretical and technical aspects of rocketry and spaceflight, grounded in Shternfel'd's genius for higher mathematics, so elegantly translated into the differential equations and trajectories to escape gravity and approach the near planets. It was a discourse on earth science and astronomy, on the physiological and psychological effects of spaceflight, and on a new orbital mechanics for the navigable rocket, applying a wide and impressive variety of French, English, German, and Russian sources.[53]

The work offers us a strategic culminating point. Shternfel'd put the human being into motion, piloting a rocket, speeding through the cosmos—triangulated between its position, the position of the earth, and the point of arrival, the crucial problem of three moving bodies. He set us traveling not wildly to the stars, as suggested by the French and American preference for astronautics, but boldly into the cosmos, the outer space between the planets, the truer science of cosmonautics. Here were elliptical trajectories into Earth's orbit, singular arcs farther into outer space, figure-eight paths to and from the moon, spiral trajectories and orbital transfers and gravity assists to Venus, atmospheric breakings back to Earth. All of these motions amounted to a wonderful human dance in space, with the object of exploring, discovering, and returning home. We became the life that belonged to the cosmos, space a "medium" within which we were meant to travel by our own assigned "routes." This was authoritative science yet with hints of the fantastic, such as colonization of the planets or even the remote possibility of flying to the stars (based on Einstein's theories of relativity). In time Shternfel'd even devised a theory of "dialectical" cosmonautics, how the several "cosmic speeds"—reaching for orbital velocity, achieving escape velocity, and proceeding to interstellar velocities—enabled humanity to leap from quantitative to qualitative dimensions of existence.[54]

In the United Kingdom, if with less intensity than Shternfel'd and with a slight delay compared to the rest of the world, a remarkable

THE FIRST FOUNDATIONS OF ASTRONAUTICS

number of smallish rocketry and spaceflight groups also formed between 1933 and 1942: the British Interplanetary Society, the Manchester Astronautical Association, the Midlands Interplanetary Society, the Astronautical Development Society, the Leeds Rocket Society, the Hastings Interplanetary Society, and the Paisley Rocketeers Society in Scotland.[55] None of them ever achieved viable rockets, in large part because of government prohibitions against the manipulation and testing of explosives, which limited their work. In one case a rocket explosion at Clayton Vale, near Manchester, brought Eric Burgess and his Interplanetary Society before the local police court on warrants of having violated the "Explosives Act" of 1875. The charges were dropped after the group vowed never again to mix potassium chlorate and sulfur in such a lethal combination.[56]

In contravention of their own laws several British authorities, namely the postmaster general and the directors of the International Air Post, were committed to the possibilities of using rockets for air mail, including a regular cross-channel postal service at the Straits of Dover, promising one-minute Royal Mail service to Calais. They promoted the German showman Gerhard Zucker, who claimed to have launched a solid fuel mail rocket in August 1933 some five kilometers (three miles) between the German towns of Hasselfelde and Stiege. By the summer of 1934 he was in Britain attempting more, helped along by an enterprising philatelist and the eager journalists of London's *Daily Express*. His first shot on 6 June 1934, at a site in Rottingdean, at Sussex Downs, claimed to have launched over a thousand letters (at a cost of two shillings sixpence a piece) several miles to Brighton. His next attempts ended in failure, including one on 31 July 1934 between Harris and Scarp, in the Western Isles off Scotland. The fifty some letters, including one addressed to King George, were all destroyed when the powder-charged rocket exploded on ignition.[57]

Although they were never really accomplished with rockets in practice, the British rocketeers were captivated with the new ideology of stratospheric and even interplanetary flight. In part this was a function of their love of science fiction. Much like their American counterparts, the British Interplanetary Society was founded in 1933 by fans of Hugo Gernsback's magazines, including a young physics student, Arthur C. Clarke, and the engineer and writer P. E. Cleator, who also visited the Verein's Rocket Flying Field in January 1933 and made plans to build rockets back home. This was a growing international movement, an exciting and building "race" for rocketry, anticipated by Tsiolkovskii, put into practice by Goddard, and being pursued in earnest by the Germans and Americans, the Russians and even the Japanese.[58]

Cleator envisioned the rocket as humanity's ultimate technological envelope to overcome the natural obstacles of altitude and gravity. Several aviation publicists and members of the British Royal Aeronautical Society offered a similar literary scenario, "Into the Ether of Space," a story about the interplanetary potential of the rocket to leave the planet behind and venture on a parabolic velocity into infinity, "to blaze the trail farther into the unknown regions of space."[59] Here was a perfect summary of the beauties and complexities of rocket science: the "host of immense difficulties" and the pioneers engaged in "long years of patient, persistent study and experiment," wrapped in their calculations of mass ratios and exhaust velocities and launch trajectories. They had to display "indomitable perseverance," making "a thousand experiments" with "unconquerable determination," amid the drama of the countdown and explosion, the "downward pouring cascade of fire." Here was a passion for the rocket as "absolutely independent," having all resources within itself, the "simplest known prime mover—without any moving parts."[60]

American and Russian Rockets

In the United States Robert Goddard's rocketry work remained at the center of national efforts, if still isolated and tenuous. When Charles Lindbergh, soon after his epochal New York–to–Paris breakthrough, decided to pursue the possibilities of rocket airplanes, he found Goddard but few other innovators besides. The idea of a rocket plane first came to him, so he remembered, during a solo flight in 1928 from New York to Missouri, as he piloted the *Spirit of St. Louis*, "daydreaming" about overcoming wings and propellers and the atmosphere, about rising into space with rockets. The memory was a bit disingenuous.

THE FIRST FOUNDATIONS OF ASTRONAUTICS

Thanks to Goddard's experiments and Valier's exploits, rockets were prominently in the news, the kinds of machines that "lift themselves by their own bootstraps," in words once applied to describe Lindbergh himself.[61] He now sought out America's best minds on the subject, without any success. The consensus was that rockets were a "fantasy," a waste of time. A conference with the Dupont Company's scientists and engineers held in Wilmington, Delaware, on 1 November 1929, ended in complete failure. "A general shaking of heads took place," Lindbergh remembered. It was only a chance reading about Goddard's rocketry work in *Popular Science Monthly* that led him to make contact. They met shortly after the Dupont fiasco, on 23 November, at Goddard's Worcester home, where Lindbergh was regaled with the possibilities of jet and rocket propulsion.[62]

The meeting was a turning point in Goddard's career. Lindbergh now introduced him to Daniel Guggenheim, whose family's Guggenheim Fund for the Promotion of Aeronautics had sponsored Lindbergh's 1927 three-month national air tour, along with a number of cutting-edge laboratories for the promotion of aviation science and technology. After a ten-minute conversation at the family's Long Island estate, Lindbergh convinced Guggenheim to finance Goddard too. In a rare act of generosity to a single scientist, the fund provided Goddard a four-year grant of $25,000 a year, eventually totaling an unprecedented $148,000 over the next decade.[63]

Thanks to both the media coverage about Germany's rocket craze and Goddard's newfound celebrity, rocketry made a comeback in America's popular science press. The revival was also spurred by the American release of *The Woman in the Moon* and the fascination with its "huge rocket," the "life dream of a bewhiskered professor." Oberth now competed with Goddard for the title of "Moon man."[64] In the context of this growing international race for rocketry, a new generation of enthusiasts began to form its own amateur rocketry groups: the American Interplanetary Society (1930), the Cleveland Rocket Society (1933), the Peoria Rocket Association (1934), and the Yale Rocket Club (1935), along with similar groups in Chicago, Illinois; Angola, Indiana; Greenwood Lake in Westchester County, New York; and the Rocket Research Society of the Massachusetts Institute of Technology. Several enterprising rocketeers also took up the challenge. On 8 March 1931 a Syracuse University student, Harry W. Bull, set up a rocket sled on frozen Lake Oneida and drove it an amazing fifty feet in two-fifths of a second (about 75 miles, or 121 kilometers, per hour), at which point it hit a snowbank and spun out of control. As one story described it, "A hiss rose to a roar, and blinding flashes of flame shot backwards from the rockets set near the snow." Bull was not hurt. But his friends Charlie Chatfield and Andy Paucek suffered minor injuries and major embarrassment, their overcoats and pants "scorched black" and their hair and eyebrows "singed." The whole experiment cost them only twenty-two dollars.

On 4 June 1931, to open the summer season and wow the tourists at Atlantic City, the stunt flyer William G. Swan attached a set of solid fuel rockets to his glider, catapulted by an elastic cord, then ignited the rockets for an eight-minute flight at 200 feet (61 meters) altitude over the boardwalk and beaches. The excitement spilled over into the popular media as well. The Westclox Company, for example, advertised its "Pocket Ben" watch by launching it in a "skyrocket" to a thousand feet in the air, "and with a deafening roar and a shower of sparks, Pocket Ben shot into space . . . Higher . . . Higher," only to survive the explosive trip unscathed . . . still ticking.[65]

Like Germany, but without its scientific intensity and scope, America experienced something of a rocket craze. It had its media excesses. One of the more spectacular boasts of the day came from Robert Condit, a graduate of Baltimore's premier technical high school, the Polytechnic Institute. He received significant media coverage in 1928 for his plan to launch a rocket to Venus; one prominent photograph showed his head popping out of the tip of the rocket. Condit was a talented student and amateur engineer and even more adept at showmanship and trickery, passing himself off as a "mathematical wizard," a fitting rival to Professor Goddard. He and two friends (a stonemason and a carpenter) actually built the rocket in a neighbor's garage over the summer. It was made out of iron and varnished sailcloth, outfitted with a "living room" and "steering gyroscope," oxygen tank, two flashlights, and a first-aid kit. It was to be powered by eight steel "rocket" tubes, air compressor, and spark plugs, filled

THE FIRST FOUNDATIONS OF ASTRONAUTICS

with fifty gallons of gasoline, costing some five thousand dollars to make, so one of the builders claimed. They "launched" it in August 1928 from the neighborhood sidewalk, though it exploded in a sudden burst of fire and smoke. The rocket itself did not budge. Condit disappeared after the event, perhaps in a quick escape by pickup truck to Florida.[66]

One of Goddard's even more famous rivals was little more than a charlatan and con man—the enigmatic Darwin O. Lyon, who claimed to be a "fellow" of Columbia University and an assistant to Goddard himself. One of his first bogus rocket launches, in 1930 from Mount Redorta in the Italian Alps, even ended in a phony disaster of one dead and three wounded. But Lyon pressed forward, leaving dramatic telegrams and news releases from Paris and Davos, Genoa and Vienna, of impending launches into "inter-terrestrial space." By perfecting his light-metal, two-stage rockets, navigated by gyroscopic stabilizer, he claimed to be mastering "the science of interplanetary flight, or cosmonautics as I call it."[67] In 1933 Lyon made extravagant claims from Italian Libya, in the desert some two hundred kilometers south of Tripoli (in the service of Benito Mussolini's government), that he was nearly finished with a "big rocket" to reach eighty kilometers (fifty miles) altitude or that he had already launched a canary and a mouse in a prototype, returning them to ground by parachute without harm. Throughout the 1930s these boasts sometimes gave Lyon priority over Goddard for achieving alleged world altitude records for liquid fuel rocket launches.[68]

There were still other rivals. Through the early 1930s John Q. Stewart, associate professor of astronomical physics at Princeton University, delivered lectures and radio addresses calling for a series of gradual human reaches into outer space. At times he proposed a spacecraft, outfitted with Goddard-type solid fuel cartridges, "cannons" on all its sides, shooting three tons of lead per second at 200 miles (322 kilometers) per hour. This was all precisely calculated for the proper mass ratio to achieve escape velocity, what he called the "hop off the Earth." In one radio lecture, delivered on the Columbia Broadcasting System, he imagined a trip to the moon by 2050, dramatized for the radio audience as if they were actually watching it on a television set, of all things. We simply needed to build a "space cruiser," achievable within one hundred years, a "spherical rocket" with exhaust jets all around, now powered by seventy thousand tons of ionized hydrogen, outfitted for a crew of sixty, to reach speeds of 25,000 miles (40,233 kilometers) per hour. Total cost: two billion dollars.[69]

In 1935 news even spread out of Europe that Otto Fischer had actually ridden a steel rocket—seven meters, or twenty-four feet long, "torpedo-shaped," and asbestos lined—to ten kilometers, or six miles, altitude, the flight lasting about ten minutes, before he and the rocket parachuted back to ground. Reporters wrote about the "sensational secret demonstration" backed by the German military, emphasizing that it took place under "absolute" and "greatest secrecy" at Rugen Island on the Baltic coast (in a strange premonition, just across the bay from the future top secret rocket base at Peenemünde). Thus, "for the first time in history," a human being had made a "journey through space," the pilot experiencing a "deafening roar," then the "unbearable weight" of acceleration, finally the intense heat of reentry. These were all lies. But they made great press as well as a great picture—in the popular French Sunday supplement *L'Illustré*.[70]

Even the American Interplanetary Society (AIS), the leading amateur group, had a rather eccentric start. Most of its founders were originally science fiction writers, including G. Edward Pendray and David Lasser. Both were in the pay of Hugo Gernsback's publishing empire, originally working out of Pendray's apartment at 450 West 22nd Street in Manhattan. With him their business was to sell exotic adventure stories, mixing old-time fantasy with the coming facts of rocket power. Yet they also shared a progressive ideology of technological development and international cooperation. The technocratic Gernsback was well-read in the German-, French-, and English-language literature on rocketry and space travel. The coverage of the issues in his magazines and books ensured that American readers stayed abreast of worldwide developments, including Oberth's and Esnault-Pelterie's and even Tsiolkovskii's work, all preparations for an inevitable "interplanetary" future. The society found further patrons in several scientists associated with the American Museum of Natural History, including H. H. Sheldon, professor of physics at New York University, and Clyde Fisher, who was also one of the science editors of the *New York Herald Tribune.*

Pendray also maintained close and friendly contacts with the Verein, especially Willy Ley, who soon immigrated to the United States to become his cochampion of rocketry. In April 1931, in a remarkable act of public diplomacy, Pendray even visited the Rocket Flying Field in Germany. Thanks to his photos and narratives, appearing in the pages of *Popular Science Monthly* and *Popular Mechanics*, bolstered by the reporting of the *New York Herald Tribune* and the *New York Times*, American popular science readers saw the ambitious Germans at work in the 1930s (including a teenage Wernher von Braun) long before they came to know them as the designers of some of America's premier ballistic missiles in the 1950s. Pendray introduced us to all the "elaborate tests" and "innumerable obstacles" of what he now called "rocket science," the first such express mention of the phrase in the media that I have found. It meant the dangerous mixtures of liquid oxygen and gasoline, the challenges of building fuel and pump systems, outfitted with light yet strong metals, not to speak of navigation and life support for eventual piloted travel.[71]

In January 1931, by special invitation of Pendray and the Interplanetary Society, Robert Esnault-Pelterie visited New York City to great acclaim. He was already well known to Gernsback's readers from a piece in the magazine *Modern Mechanics and Inventions.* Two thousand people filled the great rotunda of the American Museum of Natural History on the twenty-seventh to hear him speak. They also came to watch *The Woman in the Moon,* which Pendray and company had edited, cutting out the romantic elements and turning it into a "truer" documentary on spaceflight (they continued to use the edited film as a teaching tool into the later 1930s). Ten policemen and the museum guards helped keep the excited overflow crowd orderly.[72] Although he was felled by a cold and not able to speak (Pendray read the lecture in his stead), Esnault-Pelterie offered some dramatic predictions. Within five years and about a million-dollar investment, engineers might be able to build a "space" rocket, one that would reach from Paris to New York in about thirty minutes, flying at an altitude of 800 miles (1,287 kilometers) and at a speed of 8,000 miles (12,875 kilometers) per hour. After a few years more and another million, we might even send a spaceship to the moon. Rockets themselves were so very "simple," he admitted, with no real moving parts. But rocket science and technology were in truth "very complicated," surrounded by all kinds of "enormous contingencies" and necessary refinements of the mechanisms and processes. None of this would be easy.[73]

Inspired partly by Esnault-Pelterie's words, partly by the successes of aeronautics as the new science of flight in the air, in the spring of 1932 the society changed the name of its journal to *Astronautics*, the new science of human navigation "above the air."[74] The change also met the expectations of most American rocket enthusiasts, who were not wide-eyed dreamers but serious folk, dedicated to experimenting with this new technology and pondering all of its variables and possibilities. The A I S even renamed itself for them, becoming the American Rocket Society (A R S) in mid-1934, this to highlight a new stage of practical experimentation. Thousands of young people around the country, mostly males, were drawn to amateur rocketry, building models for the sheer fun of their explosive and ballistic power. Between 1934 and 1935 the ranks of the A R S grew by almost 50 percent, partly due to the improving economic conditions, partly to the increased press about rocketry. This was a committed and enthusiastic cadre of "rocketeers" yet still vastly ignorant of the basic truths of the science and engineering. The A R S struggled to teach them the elements of physics and calculus, filling the pages of *Astronautics* with "primers" for its growing audience. The myth of risky rocket science was born in this shotgun marriage between heady specialists and rank amateurs. The more serious-minded rocket pioneers worried that as once they had been labeled the cranks and dreamers of space travel, now they would be thrown in with all the juvenile pranksters and hooligans simply thrilled with blowing things up.[75]

Press reports cautioned readers that the rocket was no longer a Jules Verne fantasy or Fourth of July plaything. It now had potential. But the extravagant claims of 500-mile-per-hour (805-kilometer-per-hour) flights or transatlantic mail (New York to Paris in twenty-nine minutes) were quite hard to fulfill. A flight on 10 February 1936 of two winged aluminum gliders, fueled by alcohol and liquid oxygen rocket motors, proved the point. It was filled with six thousand postcards, set to fly from the Morningside Country Club at Greenwood Lake, New York, to Hewitt, New Jersey. The project was sponsored by the high-sounding group the Rocket Airplane Corporation, something of a front for F. W. Kessler, a Brooklyn philatelist out to achieve some publicity for his stamp business. Yet it was also a serious venture, supported by none other than the Daniel Guggenheim School of Aeronautics at New York University (under Alexander Klemin) and the American Rocket Society (with G. Edward Pendray's and Willy Ley's patronage). Neither could save the small rocket planes from their first disasters, the attempts ended in "fizzing," "hissing," a "burst of flames," and finally "dead silence" in the snow. After several more failures, on 23 February 1936 the mail rocket *Gloria* eventually did make its maiden flight, to about 1,000 feet, or 305 meters, fulfilling some of the promises of the "reaction motor," a simple "hollow pipe with no moving parts." Yet the flight also highlighted the "many difficulties" facing America's "rocketeers," including the correct liquid fuel combinations and velocities, the proper heat-tolerant metals to deal with the high temperature of the ejecting gases, and the right design of the pumps and valves of the rocket engine.[76]

Rocket science remained a mysterious and challenging enterprise. Yet it was becoming recognized as a legitimate new science. Even the *New Yorker* heralded America's "rocketors" for experimenting with ever more complex designs, at considerable explosive risk to their persons. "A rocket is no joke," wrote the editors.[77] On the East Coast, after 1935, the members of the A RS came to focus more and more on designing and creating "rational" and efficient liquid-fueled rocket engines. Alfred Africano, America's answer to Ari Shternfel'd, helped to turn rocketry into more of an applied science, with a remarkable range of studies in both popular and scientific journals, always serious and purposeful, filled with the calculus of velocity ratio and thermodynamic cycle efficiencies. But Africano did not lose his sense of utopian zeal, even discussing the possibilities of sending a craft beyond orbit, by parabolic trajectory, to an "infinite velocity."[78]

On the West Coast, under the mentorship of two of the country's leading physicists, Theodore von Karman and Clark B. Millikan, the Rocket Research Project formed in 1936 at Pasadena's Guggenheim Aeronautical Laboratory of the California Institute of Technology (GALCIT). Von Karman, an émigré aerodynamics expert who had participated in Germany's early debates over liquid fuel rocketry, understood the significance of the new field. This was a creative, dynamic group, including several amateurs, namely Jack Parsons and Edward Forman. They were both talented technicians. Parsons worked for the Halifax Powder Company and was also a devoted occultist, working on rockets by day and engaging in satanic rituals by night. Several formidable engineers rounded out the group— Frank Malina, A. M. O. Smith, Hsue-Shen Tsien, and Weld Arnold. Known as the "suicide club" for their dangerous mishaps and explosions, they nonetheless centered their experiments, with both solid fuel and liquid fuel rockets, on certain scientific principles and on the latest German and Italian findings. In the well-established academic forums of aeronautics engineering, Malina and Smith boldly predicted the forthcoming efficiencies of rocket engines, the coming realization of the "wingless shell of revolution" in "vertical flight."[79]

Retreating to Roswell, New Mexico, with his impressive Guggenheim grant, Goddard came to rely on a small team of devoted mechanics and assistants who helped him build and test his rockets. Yet Goddard remained aloof and deeply protective of his work, which he publicly admitted had been "copied" by foreigners without acknowledgment. In the intense competition for the "conquest of space," he was working in a "curious secrecy," while the Europeans were creating the "new science" of astronautics and surging ahead.[80] From New Mexico, for the rest of his career, he continued to shun contact with fellow engineer enthusiasts, refusing the offer of a position at the California Institute of Technology to work with its growing rocket collective at GALCIT. He disappointed one of its members, the young Frank Malina, who even visited Goddard at Roswell in August 1936. He characteristically kept the all-important details hidden, covering his rockets and engines under tarps, speaking only in vague abstractions about his experiments. Malina must have been enticed, however, by the sixty-foot spiral of a launch tower, which simply could not be hidden.[81]

Goddard's style, so secretive and tenacious, gave the American public a real sense of impending achievement, a false lead of sorts. No other nation set a standard for scientific and technological achievement. Americans lived with modern advances all around them and in certain expectation of further advances of their own making. The California Institute of Technology had the world's largest telescope. The Langley Aeronautical Laboratory had the world's biggest wind tunnel. Goddard's promises and media attention between 1920 and 1939 certainly fell within this largesse: a source of American confidence . . . and complacency. Combining stubborn American practicality and eternal optimism, he became the "original rocketeer," America's most "reticent man." The press followed his work with a lively interest in the country's premier "mass scientist." They created a kind of drumbeat of expectation and result. Goddard was always making steady progress—here developing the liquid fuel engine, there perfecting a steering device via gyroscopic control, always facing some frustrating problem or obstacle. He was touted as "meticulous and exhaustive in his methods," as "an amazing example of tenacity and purpose."[82]

These developments were confirmed by Goddard's own press releases. In early 1936, perhaps in response to media reports about rocketry in the USSR and to the rising demands of his sponsors and the reading public, Goddard began to publicize his achievements and work, first in an address to the American Association for the Advancement of Science in St. Louis. He also released the most detailed and authoritative report of his work and progress to date, *Liquid Propellant Rocket Development* (1936), covering all of his seventeen years of work on rocketry. The Smithsonian charged only twenty-five cents for the brochure. In the ensuing publicity journalists finally accorded Goddard priority for launching the world's first liquid fuel rocket: on 16 March 1926, rising to 184 feet (56 meters) in 2.4 seconds, at about 60 miles (97 kilometers) per hour. By mid-1935 his "rocket ships" were by no means ready yet to send human beings to the moon. They were only 80 pounds (36 kilograms) in weight (with 60 pounds of propellants, liquid oxygen and gasoline, injected by nitrogen gas). But they were reaching new records: heights of 7,500 feet (2,286 meters) under gyroscopic control, with amazing speeds of 700 miles (1,126 kilometers) per hour, much faster than the fastest airplane speed.[83] Goddard and the Smithsonian made quite clear that the United States was still first in the race toward space.

Russian enthusiasts, sensing the initiative slip from their grasps, did not take any of these developments well. What Kibalchich and Tsiolkovskii had originally begun, the Europeans and Americans were now completing in a burst of energy and experimentation. Russia once again was falling behind the pace of the West. But there was still hope. The work of Opel and Valier, Sänger and Goddard, promised dramatic applications for flights into the stratosphere and even outer space, an "era of rockets." Doubly inspired and threatened, Russian publicists now heralded rocketry as a matter of "super-aviation." The stratospheric plane and cigar-shaped rocket became the crafts of the future. The rocket became the "airplane without wings" or the "rocket dirigible."[84] These advances demanded a Soviet response, dictated by the Stalinist imperative to "catch and surpass."

N. A. Rynin understood that the best of Western knowledge was the key to any future Soviet achievement. From his vast private library at #37 Kolomonskaia Street in central Leningrad, he was already publishing his multivolume series, *Interplanetary Flight and Communication* (*Mezhplanetnye soobshcheniia* [1928–32]), the world's first such compendium of spaceflight theory and practice, filled with translations of the best in European and American knowledge, along with the leading Russian contributions. The various editions of Perel'man's *Interplanetary Voyages* kept a running update of German and French and American developments.[85] These serious works in popular science were supplemented by an original and compelling study, Iu. A. Kondratiuk's *The Conquest of Interplanetary Space* (1929). Kondratiuk had arrived at the basic formulas and equations for space travel on his own terms, laying out the intricacies and challenges of all of the factors affecting the launch of a liquid-fueled rocket (mass ratio, exhaust velocity, gravity, and air resistance). He turned it all

THE FIRST FOUNDATIONS OF ASTRONAUTICS

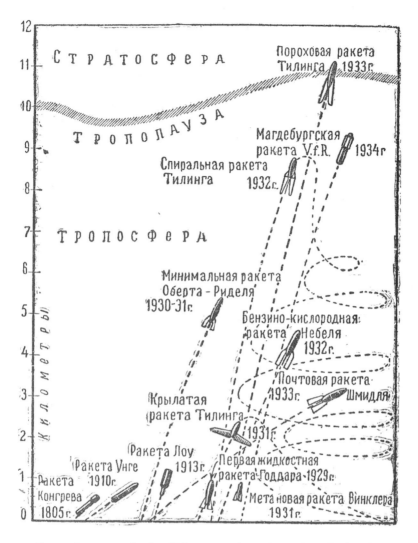

Fig. 16. Soviet cavalcade of Western rockets. An anxious Soviet view
of the West's rocket launches (some real and others hoaxes) by various altitudes in kilometers, including those of Robert Goddard (1929)
and Reinhold Tiling (1931). From *Nauka i tekhnika* 16 (1935): 3.

into the makings of what was scientifically possible and technologically achievable, designing a craft for a human pilot and making
plans for a staged program of rocket tests, flights to orbit, and even
a circumnavigation of the moon.[86] Russian enthusiasts and pioneers
were primed for innovation in rocket theory.

In the wake of these developments, and under the mounting foreign achievements in rocketry, F. A. Tsander and a small team founded the Group for the Study of Reactive Propulsion (*Gruppa izucheniia reaktivnogo dvizheniia*, or GIRD) in August 1931, an office within the civilian-based, paramilitary Society to Assist the Defense and Aviation-Chemical Industries of the USSR. Tsander essentially revived the fortunes of the old Society for the Study of Interplanetary Travel. The GIRD had a rather freewheeling culture, its young adults filled with the enthusiasm of the Young Communist League, many of them also recent graduates or students of the Moscow Higher Technical University and the Moscow Aviation Institute.[87] Tsander organized the GIRD into four "brigades": dedicated to rocket and engine design (under F. A. Tsander and L. K. Korneev); rocket engines in particular (lead by M. K. Tikhonravov); jet engines (Iu. A. Pobedonostsev); and the rocket plane (S. P. Korolev). The brigades often competed with each other to meet developmental goals, launching "storm" campaigns to promote initiative and speedier achievement. They liked to joke about their enterprise as a "Cosmic Institute," in line with Tsander's own passion for space travel and his mottoes: "Ever faster and on to Mars" and "Ever higher and higher, to the stars." But most of the enthusiasts were simply young engineers interested in building jet and rocket engines, consumed with the challenges of this altogether new technology.

Tsander was also rather eccentric in his work habits, lacking the kind of administrative focus and efficiency needed to run a team of researchers properly. He was always somewhat absent-minded and unkempt, sometimes heard mumbling in a thick German accent (he was a Baltic German from Riga, Latvia). Yet he was also the GIRD's guiding light, informing the research group with his genius for calculation and engineering design, as summarized in his book *Problems of Flight by Jet Propulsion* (1932). Tsander's utopianism was always grounded in his own sophisticated scientific and mathematical approach, which he confirmed in his readings of Goddard, Oberth, and the German pioneers, their new reach for vertical ascent and for "cosmic velocity."[88] Slowly but surely, the GIRD's work entered the mainstream press, raising the potential of reaction technologies

THE FIRST FOUNDATIONS OF ASTRONAUTICS

(both air-breathing jet engines and liquid fuel rockets). A. N. Shtern, for example, offered his signal support for the pure rocket, "direct reaction," needing no medium except its own mass and propellants. The calculus was certain. Engineers needed simply to discover the most powerful and correct mixture of fuels. Here were the foundations for a whole new science, what Shtern most figuratively called "etheronautics."[89]

For all of the publicity the GIRD had a rather modest start. It was housed eventually in the dark and damp basement of an apartment building, at #19 Sadovo-Spasskaia Street in Moscow. The hundred or so members suffered from poor funding and material shortages, low pay or none at all, and long working hours (even at night, between their other, normal jobs).[90] In time, thanks to their dedication, the GIRD became a tight-knit band of engineers. In the summer of 1932 S. P. Korolev became their manager, a demanding and effective boss, according to almost every testimony. He was also a maverick, already displaying the knack for innovation and entrepreneurship that he brought to the Soviet space program (and its *Sputnik* and Iurii Gagarin achievements) some twenty years later. This was, at least, the judgment of the government commission that investigated Korolev and the GIRD in early 1933 for questionable administrative and financial practices, including black market purchases and accounting irregularities.[91]

Tsander's rocket and engine designs, together with Korolev's leadership abilities, also had their dramatic successes. On 17 August 1933 the GIRD launched the USSR's first hybrid liquid fuel engine (designed by Tikohonravov using a gasoline gel and liquid oxygen): the GIRD-09 rocket, rising to 400 meters, eventually to some 5,000 meters (16,404 feet) altitude. It was soon followed, on 25 November, by the launch of the country's first liquid fuel engine (designed by Tsander, using liquid oxygen and alcohol): the GIRD-10 rocket, which reached only 80 meters (262 feet). The group also designed several models of the RP-1 winged rocket plane. In honor of the GIRD's successes one of the rocketeers wrote in a celebratory poem, "After a long and difficult fight, the rocket has achieved its first flight."[92]

Thus, by late 1933 the Russians had joined the Germans and the Americans in realizing the world's first respectable launches of liquid fuel rockets. With the advent of human space travel after 1957, these amateur rocket groups became the great founders, the pioneers, at the dawn of the space age: von Braun and Reidel (among others) in Germany; Pendray and Goddard in the United States; and Korolev, Tikhonravov, and Pobedonotstev in the USSR. Yet their later fame and notoriety belie the truth about their humbler origins. Each of these groups was at the margins geographically. The German Verein was situated on a half-empty ordinance base. The American Interplanetary Society did some of its rocket experiments at the Great Kills landfill, Staten Island. GIRD's home was a dilapidated building in Moscow and at a distant artillery range. They all cobbled together their pioneering rockets from salvaged parts or from free propellants donated by friendly companies. They were at the margins culturally too. Granted, each of the societies had its own journal, either public or private, or received some coverage in the newspapers and magazines. Yet official science and industry, including government and military authorities, did not show them much respect or serious consideration at first. It took a race for the stratosphere, half-peaceful and half-military, to spotlight the new science and its far horizons.

9

A Race into the Stratosphere

lthough isolated and precarious, the amateur groups had the advantage of working on a project of potentially huge impact for the aviation industry. They were reaching for altitudes and speeds that far surpassed the limits of current technology, that reached into the next great frontier of human exploitation, the stratosphere, for flight above the weather, at faster speeds. Pilots around the world had been testing the limits of human and airplane endurance at high altitudes for years: Apollo Soucek to 43,166 feet (13,157 meters) on 4 June 1930; Cyril Uwins to 43,976 feet (13,404 meters) on 16 September 1932; Renato Donati to 47,572 feet (14,500 meters) on 12 April 1934. Aviation experts understood that the challenge was to master theses ceilings, where the lack of oxygen meant the need for several innovations: pressurized airplane cabins for life support or variable pitch propellers and newly designed airplane engines (turbocompressors and superchargers) to fly in the lighter air. Goddard joined the debate, proposing a "revolutionary" stratospheric rocket plane, using its propellers to rise to altitude, where the rocket was to take over, reaching for 1,000 miles (1,609 kilometers) per hour at 30,000 feet (9,000 meters).[1]

At first the competition took peaceful forms, not so much with airplanes as with high-altitude "stratostat" (stratospheric balloon) records. This was a race for the stratosphere actually launched by an unlikely character, Auguste Piccard. He was a Swiss national, professor of physics at the University of Brussels, and a research specialist on gamma rays. On 27 May 1931, over the course of seventeen hours, Piccard and his assistant, Charles Kipfer, achieved a turning point in world history. Their stratospheric balloon, the FNRS (initials for the Belgian National Foundation for Scientific Research), made a relatively short trip from Augsburg, Germany, to the Gurgl glacier at the Austrian Tyrol. But they were also the first to reach previously unknown heights: 15,781 meters, or 51,775 feet.

The scientific objectives of the mission were mundane enough: the observation and measurement of cosmic rays (about their nature and intensity and movements), along with chemical analyses of the air and recordings of temperatures. But the flight was also filled with all the drama and danger of a science fiction story. The launch unfolded in scenes that looked as if they were cut from the movie *The Woman in the Moon*: the gondola ever so carefully transported by a small railroad track from its hangar to the launch site; huge floodlights illuminating the site deep into the night; hundreds of workers and spectators crowding the field; the pilots returning home as heroes to great public acclaim, their admirers clamoring to sign their initials to the capsule.

The spherical gondola was Piccard's unique invention, prefiguring the stratospheric gondolas to come and even the *Sputnik* spacecraft many years hence. It was the first of many kinds. Weighing 850 pounds fully outfitted, it was a seven-foot-diameter airtight ball of welded aluminum and tin (of normal atmospheric pressure and oxygen), partially based on the technology to make sealed vats for the storage of beer. Piccard provisioned it with pure-oxygen dispensers and a recirculating system to cleanse the carbon dioxide. It was raised by a giant balloon (the largest to date), some thirty-three yards in diameter and holding 500,000 cubic feet of highly flammable hydrogen gas. When fully expanded, once its gases were warmed by the sun's rays, it rose at speeds of twenty miles per hour, pear-shaped at first but eventually rounded. It was a "perfect sphere" in Piccard's words and a rival to the morning star, Venus, still visible after daylight, which several observers even confused with his craft.[2]

The flight nearly ended in disaster several times. Piccard spent about a half-hour trying to staunch an oxygen leak at the site of a one-inch hole, where a sounding instrument would not fit. He even-

A RACE INTO THE STRATOSPHERE

tually plugged it with a net and paste but only after anxiously hearing the precious air "whistling" out as the craft rose. A failed motor meant that the gondola could not turn away from the heat of the sun, internal temperatures reaching up to 104 degrees Fahrenheit. The intense heat bent the rubber joints, allowing even more air to escape. At the end of the flight the descent valve rope broke, so Piccard and Kipfer had to take extra care in watching and waiting for the setting sun and with it the cooler temperatures that allowed the balloon to descend safely. Piccard understood the drama of his own heroism, writing in his logbook: "12:12pm—All human records broken. . . . We are suffering intensely. We release more hydrogen."[3]

The media reported Piccard's achievement with bravado, what one reporter called "the greatest distance from earth ever attained by man." Here were the first humans to reach the stratosphere and return alive. Piccard had literally "raised the roof off the world." Or as he wrote in his diary of the trip, "As we rose above the blue sky, we saw the world through it in a fairylike bluish haze of extraordinary beauty."[4] He magnified the feat with a second twelve-hour flight on 18 August 1932, using the same balloon (but a different gondola) to rise to an altitude of just over ten miles, flying from Zurich to the coastline of Lake Garda in Italy (with his student Max Cosyns). They reached another world record. Cosyns, in turn, took the same balloon to 16,140 meters (52,952 feet) on 18 August 1934 (with copilot Neree van der Elst), traveling from Hour Havanne, Belgium, to Zenavelje, Yugoslavia—one thousand miles away.

American, European, and Russian news reports pictured Piccard's stratostat balloon as having risen dramatically beyond the very curvature of the earth, a human-made ascent to match and challenge the age-old meteors falling from space. Journalists now filled the *Scientific American* stratosphere chart not with Valier's imaginary rocket plane but with Piccard's real balloon. Piccard's feats taught Americans to become "stratosphere-conscious." He became their "Columbus, his balloon the Santa Maria, of the stratosphere." Both had discovered new continents—one of air, the other of land.[5] This was nothing less than humanity's ascent into the "void of space," into the "cold kingdom of mystery," from which we might survey the globe, explore cosmic rays, and test the very limits of human endurance. It was a prelude to the coming stratospheric and space rockets that would ascend to infinite altitudes.[6] For the French he was the first of the "astronauts," all the more impressive because he was putting Esnault-Pelterie's theories into action.[7] Gerald Heard offered the most poetic chords of praise: Piccard became "the first who ever burst into that silent sea," that "huge airy continent," that "new Kingdom of space."[8]

A "Cold War" of Stratostats

For Russian publicists Piccard had raised anew the demands of "super-aviation," work originally done by Tsiolkovskii so many years ago and from which Russia had now fallen drastically behind. Piccard was "the key that has opened the door leading to the stratosphere" and even to space beyond. He was a clarion call to action. Soviet Russia needed to reach for extreme altitudes: by stratostats to match the West and by rockets to leap ahead. Here was a Stalinist challenge that accompanied the debates to heighten agricultural and industrial production, to import the best American technology, the plows and reapers of International Harvester, all this amid debates to build the Moscow Metro subway system and the new industrial city at Magnitogorsk.[9]

Piccard posed a special challenge to the United States, thanks to his tour during the winter of 1932–33, at the first peak of the stratosphere craze, making his way to Chicago's "Century of Progress" exhibition, where his ascent was presented as a culminating moment in human progress, with American stratospheric ascents still to come. He brought along an "exact reproduction" of his stratostat cabin, the one he had flown to such high altitudes, photographs showing his head peeping out of the porthole. He also claimed to have invented a stratospheric rocket. The crowds were in awe. Columbia University feted him with a "gala" dinner. An Indian tribe offered him its ceremonial headdress and honorary chiefdom. But perhaps the strangest angle of all was what he did before he left Europe. The father of five young children, he allegedly kidnapped a neighbor's vicious dog and had a veterinarian remove its teeth as a safety precaution. American readers were coming to know the profile of a true eccentric scientist.[10]

A RACE INTO THE STRATOSPHERE

One person was more perturbed than impressed: Capt. Albert W. Stevens of the U.S. Army Air Corps, a record-breaking pilot and aerial photographer, with a degree in electrical engineering, and the real initiator (later hero) of the American stratostat program. Stevens was frustrated that Piccard was visiting the United States in part to gather financial support for his next stratospheric flight, as if to teach Americans a lesson about science and technology and draw from the nation's treasure and strength. As Stevens wrote to his superiors, "There is nothing that Professor Piccard has accomplished that cannot be accomplished as well, or better, by Americans." Promising to gather private support and offering one thousand dollars of his own money, Stevens vowed to get the United States to "actual elevations . . . even greater than those claimed by Professor Piccard." It was all in the name of American pride and the new science of the stratosphere.[11]

Piccard's feats and boasts were in quick time eclipsed by Russian and American stratostats, which were engaged in an international "race to the stratosphere," one that mildly prefigured their later "race to space"—always reaching for larger balloon envelopes, better gondolas, higher altitudes, and more and more scientific discoveries. Publicists in both countries fashioned the competition as a friendly but heated rivalry, exchanging boasts that "the word 'impossible' does not exist in the Soviet dictionary" or that America's stratostat was "an exclamation mark 300 feet tall, punctuating the most awesome of all man's attempts to solve the riddles of the stratosphere." Both countries openly exploited the balloon ascents for either propaganda or public relations, though at first they were racing more against Piccard than against each other.[12]

The USSR opened the race on 30 September 1933 with the launch of the *Stratostat sssr*, built by the Soviet Air Force, bigger than the *fnrs* by some 380,000 cubic feet in volume and seventeen more feet in diameter. The gondola improved on Piccard's with a unique duralumin shell (three millimeters thick), more internal space, portholes, oxygen tanks (with an improved carbon dioxide cleansing system), and electronic descent controls. It also marked the USSR's first world aviation record, beating Piccard and reaching an altitude of

18,500 meters (60,695 feet, or just over 11 miles), although for political reasons none of the Soviet stratostat records were recognized by the official body, the International Aeronautical Federation. The achievement inspired a series of forthcoming stratostat launches to debut Soviet technological prowess on the world stage and reach new records, all with the explicit approval of the Communist Party's top political bureau (*Politbiuro*).[13]

The achievement also entered the annals of domestic state propaganda and popular culture. It inspired a famous scene in the film *Circus* (1936) in which the pilot shot out of a cannon, an acrobatic performance entitled "Flight into the Stratosphere" (partly inspired by the Italian American Hugo Zacchini's act at the Leningrad Circus, the "human cannonball"). A candy was named after the *Stratostat SSSR*'s record-breaking reach, the Stratosfera, a piece of semisweet cubed chocolate with a small rocket on the wrapper, heralding the future of stratospheric flight. The term now entered the popular vocabulary as a metaphor for accomplishment: everyone wanted to achieve success with their own stratostat and reach their own personal "stratosphere."[14] The crew of G. A. Prokof'ev (a Red Army balloonist), E. K. Birnbaum (a military pilot), and K. D. Godunov (a balloon engineer) became Soviet heroes on the order of Stakhanovites and border guards, conquerors of production and distance. As "stratonauts," they enjoyed the special privilege, with the aerial rescuers of the famous Cheliushkin expedition and with Soviet pilots of the massive ANT-20 airplane, as "victors over the air." The poet Demian Bednyi celebrated the three in verse. "By the measure of collective glee, we've conquered all distance / To the heroes of the stratosphere three, we send our compliments!"[15]

Several publicists went even further, honoring the stratonauts as future cosmonauts of a kind. As one review put it, like Piccard before them but going even higher, they had raised the "roof of the world." They were new "vertical Lindberghs." They had fulfilled the "planetary" dreams of Tsiolkovskii to reach beyond the planet: first by stratospheric balloon, soon enough by rocket. The path was predetermined: "From the cultivation of one-sixth of the earth to cultivation of the whole universe, such is the future creative path of our Bolsheviks." This imagery was reinforced by the very call sign of the craft,

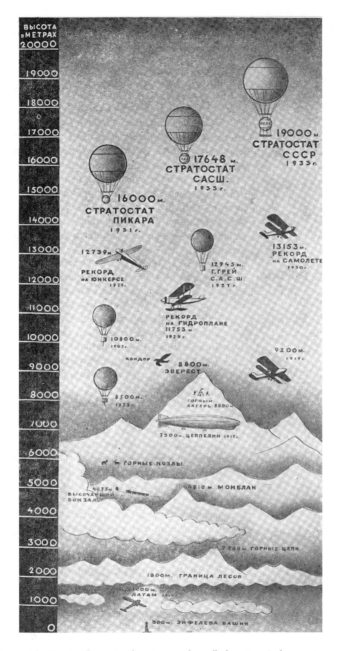

Fig. 17. The Soviet "race to the stratosphere," showing Belgian, American, and Soviet balloons at respective altitudes (in meters), culminating in a provisional *Stratostat* SSSR victory. From A. Garri and L. Kassil', *Potolok mira* (Moscow: Sovetskaia literatura, 1934), 42.

Fig. 18. The *Stratostat SSSR* as new planet. A drawing of the Soviet balloon rising to the planets and becoming one of its own, set against cascading cosmic rays. From A. Garri and L. Kassil', *Potolok mira* (Moscow: Sovetskaia literatura, 1934). A similar perspective on the American *Explorer I* (in the form of a high-altitude photograph) can be found in Capt. Albert W. Stevens, "Exploring the Stratosphere," *National Geographic* 66, no. 4 (October 1934): 422.

"Mars," which meant that the radio broadcasts from the stratostat began with the phrase "Mars calling" (*Mars govorit*). As once aliens sent interplanetary signals to Earth in the imaginings of the old science fiction and cosmic poetry, now we Earthlings were actually communicating with our own planet as nascent space beings ourselves.[16]

The United States soon responded in kind, launching the *Century of Progress* stratostat on 20 November 1933, named in honor of the Chicago fair that year. It was piloted by Lt. Cdr. T. G. W. Settle of the U.S. Navy and Major Fordney of the U.S. Marine Corps, reaching 61,237 feet (11.59 miles), or 18,665 meters (18.6 kilometers), traveling from Akron, Ohio, to Bridgeton, New Jersey, besting the Russians by roughly 542 feet (165 meters), a recognized U.S. world record. The *Century of Progress* flew again a year later, now piloted by Auguste Piccard's twin brother, Jean, and the first woman to the stratosphere, his wife, Jeanette. The pair set off from Detroit on 23

October 1934, congratulated with a wave by none other than a very excited Henry Ford (it launched from Ford Airport), accompanied by a group of children from his Greenfield Village school. The balloon reached a modest 10.9-mile altitude in its flight over Lake Erie, Sandusky, Cleveland, and Akron. Due to cloud cover, the Piccards saw little of the Ohio sites below, landing in humble circumstances on the John Fulton farm, four miles outside of Cadiz.[17]

For the Soviets the race with the West also turned into a race with themselves, a competition between the state-sponsored *Stratostat sssr* projects in Moscow and a "civilian" project in Leningrad, under Sergei Kirov's patronage, named the *Osoaviakhim 1* (for the Society to Assist the Defense and Aviation-Chemical Industries of the USSR). The civilian project was financed by a public campaign (asking for one-ruble donations) and boasted several alleged improvements beyond the *Stratostat sssr*: a redesigned gondola of thin stainless steel; the balloon made of rubber-coated muslin; the gondola and balloon attached by a reinforced rope suspension; along with a sophisticated scientific laboratory of measuring and photographic equipment.[18]

The stratostat took its maiden flight to coincide with the meeting of the infamous Seventeenth Communist Party Congress, the ironic "Congress of Victors," whose elites Stalin would target for purge and terror within a few years. On 30 January 1934, with the call sign "Sirius" (for the brightest star in the nighttime sky), it sent regular communications via wireless back to "Earth," relays that were dramatically reported on the radio, in the newspapers, and on the floor of the party congress itself. At 9:20 a.m., just after liftoff from the outskirts of Moscow, the craft was already at 1,600 meters, sun filling the cabin. At 11:42 a.m. Sirius sent a "fiery greeting" to the "tribune of the world revolution, comrade Stalin." The craft was already "storming an altitude of 21 kilometers."[19] But by morning of the next day the sorry crash of the *Osoaviakhim 1* was already known: the crew was dead.

A number of theories circulated about the cause of the crash. One leading speculation held that under the political pressure of the Communist Party, the crew had tried to rise too far and fast, even as high as twenty-two thousand meters (as one of the journal entries purportedly showed). Another early claim held that at such a height an ice buildup may have weighed the balloon down, which, when combined with the sun heating up the internal gases, may have also caused a rapid depressurization and free fall. In the end the official explanation concluded that after too high an ascent and too rapid a descent, the gondola had become unstrapped from the balloon due to poor design and construction, the apparatus crashing to the ground by around 4:30 p.m.[20]

The three crew members were given top honors, portrayed as "the best representatives of the scientific-technical intelligentsia" and the new political class. The pilot, Pavel Fedoseenko, was a flyer and Red Army officer; Il'ia Usyskin, a physics graduate student and Young Communist leader; and Andrei Vasenko, an aeronautical engineer. Together they were the "fearless stormers of the heavens." They were Bolshevik "revolutionaries of science," ready to make any sacrifice for party and country. Together they "wrote a new and definitive page in the book of history's struggle against nature."[21] But the accolades went further. These stratonauts had, according to the poets of the day, reached for the "mysterious distances" and the "fabulous heights." Indeed, "they went to distances where no man had gone before." Nikolai Bukharin teased these images, portraying the three as interplanetary travelers of a kind, who had set off for the "fathomless depths of space," who had literally discovered a "new world, even newer than the Americas." They were also the three stars who had fallen from the stars, cascading like fiery comets.[22] A song from the Communist Youth League summed up the cosmic theme:

> For those who led a starry route through the skies,
> The Komsomol will follow,
> To infinity and beyond,
> To the very stars
> It will take up its post! . . .
> Though they perished, their successors are coming
> Piloting a star-fleet their way—
> To the planets,
> As guests of the celestial host,
> We will raise our banner![23]

A RACE INTO THE STRATOSPHERE

All of this was framed by an official wake at the Great Hall of the Central Executive Committee in downtown Moscow, the crew's cremated remains placed in urns, surrounded by magnificent flower wreaths, palm plants, and red flags. Orchestral dirges, military marches, and eulogies accompanied the remains to the Kremlin Wall at Red Square. There Stalin and the top party leadership, as honor guard, watched as the ashes were finally interred in the bricks of the Kremlin wall (just like they were for the victim cosmonauts of later fame, namely the crew of *Soiuz 11*).

Both the United States and USSR continued the competition in the wake of the disaster, the United States nearly experiencing one of its own: *Explorer I*. No American insurance company agreed to underwrite the new balloon, so Lloyd's of London stepped in, to its misfortune. *Explorer I* was launched on 28 July 1934 in partnership with the National Geographic Society, piloted by Maj. William E. Kepner, along with Capt. Orvil A. Anderson and the redoubtable Capt. Albert W. Stevens, both of the U.S. Army Air Corps. The balloon was fully inflated by two o'clock that morning. As one reporter wrote: "Held to the Earth only by slender ropes, the huge bag towered overhead, a beautiful sight as the top melted into the dim shadows above the direct rays of the floodlights." Then it "cast off," speeding eastward in the direction of Omaha, Nebraska. The crew reached a modest 60,613 feet (11.5 miles), or 18,475 meters (18.5 kilometers), flying from outside of Rapid City, South Dakota, to the Reuben Johnson family farm at Holdrege, Nebraska, some 315 miles away. After a tear in the balloon envelope, the gondola made a prolonged and harrowing descent (caught by radio listeners across the United States). The crew parachuted to safety at 5,000 feet, the heroic Stevens pushing off just as the balloon exploded, all of them landing alive in time to view the crushed remains of their gondola on the ground.[24]

Nevertheless, it was a valiant effort. This was now the largest stratospheric balloon to date: 3 million cubic feet fully inflated with highly flammable hydrogen gas, 179 feet in diameter. Its fabric had been joined together with cement and tape in special clean rooms, this to avoid dust and contaminants; the assembled balloon was then laid out upon four inches of sawdust at its launch site, spread out in a 200-foot circle, this to safely support the balloon before inflation. The gondola was made of a special magnesium alloy, weighing only two-thirds as much as aluminum. To better conduct scientific studies, special valves gave the balloon equilibrium plateaus at successive altitudes. The craft carried one ton of equipment: a barometer, barograph, thermograph, spectograph, radio transmitter, and electroscope; altimeters, factographs, cameras, Geiger counters, and batteries; along with all of the environmental equipment of air dispensers and cleansers, fans and dehumidifiers, to keep the crew alive and comfortable (the craft also used liquid oxygen for breathing and a chemical screen to cleanse the air of carbon dioxide).

The entry of *Explorer I* into the race for the stratosphere certainly looks from the vantage of the present day like an intense competition with the USSR. Yet several observers and participants in the program framed it largely as a research and development effort to match Piccard's scientific challenges, not to compete with the Soviets. The U.S. military attaché in Moscow—in answer to queries from army air corps engineers at Wright Field in Dayton, Ohio—relayed his judgment to the War Department that the *Osoviakhim 1* represented no threat "to militarize the stratosphere." For the Soviets, he surmised, the stratosphere was all about science.[25]

Media outlets basked in the pride of U.S. achievements. Newspaper and magazine articles offered readers wonderful photographs of the gondola, filled with mysterious instruments and controls, many of which were designed to study outer space (detections of the mysterious cosmic rays and spectographs of the sun). The craft was a veritable "'flying laboratory' with a maze of instruments." For radio listeners who heard parts of the flight, filled with the background noise of "constant clickings and whirrings and buzzings," the photographs and sounds must have surely seemed like scenes out of the *Buck Rogers* science fiction stories.[26] The whole scope of the expedition (like the coming *Explorer II* flight) had an outer space theme, in the words of the crew, the balloon rising "far up in the heavens," where they saw a dark sky of "black velvet," as if during a full solar eclipse. Photographs of the flight in the *National Geographic* also

Table 4. The race into the stratosphere

Altitude (in miles)	1931	1932	1933	1934	1935
14				USSR *Osoaviakhim 1* 13.6 72,178 feet, or 22,000 meters (30 January)	USA *Explorer II* 13.71 72,395 feet, or 22,066 meters (11 November)
13					
12			USA *Century of Progress* 11.59 61,237 feet, or 18,665 meters (20 November) USSR *Stratostat SSSR* 11.49 60,695 feet, or 18,500 meters (30 September)	USA *Explorer I* 11.5 60,613 feet, or 18,475 meters (28 July)	
11					
10		Belgian *FNRS* 10.07 53,153 feet, or 16,201 meters (18 August)		USA *Century of Progress II* 10.9 57,579 feet, or 17,550 meters (23 October)	USSR *Stratostat SSSR Encore (bis)* 10.0 52,799 feet, or 16,093 meters (26 June)
9	Belgian *FNRS* 9.8 51,775 feet, or 15,781 meters (27 May)			Belgian *FNRS* 10 52,952 feet, or 16,140 meters (18 August)	
Year	1931	1932	1933	1934	1935

Note: The global race for higher and higher altitudes between 1931 and 1935. Compare with the misleading Soviet and American charts (figs. 17 and 20). The Belgian *FNRS* stood for Fonds National de la Recherche Scientifique (National Foundation for Scientific Research). The International Aeronautical Federation has recognized the two *FNRS* flights, the first *Century of Progress* flight, and *Explorer II* as world records. The statistics for the other flights vary depending on their media sources but are based mostly on Charles G. Philp, *The Conquest of the Stratosphere* (New York: Putnam, 1937), 36.

showed the balloon envelope as a rival to the moon or a planet all its own, as if it were rising into the sky.[27]

On 26 June 1935 the Soviets responded to the flight with a modest one of their own, the *Stratostat SSSR Encore (bis)*, an air force project that focused on a safe and achievable flight more than any reckless record breaking. It missed the mark of *Explorer I* by about two miles, yet it still helped to redeem the loss of *Osoaviakhim 1* from the year before. The crew of Kristian Zille, Iuri Prilutskii, and Aleksandr Varigo, a professor of physics, encountered trouble on descent: valve malfunctions and a leak in the envelope. As the others parachuted to safety, Zille landed the gondola successfully (though it was outfitted with a parachute as well).

This short-lived race for the stratosphere ended rather abruptly, at least from retrospect, with an American victory: the dramatic and definitive flight of *Explorer II* on 11 November 1935, Armistice Day. An earlier flight, on 12 July 1935, had ended in a near disaster with a tear in the balloon shortly after full inflation, requiring improvements to the design. The new balloon was, as one commentator put it, the "largest sphere, by far, ever constructed by man." It was the first stratostat to use safer, nonexplosive helium. But it also had less lifting power, requiring a larger balloon of two and two-thirds acres of fabric, reinforced by thin steel cables and three hundred gallons of rubber cement, carrying up to 3.7 million cubic feet of gas, reaching 192 feet in diameter when fully inflated. The gondola was a full 9 feet in diameter (larger than *Explorer I*), outfitted with electric controls for ballast and emergency parachutes, including heavy disposable batteries to run the equipment, and specially designed heated suits and gloves for the crew to withstand the severe cold (-55 degrees Celsius outside the cabin and -7 degrees within). To protect themselves from turbulence and possible injury, the crew also wore football helmets on loan from the Calvin Coolidge High School of Rapid City (Piccard and Kipfer had worn pillow-stuffed wicker baskets).[28]

A preview of the Manhattan Project and American aerospace ventures to come, *Explorer II* was a model of government, industry, and academic cooperation—but with one crucial difference: this time conservative army air corps chiefs approved official military partici-

Fig. 19. The crew of the later *Explorer II* in the gondola, revealing a "Buck
Rogers" world. From Capt. Albert W. Stevens, "Man's Farthest Aloft,"
National Geographic 69, no. 1 (January 1936): 64. Credit: Richard Hewitt
Stewart / National Geographic Creative.

pation only so long as the government was not billed. The American free market paid for the flight.[29] The scope of the undertaking was impressive. The U.S. Weather Bureau and the Coast and Geodetic Survey prepared the forecasts and maps, waiting for the favorable high-pressure systems. The Army Signal Corps provided communications. The Fourth U.S. Cavalry at Fort Meade, in Sturgis, South Dakota, offered its soldiers to move and prepare the balloon. The South Dakota National Guard helped with loading and unloading of supplies. Dow Chemical Company built the gondola; the Army Air Corps's Material Division outfitted it with controls and equipment at Wright Field, assisted by the Hamilton Watch Company and Linde Air Products Company. The Goodyear-Zeppelin Company of Akron built the balloon. The Homestake Mining Company provided the floodlights for night work. Bell + Howell, Graflex Corporation, and Eastman Cine-Kodak provided the cameras and mechanisms. Bausch + Lomb Optical Company made the porthole glass. United Air Lines and Fairchild Aviation provided aerial support, and the Shell Petroleum Corporation, Ford Motor Company, and the Burlington and Quincy Railroad Company offered their services. The Rapid City Chamber of Commerce built the roads, electric lines, and spectator platforms. Men from the Civilian Conservation Corps guarded equipment. The University of Rochester, the California Institute of Technology, the National Bureau of Standards, the Carnegie Institution, Harvard University, and the Department of Physics at Cornell all provided scientific equipment and advice.

The flight of *Explorer II* was also filled with exciting media spectacles and regalia. Like *Explorer I*, the balloon and gondola were prepared for flight outside of Rapid City, at the famed "Stratocamp" and "Stratobowl," a geographical depression in the Black Hills only 600 feet round, largely free of dangerous winds (up to 305 feet high). Teams of scientists and workers turned the barren landscape into a bustling railroad station and temporary city. Just a few days before the flight, Stevens wrote from the Stratocamp that even at two degrees below zero and with heavy snow, "we are staying at it, and plan to get the bag in the air yet. The morale is good," he said, partly because of a decent mess hall and outings to town.[30] The actual flight, reaching to a U.S. world record 72,395 feet (22,066 meters), was covered in full by the print and radio media. As with *Explorer I*, the National Broadcasting Company (NBC) relayed radio signals from the gondola coast to coast. Captain Stevens described the flight in dramatic terms as "floating in the nearest approach to a natural vacuum in which man has ever placed himself." This was the cold "alien world of the stratosphere, at the edge of space." It was "a foreign and lifeless world," one "almost divorced from Mother Earth."[31]

In the end Stevens and Anderson were mobbed by hundreds of spectators (and souvenir hunters) on their successful descent at the Cramer farm, near Stickney, South Dakota. Cars had followed the flight on the ground, leaving huge trails of dust along the country roads, clearly visible from the stratostat's heights. The two were soon feted as heroes with awards and parades, the same celebrations in life that the Soviet stratonauts had received in death. To add insult to accomplishment, one of Captain Stevens's stratosphere charts did not even include the record-breaking altitudes of either the *Stratostat SSSR* or *Osoaviakhim 1* balloons. The American media ignored the Russian Communists altogether (a myopia it repeated later in the years before *Sputnik*).

The praise for the crews of *Explorer I* and *II* also reached some rather fanciful extremes. Gilbert Grosvenor, president of the National Geographic Society, called them "gallant, resourceful, and brainy men." Gen. John J. Pershing termed their achievements as one of the greatest "assaults on the battlefront of science." Reports described the work of the ground and expeditionary crews as fulfilling "clockwork precision," the men as masters of "concentration" and coordinated effort. Stevens's wife was most proud, calling her husband "the first astronaut."[32] More impressive were *Explorer II*'s "firsts":

"The largest sphere, by far, that man had ever constructed for any purpose whatsoever."

"The largest area covered by one photograph, taken through a single lens, more than that of the state of Indiana" and which "shows a horizon farther from the lens than was ever caught on a camera plate, 330 miles."

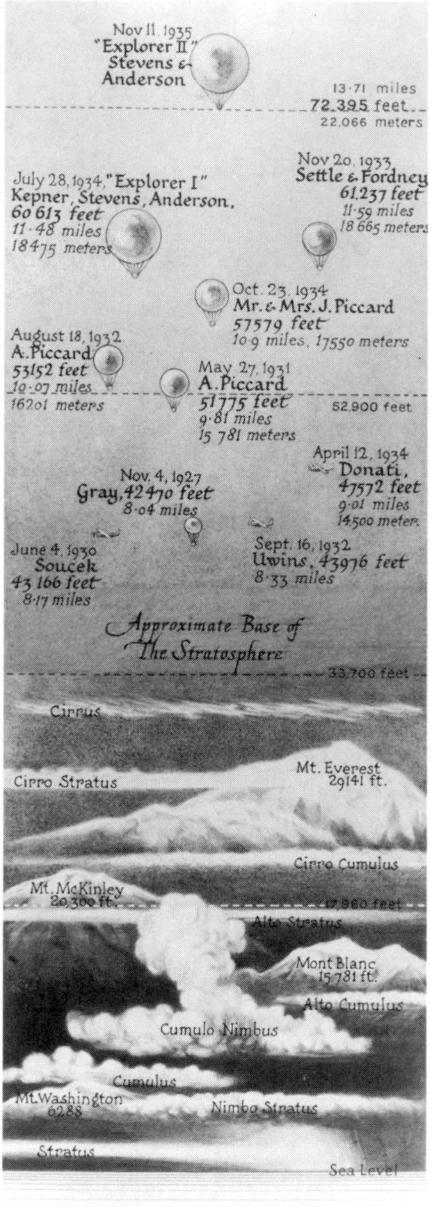

Fig. 20. "Flying High." The American "race to the stratosphere," completely leaving out all Soviet balloons. From Capt. Albert W. Stevens, "The Scientific Results of the World-Record Stratosphere Flight," *National Geographic* 69, no. 5 (May 1936): 694. Credit: Hashime Murayama / National Geographic Creative.

"The highest vertical photograph yet made by man," of the White River (at 13 miles altitude and of nearly 105 square miles).

"The first picture ever made with the line of sight between the camera and a far-distant objective—here, the arc of the dust horizon—wholly in the stratosphere."

"The first photograph ever made showing the division between the troposphere and the stratosphere and also the actual curvature of the earth: photographed from an elevation of 72,395 feet, the highest point ever reached by man."[33]

This last photograph, published as a twenty-four-by-seventeen-inch foldout in *National Geographic*, was truly remarkable. *Scientific American* and its European and Russian imitators may have drawn impressive stratospheric charts, even filled them with balloons and rockets. But it took Albert W. Stevens to actually photograph the boundary between the troposphere and stratosphere as well as the very curvature of the earth, all above the neatly plotted South Dakota farms, including a slice of the border with Nebraska. Here was the American heartland—in and from the edge of space.

The Soviets never answered *Explorer II* with another successful stratostat flight to match. They tried and failed over the next few years, but the new ceiling was never breached.[34] The brief public race with the United States faded into history.

Invention and the Coming War

Beyond balloons the race for the stratosphere had a more sinister military dimension. As Soviet analysts argued with most force, the USSR had no choice but to match wits with Western aviation and technological achievements, even engage in a race to "conquer the stratosphere" for super-aviation and super-artillery. The commander of the Soviet Air Force, Ia. I. Alksnis, justified all of this in order to defend such a mammoth country as the USSR: one-sixth of the earth's land surface and eleven thousand kilometers in distance from east to west.[35] To protect such horizons, Russia needed a new "vertical." The new threshold posed a number of daunting military challenges: how to perfect high-altitude and high-speed engines and fuselages;

how to test and train pilots to control their craft and survive at such high altitudes; how to develop "rocket planes" and "rocket artillery" (including winged bombs and cruise missiles). Here was a whole new arena beyond the reach of ground artillery and the perfect venue for surveillance of the enemy's forces or for high-altitude bombardment. Here was also a chapter in what Europeans called the "coming war"—either the *zukunftskrieg*, or *la guerra del'avvenire*, or the *budushchaia voina*. And that coming war, said the knowing Soviet commissar of defense, K. E. Voroshilov, in terms first uttered by the French marshal Ferdinand Foch, would be a "war of machines."[36]

Chemical weapons and air power were already factual achievements of the First World War. The media were filled with dire predictions: that their destructive power and strategic reach were bound to make the next war all the more terrible and global, a "war of speed, surprise, and shock," fulfilling all the "bad dreams of the horror writers."[37] In this regard German military planners recognized the decisive potential of new kinds of battlefield rockets shortly after the war. Rockets, when launching chemical weapons by smokeless powder or liquid propellant, avoided all traces of their point of origin, diminishing the potential of any counterattack. They improved distance and accuracy, so important to the lethal weaponry of chemical bombs. The USSR similarly made an early commitment to experimental work on solid fuel, smokeless-powder battlefield rockets in the Gas Dynamics Laboratory (GDL), founded in 1921 in Petrograd.[38]

According to the official Communist Party political line, the USSR was thrust into an intense competition for bigger fleets of fighters and bombers, planes that traveled ever faster and higher. Air power would decide the next war.[39] The defense planner Robert Eidemann put it bluntly at a meeting in honor of the country's first Aviation Day, 18 August 1933. Referring to Giulio Douhet's theories of strategic air power, he warned that "capitalism, having begun in history with piracy on the oceans, now completes the cycle of its development with piracy in the air." The USSR had to fight the criminals with its own aerial fleets, deemed essential by Douhet, now republished in an official Soviet version.[40]

These kinds of references were sanctioned at the highest levels.

Voroshilov reduced the problem to a pithy slogan: "He who is strong in the air will be strong everywhere."[41] The Soviet General Staff even published a massive four-volume study, *The Coming War* (1928), with precise analyses and estimates of foreign military threats, along with a sober appreciation of air power.[42] But its military planners also gave in to the temptation of drama and hyperbole, purely out of self-interest. To heighten the threat of the coming war with the West was their means of justifying better funding and status. So they sometimes took on the role of prophets of doom, weaving their own futuristic stories about the destructive marriage of chemical and aerial weapons, meaning the "significant widening *sphere* and *radius* of aerial war."[43]

This coming war of machines was partially based on historical fact, partially extrapolated from science fiction. The technological culture of the military, much like science fiction, was both known and unknown. Military innovation tottered precariously in a gray area between what was real and what was probable. The rocketry pioneer Korolev understood this, calling stratospheric flight a former fantasy about to become real.[44] As one report to Voroshilov put it, all the worst scenarios of science fiction, or "what was only possible in novels," would become true in reality. Or as another top report held, summarizing the latest Western and Russian tracts on future war scenarios: "notwithstanding a heavy dose of fantasy," they had much to teach Soviet leaders.[45] When the military translated Robert Knauss's German novel *The Aerial War of 1936: The Destruction of Paris*, its editor stripped the story of all its plotlines and characters, leaving only its scenes of future aerial war as a military primer, something befitting Douhet's own marriage of fiction and fact.[46] One Russian writer imagined waking up in the year 2050 to find a world half-destroyed by war from the air, bombardments having leveled whole cities and populations. His ironic warning: "Yes, indeed, contemporary technology develops along the lines of fairy tales."[47]

Several technological innovations, especially energy rays and rockets, were the favorite subjects of both military prognostication and futuristic storytelling. The work of military inventors was fueling a whole new kind of weapons race. English and American scientists (Harry Grindell-Matthews, Ernst Welch, and William Coolidge) claimed to be perfecting projection weapons throughout the 1920s, reported in media outlets worldwide. They promised to shoot electromagnetic beams or liquid bullets or cathode rays—to kill the enemy, stop internal combustion engines, or bring down attacking airplanes. The Soviet media constantly entertained these possible new weapons of war: "devil rays," "propeller-less planes," and "death rockets."[48] Science fiction writers set these new machines into their stories. Aleksei Tolstoi's arch-villain, P. P. Garin, invented a sophisticated "infra-red" death ray, based on a hyperbolic mirror that could slice through the earth's crust (or human beings), "like a loaf of bread." André Maurois imagined a fantastic death ray in his saga about the future "Inter-Planetary War" of 1964. It was "capable of destroying by its passage any combination of atoms," projecting far into outer space against Earth's enemies on the moon.[49]

The challenge for the military authorities was in separating fact from fiction. As a rule, military analysts doubted all the media frenzy. One found a coming war scenario as far too dramatic, a "fantasy" more appropriate for the movie house. Another found no credible scientific evidence to confirm the Grindell-Matthews devil ray. It was simply not feasible. And even if it were, the Newtonian law of action-reaction dictated that for every new offensive, there was an effective defense.[50] Yet the Soviet military kept up minor investment in "projection" weapons. The young engineer and future designer of Soviet rocket engines V. P. Glushko even promoted a "heat projector" in the GDL. It sounded an awful lot like the "repulsor" weapon in Lasswitz's *Two Planets* or like Welch's liquid death rocket. Touted as "one of the newest ideas" and a sure investment, Glushko's ray was designed to kill enemy troops and disable tanks. Rocket exhaust, in other words, could be aimed forward as well as backward.[51] Just a few years later even the famous Nikola Tesla surreptitiously approached the Soviet government with an offer to sell his "electric cannon," a matter of the "highest secrecy." It was a weapon, he promised, with the power of up to fifty million volts, enough to send a concentrated and directed ray of metal fragments, at the speed of light, as far as five thousand miles, able to destroy its target completely. Soviet military officers seriously weighed his offer.[52]

A RACE INTO THE STRATOSPHERE

The liquid fuel rocket held out the strangest military promise: the very same machine that might save humanity from a global catastrophe (by taking us to space) might also be the very means for our destruction in a total war. American and English publicists envisioned the intercontinental ballistic missile in just this way; it could travel off to Mars or jettison deadly bombs "half way around the Earth." Such destructive power, another writer warned, could "lead to conquest more absolute than anything the world has ever known," governments turning engineers into rocket-building "slaves."[53] The conservative *Liberty* magazine, backed by the authority of Gen. Billy Mitchell, colored this threat as part of the "Asiatic" communist "Red Menace." The fun-filled "Fourth of July toy" and prospective Mars rocket was about to become "the most astonishing invention and perhaps the most indispensable" and "revolutionary" weapon of war. The mad Russian inventor Tsiolkovskii was already "feverishly engaged in the development of the rocket-torpedo," illustrated by a missile's parabolic arc over the onion-dome cupolas of the USSR, headed toward the United States (and mimicking the Paris Gun of 1918).[54] Is it any surprise, then, that both the German and Russian military were already publicly entertaining the new possibilities of rocket power, the fantastic means of space travel now become a serious means of military strength?[55]

Within all of these contexts Mikhail N. Tukhachevskii began to promote more innovative research and development in liquid fuel rocketry, first as commander of the Leningrad Military District (1929–30), then as deputy peoples' commissar for defense and chief of armaments (after 1931). By 1933, partly in answer to Douhet, Tukhachevskii was establishing a strategic vision of "deep-battlefield" warfare, founded upon heavy armor and artillery, radio communications, and a variety of aerial weapons (including rockets). In other words, the coming war would see intensive and extensive strikes deep into the heart of an enemy's homeland. Well-read in the latest Western texts on military science, he understood the lethal powers of the new technologies. On a formal visit to Great Britain conservative English generals found his strategic visions unorthodox, to say the least. Said General Knox in response, "The Russians are a nation of incorrigible dreamers."[56]

Under Tukhachevskii's patronage the GDL began serious research into more powerful liquid fuel rocket engines. V. P. Glushko joined its teams in spring of 1929 to develop a series of "experimental rocket motors" (the ORM series), tested in laboratory stands by 1931, using a variety of liquid fuels and even electric power. They were never launched, but they did help to prove the basic functions and efficiencies of rocket engines. The GDL's various units also worked on solid fuel rockets for battlefield and aerial use (as takeoff assists or as pure missiles).[57] Glushko's liquid fuel rockets were its most innovative and cumbersome project. They were expensive. They were experimental. They were unreliable. Director Boris S. Petropavlovskii noted their "highly complicated construction." Rocket science was at its very origins. Yet as both he and one of his analysts noted, the USSR had no choice but to innovate and test, just as Western governments were doing, all under the cloak of top secrecy. As the analysts phrased it, "reactive action" was the technology of the future.[58]

Thanks to their clandestine military projects in place since 1922, Germany and Russia were perfectly poised to understand each other on these scores. As their pact came to a close in 1932, one of the last top-level Soviet delegations to visit Germany (before Hitler) expressed its interest in the emerging techniques of air power, including high-altitude surveillance and bombing as well as ground-to-air communications and control. But first and foremost was an interest in "experimental flights into the stratosphere."[59] Marshal Tukhachevskii even reported to Commissar Voroshilov that he had come to a high-priority agreement with the Junkers firm for development of a stratospheric jet airplane. As he emphasized for fuller effect, "This issue is of such importance, and we have fallen so far behind, that we must begin to fulfill this agreement as quickly as possible."[60]

Tukhachevskii also became the patron of the GIRD by the spring of 1932, when his Directorate of Military Inventions contracted with it for the supply of military weaponry. According to one report, the GIRD thus lived a "double life" nearly from its start, serving both civilian and military purposes. It was essentially a paramilitary organization bound to the authority, financing, and secrecy codes of the Red Army.[61] Korolov admitted, and internal documents corrobo-

A RACE INTO THE STRATOSPHERE

rated, that it was part of the civilian Osoaviakhim only "in form" but subject to the Directorate of Military Inventions "in fact." Its goals were to provide it with rocket engines and "shells"—or in Korolev's words, "the application of the rocket for defense needs."[62]

Tukhachevskii was also the guiding force in the union of the GDL and GIRD into the Reactive Scientific Research Institute (RNII), the world's first scientific research facility for jet and rocket propulsion. By the spring of 1932 he was intensely lobbying one of the Politburo's chiefs, V. M. Molotov, on the need to establish a "Reactive Institute," a proposal he framed as an answer to the growing international competition for jets and rockets and the campaign to "storm the stratosphere." The German and American militaries, he warned, were guarding every advance and achievement of Hermann Oberth and Robert Goddard with utmost secrecy. Tukhachevskii sounded the alarm that the USSR must compete too, direct its scientific and technological cadres to create new reactive "artillery, aviation, and chemical" weapons. The liquid fuel "reactive engine," he wrote, would "create unlimited possibilities for the firing of artillery shells of every caliber to every distance." It offered the surest means to achieving "stratospheric flights" of the highest altitudes and fastest speeds.[63]

The RNII set out to perfect solid fuel and liquid fuel rocket engines for both conventional and chemical warfare and to create winged rockets and rocket takeoff-assist devices for aircraft. Its first director, from 1933 to 1937, was I. T. Kleimenov; its chief engineer was G. E. Langemak. S. P. Korolev, its assistant director, was also in charge of the RNII's projects with piloted rocket planes.[64] The highest state officials valued this work as of "first-order significance." Its novel weapons were bound to be a "powerful factor in the coming war." Foreign states were working on them "intensively" and in "top secret," after all. The USSR had to respond in kind.[65] The RNII was, therefore, a closed military institution, governed by top secret rules and clearances, a forerunner of the future "post office boxes" (iashchiki) that dotted the Soviet military-industrial landscape of the Cold War. Its letterhead gave its address simply as "post office box 1027." In fact, the RNII was headquartered outside of Moscow, its buildings rather well hidden from the road, in an old institute adjacent to a crop of woods, conveniently near an airport and test field.[66] From these rather spare beginnings the institute soon achieved a number of early technical studies of the rocket. Langemak and Glushko contributed one such study, what they claimed was the first of its kind, a sober and comprehensive appraisal of the liquid fuel rocket as a potential ballistic missile in the coming war. In a basic primer about rocket science—joining physics and chemistry, metallurgy and engineering—they offered the essential rocket equations and mass ratios and exhaust velocities for this new kind of machine, which needed no medium but its own and which in its flight left a trail "tracing the very trajectory of the craft."[67]

How did these Soviet rocketry investments compare to the West? In the United States, Goddard received dramatic funding from the Smithsonian Institution and Guggenheim Fund, along with much fanfare and publicity. But he received no substantial support from the government or military. (In this, incidentally, he was not alone: Tsiolkovskii, Oberth, Tsander, Crocco, and Esnault-Pelterie all appealed to the military to build ballistic missiles but ultimately failed to receive adequate support or even build the actual missiles.) Between 1914 and 1939 Goddard made recurring appeals to the military. The coast guard and navy, army ordnance and the army air corps, were all interested in rocket artillery and planes. Goddard consulted with famed Maj. Jimmy Doolittle, worked with Brig. Gen. H. C. Brett (the patron of the *Explorer* stratostats). But in the end the military declined his entreaties, best expressed by Adm. W. H. Standley (acting secretary of the navy) that the application of rocket devices to "projectiles and bombs" was just "too expensive." In other words, let the Guggenheim Foundation pay for it all until the results are proven.[68] Ironically, because Goddard published little except for two major pieces in 1919 and 1936, with a few articles in between, the foreign media often speculated that he was actually working in top secret for the American military. One Soviet specialist even described Goddard as having "the rank of general and assigned a huge rocket laboratory."[69]

In Germany the Nazi regime took an opposite track, consolidating select persons from the amateur groups into a state "rocket team" focused on secretive and intense development. Men such as

A RACE INTO THE STRATOSPHERE

Walter Dornberger, Arthur Rudolph, and Wernher von Braun were backed by the institutional power of the German military, industry, and academia. They went on to develop the rocket engines and designs of the *Aggregat* series 1 through 3 between 1932 and 1935 at Kummersdorf (reaching altitudes of over one kilometer, or just over half a mile) and the world's first true ballistic missile with long-range trajectories: the *Aggregat 4* and *5* between 1936 and 1942 at Peenemünde.[70] Rocketry became the top secret preserve of the Nazi state, though space adventures continued to fill the venues of popular culture. They became political "space operas," for the most part, whose spaceships now never exceeded the sophistication of the Zeppelin dirigible, often applying antigravity metals and other amazing discoveries, marks of German scientific superiority. Their accent was on adventure, something like Edgar Rice Burroughs's *Princess of Mars* series, if with much sharper racist and militarist overtones.[71]

Through all of this Stalin's regime left no matter to chance. When it came to rocketry during the 1930s, no other country experienced such a commitment to both a top secret weapons program and a mass-propaganda movement as did the USSR. Individual inventors and mass enthusiasm mattered. True, the rocket pioneers tended to be somewhat eccentric both personally and professionally, often exaggerating the promises and downplaying the perils of their new inventions. The rockets they eventually built, in comparison with later achievements, were amateurish. But the pioneers, the "reactioneers" (*reaktivshchiki*) or "rocketeers" (*raketchiki*), were catalysts. The political and military establishments necessarily built upon their foundations. Organizations such as Osoaviakhim and the Society of Inventors reflected the popular base of Communist society. They also reflected the very mobilizational methods of Western governments, as one Soviet executive put it, like those of the "American militarists" who always tried to integrate scientific workers from below into the development of their new secret military technologies from above.[72]

The RNII faced precisely this problem of elite management and mass support soon after it was established. The engineers of the GIRD joined it without their agitational and propaganda cadres. The military simply did not want them. Yet administrators found it impractical to "divide the technical-research and mass-agitation work of GIRD."[73] This was quite a testimony to the rugged enthusiasm of its founders, to the double life they had led as military contractors and rocket propagandists. The public face of rocketry mattered. Engineering and propaganda were inseparable. The Soviet defense industry had no choice but to both maintain its top secret design bureaus and to promote a very public movement of inventors and amateur scientists. So the state helped to sponsor the work of the Leningrad members of GIRD (writers such as Rynin and Perel'man) with the general public. It created a Reactive Group within the Stratospheric Committee of the Aviation All-Union Scientific-Engineering Technical Society (AVIAVNITO) to help mobilize mass interest in jet and rocket technologies and to promote their teaching in the high schools and colleges. The group launched several small rockets in the summers of 1936 and 1937 and also sponsored exhibits on the "storming" of the stratosphere (and the Arctic) at Gorkii Park in central Moscow, with up to 252,000 visitors attending.[74]

The RNII worked closely with these organizations to promote rocketry. Its leading members, though bound by secrecy protocols, even signed their names and affiliations in press articles, openly advertising their rocketry work. *Pravda*, for example, celebrated one joint RNII-AVIAVNITO rocket launch with special praise for two of their engineers, future designers in the Soviet space program, M. K. Tikhonravov and L. S. Dushkin.[75] The military forged close ties with the mass journal *Inventor* to promote invention from below. In an era of total war, encompassing chemical and germ warfare and all manner of new armor and aerial weapons, no contributions were too small to help revolutionize the battlefield and gain an advantage. This included new ideas about "reactive" apparatuses (jets and rockets). In effect inventors were encouraged to think beyond the realm of the possible. In the West, they were advised, scientists were beginning to explore the "conquest of cosmic space" by "rocket ships" and "interplanetary mirrors," devices to project military power even into outer space. The USSR had to answer with interplanetary rockets.[76]

Elite scientific and military circles counted as well. RNII engineers helped to organize several signal firsts in world history: two

A RACE INTO THE STRATOSPHERE

academic conferences designed to reach "ever higher," in the words of the favorite Stalinist slogan of the day.[77] In April 1934 the Academy of Sciences sponsored the All-Union Conference on the Study of the Stratosphere, dedicated to the full range of issues related to the stratosphere. Although dozens of papers touched upon such topics as meteorology and stratostat balloons, the conference focused on a number of technical, theoretical, and historical studies of "reactive power," as applied either to stratoplanes or to pure rockets. N. A. Rynin's massive study "Methods of Conquering the Stratosphere" was presented within the volume of the proceedings, really the most comprehensive review of jet and rocket experiments to date in any language. He surveyed the current race for stratospheric flight and rocketry gripping Europe and the United States. He proposed rocket power as the coming technology to replace the traditional wing, gasoline engine, and airplane propeller.[78]

Within a year a whole new conference, the First All-Union Conference for the Development of Reactive Aircraft in the Conquest of the Stratosphere, promised jets and rockets as the top state priority. The conference, held on 2–3 March 1935 and sponsored by the RNII, AviavNITO, and the Air Force Academy, was hosted at the main headquarters of the Red Army. This was quite a turn from the first failed stirrings for rocketry in Moscow some ten years earlier. Veteran rocketeers from those days—including Perel'man, Rynin, and Vetchinkin—joined in the conference's promotion of rocket planes and long-range rockets. The country's best rocket engineers participated, including In. A. Pobedonostsev, V. P. Glushko, and S. P. Korolev, all future spacecraft designers in the Cold War. Perhaps most impressive were the contributions at both conferences of a future designer of both the R-7 rocket and *Sputnik* satellite, M. K. Tikhonravov, who delivered presentations of technical and philosophical dazzle. Based on Tsiolkovskii's and Hohmann's calculus, in terms worthy of the artists Malevich or Maiakovskii, he wrote of the liquid fuel rocket as the most perfect machine, fully independent of any other medium except its own, as opening "the possibility of movement without any point of reference." He foretold that the "interplanetary rocket" would soon chart a course on a "flight to infinity," requiring only small increases of energy (including atomic and solar) to develop greater velocities. In a rather astounding review of the future possible, Tikhonravov taught that the Soviet rocket was destined to be the first into outer space.[79]

By every measure either one of the two conferences should have won the REP-Hirsch prize for astronautics. Instead, it was awarded to two otherwise deserving winners—in 1935 to the Frenchman Louis Damblanc for his innovations in powder rockets and in 1936 to Alfred Africano and the American Rocket Society for their tests with liquid fuel rockets. This rejection of Russian achievements was really an indication of the political barriers that still separated Western Europe from Soviet Russia. No other country had offered such intense academic forums on the questions of stratospheric and interplanetary flight. Yet the conferences were officially spurned. The average American news readers was likely more impressed, learning that all of this was proof that the USSR was making steady progress in the development of "rocket propulsion machines," meant initially to reach into the stratosphere and eventually outer space, even fulfilling Goddard's original charge to get to the moon.[80]

Fascist Italy took a more serious track, sponsoring the Volta Conference on High Altitude Velocity in Aviation (1935), much like the Soviet Stratospheric Conference, dedicated to the proposition that mainstream aviation had exhausted its capacities for smarter propellers or piston engines or streamlined fuselages. Conference charts on altitude and speed records depicted this truth, as did several papers on high-speed aerodynamics (such as flying boat designs and high-altitude motors). Humanity had reached the extreme envelopes of altitude and speed. Some kind of breakthrough was necessary, so suggested several of the conference papers—a whole new human technological envelope. These studies included the innovative scientific proofs of Adolf Busemann from Nazi Germany on the advantages of the swept-back wing for supersonic flight (in reducing drag). Busemann had the most interesting perspective at Rome: having just visited both Kummersdorf, where he met with Dornberger and von Braun about Germany's liquid fuel rockets, and Vienna, where he interviewed Eugen Sänger about winged rockets. Bound to secrecy, he shared nothing of either visit.[81]

A RACE INTO THE STRATOSPHERE

Sounding very Soviet, the conference chair and veteran rocketeer G. A. Crocco proclaimed that "reaction propulsion" represented the "ultimate stage" in engine design and future transport, the "Promethean" means to fulfill "humanity's ambitious plans" for "extra-atmospheric navigation." Rocket science paved the way for what he termed (after Tsiolkovskii and Oberth) the coming age of "cosmonautics" (*Cosmonautica*). In a masterful retelling of the power of the rocket's parabolic arc into space, he spotlighted its unique kind of "motion by way of singular conveyance, by way of a fluid that completes its thermal cycle along the very same line of its advance." The conference ended dramatically with N. A. Rynin's certain calculations on the future stratospheric and space rocket, with a nod to Meshcherskii's differential calculus and Tsiolkovskii's original rocket science. In the race toward space the Italians and Russians seemed to be taking the most determined steps.[82]

As a measure of its drive to "catch and surpass," and quite unlike the German tendency for self-reliance, the Russians also made several efforts to borrow and even steal away the best achievements of the West. Government agents tried to recruit (and possibly kidnap) Oberth to the RNII. The Soviet military lured several Western specialists to work for it. Oberth's assistant, A. B. Shershevskii, so notorious for his eccentricities, returned to Leningrad, where he first lived in a deluxe suite of the Hotel Astoria, joining the Leningrad GDL as a specialist in ballistics. His contemporaries testified to his dandified dress, gourmet tastes, impeccable suits and shoes, as well as to his strange habits of working away late into the night and dozing off during the day.[83] A. A. Shternfel'd, who immigrated to the USSR from France in 1935, proved much more productive. He immediately went to work at the RNII, awarded the high rank of "senior engineer," cooperating with the chief designers Korolev, Glushko, Pobedonostsev, and Tikhonravov on rocket planes and winged rockets and also pushing several experimental studies in "android" robotics. G. E. Langemak translated Shternfel'd's unpublished work into the Russian classic *Introduction to Cosmonautics* (1937), the world's first published textbook for space travel, revised to include his findings on the dynamics of rocket flight from his work at the RNII.[84]

In another interesting episode from 1932 some former members of the Verein, led by the enterprising Rolf Engel, sent an appeal from Germany to Soviet military authorities for financial aid in exchange for their rocketry work. It came at a rather fraught turning point for Engel, who had recently been rebuffed by the German military, this amid the unemployment and anxiety of the Great Depression. Engel and his young colleagues were out of work and out of prospects, some of them homeless and hungry. Soviet military analysts received their request with interest, though nothing ever came of the proposal.[85] Engels did show a knack for self-promotion, however, extravagantly promising the coming application of liquid fuel rockets for meteorology (weather reporting and "cloud seeding"); for postal communications from Moscow to Berlin in only twelve minutes; and even for battlefield communications and troop transport. Soviet officials were impressed by Engel's engineering acumen and his passionate appeal about rockets as a "powerful weapon" of mass destruction. On this score his predictions are fascinating for their brutal candor. He foresaw the application of rocketry for chemical warfare and for long-distance attacks. These were weapons of mass production that had a wide and limitless "radius" of action, weapons of surprise and terrifying effect.[86]

Robert Goddard remained a constant foil for Soviet analysts. In an effort to justify further support and funding, the RNII even drew a fascinating table of point-to-point comparisons, centered on rocket engine weights and thrusts—between Goddard's liquid fuel rocket achievements at Roswell between 1930 and 1932 and the RNII's own achievements in 1933. The conclusion: the USSR was approaching his successes but needed more funding and support to compete. Tukhachevskii backed this judgment: "We will inevitably fall behind," he warned, if present trends continue. The imperative was to "accelerate" (*forsirovat'*) Soviet rocket work and procure more "intelligence" from the West (essentially spying more on Goddard), as Tukhachevskii scribbled in his own hand at the end of his own typewritten note and upon the RNII report.[87]

These kinds of complaints were ubiquitous. Time and again through the 1930s, lacking credible espionage on rocketry work in Europe and

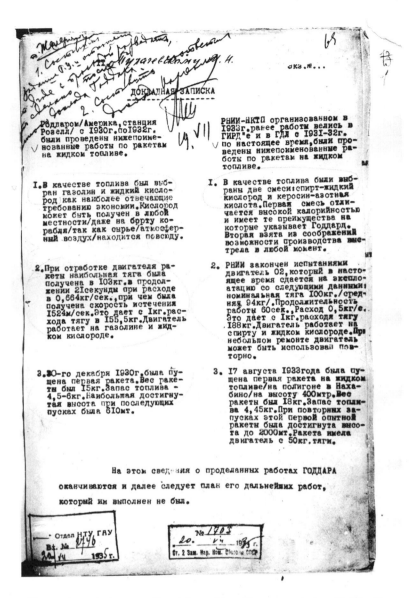

Fig. 21. America's versus Russia's rockets. Chart comparing Goddard's achievements at Roswell, New Mexico, and the rockets of the Reactive Scientific Research Institute (RNII) and its predecessors. Marshall Tukhachevskii's handwritten note (*upper left*) called for Soviet secret police (NKVD) espionage on Goddard. From I. T. Kleimenov's official RNII report, 14 July 1935, in ARAN, r. 4, o. 14, d. 245, ll. 1–4, 5–6. Credit: Archive of the Russian Academy of Sciences (Moscow).

America, Soviet planners and policy makers measured Western progress by way of press reports translated or plagiarized directly from *Field Artillery Journal* and *Scientific American* but also *Popular Science* and *Popular Mechanics*, whose content was geared to lay readers. The media hype and drama of the two pulp magazines fed Soviet fears that the West had made a "definite turn," transforming the rocket into the ballistic missile for war. The USSR could not afford to delay, for the twentieth century had already been filled with "all kinds of scientific-technological surprises," such as long-range bombing and lethal energy rays.[88] Several RNII reports made the dramatic point in 1936 that its engineers were isolated and alone, relying on only vague press reports for the latest news and advances because all the rocketry work in the West was now secret. The message betrayed a strain of self-doubt, that the work of Soviet rocketry was only based on "our own experience and achievement," that Soviet engineers desperately needed to study the best of foreign results to achieve real progress.[89]

Political Infighting and the Stalinist Purges

The initial organizational advance of the RNII had some serious setbacks. To leverage political power, Stalin transferred it from Tukhachevskii's Red Army to his own People's Commissariat of Heavy Industry shortly after it was formed. Director Kleimenov often complained that the commissariat failed to provide enough qualified personnel and financial support.[90] Its first years were marred by infighting between the disciplined military culture of the GDL and the freer paramilitary culture of GIRD. Former members of GIRD were frustrated by Kleimenov's "despotic" temperament against liquid fuel ballistic missiles, the very expertise they had brought to the institute. Overwhelmed, the leading engineers L. K. Korneev and A. Ia. Poliarnyi (with several others) quit the RNII, leaving advanced rocket research in a bind.[91] Korolev resigned as assistant director in January 1934, assuming new duties as head of the "Fifth Department," working on rocket planes. His replacement, Langemak, was a specialist in solid fuel, smokeless battlefield rockets (launched by land or by airplane), a field much more to the liking of Kleimenov and other conservatives.

A RACE INTO THE STRATOSPHERE

Tukhachevskii was frustrated by these hierarchies and conflicts. Partly in response, he promoted an altogether new institution in 1935, Construction Bureau #7 (KB-7), formed within the Red Army's Main Artillery Directorate, dedicated to the ideal of short-range, liquid fuel ballistic missiles, although it experimented with jet engines and aerial torpedoes as well. In the words of its two founders, Korneev and Poliarnyi, KB-7 was a "new GIRD." They had both been impassioned supporters of Tsander's projects, now leading their own new design bureau and collective of rocketry enthusiasts.[92]

Between 1935 and 1939, although it produced no battlefield weapons, the achievements of KB-7 were significant: a series of test stands and launching sites, precise measurements of fuel injection and engine thrusts, wind tunnel studies, and the development of gyroscopic controls. Korneev and Poliarnyi claimed to have launched the country's first short-range ballistic missile on 11 April 1937, arcing in the sky to an altitude of 2,500 meters (8,202 feet) and 12,000 meters (39,370 feet) range. Korneev wasted no time in calling it the USSR's prototype of a military stratospheric rocket, following up with a series of launches to 5- and 6-kilometer (nearly 4-mile) altitudes, flying at "angles to the horizon."[93] He wrote a barrage of letters to party and state elites between 1937 and 1938 on these scores, promising that the rockets of KB-7 would serve as "a powerful and invincible weapon in the coming military fight," missiles to "theoretically overcome any distance." The rocket was a weapon of total surprise and "demoralization," with the "colossal supersonic speed" to reach from Moscow to Berlin in only four minutes. And because Germany was working on such weapons, he warned, only defeat and "sorrow will come to that country which lags behind the conquest of the rocket."[94]

Yet KB-7 also suffered from inconsistent funding and from neglectful management. These, at least, were the constant complaints of its engineers: that the Red Army's Directorate of Military Inventions, the Main Artillery Directorate, and the People's Commissariat of the Defense Industry gave KB-7 too little funding and attention. As former members later testified, none of these overseeing agencies understood the new and complex technologies of jet and rocket engines and therefore placed the bureau as a last priority for funding and support.[95] Korneev's appeals to the higher party authorities were filled with complaints about squandered potential. The independence of KB-7 was crucial, he noted time and again. But artillery officers just did not value the promise of liquid fuel rocketry. They and other political managers still colored the new science as more fantasy than real, still too beholden to the quest for interplanetary flight. Korneev held firm, asserting that rocketry was at the very same stage as aeronautics was when the Wright brothers made their first flight in 1903, at the start of a great new development in flight technology—a difficult and dramatic turning point that required all of our "super-human will, our Bolshevik energy, and our Asian patience," as he wrote in one letter to Iosif Stalin.[96]

We do not know Stalin's response to these complaints. But we do know that his politics trumped any one person or policy or trend. As the purges intervened in Soviet political and military life between 1936 and 1939, rockets lost some of their pride of place in the mass media, along with their leading advocates in the military. The purges consumed Marshal Tukhachevskii, rocketry's champion, and the higher echelons of the military beginning in the summer of 1937. The victims included I. Ia. Alksnis, commander of the air force and one of the architects of Soviet strategic air doctrine; Robert Eidemann, head of Osoaviakhim; and M. G. Leiteizen, one of the founders of the Society for the Study of Interplanetary Travel in 1924. The Soviet secret police, now in the form of the People's Commissariat of Internal Affairs (NKVD), stripped the administrative ranks of the RNII as well. Kleimenov and Langemak were arrested on 2 November 1937, soon to follow Tukhachevskii and the others to their executions. These officers were targeted for a variety of reasons, according to the tangled logic of the purges. Tukhachevskii was accused of plotting an anti-Soviet coup and of spying for Germany. His animosity to Stalin and Voroshilov no doubt also played a role. Many of the others fell thanks to their associations with Tukhachevskii or with each other or for affiliations with Leon Trotskii or any one of the other major enemies of the regime. These confident and able military innovators were political targets, their downfall a function of what Mark Beissinger has called "the victory of the partisans of coercion over the partisans of rationalization."[97]

A RACE INTO THE STRATOSPHERE

What role did the field of rocket science and technology play in the purges? It was rarely at the center of any one accusation or conviction. But it was fraught with risk. It was subject to the criticisms of the conservative managers of artillery and aircraft production. It was also a top secret military arena, joining specialized knowledge with suspect foreign influences. In the harsh tempos and standards of the day, the climate of intrigue and intimidation, the normal trial and error of rocket experimentation easily translated into accusations of mismanagement and "wrecking" (sabotage), or into the settling of personal scores. There was little tolerance for all of the necessary failures of rocket science. So, the experimental projects of jet propulsion and rocketry readily aroused the suspicions and attentions of the secret police organs and eventually all the fury and chaos of the "Terror."[98]

Leading scientists and engineers, as persons of rare talent, were usually not executed. But there were exceptions. A. B. Shershevskii, for example, perished in the Terror for reasons that are not clear but were probably associated with his ties abroad, his long years in German emigration, and his rather eccentric personality. Like scores of other aviation and rocketry engineers, Glushko was arrested and interrogated, tortured, and convicted of fabricated crimes, then sentenced to a term in the famous "prison laboratories," there to design and build under armed guard and detention. Korolev, who inhabited the worlds of both administration and design, was initially sentenced to die, an order Stalin personally approved. But the sentence was commuted, likely because of his engineering talents. After a portion of time served in the Kolyma hard labor camps, he was removed to a prison laboratory. Through the ordeal here was a man, in the depths of imprisonment and deprivation, still dreaming of flight into interplanetary space. It was a dynamic of contrasts worthy of fiction. Arthur Koestler even appealed to it in his classic *Darkness at Noon* (1941), as his main character sat imprisoned in the Stalinist Terror, dreaming of freedom. "He had a sudden wild craving for a newspaper. It was so strong that he could smell the printer's ink and hear the crackling and rustling of the pages. Perhaps a revolution had broken out last night, or the head of a state had been murdered, or an American had discovered the means to counteract the force of gravity."[99] The radical dreams of spaceflight survived even through the worst moments of the Stalin era.

Ari Shternfel'd was more fortunate. His international prestige, from having won a version of the REP-Hirsch Prize in 1934, likely saved him from the worst excesses of the purge years. He was expelled from the RNII in 1937 and forced to work exclusively from his home office, now reproduced in the "Memorial Study of A. A. Shternfel'd" at the State Polytechnic Museum in downtown Moscow. His isolation may have saved him from further persecution, shielding him from bureaucratic and personal intrigues. He survived on honorariums from articles in the popular press and eventually from financial support sent by family members abroad, along with a small pension. The years just before the outbreak of the Second World War were not kind to him or to the other pioneers and enthusiasts. Yet through these hard times Shternfel'd became a tutor to a new generation of young readers on the mechanics and physics of rocketry and spaceflight, what he explicitly called the new science of "cosmonautics."[100] In 1940, for example, he defined the intricacies and "paradoxes of the rocket." One paradox, for example, was about proportions: how a larger rocket, with the requisite mass of fuel and exhaust velocity, would launch away from Earth more successfully than a smaller, lighter one. Another was about Hohmann's gravity assists, how the gravitational fields of the earth, sun, and planets could assist the rocket to overcome the very force of gravity, with even less expenditure of fuel, albeit if it traveled over longer distances and times. The lessons were a success, counting the hundreds of readers' letters that the publisher received, both for and against Shternfel'd's methods. Youngsters of Moscow School #91 wrote in to challenge the author's calculations, and adult readers questioned his assumptions about the laws of motion. Rocket science was not easy, but it was still captivating.[101]

Soviet rocket engineering survived, in all of these ways, just before and during the Second World War, if somewhat at the margins, below other projects of higher priority. The government's first concern was aviation proper, building the kinds of conventional, high-performance piston engine planes to compete with the best European and American fighters and bombers. Reports from the Soviet Air Force showed that they were consistently outperforming Soviet engines and airplanes, translating into stark disadvantages on the coming battlefields of war. Soviet aviation science was deficient, unable to bridge the gap between the West and Russia, which remained behind not in years but in decades. "An enormous mobilization of scientific thought and rationalization is taking place over there," said one critique. The West was achieving fantastic, astounding kinds of aerial innovations, while the USSR lumbered along. "In the case of war, we might find ourselves [flying] in old, dilapidated washtubs."[102]

When it came to reaction engines more generally, the government promoted jet propulsion over pure rocket weapons. This meant funding and developing such technologies as jet-assisted takeoff boosters or the new turboprop engines of Vladimir Uvarov and turbojet engines of Arkhip Liul'ka. Research and development of liquid fuel rockets waned, although rumors and news of their development in the West could still strike a tone of concern. During the Hitler-Stalin Pact the new Soviet research institute in charge of liquid fuel rockets requested funding for a "research trip" of two designers to Nazi Germany in order to "become acquainted with the status of rocket technology"—this in the midst of one of Hitler's top secret rocketry programs at Peenemünde and only a year before the German invasion of the USSR.[103]

What about Stalin's role through all of this and the relationship between the aviation and stratostat campaigns and the purges? We know that the Soviet leader loved learning about new aviation technologies; his support for aviators and stratonauts was on full public display. Yet the campaigns were not without their meaner political undertones. For Kendall Bailes they were a claim for popular sovereignty and state "legitimacy" by a regime without democratic foundations and with a dramatic propensity to violence (collectivization and the purges of the 1930s). The aviation campaigns were a Stalinist ploy in this sense, a false dynamism and heroism in an age of passport controls and labor camps, of purge politics and executions.[104] The 1937 Terror—against Marshal Tukhachevskii and the alleged spies and saboteurs in the Red Army—was also strategically placed between two other Soviet feats: the theories of Konstantin Tsiolkovskii and the great transpolar flights to the United States. These successes were also emblematic of the USSR's political ideology, dialectical materialism, and the foundations for a new kind of cosmism, Stalin style.

10

Stalinism and the Genesis of Cosmonautics

The Russian aesthetic of cosmic oneness, first refined by the Symbolist and futurist poets and later adapted by the proletarian writers, survived into the Soviet 1930s in various ways. F. A. Tsander expressed it when he translated the Stalinist slogan "To catch and surpass" as meaning a leap forward to a truly communistic society in outer space, a place for "free labor" and "universal creativity." G. Arel'skii, the writer of space travel adventures, even called for a whole new poetry based on mathematics and physics. "Science is building its own cathedral of Reason," he wrote, for "our earth is but one among the infinite islands in the ocean of the universe." It was an insight demanding a whole new way of thinking and writing, "a new era of planetary history for humanity."[1] Aleksandr Prokof'ev's poetry reproduced the earlier Promethean values for a new Stalinist generation. A student from the *Proletkul't* circles in 1922, he still celebrated the proletarian "We" of the revolution that "will be carried up to the heavens," predicting that communism would someday "dash off ships into flight"—and yes, even "to the stars."[2]

Official Communist ideology remained attuned to such imagery. *Pravda* valued Maiakovskii's poems for their cosmic "pathos" and "all-absorbing passion." The era of forced collectivization and industrialization was kind to the proletarian poets, their cosmist works reissued in new editions as forerunners of socialist realism. By definition this genre was all about the romanticism of heroic exploits, making miracles come true.[3] Here were the makings of an expressly Stalinist cosmism. Outer space, looking down on the planet, became one of its favorite frames of reference. "We have put socialism into practice," proclaimed one banner headline. "In place of Tsarist Russia heaves the great colossus of the USSR."[4] This extravagant globalism was a function of the very ideology of the Russian Revolution. It was built upon Marx's slogan "Workers of the World Unite." It was expressed in images of Lenin or of Bolshevik workers traversing the planet. It was screened cinematically in Dziga Vertov's film *One Sixth of the World* (1926), a visual celebration of the USSR's worldwide reach.[5] Propaganda posters featured Stalin's gigantic portrait fusing with Lenin's, like a new sun in the heavens illuminating the USSR. Stalin's own underground name, which blended the Russian *stal* (steel) with the name Lenin, was fortuitous too, allowing for a marriage between the images of the man of "steel" and the man of the "sun."[6]

Avant-garde artists retooled their techniques to the service of the Stalin regime. Konstantin Iuon repainted *New Planet* for the times, without the earlier fear and trembling of cosmic catastrophe, now with the "People" confidently at work, perhaps building a spacecraft or rebuilding their own planet, all against the background of cement mixers, searchlights, and stars. El Lissitzkii's sculpture *Red Star*, made for the International Press Exhibit at Cologne (1928), showed a planetary system revolving around the new sun of proletarian values.[7] Kazimir Malevich offered the most towering of images: a study of Lenin as orbital "architecton," his arm pointed upward, reaching for space astride a series of skyscraper monuments and against the backdrop of Malevich's cosmic *Supremus No. 56*. Here was the ultimate parabola of the revolution—Lenin as rocket.

On the ground the Soviet Union now marked several natural frontiers for conquest: the "mobilization of the ether" through radio (*mobilizatsiia efira*); the "storming of the sky" (*shturm neba*) and "the "storming of the polar north" by airplane (*shturm severa*); the "storming of the earth's depths" by mines (*shturm nedr*); the "conquest of the stratosphere" via balloon or high-altitude plane (*zavoevanie stratosfery*); and even the "storming of the universe" by rocket (*shturm vselennoi*). Inspired by the first great "storming" of the Winter Palace in October 1917, these campaigns marked the vertical horizons of

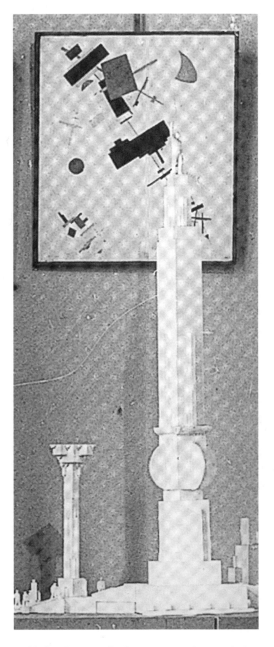

Fig. 22. Malevich's "architecton" of Lenin as rocket, with *Supremus No. 56* in the background. Credit: screen capture from the newsreel of the exhibit "Artists of the Russian Federation over the Last Fifteen Years," Russian Museum, Leningrad (November 1932).

the Soviet state. As the poet Demian Bednyi wrote, "Our strengths, they're beyond measure / Heroes of the mines become heroes of the stratosphere." Or as one youth song put it:

> Komsomolists sing to the waters
> And they sing to the heavens
> Comrade suns and stars
> We'll become your masters.[8]

The rocket became a central image of pure mechanical prowess, Tsiolkovskii the herald of the conquest of the cosmos. Both suited the Stalinist preoccupation with reaching "ever higher" (*vse vyshe*). Tsiolkovskii's rocket, together with Lenin and Stalin's revolutionary party, served the same generative purpose: moving human beings beyond Earth or moving historical events here upon it, against all odds. Astronautics, what the Soviets now began to identify more often as cosmonautics, became the science of the future, the realizable utopia of space travel.

Rockets and Mass Politics

Within these various contexts the Soviet state also promoted a broad-based campaign to educate the public in rocketry and space travel issues through the 1930s. Rocketry took center stage in the city spaces of Moscow: with lectures and exhibits at Gorkii Park, in the city planetarium, in the lobby of the Civil Air Fleet (*Aeroflot*), and at the headquarters of the Red Army. It found a special niche in the mass-circulation press. This was no fleeting movement. A generation of children and teenagers was raised on the possibilities of rocketry and space travel, symbols of scientific-technological progress.

Some of the campaign's texts were naive. The youth magazine *Knowledge Is Power* (*Znanie-sila*) devoted a whole issue to the rather far-fetched potential of Tsiolkovskii's dirigible rocket. The *Komsomol* offered rural children an uplifting cartoon about little Alesha, who dreamed of flying off to the moon in a "stratoplane-rocket."[9] Other texts were quite instructive, offering lessons on rocket physics, orbital mechanics, and basic astronomy. Iakov Perel'man's *Interplanetary Voyages* was published in its tenth edition by 1935, hailed

Fig. 23. The Tsiolkovskii dirigible rocket flies through the meteors. The front
cover of the popular science magazine *Znanie-sila* 24 (1932).

as the "world's first" popular survey to deal with rockets and spaceflight. The state publishing house translated Max Valier's and Hermann Noordung's classics, inspiring young and old with the real
possibilities of space stations.[10] It reprinted some of Tsiolkovskii's
science fiction from before the revolution. In children's magazines

he now became little "Kostia," the boy who came from nothing to become the "great Russian prodigy," the original "astronaut" (*zvezdo-plavitel'*). He was the inventor of that marvelous machine, the rocket, closed on one end, open on the other, carrying its own propulsion by purely reactive force. Thanks to him, fourth graders learned, the USSR would become the first to "conquer the Moon."[11]

Children corresponded with "grandfather Tsiolkovskii," as they called him, building models of his various air and spacecraft. These groups included the All-Union Meetings of Young Aviation Designers, the Office of Young Inventors of the Society of Inventors, and the All-Union Children's Technical Stations, dedicated to cultivating technical and engineering skills. In late 1934 fifteen-year-old Mara Malkov organized a Laboratory for Reactive Propulsion in the Kharkov House of Young Pioneers (Ukraine), gathering a handful of his mates in the ninth and tenth grades. With great excitement they wrote Tsiolkovskii, asking for "all of Your books (absolutely all of them), and signed too." From their love of physics and model plane building, they now set out to build his rockets and even test Goddard's and Oberth's models, maybe even create a "museum-exhibit on interplanetary communications." In all of these ways children became a priority audience for Tsiolkovskii's fantastic ideas. A widely reproduced photograph of the day depicted two youngsters at the old man's feet, in rapt attention, models in hand, listening to his kind wisdom.[12]

Tsiolkovskii's resurgent public fame and official recognition after 1930 were really more about the wider veneration for air power. "Man has conquered the elements" with his "metal bird," wrote the aviation publicist N. Bobrov, who was also one of Tsiolkovskii's first biographers. The regime recognized Tsiolkovskii as one of Russia's and the world's great aviation pioneers, worthy of inclusion in its "Big Life" biography series, inspirational stories for young readers.[13] His life was especially instructive because it perfectly paralleled the whole history of aviation. He was the first to conceive of an all-metal dirigible in 1892, three years before Count Zeppelin. He was the first to conceive of a functional airplane in 1894, nine years before the Wright brothers. He was the first to conceive of rocket power for spaceflight in 1903, nearly two decades before Goddard and Oberth. These historical and personal trajectories constituted Tsiolkovskii's "spirals to the sun." He would transform us, by airplane and dirigible and rocket, into points of light in the heavens.[14] For readers of the Young Communist League's newspapers, Tsiolkovskii's dirigible rocket flew highest among the great artifacts of aviation, in an ascending arc, just above the 1908 Wright *Flyer*. He had taught the "Soviet people" how to "fly farther than all, faster than all, higher than all."[15] And in one dramatic article, sponsored by the Soviet government and military, Tsiolkovskii confidently predicted nothing less than the evolutionary adaptation of the human race to "ethereal space"—our "migration" to the solar system's planets, asteroids, and moons; the "extraordinary propagation and perfection" of human beings as space colonists; even our retreat to another sun as our own began to fail.[16]

In 1932, in honor of his seventy-fifth birthday, the state awarded Tsiolkovskii the Order of the Red Banner of Labor in formal ceremonies in Moscow. He received a new home in Kaluga and a better pension. Scholarships were named in his honor; streets were renamed after him. A host of government agencies touted his achievements with meetings and discussions, telegrams and press releases. No matter that Tsiolkovskii was a thinker, an inventor of ideas more than things. In all of this his "sagacity and originality" had already matched and surpassed Western inventors. In a marriage of the personal and the national, his dreams for the "conquest of atmospheric and interplanetary space" became all-Soviet dreams.[17] He became the "patriarch of aviation and pioneer of astronautics," father of a whole "international planetary school" of rocketry pioneers. He represented the best of Soviet socialism, marking the "path to a future" of global and planetary peace, a utopia of which capitalism was capable of dreaming but incapable of achieving.[18]

Soviet propagandists also celebrated Tsiolkovskii as terrestrial and solar engineer, in league with several Soviet and American scholars who also counted Earth's energy by the measure of the sun (including astrophysicist Charles G. Abbot, director of the Smithsonian Institution and Robert Goddard's most dedicated patron). With them he appealed to the sun as the origin of universal life, worthy of ven-

Fig. 24. Tsiolkovskii's name as a "shooting star." Graphic art from Aleksandr Beliaev, "Tsiolkovskii," *Iunyi proletarii* 31–32 (November 1932): 7.

eration as the source of all energy and fuel resources.[19] He already knew that it would be the essential energy of interplanetary life and travel, powering the lush greenhouses of his space dirigibles. Solar mirrors might also be built and directed back upon Earth, to power machines and cultivate deserts. The leading science fiction writer Aleksandr Beliaev praised his projects for the "reconstruction of the Earth" and the "reconsolidation of the globe," encasing its vulnerable parts in protective and productive glass membranes, all in preparation for the future settlement of space. Tsiolkovskii was that rare kind of pioneer who saw the planet from space, who measured it by an "astronomical scale," who counted life in "billions and billions." He was the first planetary man, filled with a "cosmic consciousness," a rare "love" and goodwill for our universal home. By way of his "cosmic rocket" he had written his name as a new shooting star in space.[20]

Tsiolkovskii's writings on dirigibles and rockets were also now published as "selected works." The first volume was dedicated to his long-suffering project to build an all-metal dirigible, a project again taken up by *Aeroflot* between 1932 and 1935, which worked on designs and models under his partial supervision. For the third and final time (as in 1894 and 1925) the all-metal dirigible was debated in Russia's military circles. Once again, nothing came of the idea—except publicity. Beliaev even wrote a story about it. Thus, Tsiolkovskii's all-metal dirigible only ever flew in fiction.[21] The second volume covered rocketry, now at the center of the RNII's mission, whose leadership sought out Tsiolkovskii's imprimatur, electing him as an honorary member of its Engineering Council and publishing several of his works. In his set of terminological standards for the new field of rocketry, G. E. Langemak assigned Tsiolkovskii's name to the famous rocket equation describing the relationship between the rocket's exhaust velocity and its mass ratio.[22]

Tsiolkovskii's reputation prospered through the 1930s, a mark of the regime's optimism. The Stalinist state encouraged its people to dream. Soviet adventures targeted younger audiences with "flights of fancy," in A. R. Palei's terms, joining real achievements in aviation with imaginative storytelling about space travel. Tsiolkovskii's rocket, or some prototype of it, figured into almost all of these stories. Palei's own novel *The Planet KIM* (1930), the story of how an enterprising commune of Young Communists (he called them Soviet "Robinson Crusoes") colonized an asteroid, also featured an authoritative preface by the astronomer K. L. Baev, one of the first publicists for Robert Goddard's rocket back in 1923. Once again, Baev confirmed the legitimacy of rocket science and the real possibilities of space-flight. The certainty of calculus made it all so.[23] Aleksandr Beliaev was Tsiolkovskii's most dedicated publicist. In a series of novels and stories between 1933 and 1940, he cultivated Tsiolkovskii's dreams of space engineering via his "New Ark" (outfitted with the signature liquid buffers and solar greenhouse), a multistage "star cruiser" and "man-made comet." He made it "sail upon the waves of the ethereal ocean," a lovely and dazzling streak of golden exhaust upon the azure blue of the skies. It was a celebration of human mobility and genius and "happiness," the foundation for a new race of human beings to become "star dwellers."[24] Vladimir Vladko also took his readers to the nearby planets, speeding on such a human-made "comet," drawing an "intricate curve" through outer space. With mini-lectures on space engineering, chemistry, and biology along the way, Vladko treated readers to a series of Soviet firsts: the first All-Union Society for Interplanetary Communications, the first flights into outer space and to the moon, the first exploration of the prehistoric jungles and dinosaurs of Venus.[25]

These stories were not passing fads. At a number of local and national levels the government was committed to promoting science fiction and space fantasy. Note, for example, one radio contest for the best stories, drawings, and models on such topics as "The Arctic in 100 Years," "Aviation of the Future," and even "How to Fly to Mars."

As the announcement stated, the Mars topic owed its inspiration to Tsiolkovskii's theories, bridging such diverse fields as astronomy, physics, engineering, and chemistry. Here was a perfect model for a middle school science fair, a way for children to ponder a future of spacecraft and space stations, rocket engines and solar energy. Aleksei Tolstoi's science fiction novel *Aelita* also enjoyed a new life into the 1930s, with both official approval and a genuine youth readership, now graced with illustrations of Tsiolkovskii's rocket headed toward a Lowellian Mars, studded with the infamous canals.[26]

Tsiolkovskii's own *Beyond the Earth* was not republished in the 1930s, but it found an even better venue as a feature film, *Cosmic Flight* (1936). Tsiolkovskii flew to space yet a second time, albeit still in science fiction. This time he flew not as the love-struck Los' but as the enterprising Soviet academician Pavel Ivanovich Sedykh, director of the "All-Union Institute for Interplanetary Communications," commander of a team of Soviet "astronauts": the Young Communist Marina and the Young Pioneer Andriusha, the "first" explorers on the moon. "Forward to the Cosmos," they proclaimed. The accent here was on the real, or rather on how only the USSR could really turn fantasies into realities, on a fact-based "flight of thought," as one commentator put it.[27] Tsiolkovskii served as scientific consultant to the film, collecting his thoughts and drawings in an album for the script. He offered sketches of the rocket (the *Stalin*), launch ramp, space suits, zero gravity environment, liquid acceleration barriers, and spacewalks; corrections about the look of the stars and sun and Earth from space; and strict advice on the mechanics and physics of spaceflight.[28]

One of the last Soviet "silents," the film was a popular success, filled with captivating technology and comedic touches, including an "Earthrise" from the moon, some death-defying scenes, and the rescue of a cat. The crew even sent a Goddard-like signal flare back to prove their achievement: the bright letters *USSR*. When it premiered to Moscow's youngsters during the cold winter holidays of 1936, they broke into waves of cheers and laughter. The movie's launch ramp was especially emblematic of the Soviet future. Built at "Star City" (*Astrogorod*), it and the rocket dwarfed the magnificent city of Mos-

Fig. 25. Moscow's catapult ramp to outer space; Tsiolkovskii's rocket rises against the background of downtown Moscow and the Palace of Soviets (with Lenin statue). Screen capture (still shot) from the film *Cosmic Flight* (1936). Credit: Archive of the Russian Academy of Sciences (Moscow).

cow itself, in the distance the planned "Palace of Soviets" and gigantic Lenin statue (to be larger than the Eiffel Tower and Empire State Building). Yet this ramp was not original. It was already a staple in European media and books, thanks largely to Max Valier, who first popularized it. Soviet graphic artists had even stolen Valier's ramp image and rocket flight in 1934—for a celebratory piece on flight into the stratosphere—Lenin's statue and the Moscow city center again conspicuously in the background.[29]

Tsiolkovskii's death on 19 September 1935, at "22 hours and 34 minutes," the beloved scientist reaching seventy-eight years of age, marked a peak in the Stalinist campaign for the cosmos. Kaluga honored him with a grand funeral. Fifteen thousand people attended, making their way along a cortege two kilometers long. Leaders of civil and military aviation gave speeches. An escadrille of airplanes from Moscow dropped leaflets about his life and lowered a wreath to his grave. His brain, weighing a full 1,350 grams, was turned over to the Moscow Institute of the Brain for safekeeping and study, not

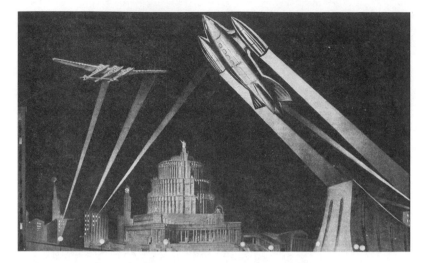

Fig. 26. Valier's catapult ramp to outer space (at right), Russian style, also against the background of downtown Moscow and the Palace of Soviets (with Lenin statue). From A. Garri and L. Kassil', *Potolok mira* (Moscow: Sovetskaia literatura, 1934), 24.

too far from Lenin's own. Tsiolkovskii's personality cult was on full display: the dreamer spurned by Tsarist authorities; the half-deaf genius struggling on alone; the enemy of gravity; the dirigible and rocket designer backed by rigorous mathematical proofs. It was a cult of stratospheric and space travel honoring the "all-metal interplanetary name of Tsiolkovskii." He was buried at Kaluga's outskirts. An obelisk, not yet a rocket, was mounted at his grave, amid birch and fir trees. Its inscription read, "Founder of the theory of reactive motion" and "Pioneer of the conquest of interplanetary space," along with Tsiolkovskii's own claim, from 1911, "Humanity will not remain forever on Earth."[30]

During this campaign of mourning (and for years afterward) the media also gave wide coverage to the letters Stalin exchanged with Tsiolkovskii just before his death, with the strange effect, given their ages, of Stalin playing the role of "wise leader," the father, and Tsiolkovskii the adoring and appreciative citizen, the son. These letters became centerpieces of the Tsiolkovskii postmortem cult. In grandiloquent terms he bequeathed his papers and legacies to the "Bolshevik party and Soviet power" so as to promote the further "progress of human culture." In their own professional correspondence to Stalin, the administrators of Soviet rocketry tapped into the hyperbole to justify more funding. I. T. Kleimenov, director of the RNII, warned that liquid fuel rocketry, the project closest to Tsiolkovskii's heart, should not die with him. A. K. Korneev, head of KB-7, wrote to Stalin that "the hour will soon come when our Bolshevik interplanetary ships will rise up to the unbounded vacuum of space."[31]

Stalin's own public persona also became a cult of "cosmic" force. In a wildly imaginary lecture from a future "School of Interplanetary Communications," the propagandist Karl Radek celebrated Stalin for the "daring of a great rebel" and the "cool calculation of a mathematician," a young man who was a "thirsty student of the algebra of revolution," images that recalled Stalin's early years at the Tiflis Geophysical Observatory.[32] One of the more infamous of appeals came from Osip Mandelshtam in his panegyric the "Ode to Stalin" (1937), which drew Stalin's profile as lines in the sky. He became the one "who has shifted the world's axis." He became a giant towering over mountains, a "Prometheus" bridging countries and continents. He became the great cultivator, sowing progress "like tomorrow out of yesterday— / The furrows of a colossal plow reach to the sun."[33] After the hagiography of Richard Maurice Bucke and John Addington Symonds from the turn of the century, Mandelshtam turned Stalin into a modern-day Walt Whitman. A poem in *Pravda* made much the same point: "Between the heavens and the earth / He fills the whole world with his girth." Stalin became the quintessential "vertical" man, standing upon the mausoleum as the dead Lenin lay horizontal within it, at one point towering above Red Square, his portrait projected onto a tethered balloon, as if a new planet in the skies.[34]

These kinds of images help us better to understand H. G. Wells's second visit to the USSR in 1934. As a British celebrity with Soviet sympathies, he offered a reference point for the world, confirming just how dramatically the country had changed since his first visit with Lenin in the troubled year of 1920. He offered a "before and after" picture of Russia's long revolution. Wells arrived in Moscow by air, no longer the dilapidated site of one of his apocalyptic novels. Now he was flying into a "rigorous," vibrant city surrounded by a "patchwork of aerodromes" and many "hundreds of planes," to meet Iosif Stalin, one of the great representatives of the "human future." True enough, as described in his "alternative" history, *The Shape of Things to Come* (1933), Wells saw both the United States and USSR as utopian civilizations in the making, each with a "major mass of human beings" ready to build the foundations of "an organized world-state."[35] Yet he favored Stalin and a "theory of world revolution" (one he shared with J. B. S. Haldane) meant to fulfill a "socialistic, cosmopolitan and creative" global government. Progress meant "abolishing distance"—by land and sea and air, among peoples and states, even between death and life. It meant mastering all life on the planet ("geogonic planning"); it meant reaching for outer space and immortality. William Winwood Reade's prophecies would come true: "This is the day, this is the hour of sunrise for united manhood. The Martyrdom of Man is at an end. From pole to pole now there remains no single human being upon the planet without a fair prospect of self-fulfillment, of health, interest and freedom."[36]

The film version of this fancy, *Things to Come* (1936), represented the future by a rocket, launched initially by Verne's cannon but piloted by courageous young people setting out to create a new civilization in outer space. It was a story line worthy of Stalinist socialist realism. Yet what might seem positively Fedorovian or Stalinist here was really at one with the very transformism at the heart of the Western experience. The aviation engineer and science writer Waldemar Kaempffert perfectly summarized this futuristic vision as encompassing the cosmic: the reach for new sources of terrestrial and solar energy to power the industrial globe; the reach for longevity and even a kind of immortality through the new chemistry and biology; the reach for outer space and the planets by rocket. Thus, "the romances of yesterday," he wrote, become "the realities of today."[37]

Dialectical Materialism and Astronomy

Besides all of these investments in practical and symbolic rocketry, the Stalin regime also perfected a corresponding ideology of state power, "dialectical materialism," between 1935 and 1938. The system had its foundations in the political writings of Marx, Engels, Lenin, and Stalin, but it also pretended to a "scientific socialism." Friedrich Engels's newly published *Dialectics of Nature* was especially relevant, a celebration of the "greatest progressive revolution that mankind has so far experienced"—meaning Isaac Newton's "general laws of motion and matter" and the Kant-Laplace "nebular hypothesis" on the origins of universe.[38] Engels spoke admiringly of the "relative equilibrium" in nature, "where motion is reciprocally determined," whereby "all attractions and all repulsions in the universe must mutually balance one another." Newton's parallelogram of forces acted both in nature and through history, both of which moved according to predictable patterns. Or as one obituary of V. I. Lenin confirmed, "As the astronomer has studied the heavenly bodies, so Karl Marx has established the objective paths by which Capital arises, develops and dies out." The Stalinist ideologue G. F. Aleksandrov put it much the same way: "Marxism-Leninism has proven scientifically that capitalism will give way to socialism, just as inevitably as night is followed by day."[39]

For Engels, Newton's third law of motion was a simple scientific paradigm for human force and labor through history: "the action of the human organism on the external world." He even fashioned the human being as the first and foremost "cause" in history, like the "explosive charge" of a firing gun: "His normal state is one appropriate to his consciousness, *one to be created by himself*."[40] For Engels the human being was like the rocket, sui generis. This image was consonant with the philosophical mandate of Soviet dialectical materialism. It held that all matter arises and moves spontaneously, by its "self-movement," thanks ultimately to the "law of the unity of opposites." Life was self-originating, self-sustaining, and self-replicating. These were the natural and historical laws that defined all matter and mind in motion, that presupposed life's ascent from the lowest and simplest to the highest and most complex. All historical progress, too, represented the "continual ascent of society to ever higher forms of life, till the reign of necessity to which the world is still subject is inevitably compelled to give place to the reign of freedom." This trajectory, which Lenin adopted as well, took the shape not of a strict parabolic arc but of a spiral, essentially a series of parabolic arcs, lined with turns and returns but always moving ever higher. These are the shapes of dialectical materialism.[41]

Dialectical materialism also depended on the findings of modern astronomy, which had dealt a mortal blow to the religious worldview. It was "blood of the blood" of the proletarian revolution and of Soviet socialism. Karl Marx and Vladimir Lenin had very little to do with this. The Soviet state's official atheism was founded upon an older provenance: Copernicus and Galileo, Bruno and Newton, whose theories and findings the state now republished in mass editions, several in the series edited by Maksim Gorkii, "Lives of Extraordinary People" (which included B. N. Vorob'ev's biography of Tsiolkovskii).[42] Copernicus's geocentric and "anthropocentric" theories of 1543 were a "revolutionary act," wrote one leading propagandist. Newton's law of universal gravity was a "great achievement for atheism." Their novel scientific visions had displaced the Earth-centered universe, humanity's "exclusivity," opening a sun-centered planetary system within a universe of other possible worlds and life forms. Astronomical science had undone all that was superstitious, idealistic, and godly. The universe was not created, had no origin or finale. It was eternal and infinite. The recent discoveries of astrophysics had verified the "truth of the material unity of the universe," that matter depended upon the laws of the "stability and transformation of energy."[43]

These principles were built into the very cultural geography of Moscow. After Lenin's Mausoleum, which received some ten million visitors between 1924 and 1936, the Moscow Planetarium was one of the most visited city sites, especially for Soviet tourists from the country's distant towns and villages, offering lectures and tours to five million visitors between 1929 and 1937. Both places were irreligious utopian temples of a kind: one to a corpse become revered cult figure, the "eternal" Lenin; the other to a site of exhibits and dioramas, slide shows and presentations, on the wonders of the self-sustaining, secular, infinite heavens.[44]

None of this (except for the mummy) was so unique to the Soviet Union. Between East and West the new astronomy was already divesting the supernatural from natural science. Popular perceptions about space and time were shifting—from the local to the global and even from the global to the galactic. Ours was but one world among many. We were all part of something big. One Russian publicist even wrote his address as "#9 Vozdvizhenka Street, Moscow, the USSR, Europe, Earth, the Solar System, the Milky Way, the Universe." Graphic artists represented the solar system in terrestrial terms. If Moscow's Kremlin was the sun at the center, Earth was simply Kaluga, Mars was Orel or Kursk, and Jupiter no farther than Kharkov. From the United States one writer featured a similar perspective: if the sun was the dome of the Boston State House, Mars was only 1.63 miles away at the YMCA on Huntington Avenue, Uranus in the suburbs at Framingham.[45] These images brought the earth down to size, shrunk it but also ennobled it, made the near planets all the more accessible to us.

Both Russian and American scientists still entertained the possibilities of extraterrestrial life. The Leningrad Stratosopheric Conference raised the question of what we now call "extreme" life, the physical boundaries at which organisms might live or die. Its scope included the human being as a kind of "x life," with research into the effects of acceleration and high altitudes on human physiology. But the endeavor also meant raising the issue of the very origins of life, whether it began by Arrhenius's interplanetary seeding or by Oparin's spontaneous generation on Earth. The Soviet academician G. A. Nadson recognized that science was divided on the issue. But he was sure of two probabilities: the eventual death of the earth in some fashion and the tenacity of life to somehow survive, perhaps by breaching the stratosphere for outer space.[46]

Academician Vernadskii contributed a remarkable piece at the conference on the stratosphere as the outer boundary of the biosphere, emphasizing how life evolves in decreasing spirals and envelopes outward to the ozone layer and ionosphere. Yet this was a frontier that we were eventually bound to conquer as a distant zone of human life. In one dramatic reading of its allure, the rocket enthusiast I. P. Fortikov soon recast the stratosphere itself as but one part of the earth's greater "biosphere," the terrestrial globe as medium for life on and above and below its surface. Humanity was now reaching,

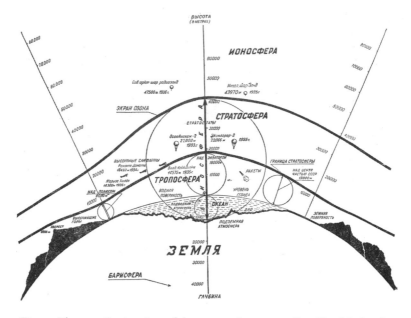

Fig. 27. The new Soviet view of the stratosphere, revealing Earth's depths and heights, including airplane altitude records (in meters), the feats of the *Osoaviakhim 1* and *Explorer II* balloons, and the coming age of rockets (*center right*). From I. P. Fortikov, "Biosfera," *Priroda* 9 (1936): 29. Credit: *Priroda* (an official organ of the Russian Academy of Sciences).

through stratostats and deepwater submersibles, "to conquer those farthest heights and depths at the limits of the biosphere," wrote Fortikov. We were about to test how life might survive at the rarified heights and depths, possibly even confirming Arrhenius's theories about organic life in outer space. We were on the cusp of creating, at the edge of space, an "altogether new medium for human existence." Humanity was pushing the limits of the biosphere beyond Earth itself, the rocket now part of our very extraterrestrial being.[47] Here was a whole new Soviet way of envisioning the stratosphere.

This very theme of the habitability of the stratosphere (and outer space) had actually been a concern of several stratostat flights. Attached to the *Explorer II* gondola, for example, were test tubes carrying spores of seven types of fungi, sent along to see if they would survive the high altitude. Five did, and they continued to grow after their return to laboratories at the Department of Agricul-

STALINISM AND THE GENESIS OF COSMONAUTICS

ture. The University of Wisconsin also provided the flight with a set of *Drosophila* fruit flies, placed on board to study the effects of cosmic rays. The flies died, but the eggs and larvae survived for study. One of *Explorer*'s specially outfitted sterile tubes also collected five species of common bacteria and five of terrestrial molds at altitudes between seventy thousand and thirty-six thousand feet. Simple life, the experiment proved, was resilient at those heights.[48]

The specific question of Martian life remained in academic dispute. In a powerful combination of evidence and argument, E. M. Antoniadi had already revealed the canals as "illusions." Yet the popular press in the United States and USSR, with the support of a few astronomers, still toyed with the possibilities of life on Mars and the planets.[49] Soviet dialectical materialism presumed the plurality of worlds. Even academic science remained interested. G. A. Tikhov, whom we remember as an early supporter of Tsiolkovskii's spaceflight theories in 1913, claimed to have discovered bands of plant life on Mars by 1946, the foundations for a whole "new science" that he was soon calling "Astrobiology," yet another first in the Soviet arsenal.[50] But none of these endeavors were colored by the fantastic or wonderful. They all tended to spotlight the significance of life here on Earth. Take the front cover of *The Truth about the Heavens* (1941)—written by the indomitable Baev—which offered a telltale view of the earth from space. Aliens might exist, but we were the beings who counted.[51]

In the Soviet Union the works of leading Western astronomers remained well respected. Their findings often graced popular science journals.[52] James Jeans's *The Stars in Their Courses* went through several Soviet translations between 1933 and 1937. True, the editors cautioned that he was a bourgeois scholar, beset by a class ideology and a "dark pessimism." Yet he was also a "master of his science" and of the objective "worlds around us." Jeans took his Soviet readers through the solar system on his "magic rocket," first traveling at about seven miles (over eleven kilometers) per second, later supercharging to Einsteinian speeds and even going back in time to the origins of the planet and life upon it. Earth, after all, was a "little colony" in the cosmos, a mere point of departure toward the vast "star cities" of the greater universe.[53] As Jeans's star rose in the East, so A. I. Oparin's did in the West, where he republished a more scientific version of his 1924 work on spontaneous generation (abiogenesis), now titled *The Origin of Life* and soon accepted as the new global standard. Oparin's chemical reactions were part of an "endless chain of transformations of matter," what Laurence La Fleur of Brooklyn College termed "the accident of the appropriate chemical structure arising." At home he became a standard-bearer of dialectical materialism and scientific atheism.[54]

In the United States believers and agnostics both were open to the Kant-Laplace theory of cosmogony or to Darwin's theory of evolution or to the theory of the many "island universes" inhabiting the greater cosmos. All matter in the universe was eternal and indestructible, dependent upon the selfsame laws of "incorporation and disintegration," as one editorial put it. Science and religion had come to mutually agreeable terms. Greek or Hindu pagan theories of our origins were dismissed. Jewish and Christian doctrines of Genesis were respectfully ignored. A kind of provisional intelligent design was now in vogue.[55] The average Soviet publicist of dialectical materialism or scientific atheism would have probably felt quite comfortable, for example, at the lecture by E. G. Davis, president of the local astronomy club, for the First Central Congregational Church in Kansas City. "The visible universe is a vast inconceivable cosmic precipitate in which chemical changes are constantly taking place in all worlds and suns," Davis said. "All matter is in constant evolution or motion," subject to the "law of physical dissolution and resurrection of worlds." Or as the astronomer Harlow Shapley put it: our "higher immortality" means that we are "made of the same undying stuff as the stars."[56] Both dialectical materialism and Western science were predisposed to such an intelligent design, created or not.

No less than Albert Einstein expressed these principles in a famous address. Paraphrasing Richard Maurice Bucke from the turn of the century, Einstein raised "the cosmic religious experience" as "the strongest and the noblest driving force behind scientific research," the alpha and omega point in the achievements of such luminaries as Kepler and Newton and himself. Cosmic consciousness was the pinnacle of human self-awareness, that recognition of our singular place in the plural universe. The Reverend John Haynes Holmes of the Manhattan Community Church called it being in "communion with the vast harmony of the illimitable universe." Wrote Episcopalian reverend Robert Norwood, "Real knowledge leads us into cosmic freedom, for we cannot be free if we are imprisoned on a planet." We are, rather, "citizens of infinite space," a quote straight out of the lexicon of Soviet cosmism. The *New York Times* pictured these ideals with a lonely scientist working at his desk, watching comets streak through the sky while plotting his own rocket craft's trajectory into outer space.[57] The dramatic image coincided well enough with the new worldview of relativity, which transformed space (in Einstein's own words) from something rather static and predictable into something "changeable and capable of being influenced"; a "metric structure" measurable and malleable; a space of new, human-made, curving latitudes and longitudes.[58]

Rocketry enthusiasts in Europe and America shared in this new "cosmic philosophy." From France, Alexandre Ananoff educated the public on the basic facts of rocket power, helping to popularize Tsiolkovskii's "cosmic rocket," "cosmic ship," and "cosmic station," the building blocks of the new science of cosmonautics, getting to and living in outer space. He also indulged in the romantic, seeing the new rocket science as ultimately about the exploration of the "beauties of infinity," the "immensities of space," and the possibilities of discovering new worlds and peoples. Rocket science was humanity's most perfect and total task.[59] Ananoff's rocketry displays at the Paris International Exhibition (1937), in the famous Palace of Discovery, were framed against the backdrops of lunar landscapes painted by the renowned illustrator Lucien Rudaux, drawn from his recent survey of astronomy *Upon Other Worlds* (1937). Here was an update of Flammarion's voyage through the solar system, with imaginary perspectives on the planets from the porthole of a rocket spaceship, its parabolic arcs new rivals to the comets. Here were also fitting tribute to another backdrop at the Palace of Discovery, the sculpture of the "spiral of evolution," illustrating life's origins at the depths of the planet, ever rising through evolutionary stages to a summit in humankind, now reaching for the stars.[60]

From Britain the religious writer Gerald Heard revived William Winwood Reade's evolutionary optimism and Richard Maurice Bucke's cosmic consciousness for a new generation. Humanity was beset by the challenges of world war and fascist dictatorship, but it was nevertheless set on an inevitable path of progress, ever secularist and humanist. His "ascent of humankind" was to peak with a "complete co-consciousness," the "super-consciousness" of humanity's small place in the vast universe. For Heard historical progress took the shape of an ascending spiral, a sequence of curves and parabolas moving ever higher and smaller, a modern-day "Tower of Babel," whose arches were to "span" the "chaos of modern life." The spiral expressed nothing less than the evolution of the human psyche, the union of the individual with the collective, of mind with nature, a consciousness of our planet and of its place in the cosmos.[61] He pictured it using an inside shot of one of Robert Goddard's launch towers at Roswell, New Mexico.

In its overarching metaphors Heard's "ascent" mirrored the historical trajectories of the Russian Revolution and Soviet dialectical materialism: human history as a process of self-creation, of radical leaps from quantity to quality, from necessity to freedom. For Heard modernity represented a revolutionary surge, a release of human energy that he variously described as the "new effervescence," a "frenzy of discharge," a "volatilizing energy," and a "convulsive condensation" upward. So he wrote, "Evolving consciousness, at each turn and crest of its cycle, discharges with an intensifying force." Heard entertained an absolute confidence in the human capacity to shape mind over matter, to perfect the "divine" element in our very beings.[62] This was not some empty ideology of false hope. It was an ideology aligned with the real, with the concrete achievements of modern science and technology. Chemistry and biology had proven Darwinian evolution true. Inventors and industries were building higher and faster planes, even for rockets to outer space. For Heard and publicists like him, rocket power represented the culmination of this process of discovery and invention, of the human mastery over space and time. The "Newtonian law" of "action and reaction" was a metaphor on the power of the human mind as "sui generis"

Fig. 28. A spiral toward space—"the tower" that Robert Goddard used to mount his rockets for launch, as seen from within (at Roswell, New Mexico). From Gerald Heard, *Exploring the Stratosphere* (London: Nelson, 1936). Credit: Associated Press.

fulcrum. Our "self-knowledge," the reach for understanding within, was mirrored in the power of rockets to reach outward in the "new vertical exploration." Both would achieve immortality and infinity.[63]

Olaf Stapledon explored the same themes in his influential science fiction novel *Starmaker* (1937). Its main character discovers myriad worlds as he speeds along through time and space by perfect telepathic projection and stream of consciousness, all mind without body. Stapledon thus fulfilled the dreams of Reade and Bucke. His star traveler literally melds the thinking human "I" with the feeling cosmic "We," rising to a near perfect state of "communal consciousness."[64] Along the way he meets winged aliens, fish beings, "six-legged" monsters, "mollusk-like" creatures, and plant beings of various sorts. Stapledon found that the archetypical technologies of rising and "waking worlds" were radios and rockets. His own star traveler was a being straight out of a Vladimir Maiakovskii poem: a being in "headlong flight" by a "new power of locomotion," striking out "into the ocean of space," "sweeping hither and thither among the stars."[65] Stapledon's star traveler was the human being become spacecraft, a flash of light speeding through space, whole planets approaching or receding, trillions of years turned into an instant, a culmination of the Russian revolutionary dream about the total human mastery of time and space and the elements.

Stapledon's price for this instantaneous human perfection was to visit worlds beset by extravagances and lusts, ecological decay and social calamities, senseless risings and fallings, exploding stars and ice deaths. The whole universe was punctuated by the births and deaths of planets and stars, by the death of whole galaxies, by a final "cosmical decline." For all his secular faith in a cosmic consciousness, Stapledon's Gnosticism was overpowering. He became the spokesman for a self-hating world.[66] Such bleak prophecies were often the rule in the Western mass media, especially in the years of the Great Depression. The sun was sure to die out or explode. Natural disasters were bound to happen. Life on Earth was terminal. Here was pessimism in line with the times, worthy of the great H. G. Wells and his *War of the Worlds*, still a favorite among European and American readers. The dramatist Orson Welles seized the moment with his famous Halloween night radio broadcast in 1938, a parody of Wells's Martian invasion, authentic enough to scare thousands of listeners, who thought it was the real thing. Audiences were primed for apocalypse.[67] And in an interesting twist on the biblical studies of Nikolai Morozov and the solar theses of Aleksandr Chizhevskii, which he had read in his youth, the Russian Jewish émigré Immanuel Velikovsky set out to prove the stories of the Old Testament by his new school of "historical Cosmogony." He discovered presumed correspondences between electromagnetic divergences in the orbits of the planets and comets, causing near collisions with planet Earth, natural disasters, and mass disturbances in our history. The wayward revolutions of the planets, especially Venus, had caused revolutionary events such as the exodus of the Jews to Egypt, with its attendant plagues and partings. No matter that all of this was spurious science, American readers were enthralled, turning Velikovsky into a best-selling author of doom.[68]

Stalin's regime dispensed with such dystopias, except perhaps in official ideology, which marked the West as a nightmare civilization all its own, corrupted by its capitalist and imperialist excesses, preparing for a new war of mass destruction. From the United States, David Lasser's classic treatise *The Conquest of Space* (1931) made a passionate appeal to these "pacifist" values, Soviet style. Besides his work as a science writer and editor for Gernsback's science fiction magazines, Lasser was also a dedicated labor activist and socialist. In his book he celebrated the human project for rocketry as a "revolutionary technology," a "plunge upward" into the reaches of "outer space." The piece reads in part like a gloss of Zamiatin's *We*, with pointed references to an imagined rocket flight by the "Chief," the great designer who was also "master of half a dozen sciences and a leader of men." He tamed the "metal monster" and set it on a course for the moon. At times Lasser perfectly expressed the tropes of Soviet socialist realism, with dramatic references to a new race of super humans who would "circle the globe faster than the sun," a breed of "zealous astronauts" ready for any risk, ready to "perform feats of strength and endurance never before asked." Rocketry and space travel were hallmarks of a new human era, tapping into the energy of the sun and the atom to conquer all of nature by machine.[69]

Lasser even planned the formation of an International Interplanetary Commission to unite all of the world's pioneers, and Robert Esnault-Pelterie and N. A. Rynin agreed to join it. In this endeavor Lasser shared with his fellow rocket enthusiasts a sense of the revolutionary and utopian possibilities of the rocket to unite people, remake us for the better, and liberate us from petty parochialisms and earthly gravity.[70] As one of his comrade American rocketeers generously put it, they were all zealots for the cause, "brothers" and "missionaries," part of an international fraternity that included such signal Soviet achievers as N. Kibalchich and K. E. Tsiolkovskii, F. A. Tsander and M. K. Tikhonravov.[71]

These utopian visions of a future international or interplanetary state, built upon sophisticated technologies and a socialist ethic, were one dimension of an American cosmism, what De Witt Kilgore has called "astrofuturism." These were only somewhat radical proposals, to tell the truth, in a day when socialist and corporatist solutions to the Great Depression were in wide circulation. They were echoed in Gernsback's science fiction. One of his authors, Lilith Lorraine, imagined a fantastic new society built on mind control, applying the forces of "the action and the reaction" in order to force evolutionary progress and implant new thoughts of love ("chains of roses") in people's minds. But in the end her goal was the same as Lasser's: to create a society of perfect "Socialism" in which "all the mighty energies of man's superhuman machinery were enlisted on the side of progress." Lorraine called this a society of free labor, free faith, and free love. A society of "a perfect race for a perfect world, a race that having overcome the Earth, pierces the heavens with an endless arc of light seeking new wrongs to right, new worlds to conquer."[72]

The libertarian Charles Lindbergh, Goddard's most important patron, remained committed to much the same vision. In a letter read before commencement exercises at Clark University in 1937, he envisioned humanity as standing at the edge of a whole new world. Man might soon be able to "lose himself in interstellar space." Lindbergh predicted the rocket's revolutionary and "far-reaching effects on the future of civilization." As the *New York Times* put it, rockets would give humanity "freedom from the Earth" just as planes had given it "freedom from the air." Or as the *New York Herald Tribune* had it, rockets turned us into "arrows into space," riding "the breathless swish of the rocket's tail," people "self-propelled" to infinity. The conservative *American Boy* magazine featured just such an image for its November 1937 issue: rocket and man in parabolic trajectory through space.[73] The New Deal artist Carlo Ciampaglia had already crafted all of these hopes into his mural for the Texas Centennial Exposition in Dallas in 1936, somewhat strange for this Italian American of rather conservative and capitalist tastes, son of a Hoboken barber and no friend of Bolshevism. Nevertheless, he painted a prescient symbol for America's heartland, framing Texan frontier history between its early stagecoaches, boats, and railroads and its imminent space promise (this thirty years before Houston became a NASA center). The central image of the three porticoes of the exposition's Transportation Building revealed "Future Transportation," what Ciampaglia said revealed "man's final mastery of the heavens. A rocket, guided by a man and a woman, leaves the earth and sea far below in its journey to the moon. About it are the planets, clouds, and stars; ahead of it the Milky Way."[74]

Russian and American Cosmism

Given the immense powers of the Communist "propaganda state" to speak in one voice and to mobilize assent from above, we ought to take some pause in weighing Soviet ideologies about science and technology.. Yes, its monoliths and decrees are impressive. We illustrate our history books with them. We quote them at length. But they are also echoes from the culture of industrial achievement that already filled the European and American media. Soviet propaganda about science and technology, if in a more concentrated form, mirrored the West's own longings about the future. It was not some freak mutation of Marxist philosophy or of European history. It was something at the very heart of the modern experience.[75]

Take Soviet science fiction, which lost its visionary social edge in the 1930s, instead focusing on the traditional stories of Jules Verne and H. G. Wells, or on dramatic technical or engineering achievements. Writers bowed to the Stalinist "administrative utopia," as Richard Stites has called it, a utopia of discipline and hierarchy, science and technology, and the "magic of rationality."[76] Yet these developments also followed a worldwide trend, the "hard science" approach that began fitfully with the magazine *Amazing Stories*, first published in 1926, and eventually dominated the golden age of science fiction, from 1939 to 1959. The approach spanned a range "from U.S. pulp magazines to the Soviet Agitprop," as Darko Suvin has argued. Real "science" in the new fiction was a thread common to the mass print

Fig. 29. "Future Transportation." A detail of Carlo Ciampaglia's 22' x 40' mural for the Texas Centennial Exposition in Dallas (1936), illustrating the human being as rocket. Credit: Carlo Alberto Ciampaglia Papers / unidentified photographer, Archives of American Art, Smithsonian Institution.

culture of free market capitalism and propaganda state communism. Czesław Miłosz recognized the same dynamic: "Dialectical materialism, Russian-style, is nothing more than nineteenth-century science vulgarized to the second power," packed with "emotional and didactic" force.[77] They both shared the same core value of transformational change—the fantastic becoming real. The Western scientific romance became the "revolutionary romance" of the Bolshevik regime, married to the grand historical plotline of Marxism-Leninism.

Stalinist culture was imbued with an ideology of material progress set by European and especially American standards. The Soviets co-opted the values and slogans of Western popular science to the level of official ideology and state policy. Stalinist cosmism in this sense was a kind of "Americanism." Russians were reading in their newspapers and magazines and school texts or seeing on their banners and posters in public what Western readers were already well accustomed to in their popular science media. The Soviet propaganda machine read something very much like *Science and Invention* or *Popular Science Monthly*, filled with the American obsession over "SPEED, SPEED, SPEED, SPEED, SPEED"; the fixation upon "high speed production with split-hair precision," as an advertisement of the Norton Grinding Wheels Company boasted; and evidence of "man's leaping knowledge," embodied in the "giants out of the earth" such as railroads and skyscrapers, as an advertisement of the Bell Telephone Company put it.[78] The language of American exceptionalism about science and technology was often striking in its bombast. One short story in *Popular Aviation* predicted the rocket as the future shape of flight, offering a vision by decade-long leaps, only a bit less bold than Stalin's Five-Year Plans. In a special section devoted to the amazing achievements of the twentieth century, the editors of *Popular Mechanics* compared American inventors to the "shock troops" of the wondrous future.[79] It all sounded nearly Soviet. The Stalinist slogan of "further, higher, faster" was something straight out of the commercial advertisements of the Lockheed or Boeing corporations.

Yet these points of reference already hint at a crucial difference between the United States and USSR, at least with regard to rocketry and spaceflight. The United States was more fixed on speed, on the "faster," a function of movement through time. The USSR, coming from behind, was instead more occupied with velocity, the "further," a function of movement through time *and* space. The Soviets were also obsessed with altitude. Their graphs of aviation "world records" represented, time and again, the same parabolic curve of rising achievement, culminating in higher and higher altitudes.[80]

Russian and American relations, at least through the public diplomacy of aviation contacts, remained mutually deferential. In part this was a function of the shape of the world and of the aviator's zeal for conquering distance. Like astronomers, fliers were part of a close-knit international fraternity, one strong enough to overshadow their political and ideological differences. Distance records captivated aviators, governments, and the public, part of a dream to stitch East and West, North and South, into new transport skyways. The media loved to frame these projects as fulfilling Jules Verne's fantastic stories, in terms that every literate person could understand. Cartographers remapped the world by new "azimuth" projections, centered on the North Pole, revealing the gently sloping arcs (parabolas) that pilots were now flying over parts of a rounded Earth.[81]

Soviet aviators set out to make their own world distance records. They had many points of arrival, but their most meaningful ones were over the Arctic, on a flight plan toward the United States. The summer of 1937 witnessed two such dramatic events. On 18 June a Soviet crew piloted by Valerii Chkalov set off from Moscow for Oakland, California, flying over the North Pole, the "top of the world." After sixty-three hours and twenty-five minutes, the exhausted crew was forced to make an emergency landing in Vancouver, Washington, where they had a hot breakfast (bacon, eggs, and cognac), a nap, and then a parade. This was but the first in a host of victory celebrations as the crew made a victory circuit through Portland, San Francisco, Hollywood, Chicago, Washington DC, and New York City. Chkalov remembered the tour fondly: the police escorts, sirens blaring; the banquets upon banquets; the impromptu and mangled playing of the *Internationale*; the adoring crowds. On 12 July a second crew broke a world distance record by flying, via the North Pole, from Moscow to Los Angeles in sixty-two hours and seventeen minutes. Americans applauded once again, the fliers photographed towering over Hollywood's latest star, Shirley Temple.[82] These aerial exploits were a clever mixing of several Stalinist challenges: the technical mastery of aviation, the conquest of the Arctic, and the rediscovery of

America. To race into the air was literally to conquer new heights, new ranges across space.

By the sheer coincidence of metaphor, the poetic images about these transpolar flights also approached the coming age of space-flight. As one booklet put it in 1939, "No free spaces remained here on earth." Communism swept "away all boundaries." Songwriter Vasilii Lebedev-Kumach promised that for an "immense" country such as the USSR, there were "no limits for the capable and brave." The trajectory was "ever higher and higher," always "forward and forward." The Soviets were a "winged people," breaking all human "ceilings and celestial envelopes." His companion poets joined the call to reach for the "aerial," for the "blue expanses" and the "heavenly depths." In all of this the USSR was master of the "leap" (*pryzhok*) into the air, the stratosphere, and even outer space. If aviation was the alpha of this Promethean spirit, space travel was its omega. The only way forward was up, to reach into the "solar heights," to fly "even to the stars."[83] Part of this was artistic license, poetic symbolism. But given the celebration of Tsiolkovskii and his rocket, part of it was realistic expectation too. The transpolar flights proved the pilots' unbounded love of "interstellar spaces," their wish to "rush along upon a stellar parabola," ultimately "to open a dazzling path to the universe."[84]

Boris Chertok, future Soviet spaceflight administrator, remembered the two great transpolar flights with a special nostalgia, experiencing firsthand the "popular jubilation" for the aviators in the summer of 1937, what he said was "comparable to the public rejoicing that took place on 12 April 1961, the moment of Iurii Gagarin's first flight into Earth orbit."[85] Hero fliers returning from the United States paved the way for a hero cosmonaut returning from outer space. Yet Chertok's memory was not purely retrospective. It was already seeded with cosmic values and images from that very summer of 1937. Poets celebrated the transpolar fliers for circling the planet, reaching from Moscow back again to Moscow, flights by which "they ascend to the starry heights." Georgii Baidukov even dedicated a fictional short story to his factual exploits, a story about a transglobal flight, from pole to pole, by a Soviet high-altitude, high-speed airplane—its name, *Forward to Communism*, a reference to the planned Lenin statue atop the spiraling Palace of Soviets, raised skyward and pointing into the future with his outstretched arm. He illustrated the story with a drawing of the fliers as the world's first cosmonauts, taking their aviation accomplishments from the North Pole into space, all the way to the moon.[86]

These cosmic values and images survived into coming years. What had once been sensational material for science fiction stories now became centerpieces of Soviet state propaganda. In one story for young adult readers, Baidukov's imagined plotline was rewritten for the rocket, the transglobal flight through the Americas, a prelude to coming interplanetary conquests. By the spring of 1939 Vladimir Kokkinaki and his actual transpolar crew became, twenty years before the *Sputnik* of 1957, new "sputniks" of the earth and "fellow travelers of the Sun." They set off, these "people of the new New World," Communist Russia, to conquer the old New World, capitalist America, by way of the poles. Flying off for the New York City World's Fair, "as if in a star-crossed fable," wrote one poet, "they leapt into a quick arc."[87] Their parabolic flight to America presaged the coming parabolic arcs to outer space (although Kokkinaki's plane crash-landed in Canada).

The United States did eventually catch up to the USSR in terms of its own cosmic sensibilities, peaking with the New York City World's Fair in 1939. This cosmism took shape in the fair's Theme Center, which included the "Perisphere," a 180-foot diameter steel and stucco globe (the world's largest), a planet all its own; the "Trylon," a 610-foot-high obelisk, standing alongside the Perisphere, reaching to the heavens like a rocket; and the "Helicline," a 950-foot-long spiral ramp, joining the two. Loudspeakers played a soft, celestial music of bells and strings around these displays, and at their exit stood Carl Milles's 30-foot-tall sculpture *The Astronomer*, the figure holding a compass and looking up to infinite space.[88] Joseph Binder's award-winning poster for the fair shrunk New York City before the Perisphere and Trylon, airplanes in vertical flight, headed for the stars (or perhaps just around the world, as the marvelous Howard Hughes did in July 1938 in a plane named the *1939 New York World's Fair*).

These monuments were literally at the fair's geographic and symbolic center, the core logo around which the whole event radiated. One reporter remembered that when seen together, they joined in a cos-

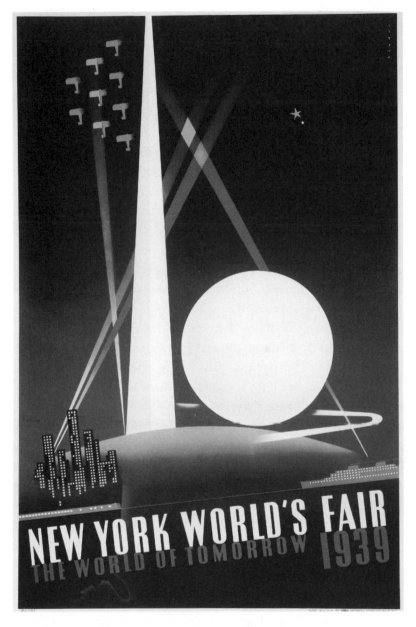

Fig. 30. The Perisphere and Trylon, Joseph Binder's cosmic poster for the
New York World's Fair (1939). Credit: © David Pollack / Corbis. For an early
Soviet precursor to this style (not reproducible here), see Ivan I. Leonidov's
model for the Lenin Institute (1927), in Selim Khan-Magomedov, *Pioneers of
Soviet Architecture* (New York: Rizzoli, 1987), 221.

mic pose of point and curve, drawing the eye forward and upward in a parabola toward the heavens.[89] Here were also America's answers, if in the shape of passing fairground exhibits and souvenir trinkets, to the very radical forms of Russia avant-garde futurism. The Perisphere and Trylon had their precedents from some ten years earlier, in Ivan Leonidov's cosmic model for a "Lenin Institute" (1927), designed to be built in the Lenin Hills overlooking Moscow, replete with library and a scientific research institute for interplanetary communications.[90] Much like Malevich's famous *Black Square*, designers touted the Perisphere and Trylon structures as pure form, the sum of simplicity and abstraction. Like the abstract canvases of Malevich's students, the Perisphere even seemed, thanks to the fountains and reflections at its base, to hover in planetary space or, as one newspaper piece put it, as if "ready to float gently away for a flight to Mars." One sketch of the Perisphere, on an imaginary "pageant night," drawn by America's premier cityscape artist, Hugh Ferriss, looked eerily just like K. F. Iuon's *New Planet*.[91]

The Perisphere also united form with symbol. It featured "Democracity" within its shell, the centerpiece of the fair's slogan, "Building the World of Tomorrow." Audiences arrived at the year 2039 by way of the world's longest escalator (made of stainless steel) and a spiraling series of sky rides, treated to a movable feast of cosmic sights and sounds. The urban diorama, set within the lower shell of the Perisphere as if it also floated in outer space, incorporated a film toward the end of the presentation, projected onto the upper shell, as hundreds of distant stars, a "celestial conclave," transformed cinematically into masses of workers and farmers, marching from the "heavens" toward the future city, a "mammoth size" living mural. They sang about conquering the chaos of nature and traditional culture, about building a "brave new world. Tomorrow's world, / That we shall build today." It was as if the United States, in a moment of festive grandeur, had co-opted the hyperbole of the USSR propaganda state. Both shared, after all, what Anthony Swift has called a "language of technological progress."[92]

The closest the USSR came to such cosmic strains was the statue that graced the front yard of its pavilion buildings, a male worker standing some 269 feet (82 meters) high (nicknamed "Uncle Joe"), holding up a five-pointed red star, the second highest structure after the Trylon. It glowed at night, just like the selfsame red stars that hovered over the Kremlin. Like the Trylon, it reached upward, ever higher, in an even more heroic pose of aspiration and expectation. Befitting the theme, on display inside the pavilion was Chkalov's 1937 transpolar plane; a full-sized replica of the Maiakovskii metro station in Moscow; and a twenty-ton, thirty-foot-high, bejeweled and marbled model of the Palace of Soviets with Lenin's statue on top (only one-seventy-fifth of its proposed size).

For all its utopian dressings the fair was mostly consumed with advertising the best of American capitalism (somewhat like the *Explorer* stratostats), displayed in the commercial promotions of the Ford and Dupont corporations, Bell Telephone and General Electric, Eastman Kodak, American Tobacco, and Borden Foods. Besides the world's longest escalator at the Theme Center, the fair boasted the world's largest cash register (National Cash Register's); the world's largest typewriter (Underwood's); and the world's largest robot, Elektro, with his robotic dog, Sparko (Westinghouse Electric's). The Heinz Company also featured a six-foot-tall robot, "Tomato Man," in formal "top hat and tails" doing a song and dance routine. Thanks to Norman Bel Geddes, W. D. Teague, and Raymond Loewy, art deco streamlining helped to define the fair: the aerodynamics of elongated pointed ends, of teardrops and rounded corners, in all manner of automobiles and planes, buses and ships, buildings and things. Bel Geddes called this look our glimpse into a better-planned, Soviet-style future.[93] These shapes were already transforming into affordable purchases for our homes: radios and cooling fans, toasters and refrigerators (such as Loewy's design for the Sears "Coldspot"). Here may be a one of the reasons for America's fickle affair with the space rocket. It was but one of the "looks," one of the celebrated streamlined shapes that enclosed us.[94]

In U.S. science fiction, too, the rocket tended to serve an auxiliary role, just a means to engage in more colorful storytelling. Hard science often gave way to the space opera. J. M. Walsh's *Vandals of the Void* (1931) was an archetypical space opera for young readers, filled with fun characters and plotlines and nifty gimmicks such as televisions, ray guns, magnifying eyes, see-through glasses, and cloaking force fields. Based in the year 2001, its story revolved around the authoritarian "Inter-Planetary Board of Control" and its courageous "Guard," their slogan "Peace in the Universe." Bob Olsen's goofy tale about the adventures of Captain Brink to Jupiter (to suppress a revolution in the lunar mines of Io) set the perfect tone for these kinds of stories: "At the door of his rocket-ship hangar," he wrote, "Captain Brink jabbed his knuckles into his lean hips and gazed smilingly at the sky."[95] These stories were also the models for the immensely popular *Flash Gordon* and *Buck Rogers* series in print, radio, and film. When, for example, the Fels Planetarium in Philadelphia put together a special-effects presentation in 1939, "To the Moon by Rocket Ship," it featured a space trip in the year 2033, complete with a "Buck Rogers Rocket Ship Control Cabin," with pretend devices such as the Cosmic Relativator Control and the Outer Space Compass. Nearby bars offered a new mixed drink for the occasion, the "Rocket Ship Special," promising that patrons would "see the stars." Robert Goddard even made a special one-day trip to see it all. Given his love of martinis and a good cigar, we can imagine him sampling the cocktail too.[96]

In all of these ways, for many Americans rocketry and spaceflight themes were locked into the realm of science fiction, not science fact. Even the term *rocket* carried its own pop cultural baggage. After all, 27 December 1932 saw the opening night for the Radio City Music Hall "Rockettes" in Manhattan, thus named because they were all so tall and straight, precise and perfect in their chorused dance, even gravity-defying in some of their moves. Just like rockets. America's most serious pursuit, rocket science, became conflated with pure kitsch.[97] In popular culture rocketry often had more to do with carnival stunts than with outer space. Spectacles were the rule. One enterprising pilot made his way between county and state fairs, flying a stunt plane that blew smoke out of its tail, only imitating rocket flight but pleasing the audiences all the same. At the Century of Progress Exposition in Chicago in 1933, a train of "bullet-shaped," "streamlined cars" moved on cables two thousand feet above the exhibits, suggesting "rocket planes of the future" but puffing only steam to mimic reaction power. The Golden Gate International Exposition in San Francisco in 1939 featured a "rocket-gun thrill ride" that "launched" 250 people at a time beyond Earth's gravity. Thus, the sober editors of *Aircraft Engineering* put it best when they cautioned that "there is nothing inherently funny about rocket propulsion and yet it has undoubtedly assumed a place among the comic things of aeronautics."[98]

If cosmist values, American style, enjoyed something of a central place at the New York World's Fair, rocketry and spaceflight remained sideshow amusements, like the fair's parachute jump and its many peep shows or like two of its fun-rides, the "Stratoship" and "Meteor Ride." Designer Raymond Loewy's "Rocketport of Tomorrow," the climax of the Chrysler Corporation's "World of Tomorrow" site, also featured a "meteoric" stratospheric passage from New York to London by rocket. Mixing part Verne and part Wells, the "rocketship" was launched by cannon. "A flash, a muffled explosion, and the ship vanishes into the night," so one description went. Even so, Loewy did allow the American Rocket Society to display one of its test models, the ARS Experimental Rocket No. 3, at the exhibition, dents and all. The point was "to lend reality to a program considered by some to border on the fantastic," as the placard read. Thus, the United States, too, had its own American blend of socialist realism, of fiction and fact, highlighting the realities of "jet propulsion" on the path to "man's age-old battle to conquer space."[99]

At the World Fair's Theatre of Time and Space, the American Museum of Natural History and the Longines-Wittnauer Watch Company also organized a space ride, the Inter-Universe Grand Tours, a "thrilling journey over vast cosmic seas to the shores of island universes into the depths of space." The points of arrival were the near planets and the galaxies beyond, "past the dark nebula in the constellation of Orion."[100] As with Tsiolkovskii's consultations for the Soviet film *Cosmic Flight*, the promoters of the ride based the attraction on formal science. William H. Barton created realistic "moon crater scenery" with special lighting. "Trick photography" simulated rocket flight to the moon by an "ultra-scientific craft" of control panels and dials, helped along by motion pictures and sound effects and fans, the hissing and whizzing of reaction flight at 250,000 miles per minute. The front cover and lead article of *Popular Science* in April 1938 featured a design of the ride. The corresponding Soviet issue of *Science and Technology*, from May 1938, reproduced it in outer space—the image inverted, as if held before a mirror, in a way symbolic of the World's Fair as event. The Soviets took the part, the one small part, for the whole. This was not simply a question of graphic design on the cheap. It was also a question of a shared perspective. Russia's imagination of rocketry and spaceflight was still America's. And America, at least so far as amusement rides went, was better at it.

In one interesting science fiction story, *Zero to Eighty* (1937), the two powers even meet in space, thanks to E. F. Northrup, a former professor of physics at Princeton University. The plot and characters reflected the American passion for a coming flight to the moon via a "Goddard-type rocket." It launches into a mystical "Parabolic Velocity," meaning "the velocity at which a body leaves the earth along the path of a parabola, and hence never returns," by way of an electromagnetic cannon. Yet the Russians steal its designs and plans in a reckless and fatal attempt to beat America, "to be the first humans to attempt an escape from earth, where gravity has imprisoned man . . . a greater adventure than Prometheus undertook when he stole fire from the Olympian gods." Although they ultimately lose this imagined race to space, their craft fated to drift helplessly in the ether, Northrup nevertheless credits the Russians as "a virile, brave, and forward-looking people," worthy rivals to the Americans. In the end both sides boldly exhibit the human power to project themselves and their environment beyond the planet, to fulfill evolution by returning to that space from whence Arrhenius's seeds of life first came.[101]

So long as the West was interested in rocketry and spaceflight, to one degree or another, the USSR was interested too. Such was the imperative of international competition. But the imperative, we have seen, was also a function of Russian national traditions. Between 1931 and 1940 the Stalin regime published three official biographies of K. E. Tsiolkovskii by none other than his three original publicists—B. N. Vorob'ev, Ia. I. Perel'man, and N. A. Rynin—from the years just before and during the Russian Revolution.[102] These biog-

Fig. 31. The American educational ride Inter-Universe Grand Tours at the Theatre of Time and Space, New York World's Fair. From the front cover of *Popular Science Monthly* (April 1938). Credit: Transcendental Graphics / Getty Images.

Fig. 32. The Soviet copy of the American educational ride Inter-Universe Grand Tours. From the front cover and featured article "Raketa v planetarii," *Nauka i tekhnika* 5 (May 1938). Credit: the family of the artist E. V. Voishvillo (with special thanks to El'vina Evgen'evna and Georgii Askol'dovich).

raphies return us full circle, back to beginnings. Vorob'ev had been a promoter and friend of Tsiolkovskii starting in 1911, one of the first of the Russian aviation journalists to disseminate his theories. Now he became Tsiolkovskii's leading biographer, packaging him as the original founder of what the regime was now regularly calling "cosmonautics," the mathematical, applied science of flight into outer space.[103] These contributions to Stalinist cosmism remind us of its scope, of its near and far horizons, how it competed with the West and what it inherited from the past. Stalinist cosmism was based upon origins, upon the enthusiasms for rocketry and spaceflight reaching back to the turn of the century, to the late Russian Empire, if also always reaching across the continent to Western Europe and across the Atlantic to America. On this score something of a global "utopian" project, interplanetary travel by rocket, thrived across the span of three decades, between the early 1910s and into the late 1930s. Stalinist cosmism testified to Russia's enduring gaze, looking spaceward by looking westward—and back again.

Conclusion

There, to the silver ice between the orbs,
Through time, through death, through storms,
There—we rush! For no better fate awaits,
Than for us to become—an interplanetary race.
—PAVEL ANTOKOL'SKII

The outbreak of the Second World War in 1939 offers a dramatic pause—and punctuation—to our story. Some thirty years of vibrant debates on rocketry and spaceflight theory went silent. In Russia and America the war saw the momentary eclipse of liquid fuel rocketry, its pioneers and societies. But in Germany the rocket was reborn as the ballistic missile, one of the touted "wonder weapons" and "V [vengeance] weapons" that were supposed to turn the tide of war Germany's way. When they became vaguely known to the general English-speaking public in the middle of 1943, rocket power was no longer a topic of distant promise. "Buck Rogers' World Comes True as Warring Powers Devise Self-Propelled Projectiles," proclaimed one banner headline, introducing a truly new weapon, one that "drives itself along." The war was fulfilling the magnificent "dreams" of the Sunday supplement writers of the 1930s.[1]

Walter Dornberger, one of the directors of the v-2 program, certainly dreamed so. His memoir recalled a genuine enthusiasm at Peenemünde for the rocket as a means of reaching space. He said as much on 3 October 1942, the day of the v-2's first successful flight.

Its very form represented a perfect parabolic trajectory, if in rather medieval terms: "The slender sharp-pointed nose took on the shape of a Gothic arch as it joined the cylindrical body." When it flew, he saw a shining rocket following its guided path upward, true to its course, the exhaust fire "clear-cut and self-contained," until it was but "a tiny dot glittering dazzlingly white at the end of a small dark streak."[2] Newton's circumspect model of attraction and repulsion had finally given way to Dornberger's aura of technological seduction, the rocket in mystical flight.

Germany was both a winner and loser in this final sprint of the race toward space. Twice in the twentieth century, it had bargained on war and failed, risking the newest and most spectacular of military technologies: the Paris Gun of 1918 and the "V" weapons of 1944.[3] Both incited fear but left relatively minor human and material damage. In official terms the v-2 rocket was a vengeance weapon to answer the strategic bombing campaigns against German military and civilian targets, unleashed by the Allies with full fury in 1944. In this sense the v-2 was not inaugurated on 3 October 1942, its first successful flight, but on 8 September 1944, the day the German military forces first launched it against a civilian population, the city of Paris, fulfilling the very purpose for which it was originally made. Parisians awoke shortly after 8:30 a.m. to the explosion of a v-2 missile, fired from about 180 miles (290 kilometers) away. Londoners experienced the same effect a bit later in the day. In remarks to the Peenemünde team Dornberger honestly defined the v-2 as a weapon of war: "from the artillery man's point of view," a successor to the Paris Gun. "We have invaded space with our rocket and for the first time—mark this well—have used space as a bridge between two points on the earth."[4] He was essentially describing the coming intercontinental ballistic missile.

The trajectories and targets of the v-2 raise an interesting query. Why was it never used on the eastern front, against the Red Army or the civilian populations under its occupation? We can make one supposition, based on the broad findings gathered here. The v-2 was an element of high-technology terror reserved exclusively for the advanced West. "What I want," proclaimed Adolf Hitler to Walter Dornberger on 7 July 1943, "is annihilation—annihilating effect," primarily against England.[5] Launching it eastward would have been like sending one of Germany's most sophisticated weapons straight into the past, into oblivion. The eastern front saw its share of German high technology, in the tanks and airplanes and artillery of "lightning warfare" during 1939 and 1941 and in the labor and death camps that followed. But the v-2 was meaningless in the East, with few fixed targets on a fluid front, where violence and brutality were already the norm. Terror in the East was blunt and barbaric, racist and genocidal, annihilation from the past. Against the West the v-2 was meant to be a precise means of destruction, awe inspiring and cowering, annihilation from the future. It was the centerpiece of Thomas Pynchon's half-imagined, half-real "Rocket State" (*Raketen Stadt*), that government machine so grotesquely representing Newton's law of action-reaction and Pavlov's law of stimulus-response.[6]

Russia and America, banking on the saner investments of conventional infantry and munitions, received far greater returns than Germany's risky high-technology investment. Stalin's military depended not on innovative ballistic missiles but on more modest solid fuel rocket weapons for air and battlefield combat (for example, the famous "Katiusha"), all to repel the German invasion. Only the Manhattan Project matched Germany's investment in fantastic weaponry. As Mark Harrison has argued, the U.S. effort to build and deploy the atomic bombs roughly equaled the German effort with the v-2 missiles, the cost at around two billion dollars each; in contrast, the USSR likely spent only about ten million dollars on various "jet propulsion" projects in the 1930s and 1940s.[7] Both Russia and the United States would likely have developed medium-range and intercontinental ballistic missiles without German intervention. They each had the scientific cadres, the institutional arrangements and experiences, the industrial might, and the traditions of complex enterprises in place to succeed (canals and hydroelectric dams, transcontinental railroads and atomic bombs).[8] Getting to the Germans first was simply a closing round, a competitive edge, in the arms race of the Second World War.

Yet both countries learned a crucial lesson from Germany, that the ballistic missile was already a mechanism of force and counterforce.

In the last months of the war the race toward space transformed into a race for the remains of the v-1 and v-2 weapons, together with a variety of other innovations, from jet engines to advanced electronics, from remote guidance to atomic power.[9] As each side began to inventory and test its v-2 rockets, American and Russian rocket science essentially became German rocket science, whose engineers (men such as Wernher von Braun) became vested cadres for the development of rockets and missiles in both countries. German influence was decisive on a range of issues. The v-2, in parts and in sum, had set a revolutionary standard of proven achievement.[10] The world had finally found that elusive artificial international language—in the differential calculus that framed the designs of the German rocket team and that never really needed any translating. The three hundredth anniversary of Isaac Newton's birth in 1943 offered the Soviets a fitting turning point. Up to then they had been "thinking and speaking" in "Newton's language," as one tract put it. Now, alongside the Americans, and thanks to a marriage of necessity with atomic rockets, they were about to "create the new languages" of relativity and quantum mechanics.[11]

In America publicists lectured interested readers on the nature of rocket science, in part to make sense of Germany's innovations, in part to confront the lingering misconception that rockets moved by pushing themselves against either the ground or the air. In the pages of the *American Journal of Physics* the mainstream scientific establishment finally recognized the legitimacy of rocketry and spaceflight theories, if still beset by "many diverse problems." Rocket science was hard even for normal science.[12] Willy Ley and Wernher von Braun introduced American readers to the befuddling notions of the "rocket scientist," immersed in all the differential equations and celestial mechanics that made rocket travel in space achievable.[13] Boris Chertok, too, remembered just how challenging rocket science was in these early days, notwithstanding German achievements. Russian engine designers had no comprehensive theoretical treatises against which to test their models. They were still creating a science largely from scratch and struggled with myriad trials and errors and all the tangled systems of rocket engines.[14]

The excitement for space travel, it is worth noting, was not universal between West and East. Several authors defied it. C. S. Lewis pilloried the whole space craze in his adventures of Dr. Arthur Ransom on the planets Mars and Venus. He satirized all of the fanatical interest "in little Interplanetary Societies and Rocketry Clubs, and between the covers of monstrous magazines." Here was the thrill of the "false infinite," the rehashed dreams of spiritualists and cosmists in plurality and personal immortality. This kind of critique was not published in the USSR. But it was written—in Andrei Platonov's *Happy Moscow* (1936), all the more poignant because he had valued the hopes of science and technology during the Russian Revolution. His parody of results under Stalin was severe. Mimicking the exaggerated rhetoric of the day, he offered to "let Stalin himself, let wise old Stalin, direct the velocity and thrust of human history beyond the bounds of earth's gravity." In this story the cast of quirky Soviet characters was caught between the drudgery of weights and measures and the continuing dreams of rejuvenation and immortality, between "scales and stars." He set them amid the "mown spaces of an empty, frenzied earth," between the "spherical thought" of "its own despair" and the "arrow of action and hope, tensed for irrevocable movement into the distance, into space that was straight and severe."[15]

Yet enthusiasts of the liquid fuel rocket continued to share an extreme optimism. G. Edward Pendray, now an executive with the Westinghouse Corporation, celebrated the "amazing possibilities of locomotion without wheels." The rocket, he reminded readers, was still the province of American expertise and efficiency, Robert H. Goddard still its founding father. With the heady air of the occult, the members of the new United States Rocket Society championed rocket power as the culmination of human ingenuity, whose "motive power is carried wholly within itself." Although Americans were destined to be first in space, they nevertheless paid homage to the first martyr for the cause, the Russian engineer and assassin Nikolai Kibalchich. His "Rocket plans" were "Star stuff," a point of departure along the path "toward infinity." His rocket pointed the human way to the universe, seizing space as it leaped through it, leaving the telltale trail of exhaust for others to follow.[16]

The astrophysicist Fritz Zwicky envisioned his own "revolutionary" project based on rocketry's potentials: our "active interference in material celestial affairs and the reconstruction of sections of the universe other than the surface of the Earth." He foresaw humanity changing even the orbits of the near planets in relation to the sun, this to make them more habitable "earths." Zwicky added that "these thoughts are today perhaps nearer to scientific analysis and mastery than were Jules Verne's dreams in his time." Rocketry was a science of "what can still be done, of what is possible with available means and manpower and of what might come if these means were radically expanded." We stood at the dawn of "the morphological reconstruction of both the human society and the material universe."[17] The Russian cosmist Nikolai Fedorov would have approved.

These dreams of rocket science found a ready forum in popular culture. Books by Willy Ley, Herbert S. Zim, and Arthur C. Clarke all proposed outer space as the scene of humanity's redemptive future. The rocket was the means. Robert Heinlein's various science fiction stories translated into *Destination Moon* (1950), a postwar hit, America's late answer to Germany's *The Woman in the Moon* and Russia's *Cosmic Flight*, with realistic scenes of the rocket launch, life in zero gravity, and distant views of the planet. The movie warned of a "race" with the Soviets for "control" of outer space, the moon, and ultimately Earth. It raised the allure of "rocket engineering" as the "big stuff" of "pretty smart men," physics professors at work with their blackboards and slide rules, pondering all the differential equations of "reaction mass" and "initial velocity." In terms straight out of Stalinist socialist realism, the popular film challenged America to achieve the "fantastic" and "incredible," to reach for the ultimate envelopes of "higher and faster."[18]

The classic space operas of the 1930s also translated well into television, so well that by the early 1950s several million young people were watching a whole variety of entertaining programs on space adventure themes (not to mention the reruns of *Buck Rogers* and *Flash Gordon* films). They included *Space Patrol* on ABC, featuring Cdr. Buzz Corry (sponsored by Ralston Purina); *Space Cadet* on ABC with Tom Corbett (sponsored by the Kellogg Company); and *Captain*

Video and the "x-9" spaceship on the Dumont network (sponsored by General Foods). Together they introduced a number of fantastic inventions: the remote carrier beam, cosmic ray vibrator, atomic rifle, thermoid ejector, electronic straight jacket, nucleamatic pistol, radio scillograph, opticon scillometer, study machine, discotron portable TV, and the amnesia helmet. Accompanying them was a whole new way of speaking, an adolescent idiom of the "rocket age": phrases such as *blow your jets, spaceman's luck, smoking rockets,* and *blast off.* Among the programs *Space Cadet* proved the most educational, with science consultants in Willy Ley and the astronomers at the Hayden Planetarium keeping it all honest. Children wrote in to the studio too, with numerous complaints if there was ever a hint of a mistake in the science.[19]

America's magazines joined the fray. True, *Collier's* was not beneath the occasional satire of the popular craze for space travel. One short story, about launching the starlet Laurie Lane to the moon in her "little plutonium sunsuit," poked fun at the mania for "the moon, flying saucers, little men from Mars, and other interstellar nonsense," what it called the "rocket racket," fed by the character of the German professor Waldo Zoom (Wernher von Braun). Kurt Vonnegut also parodied the burgeoning space race, driven by the government's frenzied propaganda to send the first mechanized rocket man into space. There he discovered not some wonderful arena for human fulfillment but a cemetery, the "Thanasphere," a ring of dead souls orbiting Earth, the realm so long sought after by the spiritualists.[20] But these critiques were the exception. The amazing potential of contemporary science and technology (wonder technologies such as the X-ray, new hormonal therapies, and the rocket), along with the mounting challenges of the Cold War, convinced *Collier's* editors that these topics were no longer in the realm of fantasy, that the age of space travel was indeed at hand. "Science fiction" was becoming "science fact"; a rocket launch beyond the planet was but "the first step in a series of infinite and perhaps unimagined possibilities." As a popular magazine with stridently conservative views, it saw the critique of Soviet communism and the challenge of "World War III" with the USSR as national patriotic priorities.[21] *Collier's* thus raised a far-reaching campaign to achieve American supremacy in rocket science and space travel, von Braun and Ley offering sketches and rationales of their circular stations, torus style, as America's rocket-driven stepping-stones into space. Walt Disney even turned these essays into a series of capstone television programs for ABC, premiering just a few months after the Soviet launch of *Sputnik*.[22]

For his part Stalin revived rocketry and cosmism once again after 1945, challenging his scientific establishment to "catch and surpass" all these best achievements of European and American science. The reasons for this renewed competition were clear enough: the race for the "annihilation bomb" and for "rocket power," as the U.S. media were already calling them. Russia was clearly behind in nuclear weapons and in long-range bomber capability, a potentially lethal combination given America's advantages. But as for rockets, the experience of the 1930s, along with the borrowing from the German rocket team, meant that the two countries were rather evenly matched. Stalin presumed that when it came to rocket science, his designers and engineers might just be able to outstrip the United States. This was the context for the Council of Ministers' top secret resolution of 1946 establishing the Soviet missile industry as a signal state imperative, including its scientific-research, manufacturing, and military dimensions.[23] The "coming war" was again in play. Stalin's old object of admiration, the United States, became his new nemesis.

What with its rising campaigns for Russian patriotism, against cosmopolitanism, and for Promethean science, Stalin's regime gained a new confidence. Russian science was now its own gold standard and had its own inventors and innovators, its own "founding fathers" of world renown. We might question most of the facts, of course, but as for marking originality, this was something American popular science writers had already been doing since the turn of the century. Russia was merely catching up again, not just in the history but in the hagiography too. Konstantin Tsiolkovskii joined this elite cadre of "firsts," the premier inventor of "cosmonautics" as a particularly national, "Soviet Russian" version of astronautics.[24] The Central Committee of the Communist Party stage-managed the revival and retooling of his personality cult in honor of the ninetieth anniversary of Tsiolkovskii's birth in 1947. It ordered biographies to be written, a portrait painted, scholarships and prizes to be funded, medals to be struck, his collected works to be published, films and radio and media presentations to be made.[25]

Soviet popular science magazines from this time, in the long tradition of the genre reaching back to the late imperial and early Soviet periods, also celebrated Tsiolkovskii and rocketry in a cavalcade of images and texts—sometimes fictional, at other times factual, always patriotic. The magazine *Knowledge Is Power* served these purposes, essentially becoming the Soviet version of the American *Collier's*. Speeches and portraits by Iosif Stalin punctuated the campaign around "our great Future," a Soviet society of streamlined and orderly cities, of helicopters and planes moving freely about, of rockets reaching into space.[26] Stalinist science fiction, such as Viktor Saparin's *New Planet*, predicted that Soviet communism would soon fashion fully automated and computerized societies—with plentiful sources of energy and newly cultivated lands, diverting Siberia's rivers to flood Central Asia with water and life, making for a whole new planet. This coming USSR, already one-sixth of the globe, was also destined to expand on a "cosmic scale," to become the "first in the history of the earth to launch a human being into interplanetary space." The first "cosmonaut" would then travel by rocket to the moon, Mars and Venus and create new earths there as well.[27]

For Russian popular science readers at the start of the Cold War, the Tsiolkovskii rocket became a symbol of Soviet power and of its most perfect utopia: space travel. Here was an achievement of real science and technology, one that opened a whole new series of fantastic adventures and wonderful possibilities. Vasilii Zakharchenko's *Voyage to Tomorrow* (1952) imagined a journey around the future USSR, filled with colossal engineering projects (mechanization, wind and solar power, huge canals), culminating in a voyage into outer space by Tsiolkovskii's rocket craft and the construction of a torus-style Soviet "space station" (*sputnik*).[28] Boris Liapunov laid out these premises in his authoritative review, *The Discovery of Worlds* (1954). With myriad drawings and pictures, he visualized humans in outer space, a new optics as much as a new physics. The USSR would build the

342   CONCLUSION

... ГРОМАДНАЯ СТАЛЬНАЯ СИГАРА, ГОТОВАЯ К
ДАЛЬНЕМУ ПЕРЕЛЕТУ, ЛЕЖАЛА НА СПЕЦИАЛЬНОЙ
ТЕЛЕЖКЕ, КАТИВШЕЙСЯ ПО РЕЛЬСАМ.

Худож. С. КАПЛАН.

Fig. 33. Space rockets in the city of the future. From the popular science
magazine *Znanie-sila* 10 (October 1948): 41.

world's "first" space rockets and orbital stations, moon and planetary
colonies, even venturing out to the stars. None of this was fantasy.
All of it was opportunity, brought on by the advent of atomic power
and the ballistic missile of the Second World War. "The impossible
has become possible," wrote Liapunov. "The might of Soviet science

Fig. 34. Stalin's parabolic arc into outer space. From B. Liapunov, *Otkrytie mira* (Moscow: Molodaia gvardiia, 1954), inside front cover.

is known the world over. In the hands of the Soviet people, it will create miracles." Space was filled with infinite horizons. The rocket, "like the tail of a comet," only now human made and outward bound, opened up unlimited potentials, like time travel as envisioned in Tolstoi's fictional *Aelita* or the discovery of organic life on Mars as predicted by Tikhov's scientific "Astrobiology."[29]

Here were in essence Soviet versions of what American and European publicists were already doing in their rocketry and spaceflight works. Soviet publicists even took some of their cues, at least in graphic design, from the West. Their visions of terrestrial and other planetary landscapes from space, from the portholes of rocket craft—or their visions of future orbital stations and moon colonies—came straight out of *Destination Moon* and Ley's *The Conquest of Space* and the pictorial spreads of *Collier's* magazine. Soviet imaginings of space travel were, quite literally, America's too. What Walt Disney did for the United States, Iosif Stalin was also doing for the USSR. Both became the patrons of competing "tomorrowlands": one in the "Moonliner" rocket ride at Disneyland in Anaheim, California; the other in the pictorial imaginings of future Lenin monuments, cosmodromes, and space catapults in Moscow. Iosif Stalin became the Soviet Union's Walt Disney.

But Stalin's was also an ideology of a higher order. His and Lenin's works were presumably equal in weight to any of the great classics of modern science. Soviet dialectical materialism derived its ultimate legitimacy from the achievements of science generally, which discovered all the microscopic facts about atoms and molecules, all the macrocosmic facts about suns and galaxies. All matter everywhere was united, multi-varied, and in motion. We human beings were matter in motion too. And just as comets and meteors streaked through the night skies as emblems of these truths, we were now reaching into the universe itself by way of interplanetary rockets, by comets and parabolas of our own making.[30] Several writers even suggested that the great Tunguska meteor of 1908 was actually an alien spaceship, a vast interplanetary rocket powered by atomic energy, crashed to Earth. The rising science fiction star Ivan Efremov built this premise into his story about interstellar travelers visiting our planet. These imagined aliens revealed truths about the unity of human history with universal evolution, about global progress toward order and justice. They were an intelligence reaching across the eons of time and the "endless vistas of universal space," like a great parabolic arc of "cosmic" communication.[31]

After 1945 the fascination with the rocket's potential to liberate humanity from a dying Earth sometimes turned dramatically into the horror of its capacity for global destruction. In the first Russian edition of H. G. Wells's *War of the Worlds* to appear after the war, in an interesting act of artistic license and creative foretelling of doomsday machines, the graphic designer now outfitted the Martian craft with rocket motors. But the editor, Ia. I. Perel'man, comforted his readers, amid the novel's devastation, that the atmospheric conditions of Earth and the probable biological nature of any Martian beings would send any invasion force to easy defeat. Two scientists at the Mount Wilson Observatory had made nearly the same point at the beginning of the Second World War, reassuring their American readers that because of the differences in gravity between Earth and Mars, we humans would be as much as three times stronger than them. "And if there were too many of them to fight, we should also be able to run faster."[32]

The Stalin regime gave similar comfort from the pages of its popular science texts that the human being enjoyed immense reservoirs of self-mastery. True, all the extravagant hopes of the 1920s for immortality were over. Human beings were not like the single-celled wonders in Alexis Carrel's laboratory test tubes. They were mortal. For those who had survived the Second World War, science offered more realistic hopes of simply improving and prolonging their temporary lives. Meanwhile, Soviet communism delivered them a higher, plural, eternal cause.[33] Yet in a remarkable marriage between physical rejuvenation and space travel, the popular science magazine *Knowledge Is Power* celebrated the power of Newton's third law of motion in extending humanity's reach, both in physiology and in rocketry. The short story "Rocket Man" predicted that Soviet scientists would soon discover how to master the ultimate strengths of the human body and overcome its "fatigue" with hormonal therapies, tapping into its capacity for electrochemical and physical "reactions," much like the techniques of the steam engine. The very next article remembered the theoretical advances in the science of "reactive motion" made by K. E. Tsiolkovskii, the father of the Soviet Union's rocket plane and space rocket, the "patriarch of astronautics." Two colorful drawings, of the "rocket man" sprinting to the finish line and of the country's first rocket plane reaching into the heights, completed the scene.[34]

The regime made a similar case for the presumed mortality of the earth. The "end of the world" was not near. Ends were as nonsensical as beginnings when it came to the natural world. "Matter is eternal, infinite, and indestructible," testified two of the country's leading astronomers. "Science proves this." Modern science promised to stretch time more than fully conquer it. Humanity had little to fear from the death of the sun or from dramatic "climate change." Our world had little chance of dislodging from its orbit or being destroyed by catastrophic meteor or asteroid impacts. The "peaceful coexistence of the Earth and Sun" were assured "over the course of a very long time."[35] Peaceful coexistence here on the planet, given the challenges of the Cold War, was not so easy.

Why, in that Cold War, did the Russians reach space first? One answer lies in the ideologies, enthusiasms, and experiences accompanying the Russian Revolution of 1917. They help to account for that remarkable phenomenon of firsts to which the country made legitimate claim after 1903. These firsts were in part a measure of the West's influences, in part a measure of the East's own initiatives, of its fearful drive to become more like the West. What else accounts for the remarkable public acclaim and attention paid to Tsiolkovskii between 1903 and the present or the tenacity of Russian cosmism from then to now? The late empire's spaceflight utopia belonged to the Bolshevik and Stalinist regimes too. When it came to space travel, the utopia was nearly always the same because in each case the line of reference was the same. It pointed westward. It pointed spaceward. It was not so much a fantastic leap forward but a practical matter of keeping one step ahead of Europe and America. Aleksei Fedorchenko's film *First on the Moon* (2005) made light of this truth, mixing pretend facts and absurd fictions—including scenes from Tsiolkovskii's *Cosmic Flight*—its story built around the pretense that the Soviet Union first landed a man on the moon in 1938. Alexander Solzhenitsyn's "zek" (prison laboratory) engineers in *The First Circle* imagined the same "first flight to the Moon," with all the speed and spectacle of the Stalinist "plan," the irreverent among them breaking out into "clear, childish laughter" about the Americans getting there first. These parodies spoke ironic truth to the depth of Stalinism's attraction to cosmic flight. Russians were already well attuned to the theme before the Cold War ever broke out.[36]

America lagged behind in 1957 for many reasons, one of which was that it had already been behind some forty years earlier. The Russians achieved so much in the later race to space because they had joined the race first. They were reading about American efforts to develop space technologies in the 1920s and 1930s, long before Americans began reading about Russia's efforts, during the 1960s and 1970s, in the heyday of translations of Russian-language rocketry and space texts by the National Aeronautics and Space Administration (NASA). Both interventions and readings were fraught with mistranslations and misunderstandings. In 1965, for example, the U.S. Air Force translated Aleksandr Beliaev's novel *The Struggle in Space* (1928), thinking it the "Red Dream" of a "Soviet-American War." But what seemed like such a threat was actually little more than a Soviet version of a mainstream Western cosmic romance or space opera.[37] Or take the archivists at the National Air and Space Museum (NASM), who made a startling discovery in the 1970s: prescient Russian articles from 1924, published in the Russian popular science magazine *Technology and Life*, boldly predicting the possibilities of rocketry and space travel. The archivists translated them into English and cataloged them in the vast new archive of Russian-language sources, this to help Americans better understand the enemy and fight the mounting Cold War. Little did they know that the articles were actually Russian translations from English, first published in the American popular science magazine *Science and Invention*.[38] Americans looked for distant origins and priorities in the Russians, only to find nothing more than themselves.

Something similar happened in 1970, when NASA distinguished historian Eugene Emme lobbied to have Nikolai Rynin's nine-volume *Interplanetary Flight and Communications* (1928–32) translated from Russian into English. "No single work of greater historical significance in any language pre–World War II exists," he wrote. "NASA historians require translation of this work to document the origins of space technology and science."[39] Rynin's volumes contained their share of original Russian sources and plenty of clues about why the Russians maintained such early and abiding interest in these fields. But significant portions of Rynin's books were also simple translations, or summary descriptions, of scientific and technological advances already made in the West, in Europe and the United States. In its historical translations NASA archivists thought they had found a prodigious and implacable foe in the Cold War. Instead, they really found a considerable amount of good old American and European know-how and technology, twice removed. Or perhaps we might say that rocket science was not just a mirror but a two-way mirror, in which both sides saw fleeting images of each other and ourselves.

These contexts help to make sense of the popularity of Tom Wolfe's best seller *The Right Stuff* (1979) and Walter McDougall's prize-winning *Between the Heavens and the Earth* (1985). Both weighed the early American space program upon the scales of Russian achievement. Wolfe's test pilots and astronauts looked more like characters out of early Soviet cosmism and Stalinist hagiography than the American experience. These were heroes who defied gravity and conquered space, nearly fused to their rocket planes and rockets, "revved up with adrenalin," "'booming and zooming'" by the power and "surge of the rockets." Their nemesis was Evgenii Zamiatin's *We*, the full "sorcery" and "magic" of the Soviet space designers, masters of the Integral become R-7 rocket, that "thing of misty but stupendous dimensions." Their totem was the "great ziggurat" of challenge and achievement, something almost like America's version of Lenin's tomb, by which they cheated death in mortal honorific combat with the heathen Russians. The object, of course, was to "catch up," to close "*the space gap*."[40] McDougall translated this interpretive model into compelling history, a story about how we Americans became something more like the Soviet Russians to close the gap, this to recover from *Sputnik*'s shame, not at all pleased by what we had become in the mirror of Soviet technocratic achievement.[41]

The mirror even survived the end of the Cold War and the collapse of the USSR. At this moment of reflection upon the legacies of the race to space, publicists began to extol Tsiolkovskii's originality and priority in aiming humanity toward the planets and stars. He became the great predecessor, master of the new cosmism, the property no longer of one side in the Cold War but of all humanity. He became the catalyst that set even contemporary minds afire, including Carl Sagan's, with the possibilities of alien worlds, of pan-spiritualism and immortalism. Tsiolkovskii was the great author of humanity's "manifest destiny" in space.[42]

Goddard occupies a similar place in the history: one of reflections and refractions. He is either everything or he is nothing. With the occasional NASA news release, he is the object of routine hyperbole, as if he alone was the first father of rocketry, who created the "underpinning of everything that we are able to do in space today" and who "recognized before virtually anyone else" the importance of liquid fuel rockets. On the fortieth anniversary of the *Apollo 11* moon landing, astronaut Neil Armstrong celebrated Goddard's priority, noting how even "Germany used his technology" to develop the v-2.[43] For thousands of youngsters over the generations, he has been a favorite study of juvenile literature, a model of perseverance and fortitude, every boy's hero. He has been the subject of dozens of children's books and inspiring documentary films, America's own Tsiolkovskii.

Goddard has also been the object of a remarkable calumny, marking him as an eccentric inventor and lone pioneer. "There is no direct line from Goddard to present-day rocketry," wrote the feisty Theodore von Karman in his memoir. "He is on a branch that died. He was an inventive man and had a good scientific foundation, but he was not a creator of science." In the spirit of von Karman's judgment, a number of historians have diminished Goddard's influence as if he did not matter at all.[44] The commentary has some merit. By his obsession for secrecy and his rejection of teamwork, Goddard condemned himself to a kind of oblivion. Beyond several classic works on rocketry, he left no lasting legacy or school. His P series rocket of 1939 stands at the west entrance to the National Air and Space Museum like some ancient obelisk from the dawn of the space age.

Yet the broader historical record suggests that Goddard did have a profound influence on the Russians, who moved with deliberate speed to compete with America based on his work, as if he was all that mattered. Even into the 1970s and 1980s, Goddard remained a topic of interest and attraction, an echo of his heyday in the 1920s. Russian historians, with righteous indignation, faulted America for not valuing Goddard's legacies enough, guarding his legacies less as America's, more as their own.[45] To this extent, when we look at *Sputnik*, we see a little bit of Goddard and a little bit of ourselves. In the long run he was as much of a guiding inspiration for *Sputnik* as any of the Russian pioneers. He was the catalyst for a remarkable set of mixed signals and conflicted interests that lie at the origins of the race toward space.

In effect Goddard's rockets helped to point the Russians spaceward, metaphors as prospective as any of the space parabolas introduced in this book. These parabolas, after all, were stories: parables. As arcs, they positioned the human being "side by side" (*parabolē*) with the rocket, both in motion through the universe. The spacecraft's expanding arcs to the planets became the human form writ large, fulfilling the human form writ small, that speck of dust in the vacuum of the cosmos, now tracing new forms across its vast expanses. By way of the rocket we became the vector pointed beyond the planet, the microcosm seeding the macrocosm, the pathogen humanizing outer space. The rocket became humanity's vanishing point in outer space, our self-representation of eternity and infinity, the wayward comet outward bound.

The Soviet monument *To the Conquerors of Space* (1964) represented this parabolic arc. Adorning the Memorial Museum of Cosmonautics in northeast Moscow, its one-hundred-meter high titanium arch sculpting a stream of exhaust leading a rocket into outer space. The image was more than a pathway. It was also an ideology about the revolutionary priority and politics of Soviet materialism and atheism. By its logic, multiplied in similar images throughout Soviet popular culture, human history was turning biology into technology, the human being becoming a star traveler after Maiakovskii and Stapledon, now transformed and reborn as pure, immortal spirit, a "spaceship" all its own. This arc, too, was at the center of Arthur C. Clarke's *2001: A Space Odyssey* (1968), first conceived in several short stories during and just after the Second World War. Clarke conjoined the evolutionary "ascent of man" with humanity's astronautic pathways to Earth's orbit, to the moon, and to the planets beyond.[46] Or take Carl Sagan's design for the plaques on the *Pioneer 10* and *11* spacecraft (1972–73), picturing it as an arrow curving away from Earth to the edges of the solar system, a glyph he borrowed from rocket pioneer Willy Ley. Here was humanity's greeting to alien life and infinity beyond, fulfilling all of the dreams of the interplanetary signalers from the turn of the century. Here was a spacecraft, in Sagan's words, "moving, compared to the immense interstellar distances, with the slowness of a race in a dream."[47] The official emblems of the Centennial of Flight (2003) and of the Ansari X Prize (2004) show the same ascending arc, the space dream as hyperbole. It has become the universal symbol for humanity's greatest hopes, its mastery of aviation, its progress in astronautics.

All of these deep signs and moving pictures really remind us once again that the race toward space was more about headings, going there as much as getting there, more about plotting our way. These images had their provenance: in K. E. Tsiolkovskii's "vertical ascent" of 1903, a fitting herald of the coming revolutionary era; in M. Ia. Lapirov-Skoblo's "parabolic" trajectory of 1924, right at the start of the Soviet regime; and in the genesis of "cosmonautics" during the Stalinist 1930s. Whatever postmortems we might declare over the collapse of the USSR, now that it is gone, one must be that it appreciated and fostered rocket science and cosmonautics with a singularity of commitment and a priority of achievement, thanks in significant part to its race with the United States. The USSR had no ultimate future. But it did have a sometimes visionary, however violent and troubled, past. Communism, thanks to its inherent sense of inferiority and rivalry, was far better suited to the initial conquest of space than was capitalism.

Notes

Several sources below use common spellings—e.g., *Tolstoy* for *Tolstoi* and *Tsiolkovsky* for *Tsiolkovskii*—that differ from my Library of Congress transliterations.

Introduction

Epigraph: Vl. Maiakovskii, "Protestuiu," *Krasnaia niva* 3 (1924): 72. My thanks to Olga Shchennikova (Moscow) for her help in translating the poetry in this work as well as for her crucial research assistance.

1. Roger R. Bate et al., *Fundamentals of Astrodynamics* (New York: Dover, 1971), 3.

2. See Thomas Kuhn, *The Structure of Scientific Revolutions* (Chicago: University of Chicago Press, 1962); and William Sims Bainbridge, *The Spaceflight Revolution* (New York: Wiley, 1976).

3. K. L. Baev and V. A. Shishakov, *Pravda o nebe* (Moscow: OGIZ, 1941), 14–16, 47.

4. A. Abramov, *Raketa* (Moscow: Molodaia gvardiia, 1931), chapter heading; Ia. Perel'man, *Mezhplanetnye puteshestviia*, 9th ed. (Leningrad: GTTI, 1934), 154. For appreciations of Newton, see *Iskra* 3 (1927): 2–4; and *Popular Science Monthly* (March 1928): 34.

5. Quoted from Goddard's correspondence in M. A. Stuart, "Heavy Artillery vs. Rockets," *Field Artillery Journal* 21, no. 6 (November–December 1931): 635. On "*la fusée auto-propulsive*," see Robert Esnault-Pelterie, "On prépare vraiment des expeditions planétaires," *Je sais tout* 288 (December 1928): 527.

6. Henri Bergson, *L'évolution créative* (Paris: Alcan, 1907), with Russian translations between 1909 and 1914. See Hilary L. Fink, *Bergson and Russian Modernism* (Evanston IL: Northwestern University Press, 1999), 26, 142.

7. Henri Bergson, *Creative Evolution*, translated by Arthur Mitchell (New York: Random House, 1944), 37, 207, 210.

8. Bergson, *Creative Evolution*, 295.

9. Bergson, *Creative Evolution*, 270–73. On how life "is free at all times to modify its course, to change its direction. . . . Like a shell bursting as it flies, each frag-

ment again bursting, and so on," see Harvey W. Shimer, "Bergson's View of Organic Evolution," *Popular Science Monthly* (February 1913): 164–65.

10. Bergson, *Creative Evolution*, 14, 21, 212–19, 274, 280, 293, 401.

11. Quoted from A. G. Cherniakov, *The Ontology of Time* (Dordrecht: Kluwer, 2002), 158.

12. Marshall Berman, *All That Is Solid Melts into Air* (New York: Penguin, 1982), 15, 22, 129, 345.

13. Robert Wohl, *A Passion for Wings* (New Haven: Yale University Press, 1994), 1–2.

14. H. G. Wells, *The World Set Free* (New York: Dutton, 1914); Langemak quoted in V. F. Rakhmanin and L. E. Sternin, eds., *Odnazhdy i navsegda* (Moscow: Mashinostroenie, 1998), 66–67; *The Papers of Robert H. Goddard*, edited by Esther C. Goddard and G. Edward Pendray, 3 vols. (New York: McGraw-Hill, 1961), 1:158.

15. Hermann Oberth, *Die Rakete zu den Planetenraumen* (Munich: Oldenbourg, 1923); Goddard and Pendray, *Papers of Robert H. Goddard*, 1:498.

16. For an earlier use of the term, see Frederick C. Durant and George S. James, eds., *First Steps toward Space* (Washington DC: Smithsonian Institution Press, 1974).

17. V. E. L'vov, "Pervoe nauchnoe obshchestvo mezhplanetnykh soobshchenii v SSSR," *Vestnik znaniia* 5 (1929): 204.

18. Louis Althusser, *For Marx*, translated by Ben Brewster (New York: Penguin, 1965), 97; Berman, *All That Is Solid*, 175, 217.

19. N. N. Bobrov, *TsAGI* (Moscow: Molodaia gvardiia, 1934), 12. On these issues, see Alan M. Ball, *Imagining America* (Lanham MD: Rowman & Littlefield, 2003).

20. A. R. Beliaev, *Bor'ba v efire* (Moscow: Molodaia gvardiia, 1928).

21. Walter A. McDougall is one of the first historians to recognize the dynamic between "rocketry and revolution" (*Heavens and the Earth* [New York: Basic Books, 1985], 19), which I have paraphrased in my own title.

22. Michael Stoiko, *Soviet Rocketry* (New York: Holt, 1970), x.

23. Frank H. Winter, *Prelude to the Space Age* (Washington DC: Smithsonian Institution Press, 1983); William Burrows, *This New Ocean* (New York: Random House, 1998); Mike Gruntman, *Blazing the Trail* (Reston: AIAA, 2004); and Chris Gainor, *To a Distant Day* (Lincoln: University of Nebraska Press, 2008).

24. Stephen Kern, *Cultures of Time and Space* (Cambridge: Harvard University Press, 1983), 6–7. I thank Whitney Walton (Purdue University) for sharing this book with me and for reading my book manuscript and offering many valuable insights.

25. Willi Ley and Chesley Bonestall, *The Conquest of Space* (New York: Viking, 1949), 21–23.

26. As in abbreviated ways it was by the high-ranking defector Col. G. A. Tokaty, in "Soviet Rocket Technology," *Technology and Culture* 4, no. 4 (Fall 1963): 515–28. See also Peter A. Gorin, "Rising from the Cradle," in *Reconsidering Sputnik*, edited by Roger D. Launius et al. (Amsterdam: Harwood, 2000), 11–42.

27. Quotes from Camille Flammarion, *La pluralité des mondes habités* (Paris: Mallet, 1862); and K. Flammarion, "Obitateli planet," *Priroda i liudi* 40–41 (1892):

636–53. The Russian versions were published in 1895 and 1908, along with many of Flammarion's other works.

28. Jules Verne, *From the Earth to the Moon*, translated by Lowell Blair (New York: Bantam, 1993), 3, 43, 112, 120, 148 (originally published in French in 1865, with English and Russian editions in 1873). For rockets, see Jules Verne, *Autour de la lune* (Paris: Hetzel, 1870); and Verne, *Around the Moon* (London: Ward, 1885).

29. Darko Suvin, *Metamorphoses of Science Fiction* (New Haven: Yale University Press, 1979), 22.

30. The hoax amounted to a series of false news reports. See Michael Crowe, *The Extraterrestrial Life Debate* (Mineola NY: Dover, 1999), 210–15.

31. Alexander von Humboldt, *Cosmos*, translated by E. C. Otté, 4 vols. (New York: Harper Brothers, 1863), 1:viii, xviii, 40, 69, 79, 359; also in Russian as Aleksandr fon Gumbol'dt, *Kosmos*, translated by Ia. Veinberg (Moscow: Frolov, 1848–63). For context, see Laura Dassow Walls, *The Passage to Cosmos* (Chicago: University of Chicago Press, 2009), 129, 218.

32. Georges Le Faure and Henri de Graffigny, *Les aventures extraordinaires d'un savant russe* (Paris: Edinger, 1889), v–vi, 13. The Russian translations were first published in *Priroda i liudi*, issues 1–42 (1890); later as *Puteshestvie na lunu* and *V nevedomykh mirakh* (St. Petersburg: Soikin, 1895); and *Vokrug sol'ntsa* (Moscow: Puchin, 1926).

33. See *Science* 26, 20 September 1907, 388. Anindita Banerjee, "The Genesis and Evolution of Science Fiction in *Fin de Siècle* Russia" (PhD diss., UCLA, 2000), 3–6; and Banerjee, *We Soviet People: Science Fiction and the Making of Russian Modernity* (Middletown CT: Wesleyan University Press, 2012), 11, 14.

34. J. O. Bailey, *Pilgrims through Space and Time* (New York: Argus Books, 1947), 119, 191; and W. H. G. Armytage, *Yesterday's Tomorrows* (London: Routledge, 1968).

35. Goddard and Pendray, *Papers of Robert H. Goddard*, 1:66; masthead for *Amazing Stories* 1 (1926); editorial from *Scientific American* (July 1927): 3.

36. I take these terms from Suvin, *Metamorphoses*, 62–74.

1. Envisioning the Biological Universe

1. Hannah Arendt, *On Revolution* (New York: Viking, 1965), 34–35; Jean Starobinski, *Action and Reaction*, translated by Sophie Hawkes and Jeff Fort (New York: Zone, 2003), 42–44.

2. Leo Tolstoy, *War and Peace*, translated by Constance Garnett (1869; repr., New York: Modern Library, 1950), 1118, 1142–45.

3. Edward Holden, "Copernicus," *Popular Science Monthly* (May 1904): 131.

4. Abbé Théophile Moreux, *A Day in the Moon* (London: Hutchison, 1913), 42.

5. Robert Hooke, "Cometa," in *Lectures and Collections* (London: Royal Society, 1678), 35; Sara Schechner Genuth, *Comets, Popular Culture, and the Birth of Modern Cosmology* (Princeton: Princeton University Press, 1997), 3, 140, 152–56.

6. See *Vestnik inostrannoi literatury* 2 (February 1910): 283–86; and 5 (May 1910): 188–92.

7. Camille Flammarion, *La fin du monde* (Paris: Flammarion, 1893), published in three Russian editions after 1894. I have quoted from the English version, *Omega* (New York: Cosmopolitan, 1894), 8, 77. See also *Je sais tout*, 15 June 1906, 512; and 15 July 1908, 746–48.

8. S. Bel'skii, *Pod kometoi* (St. Petersburg: Pechatnyi dvor, 1910), 108–20. N. N. Kholodnyi, *Bor'ba mirov* (St. Petersburg: Evstifeev, 1900), also built his story around a killer comet. On the eclipse, see *Sinii zhurnal* 16, 13 April 1912, 10–12; and *Vestnik inostrannoi literatury* (October 1912): 84–85.

9. Arendt, *On Revolution*, 34–35. Karl Griewank, "Emergence of the Concept of Revolution," in *Revolutions in Modern European History*, edited by Heinz Lubasz (New York: Macmillan, 1966), 55–61.

10. E. Iu. Grigorovich, *Zarnitsy* (Leningrad: Sabashnikovykh, 1925), 32. On this Russian application of Newton's third law of motion to human history, see also Gustav A. Wetter, *Dialectical Materialism*, translated by Peter Heath (New York: Praeger, 1958), 81.

11. Jean Starobinski, *1789: The Emblem of Reason*, translated by Barbara Bray (Charlottesville: University Press of Virginia, 1979), 43–50; Dmitri Shlapentokh, *The French Revolution in Russian Intellectual Life* (Westport CT: Praeger, 1996).

12. I. V. Stalin, "Rabochie kavkaza, pora otomstit'!" *Sochineniia*, 13 vols. (Moscow: OGIZ, 1946), 1:78. Stalin worked at the post for only three months, beginning in December 1899. See the descriptions in Robert Service, *Stalin* (Cambridge: Harvard University Press, 2005), 43. Quoted from Vano Ketskhoveli, "Druziia i soratniki tovarishcha Stalina," in *Rasskazy o velikom Staline* (Tbilisi: Zaria vostoka, 1941), 75–86.

13. J. Norman Lockyer, *Elements of Astronomy* (New York: Appleton, 1870), with a Russian translation in the same year and several to follow.

14. See "Chto chitat' po astronomii?" *Nauka i zhizn'* 1 (January 1904): 262–70. After France itself, Russia had the second most members in the French Astronomical Society. On the new "faith" in science, see Dave Pretty, "The Saints of the Revolution," *Slavic Review* 54, no. 2 (Summer 1995): 301–2.

15. Auguste Comte, *Traite philosophique d'astronomie populaire* (Paris: Apostolat, 1893); O. M. Mitchel, *The Orbs of Heaven* (London: National Illustrated, 1851), 1, 14, published in Russian in 1859.

16. Mitchel, *Orbs of Heaven*, 148.

17. Mitchel, *Orbs of Heaven*, iv–v, 3, 60, 219.

18. Lockyer, *Elements of Astronomy*, 173. David Starr Jordan, "Comrades in Zeal," *Popular Science Monthly* (February 1904): 315. For more examples of this paradigm, see Crowe, *Extraterrestrial Life Debate*, 364, 436, 448.

19. F. S. Gruzdev, ed., *Vselennaia i chelovechestvo* (St. Petersburg: Soikin, 1904), 8.

20. From *Vestnik inostrannoi literatury* (April 1894): 164; and (November 1907): 313.

21. See the images in Jean Clair, ed., *Cosmos* (Munich: Prestel, 1999), 41, 174. C. W. Woodridge, *Perfecting the Earth* (Cleveland: Utopia, 1902), 13, 214, 323–25.

22. See Steven J. Dick, *The Biological Universe* (New York: Cambridge University Press, 1996), 38–49.

23. N. N. Strakhov, *Mir' kak tseloe* (St. Petersburg: Zamyslovskago, 1872), iv–viii, 304, 313.

24. Strakhov, *Mir' kak tseloe*, 177, 253–58.

25. Strakhov, *Mir' kak tseloe*, 187–89, 206–7.

26. Strakhov, *Mir' kak tseloe*, ix–x.

27. Alexander Vucinich, *Darwin in Russian Thought* (Berkeley: University of California Press, 1988), 3–4.

28. F. J. Allen, "Life in Other Worlds," *Popular Science Monthly* (November 1903): 26–31.

29. James H. Billington, "The Intelligentsia and the Religion of Humanity," *American Historical Review* 65, no. 4 (July 1960): 809; Reginald E. Zelnik, ed. and trans., *A Radical Worker in Tsarist Russia* (Stanford: Stanford University Press, 1986), 32.

30. Winwood Reade, *The Martyrdom of Man* (London: Trubner, 1872).

31. See Niles R. Holt, "Ernst Haeckel's Monistic Religion," *Journal of the History of Ideas* 32, no. 2 (April–June 1971): 265–80. Haeckel's primary works were published in Russian between 1905 and 1913.

32. Max Wilhelm Meyer, *The End of the World*, translated by Margaret Wagner (Chicago: Kerr, 1908), 109–40; and Meyer, *The Making of the World*, translated by Ernest Unterman (Chicago: Kerr, 1906), 18–26. See also *Je sais tout* (August 1921): 995; and *Scientific American* (February 1925): 80–81.

33. Meyer, *Making of the World*, 9–22.

34. Meyer, *Making of the World*, 6–7, 82, 127.

35. I. Melekhinskii, "Proshedshee i budushchee nashei planete," *Priroda i liudi*, a series beginning with 12, 23 January 1892, 189–91; Horace Clark Richards, "The Structure of the World-Stuff," *Popular Science Monthly* (March 1910): 269–79.

36. V. I. Lenin, *Materialism and Empirio-Criticism* (1909), *Collected Works*, 45 vols., edited by Clemens Dutt and translated by Abraham Fineberg (Moscow: Progress, 1977), 14:45, 75, 155–57, 169, 175–78, 253.

37. Lenin, *Materialism*, 346–56. Lenin mentioned Haeckel favorably several times in the text (46, 95, and 274).

38. See Daniel Todes, *Darwin without Malthus* (New York: Oxford University Press, 1989), 72, 146.

39. Stalin, "Anarkhizm ili sotsializm" (1906–7), *Sochineniia*, 1:294–372.

40. Arthur Brisbane, *Editorials from the Hearst Newspapers* (New York: Albertson, 1906), 113, 276–78.

41. Brisbane, *Editorials*, 15.

42. Helga S. Kragh, *Entropic Creation* (Burlington VT: Ashgate, 2008), 23–46.

43. Meyer, *End of the World*, 2, 86; Wilhelm Boelsche, *The Triumph of Life*, translated by May Wood Simons (Chicago: Kerr, 1906), 147–57. See also Camille Flammarion, "La fin du monde," *Je sais tout* 1, no. 1, 15 February 1905, 62.

44. Flammarion, *Omega*, 219–20, 231.

45. Edward Bellamy, *Looking Backward* (1888; repr., New York: New American Library, 1960), 31; Jules Verne, *L'éternel adam* (Paris: Mille et une nuits, 2001).

46. These quotes are from H. G. Wells, *The War of the Worlds* (Mineola NY: Dover, 1997), 2, 82, 144. An early Russian translation was G. Uells, *Bor'ba mirov* (St. Petersburg: Skorokhodov, 1898).

47. Wells, *War of the Worlds*, 3, 132.

48. J. H. Rosny, *La mort de la terre* (Paris: Plon-Nourrit, 1912); also *Konets zemli* (St. Petersburg: Semenova, 1912); and *The Xipehuz and the Death of the Earth*, translated by George Slusser (New York: Arno, 1978).

49. "Vozdushnaia armiia," *Vestnik inostrannoi literatury* 10 (October 1910): 36.

50. August Niemann, e.g., author of *Der Weltkrieg* (Berlin: Voboch, 1904) (translated as *The World War* [New York: Putnam, 1904]), also wrote a space travel adventure tale for young readers, *Aetherio* (Regensburg: Wunderling, 1909). George Griffith, author of a number of future war stories—*Outlaws of the Air*, *The Stolen Submarine*, *The Angel of the Revolution*, and *Olga Romanoff*—also wrote the space adventure *A Honeymoon in Space*. Paul Scheerbart was author of an antiwar "future war" essay, *Die Entwicklung des Luftmilitarismus* (Berlin: Oesterheld, 1909), and of several wonderful novels and short stories on space travel and other worlds.

51. I. F. Clarke, ed., *The Tale of the Next Great War* (Liverpool: Liverpool University Press, 1995).

52. Kurd Lasswitz, *Two Planets*, edited by Erich Lasswitz and translated by Hans H. Rudnick (Carbondale: Southern Illinois University Press, 1971), 380–84 (originally published as *Auf zwei Planeten*, 2 vols. [Leipzig: Elischer, 1897]; with a revised Russian translation, Kurd Lasvits, *Na dvukh planetakh*, translated by Sofiia Parnok and Boris Gornung [Moscow: Gosizdat, 1925]). See also H. Bruce Franklin, *War Stars* (New York: Oxford University Press, 1988), 19–77; and Peter Daniel Smith, *Doomsday Men* (New York: St. Martin's, 2007).

53. Albert Robida, *The Twentieth Century*, edited by Arthur B. Evans and translated by Philippe Willems (Middletown CT: Wesleyan University Press, 2004) (originally published as *Le vingtième siècle* [Paris: Decaux, 1883]).

54. A. Belomor, *Rokovaia voina 18?? goda* (St. Petersburg: Sudokhodstvo, 1889); Sergei Sharapov, *Cherez polveka* (Moscow: Vasilieva, 1902).

55. Vl. Semenov, *Tsaritsa mira* (St. Petersburg: Vol'f', 1908); and *Tsari vozdukha* (St. Petersburg: Vol'f', 1909).

56. Sergei Solomin, "Bor'ba zlykh' i dobrykh' na sushe, na more, v' vozdukhe i pod' vodoiu," *Sinii zhurnal*, beginning with 7, 10 February 1912, 2–4.

57. D. Brushkoskii, "Posledniaia voina," *Argus* 21 (1914): 88–91. See also N. Skvortsov, "Pervaia bitva v vozdukhe," *Putevodnyi ogonek* 15, 7 August 1914, 474; G. D. Uells, *Voina v' vozdukhe*, in *Sinii zhurnal*, beginning with 1, 3 January 1915.

58. I. S. Bliukh', *Budushchaia voina*, 2 vols. (St. Petersburg: Effron, 1898), 1:172–78. Quoted from Jean de Bloch, *The Future of War* (Boston: Ginn, 1903), xviii–xix.

59. Some of these images are reproduced in *Images of Revolution*, edited by David King and Cathy Porter (New York: Pantheon, 1983), 98–114. V. Briusov and

M. Gorkii, quoted from N. L. Brodskii and V. L'vov-Rogachevskii, eds., *Revoliut-sionnye motivy russkoi poezii* (Leningrad: Kolos, 1926), 180–81.

60. Viacheslav Ivanov, "The Symbolics of Aesthetic Principles," *Selected Essays*, translated by Robert Bird (Evanston: Northwestern University Press, 2001), 5.

61. Valerii Briusov, "Novye grezy," "S komety" (1895), and "Astrolog" (1899), *Sobranie sochinenii*, 7 vols. (Moscow: Khudozhestvennaia literatura, 1973), 1:42–43, 70, 157.

62. Valerii Briusov, *Zemnaia os'* (Moscow: Skorpion', 1907), vii–x.

63. Andreev's play *K zvezdam* (3 November 1905), in *Sobranie sochinenii*, 6 vols. (Moscow: Khudozhestvennaia literatura, 1994), 2:319–71, was banned in Russia until 1917.

64. Alexander Bogdanov, *Red Star: The First Bolshevik Utopia*, edited by Loren Graham and Richard Stites and translated by Charles Rougle (Bloomington: Indiana University Press, 1984), 76, 86, 96, 106, and 117.

2. Mystical Economies of Earth and Space

1. On Richter's theories between 1865 and 1871, see Max Verworn, *General Physiology*, edited by and translated by Frederic Lee (London: Macmillan, 1899), 300–301. For contexts, see James Strick, *Sparks of Life* (Cambridge: Harvard University Press, 2000).

2. Alphonse Berget, "The Appearance of Life on Worlds and the Hypothesis of Arrhenius," *Smithsonian Annual Report* (1912): 547.

3. Svante Arrhenius, *Worlds in the Making* (New York: Harper, 1908), 217–18 (originally published as *Väldarmas Utveckling* [Stockholm: Geber, 1906]; with a Russian translation in *Obrazovanie mirov* [Odessa: Mathesis, 1916]).

4. Boelsche, *The Triumph of Life*, 15, 23; and Boelsche, *The Evolution of Man*, translated by Ernest Untermann (Chicago: Kerr, 1905), 140–41. Meyer, *The Making of the World*, 86, wrote of life as "rain" from the "heavens."

5. Between 1868 and 1893 Fedorov was a cataloger at the Special Reading Room of the Rumiantsev Library (Moscow), where he prepared reading lists for some of Russia's leading writers and scholars. See N. F. Fedorov, *Filosofiia obshchego dela*, edited by V. A. Kozhevnikov and N. P. Peterson, 2 vols. (1906–13; repr., Paris: Homme, 1985), 1:9, 54, 283, 656–68. For a comprehensive study, see George Young, *The Russian Cosmists* (New York: Oxford University Press, 2012), 76–91.

6. Fedorov, *Filosofiia obshchego dela*, 1:56, and vol. 2, pt. 3. Stephen Lukashevich, *N. F. Fedorov* (Newark: University of Delaware Press, 1977), 15, has noted the similarities between Reade and Fedorov.

7. The painting was part of a much larger unfinished mural on the topic of Fedorov's "cosmism." See Georgi Costakis, *Russian Avant-Garde Art* (New York: Abrams, 1981), 92.

8. Fedorov, *Filosofiia obshchego dela*, 1:54.

9. Lukashevich, *N. F. Fedorov*, 48; and Fedorov, *Filosofiia obshchego dela*, 2:251–52.

10. Fedorov, *Filosofiia obshchego dela*, 1:284, 511; and 2:251–52, 348, 379. For

context, see Irene Masing-Delic, *Abolishing Death* (Stanford: Stanford University Press, 1992), 76–104.

11. Fedorov, *Filosofiia obshchego dela*, 2:250–51, 269–70, 350–51.

12. Fedorov, *Filosofiia obshchego dela*, 1:282–83, 291; 2:218.

13. Masing-Delic, *Abolishing Death*, 76–104; Bernice Glazer Rosenthal, ed., intro., *The Occult in Russian and Soviet Culture* (Ithaca NY: Cornell University Press, 1997), 11. Dmitry Shlapentokh, "Bolshevism as a Fedorovian Regime," *Cahiers du monde russe* 37, no. 4 (October–November 1996): 429–66, even makes a case for Fedorov's influence on Leon Trotskii and Iosif Stalin.

14. On the privileged "Russian origins" of "Cosmic Philosophy," see *Russkii kosmizm*, edited by S. G. Semenova and A. G. Gacheva (Moscow: Pedagogika, 1993); Vladimir Lytkin, "Tsiolkovskii's Inspiration," *Ad Astra* (November–December 1998): 35; Svetlana Boym, "Kosmos," *Kosmos*, photos by Adam Bartos (Princeton: Princeton Architectural Press, 2002), 83–86; and Young, *Russian Cosmists*, 235, 263.

15. Of these times "there was no unity, no consistency, only a flood of individual philosophizing." Leonid Sabaneeff, "Religious and Mystical Trends in Russia at the Turn of the Century," *Russian Review* 24, no. 4 (October 1965): 360.

16. James Billington, *The Icon and the Axe* (New York: Vintage, 1970), 43, 443, 478; Richard Stites, *Revolutionary Dreams* (New York: Oxford University Press, 1989), 170; Michael Hagermeister, *Nikolaj Fedorov* (Munich: Sagner, 1989), 241.

17. Berdiaev ultimately critiqued Fedorov's ideas as a "utopia" and "fantasy," filled with all of the "contradictions" and "detritus" of the nineteenth century. Nikolai Berdiaev, "Religiia voskreshcheniia," *Russkaia mysl'* 7 (July 1915): 76–77, 120; Flammarion, *Omega*, 125–32; Northrop Frye, *Anatomy of Criticism* (Princeton: Princeton University Press, 1957), 119.

18. *Vselenskoe delo*, no. 1 (Odessa: Venskie i Liubek', 1914), 107. See Prentis Malford's Russian translations: *Vashi neopoznanennye sily* (Kiev: Kul'zhenko, 1904), *Na zare bessmertiia* (Odessa: n.p., 1912), and *K zhizni* (St. Petersburg: Ulei, 1913).

19. Quoted from the chapter "Immortality in the Flesh" by Prentice Mulford, *Thoughts Are Things* (1889; repr., London: Bell, 1911). See also Prentice Mulford, "Regeneration," in *The God in You* (London: Rider, 1918).

20. Porfirii Ivanovich Bakhmet'ev (1860–1913) was trained as an entymologist at the University of Zurich and taught from 1890 to 1907 at the University of Sofia, Bulgaria. Quoted from A. Bushtein, ed., *Anabioz* (Odessa: Barshakh, 1913), 5, 13–15. See also P. I. Bakhmet'ev, "Kak ia nashel anabioz u mlekopitaiushchikh," *Priroda* (May 1912); and N. Kulagin, "Pamiati P. I. Bakhmet'eva," *Priroda* 10 (1913). For an expert survey of Bakhmet'ev's life and accomplishments in historical context, see Nikolai Krementsov, *Revolutionary Experiments* (New York: Oxford University Press, 2014), 66–82.

21. James Dewar, "A History of Cold and the Absolute Zero," *Smithsonian Annual Report* (1902): 207–40; Allan Macfadyen, "On the Influence of the Temperature of Liquid Air on Bacteria," *Proceedings of the Royal Society of London* 66 (1899–1900): 180–82; I. T., "O proiskhozhdenii zhizni," *Vokrug sveta* 4 (1911): 222–23.

22. P. I. Bakhmet'ev, "Zaveshchanie milliardera," *Estestvoznanie i geografiia*, beginning with 8 (October 1904): 1–24. The work was a gloss upon Sir Francis Bacon's "Salomon's House," from *New Atlantis* (1624).

23. For reviews of Bakhmet'ev's work, see *Priroda* 10 (October 1914): 1169–90; and P. I. Bakhmet'ev, "Sedalishche dushi (Anabioz)," in *Vselenskoe delo*, 59–85.

24. From the poem by A. Gornostaev, "Novoe nebo. Pamiati P. I. Bakhmet'eva," in *Vselenskoe delo*, 92–94.

25. Chandak Sengoopta, *The Most Secret Quintessence of Life: Sex, Glands, and Hormones, 1850–1950* (Chicago: University of Chicago Press, 2006), 36–37.

26. On Kuliabko, see R. Legendre, "The Survival of Organs and the 'Culture' of Living Tissues," *Smithsonian Annual Report* (1912), 413–20; and A. V. Nemilov, *Chto takoe smert'?* (Moscow: Gosizdat, 1923), 60. On Carrel, see David M. Friedman, *The Immortalists* (New York: HarperCollins, 2007), 13, 29.

27. Bert Hansen, "New Images of a New Medicine," *Bulletin of the History of Medicine* 73, no. 4 (1999): 629. Quoted from P. Iu. Shmidt, *Bor'ba so starost'iu* (Petrograd: Soikin, 1915), 32; and *Na granitse zhizni i smerti* (Petrograd: Panafidina, 1916), 55–58.

28. Il'ia Il'ich Mechnikov (1845–1916) also held research and teaching posts in Odessa and St. Petersburg. See Elie Metchnikoff, *The Prolongation of Life* (New York: Putnam, 1907); and Metchnikoff, *The Nature of Man* (New York: Putnam, 1903), both published in French and Russian.

29. S. Metal'nikov, "I. I. Mechnikov, 1845–1916," *Russkaia mysl'* 37 (October 1913): 15.

30. Laura Goering, "'Russian Nervousness,'" *Medical History* 47 (2003): 34–38, 41. See also Daniel Beer, *Renovating Russia* (Ithaca: Cornell University Press, 2008), 62–63; Eugene Sandow, *Life Is Movement* (London: Family Encyclopedia, 1922); and A. A. Suvorin, *Novyi chelovek* (St. Petersburg: Uspenskii, 1913).

31. On this thesis and its dissemination in Russia, see August Weismann, "The Duration of Life," *Essays upon Heredity and Kindred Biological Problems*, edited by Edward B. Poulton et al. (1881; repr., Oxford: Clarendon, 1891); Avgust Veisman, "O zhizni i smerti," in *Smert' i bessmertie*, edited by V. A. Vagner and E. A. Shul'ts (St. Petersburg: Obrazovanie, 1914); and N. M. Kulagin, "O prichinakh vymiraniia vidov," *Priroda* 1 (1914): 33–52.

32. V. V. Zav'ialov, "Smert' i bezsmertie," *Priroda* 1 (January 1914): 52–60.

33. See *Scientific American* 29, 15 November 1873, 309. For the broader historical contexts, see Crowe, *Extraterrestrial Life Debate*, 205, 489; and Dick, *Biological Universe*, 82.

34. See *Nature* 55, no. 1411, 12 November 1896, 39; *Zhurnal noveishikh otkrytii i izobretenii* 20, 18 May 1897, 634; and *Putevodnyi ogonek* 6, 22 March 1912, 208.

35. From S. Frederick Starr, "New Communications Technologies and Civil Society," *Science and the Soviet Social Order*, edited by Loren Graham (Cambridge: Harvard University Press, 1990), 25. For context, see Marsha Seifert, "'Chingis-Khan with the Telegraph': Communications in the Russian and Ottoman Empires,"

in *Comparing Empires: Encounters and Transfers in the Long Nineteenth Century*, edited by Jörn Leonhard and Ulrike von Hirschhausen (Göttingen: Vandenhoeck & Ruprecht, 2010), 78–107.

36. Camille Flammarion, *La planète Mars et ses conditions d'habilité* (Paris: Gauthier-Villars, 1892); Percival Lowell, *Mars* (Boston: Houghton, 1895); *Mars and Its Canals* (New York: Macmillan, 1906); and *Mars as the Abode of Life* (New York: Macmillan, 1908), with a 1912 Russian translation. For a survey of the topic, see Robert Markley, *Dying Planet* (Durham: Duke University Press, 2005), 61–97.

37. Gruzdev, *Vselennaia i chelovechestvo*, 471–500. The Lowell thesis and Martian canals were regular news items in the leading Russian journals—*Zhurnal noveishikh otkrytii i izobretenii*, *Vestnik inostrannoi literatury*, and *Priroda i liudi*—between 1896 and 1907.

38. V. Uminskii, *Nevedomyi mir*, translated by F. V. Dombrovskii (St. Petersburg: Liberman, 1897), from the 1895 Polish original.

39. Fedorov, *Filosofiia obshchego dela*, 1:348.

40. On Esperanto as a possible new language for aviation and astronautics, see Ferdinand Ferber, *L'aviation* (Paris: Berger, 1908), 148. On other global and "interplanetary languages," see Charles Torquet, "L'appel d'un autre monde," *Je sais tout* 2, no. 22 (November 1906): 410; A. G. Liakide, *Novyi vseobshchii iazyk "Franseen"* (St. Petersburg: Riman, 1893); and A. G. Liakide, "Soobshchenie mezhdu nebesnymi mirami," *Priroda i liudi* 45–46 (1892): 720, 738–40.

41. "The Scheme to Signal Mars," *Popular Mechanics* 12, no. 1 (July 1909): 10.

42. Percy Greg, *Across the Zodiac* (London: Trubner, 1880), 110.

43. Kurd Lasswitz, *Two Planets*, edited by Erich Lasswitz and translated by Hans H. Rudnick (Carbondale: Southern Illinois University Press, 1971), 16, 20, 169.

44. Quoted from M. Aleksandrov, "Proekt snoshenii s Marsianami," *Priroda i liudi* 40 (1909): 644. Remarks in "Sushchestvuiut li obitateli Marsa?" *Priroda i liudi* 52 (1909): 834–36. The quote—*pochemu oni k nam' do sikh' por' ne iavilis'?*—is from "Mezhplanetnye soobshcheniia," *Vestnik inostrannoi literatury* (May 1903): 332. In his famous "paradox," spoken in lunchtime conversation at a Los Alamos dining hall in the summer of 1950, Fermi asked, "If there are extraterrestrials, where are they?" See Dick, *Biological Universe*, 443.

45. Smith's Mars visitations occurred between 1892 and 1901. See Theodore Flournoy, *From India to the Planet Mars*, edited by Somu Shamadansi (1900; repr., Princeton: Princeton University Press, 1994).

46. Charles Leadbeater, *The Inner Life* (Chicago: Rajput Press, 1911); summarized in "Puteshestvie na Mars'," *Vestnik inostrannoi literatury* (April 1913): 43–45.

47. Quoted from Wladislaw S. Lach-Szyrma, "Letters from the Planets," *Cassell's Family Magazine* 4, no. 11 (November 1887): 689. His space travel adventures include *A Voice from Another World* (London: Wyman, 1882); and *Aleriel, or a Voyage to Other Worlds* (London: Wyman, 1883).

48. Wladislaw S. Lach-Szyrma, "Corresponding with the Planets, *Cassell's Family Magazine* 10, no. 6 (June 1893): 403–5.

49. A. G. Liakide, *V okeane zvezd* (St. Petersburg: Stasiulevich, 1892).

50. Al'bert Debeier, *Tri goda na planete Mars*, translated by B. Pegelau (Moscow: Mamantova, 1909), a supplement to the youth magazine *Putevodnyi ogonek* (1909). The story was part of the series (soon translated into Dutch and Swedish): Albert Daiber, *Die Weltensegler* (Stuttgart: Levy Müller, 1910); and *Vom Mars zur Erde* (Stuttgart: Levy Müller, 1910). For a classic approach to Mars under "ideal Socialism," a planet governed by environmental harmony and civic freedom, see Mark Wicks, *To Mars via the Moon* (Philadelphia: Lippincott, 1911).

51. L. B. Afanas'ev, *Puteshestvie na Mars* (St. Petersburg: supplement to the journal *Niva*, 1901).

52. P. Infant'ev, *Na drugoi planete* (Novgorod: Gubernskaia tipografiia, 1901). Porfirii Pavlovich Infant'ev (1860–1913) was a political radical and ethnographer. Tsarist censors pared down much of the story for its subversive topics, probably related to Martian politics. All that remained were a few vague references to progressive education and civil rights.

53. V. Bariatinskii, "Pis'ma s Marsa," *Vsemirnyi vestnik* 1 (1904): 115–23.

54. See Maria Carlson, "Fashionable Occultism," in Rosenthal, *Occult in Russian and Soviet Culture*, 135; and Maria Carlson, *"No Religion Higher than Truth"* (Princeton: Princeton University Press, 1993). Jeffrey Brooks, *When Russia Learned to Read* (Princeton: Princeton University Press, 1985), 259–62.

55. Cited from John Trowbridge, "Wireless Telegraphy," *Popular Science Monthly* (November 1899): 72. For the contexts, see Deborah Blum, *Ghost Hunters* (New York: Penguin, 2006).

56. See *Vestnik inostrannoi literatury* (December 1897): 9. Camille Flammarion, *Recits de l'infini* (Paris: Didier, 1873), published in English (1873) and Russian (1893).

57. Carlson, *"No Religion Higher than Truth,"* 114–36.

58. Annie Besant, *Why I Became a Theosophist* (London: Freethought, 1889), 7–8, 14–18, 23–24.

59. Besant, *Why I Became*, 28. See the Russian versions of these passages in Annie Wood Besant and S. Tatarinova, *Stroenie kosmosa* (St. Petersburg: Viestnik teosofii, 1914); Annie Wood Besant, *Zakony vysshei zhizni* (Kaluga: Lotus, 1913); and Besant, *Anni Bezant, Avtobiografiia* (St. Petersburg: Viestnik teosofii, 1912).

60. V. Kryzhanovskaia, *Na sosednoi planety*, 2 vols. (1903; repr., Riga: Gudkov, 1920), 1:11, 20–30, 36, 75, 154; 2:39.

61. V. Kryzhanovskaia, *V inom mire* (1911; repr., Riga: Gudkov, 1929), 22–23, 32, 64.

62. V. Kryzhanovskaia, *Gnev bozhii* (1909; repr., Krasnoiarsk: GRIG, 1995). Her *Magi*, a five-part "occult-cosmological cycle" of novels, included *Zhiznennyi eliksir* (1901), *Magi* (1902), *Gnev bozhii* (1909), *Smert' planety* (1911), and *Zakonodateli* (1916). E. Kharitonov, "Pervaia ledi nauchnoi fantastiki," *Bibliografiia* 1 (1997): 56–61; V. Kryzhanovskaia, *Smert planety*, 2 vols. (1911; repr., Riga: Vieda, 1992), 1:89–91.

63. *Na sosednoi planety*, 11–14; *Gnev bozhii*, 83–84; *Smert planety*, 1:90, and 2:260.

64. The Ross Winan family of Baltimore, Maryland, built several of these sleek, metal, steam-driven ships between 1858 and 1866. Among many other science fic-

tion writers, Oskar Hoffmann featured such a cigar-shaped airship in his whimsical tale *Macmilfords Reisen im Universum* (Roda: Weller, 1902).

65. H. G. Wells, "The Discovery of the Future," *Nature* 65, 6 February 1902, 380–81, 389–92.

66. Editorial, "Padaiushchaia zvezda," *Putevodnyi ogonek* 14, 22 July 1909, 422.

3. The Mechanics of Interplanetary Travel

1. See William Burrows, *This New Ocean* (New York: Random House, 1998), 37–39, who argued that "Fyodorov's seeds were deeply planted." In contrast, affirming Tsiolkovskii's independence, see B. Vorob'ev, *Tsiolkovskii* (Moscow: Molodaia gvardiia, 1940), 29–30; Young, *Russian Cosmists*, 145–49, 151–52; and Asif Siddiqi, *The Red Rockets' Glare* (Cambridge: Cambridge University Press, 2010), 80–81.

2. K. E. Tsiolkovskii, *Cherty iz moei zhizni* (1935; repr., Kaluga: Zolotaia alleia, 2002); and "Znamenitel'nye momenty moei zhizni," in *K. E. Tsiolkovskii*, edited by I. A. Islent'ev (Moscow: Aeroflot, 1939), 44.

3. N. Moiseev, "K. E. Tsiolkovskii," in K. E. Tsiolkovskii, *Tsel'nometallicheskii dirizhabl'*, edited by Ia. A. Rapoport (Moscow: ONTI, 1934), 32. See also Ia. I. Perel'man, *Tsiolkovskii* (Moscow: ONTI, 1937), 69. Also quoted from S. Grishin, "Razvitie raketno-kosmicheskoi tekhniki v SSSR," in S. Getland, *Kosmicheskaia tekhnika* (Moscow: Mir, 1986), 269.

4. On Tsiolkovskii's pessimism, best expressed in his self-published work *Gore i genii* (Kaluga: Izd. avtora, 1916), see the various comments in Islent'ev, *K. E. Tsiolkovskii*, 96, 181. On his martyr complex, see Aleksandr Chizhevskii, *Na beregu vselennoi* (Moscow: Mysl', 1995), 153, 165, 302.

5. The first quote is from Tsiolkovskii's letters to Aleksandr Chizhevskii, 20 November 1925 and 3 July 1934, Arkhiv Rossiiskoi Akademii Nauk (ARAN), f. 555, o. 4, d. 28, ll. 18, 24–25. The second quote is from Tsiolkovskii's letter to Perel'man, 8 September 1913, ARAN, f. 555, o. 4, d. 20, l. 1. For a study of Tsiolkovskii's myths, see James T. Andrews, *Red Cosmos* (College Station: Texas A&M University Press, 2009).

6. These journals included *Nauka i zhizn'* and the *Vestnik opytnoi fizikii i elementarnoi matematiki*. He delivered a report in 1890 before the Imperial Russian Technical Society. "Aeroplan ili ptitsepodobnaia (aviatsionnaia) letatel'naia mashina," in *Nauka i zhizn'*, 43–44 and 45–46 (1894).

7. K. E. Tsiolkovskii, *Aerostat metallisticheskii, upravliaemyi* (Moscow: Chertkova, 1892).

8. Kh., "Zheleznyi upravliaemyi aerostat na 200 chelovek K. Tsiolkovskogo," *Zhurnal noveishikh otkrytii i izobretenii* 41, 13 October 1896, 271–20.

9. Letter from Tsiolkovskii to Perel'man, 9 January 1932, ARAN, f. 555, o. 4, d. 20, l. 14.

10. "From the Manuscript 'Free Space' (1883)," in K. E. Tsiolkovsky, *Selected Works*, edited by A. A. Blagonravov and translated by G. Yankovsky (Moscow: Mir, 1968), 28.

11. See the separate editions: K. E. Tsiolkovskii, *Na lune* (Moscow: Sovetskaia rossiia, 1957), written in 1887 and published in the popular science magazine *Vokrug*

sveta (1893); and K. E. Tsiolkovskii, *Grezy o zemle i nebe*, edited by B. N. Vorob'ev (Moscow: Akademiia nauk, 1959), first published in 1895. I have quoted from the English versions in Konstantin Tsiolkovsky, *The Call of the Cosmos* (Moscow: Foreign Languages, 1960).

12. See the photograph in K. Tsiolkovsky, "Dreams of Earth and Sky," *Call of the Cosmos*, 65. He was a teacher first in Borovsk (1880–92), later in Kaluga (1892–1935). On his love of popular science, see the letters of Tsiolkovskii to Perel'man, 26 August 1928 and 31 January 1932, ARAN, f. 555, o. 4, d. 20, ll. 37 and 17.

13. K. Tsiolkovsky, "On the Moon," *Call of the Cosmos*, 14–26.

14. Tsiolkovsky, "Dreams of Earth and Sky," *Call of the Cosmos*, 79, 54–57.

15. Moreux, *A Day in the Moon*, 1, 69–73, 82–152; Henri de Graffigny, "Une fusée péri-lunaire," *Je sais tout* 256 (April 1927): 68–70.

16. *Le Voyage dans la lune*, directed by Georges Melies (1902; France: Star Film) was only sixteen minutes long, but it was the world's first science fiction film and a costly innovation in sophisticated visual effects.

17. Zulawski's works were translated and serialized in Russian as Iurii Zhulavskii, *Na serebriannoi planete*, *Pobeditel'*, and *Staraia zemlia* in the journal *Vestnik inostrannoi literatury* (1908).

18. Al. (Aleksandr Petrovich) Fedorov, *Novyi printsip vozdukhoplavaniia, iskliuchaiushchii atmosferu, kak opornuiu sredu* (St. Petersburg: Trunov, 1896), 3–16. See K. E. Tsiolkovskii's self-published *Issledovanie mirovykh prostranstv reaktivnymi priborami* (Kaluga: Izd. avtora, 1926), 2; Vorob'ev, *Tsiolkovskii*, 159–61; and A. A. Rodnykh, "Iz istorii reaktivnogo letaniia," *V masterskoi prirody* 3 (1924): 9–13.

19. I. Meshcherskii, *Dinamika tochki peremennoi massy* (St. Petersburg: Akademiia nauk, 1897), 1, 80–82. On Meshcherskii's significance, see Werner Brügel, ed., *Männer der Rakete* (Leipzig: Hachmeister & Thal, 1933), 80, 137; and A. E. Fersman, ed., *Rasskazy o nauke i ee tvortsakh* (Moscow: Gosizdat, 1946), 248–49.

20. K. Tsiolkovsky, "Investigation of World Spaces by Reactive Vehicles (1903)," *Selected Works*, 53–56, 61–63 (originally K. Tsiolkovskii, "Izsledovanie mirovykh' prostranstv' reaktivnymi priborami," *Nauchnoe obozrenie* 5 [May 1903]: 45–75).

21. Tsiolkovskii, "Investigation of World Spaces" (1903), 59, 65–66, 75, 82.

22. Tsiolkovskii, "Investigation of World Spaces" (1903), 55. On Ganswindt's 27 May 1891 "rocket" lecture (at the Berlin Philharmonic Concert Hall), see T. M. Mel'kumov, ed., *Pionery raketnoi tekhniki* (Moscow: Nauka, 1977); and Daniel Brandau, "Cultivating the Cosmos," *History and Technology* 28, no. 3 (September 2012): 235, a pioneering approach to the German contexts.

23. A. Le Mée, "Sur les communications interplanétaires," *La revue* 45, 15 April 1903, 227–33; and the translation, "Mezhplanetnye soobshcheniia," *Vestnik inostrannoi literatury* (May 1903): 329–32. There is an intriguing possibility that although published first (in April), Le Mée's article was itself a partial translation and commentary on a manuscript of Tsiolkovskii's later article, "Investigation of World Spaces by Reactive Vehicles," published in May but perhaps already in the hands of editors at *La revue* beforehand.

24. Abstracts of Le Mée's article were also published as "Messengers to Mars," *Review of Reviews* 27 (January–June 1903): 500; and in *American Monthly Review of Reviews* (June 1903): 755–56.

25. John Munro, *A Trip to Venus* (1897; repr., Westport CT: Hyperion, 1976), 37–39, 50, 53, 61.

26. Munro, *Trip to Venus*, 10–13, 108–9, 174–75.

27. For a biography, see B. M. Filippov, *Ternistyi put' russkogo uchenogo* (Moscow: Nauka, 1982), 82.

28. On Filippov's life and these rumors, see Filippov, *Ternistyi put'*, 144–50.

29. Quoted from Jim Rasenburger, "1908," *Smithsonian* 38, no. 10 (January 2008): 42; and from the editorial "Aerial Navigation," *Popular Science Monthly* (October 1908): 381.

30. The drawing is in Henri Farman, "Comment je suis devenu aviateur," *Je sais tout* 42, 15 July 1908, 725. For a rare recognition of Esnault-Pelterie's priority in conceiving this rocket plane, see A. B. Scherschevsky, *Die Rakete für Fahrt und Flug* (Berlin: Volckmann, 1929), 76–77.

31. René Lorin, "Note sur la propulsion des véhicles aériens," *L'Aérophile* 15, no. 11 (November 1907): 321–22. See also Lorin, "Le propulseur à échappement et l'aéroplane à grand vitesse," *L'Aérophile* (September 1908): 332–36.

32. Ferber, *L'aviation*, 142–47, 161.

33. K. E. Veigelin, *Zavoevanie vozdushnago okeana* (St. Petersburg: Soikin, 1910), 116. See the cover of *Sinii zhurnal* 3, 8 January 1911; and *Putevodnyi ogonek* 12, 22 June 1914, 405. For the full context, see Scott Palmer, *Dictatorship of the Air* (New York: Cambridge University Press, 2006), 27–29.

34. See *Sbornik pamiati L. M. Matsievicha* (St. Petersburg: Suvorin, 1912), 7–27, 117, 159–72.

35. *Sbornik pamiati L. M. Matsievicha*, 16–17, 27, 48.

36. Leonid Andreev, "Polet" (1914), *Sobranie sochinenii*, 6 vols. (Moscow: Khudozhestvennaia literatura, 1994), 4:301–6.

37. See the sketch and a discussion of the poem "The Flight of Vasya Kamenskii in an Airplane over Warsaw" (1914), in Robert Wohl, *A Passion for Wings* (New Haven: Yale University Press, 1994), 153. Quoted from *Sbornik pamiati L. M. Matsievicha*, 167.

38. "Letatel'nyi apparat budushchego," *Putevodnyi ogonek* 9, 7 May 1912, 284.

39. Aleksandr Gorokhov, "Mekhanicheskii polet budushchego," *Vozdushnyi put'* 2 (February 1911): 23–32.

40. The pieces appeared in *Vestnik vozdukhoplavaniia* 19–22 (1911) and 2–9 (1912) and were also publicized in leading newspapers. See Tsiolkovsky, "Investigation of World Spaces by Reactive Vehicles (1911–1912)," in Tsiolkovsky, *Selected Works*, 84–89, 95, 105–8, 123.

41. V. V. Riumin, "Na rakete v mirovoe prostranstvo," *Priroda i liudi* 36 (1912): 556–58. Riumin was editor of the magazine *Elektrichestvo i zhizn'*, in which he promoted Tsiolkovskii's spaceflight theories between 1913 and 1914.

42. Tsiolkovsky, "Investigation of World Spaces" (1911–12), 102–5, 106–7, 127.

43. Esnault-Pelterie probably learned of Tsiolkovskii while in Russia but ignored him until 1928. He probably also knew about the work of the Belgian inventor Andre Bing, who had designed an atomic energy spaceship in 1910–11. On these disputes, see Alexandre Ananoff, *Les mémoires d'un astronaut* (Paris: Blanchard, 1978), 46–55.

44. He presented "Les considérations sur les résultats d'un allégement indéfini des moteurs" again to the Société Française de Physique on 15 November 1912, later published in *Journal de physique* 5, no. 3 (March 1913): 218–30.

45. Goddard returned home to Massachusetts from Princeton University on 19 March 1913 and recuperated from a bout of tuberculosis until the end of May. The source of Esnault-Pelterie's work, the *Journal de physique*, was readily available to him. He submitted his first rocket patent to his attorneys on 2 July and wrote his first significant article on rockets and space travel in September and October. See his diary entries, the explanatory notes, and the article (as well as his denials of ever having read Esnault-Pelterie's 1913 work) in Goddard and Pendray, *Papers of Robert H. Goddard*, 1:116–23, 436; 2:643; and 3:1590.

46. Giulio Costanzi, "Sulla possibilità di un aumento quasi indefinito della velocità degli aeroplani nella stratsofera," *Aer* 5 (1914). The piece was republished in *Rivista di aeronautica* (1916).

47. K. E. Veigelin, "Kak mozhno doletet' do luny," *Priroda i liudi* 4 (1914): 53–55, against whom the editors inserted a note that Tsiolkovskii's work came first. N. Tolstoi, "Puteshestvie k planetam'," *Vokrug sveta* 20 (1914): 314–15; Anri Grafin'i, "Vozmozhny li puteshestviia na planety," *Priroda i liudi* 13 (1916): 204.

48. K. Tsiolkovskii, *Issledovanie mirovykh' prostranstv'e reaktivnymi priborami (dopolnenie k' I i II chasti truda togo-zhe nazvaniia)* (Kaluga: Semenova, 1914), 1–2. An English translation of the new material, with the drawing but without the preface, is offered as "Investigation of World Spaces by Reactive Vehicles (Supplement to First and Second parts, 1914)," in Tsiolkovsky, *Selected Works*, 128–39.

49. Ia. I. Perel'man, *Zanimatel'naia fizika* (St. Petersburg: Soikin, 1913–16). Compare with Richard A. Proctor, *Easy Lessons in the Differential Calculus* (London: Longmans, 1887); and Abbé Théophile Moreux, *Pour comprendre le calcul different-ential* (Paris: Bibliothèque d'éducation scientifique, 1924).

50. "Khronika," *Rech'*, 22 November 1913, 5. The lecture was widely disseminated in the press, as, e.g., in "Mezhplanetnyia puteshestvyiia," *Priroda i liudi* 8 (1914): 126–27.

51. Bruno Bürgel, *Aus Fernen Welten* (Berlin: Ullstein, 1910); Felix Linke, *Ist die Welt bewohnt?* (Stuttgart: Dietz, 1910); and Linke, *Kann die Erde untergehen?* (Stuttgart: Dietz, 1911); Edmond Perrier, *La vie dans les planètes* (Paris: La revue, 1912), translated into Russian in 1914.

52. Ia. I. Perel'man, *Mezhplanetnye puteshestviia* (Petrograd: Soikin, 1915). Siddiqi, *Red Rockets' Glare*, 39, also gives credit to Perel'man's priority.

53. Bogdanov, *Red Star*, 35–39, 51, 59.

54. "Vecher futuristov," *Rech'*, 21 November 1913, 6.

55. The sound poem is in *Russkaia mysl'* 3 (1914): 91. On Khlebnikov, see Patricia Railing, *From Science to Systems of Art* (Forest Row: Artists' Bookworks, 1989), 79–81, 106–9. For the context, see Tim Harte, *Fast Forward* (Madison: University of Wisconsin Press, 2009), 18, 36.

56. See the disputes in Jane A. Sharp, "The Critical Reception of the 0.10 Exhibition," in *The Great Utopia* (New York: Guggenheim Museum, 1992), 45.

57. Vasilii Rakitin, "The Artisan and the Prophet," in *Great Utopia*, 26–27. For the contexts, see Linda Dalrymple Henderson, *The Fourth Dimension and Non-Euclidian Geometry in Modern Art* (Princeton: Princeton University Press, 1983).

58. For these quotes and their contexts, see Rainer Crone, *Kazimir Malevich* (Chicago: University of Chicago Press, 1991), 161; Charlotte Douglas, *Swans of Other Worlds* (Ann Arbor MI: UMI, 1980), 53–54; Kasimir Malevich, *Malevich* (Copenhagen: Borgans, 1978), 15; Kazimir Malevich, *Sobranie sochinenii*, 5 vols. (Moscow: Gileia, 1995), 1:44; Christine Lodder, *Constructive Strands in Russian Art* (London: Pindar, 2005), 78–110; and Charlotte Douglas, *Kazimir Malevich* (New York: Abrams, 1994), 92. See also the sketches in Kazimir Malevich, *The Non-Objective World* (Chicago: Theobold, 1959), 92–93.

59. Edward J. Brown, *Mayakovsky* (Princeton: Princeton University Press, 1973), 83, 96, 113, 184.

60. Charles Howard Hinton, *The Fourth Dimension* (1904; repr., London: Sonnenschein, 1906) (translated as *Chetvertoe izmierenie* [Petrograd: Novyi Chelovek, 1915]); P. D. Uspenskii, *Tertium organum* (St. Petersburg: Trud, 1911) (translated as *Tertium Organum* [London: Routledge, 1914]).

61. See Wohl, *Passion for Wings*, 138–43.

62. See Paul Scheerbart, *Die grosse Revolution* (Leipzig: Insel-Verlag, 1902), which features lunar beings with their own sense perception of the cosmos; Scheerbart, *Lesabéndio* (Munich: Müller, 1913), which features the planet "Pallas," whose inhabitants are building a giant tower to peer into space. See also Scheerbart, *Astrale Novelletten* (Leipzig: Müller, 1912). Quoted from Rosemarie Haag Bletter, "Paul Scheerbart's Architectural Fantasies," *Journal of the Society of Architectural Historians* 34, no. 2 (1975): 92.

63. See Constance Naubert-Riser, "Cosmic Imaginings, from Symbolism to Abstract Art," in Clair, *Cosmos*, 220–22, 365, 387, who argues that Hablik anticipated the architectural designs of Malevich and his students.

64. Richard Maurice Bucke, *Cosmic Consciousness* (Philadelphia: Innes, 1905), 3–4 (translated as R. M. Bekk, *Kosmicheskoe soznanie* [Petrograd: Novyi chelovek, 1915]).

65. Bucke, *Cosmic Consciousness*, 96, 14. His influence in Russia was widespread: from Pavel Florenskii and Kornei Chukovskii to Velemir Khlebnikov and Ivan Filipchenko.

66. On these images of Whitman, see Mila Tupper Maynard, *Walt Whitman* (Chicago: Kerr, 1903). For more about Whitman's influences on Iosif Stalin, see Michael G. Smith, "Stalin's Martyrs," in *Redefining Stalinism*, edited by Harold Shukman (London: Frank Cass, 2003), 95–126.

67. Walt Whitman, "On the Beach at Night Alone," *Leaves of Grass and Selected Prose*, edited by John Kouwenhoven (1855; repr., New York: Modern Library, 1950), 209; and Uol't' Uitman', *Pobegi travy*, translated by K. D. Bal'mont (Moscow: Skorpion', 1911), 3.

68. John Addington Symonds, *Walt Whitman* (London: Nimmo, 1893), 155–56. Kornei Chukovskii, *Uot Uitmen*, 4th ed. (Petrograd: Izd. Petrogradskogo soveta, 1919), 110–11, noted that K. Bal'mont, "Pevets lichnosti i zhizni," *Vesy* 7 (1914), plagiarized these exact phrases from Symonds.

69. Whitman, *Leaves of Grass and Selected Prose*, 484, 496, 503.

70. From Poem "29" (1912), with my revised translation, in *The Complete Poetry of Osip Emilevich Mandelshtam*, translated by Burton Raffel and Alla Burago (Albany: State University of New York, 1973), 46.

71. "The Morning of Acmeism" (1912–13, published in 1919), in *Osip Mandelshtam*, translated by Sidney Monas (Austin: University of Texas Press, 1977), 128–31.

72. Fyodor Sologub, *Smoke and Ashes*, pt. 3 of *The Created Legend / Tvorimaia legenda* (1907–14), translated by Samuel D. Cioran (Ann Arbor MI: Ardis, 1979), 38.

73. Sologub, *Smoke and Ashes*, 13, 33–34, 121–22. Chapter 81 of *Smoke and Ashes* is a lecture on gravity straight out of Tsiolkovskii. Friedrich Wilhelm Mader, *Wunderwelten* (Stuttgart: Volkskunst, 1911), also employed a planet-shaped, antigravity ship, speeding along on a parabolic "voyage into infinity."

74. From one of the manifestos of the group, "Turbopaean" (1914), in Anna Lawton, ed., *Russian Futurism through Its Manifestoes*, translated by Anna Lawton and Herbert Eagle (Ithaca: Cornell University Press, 1988), 161.

75. Velemir Khlebnikov, "Trumpet of the Martians" (*Truba Marsian*, 1916), in the *Collected Works of Velemir Khlebnikov*, edited by Charlotte Douglas and translated by Paul Schmidt, 3 vols. (Cambridge: Harvard University Press, 1987), 1:321–23.

76. "A Martian Stranded on Earth," in Bogdanov, *Red Star*, 238; letter from Khlebnikov to Mikhail Matiushin, 18 June 1913, in Khlebnikov, *Collected Works of Velemir Khlebnikov*, 1:77.

77. David F. Noble, *The Religion of Technology* (New York: Knopf, 1998), 122, 128.

78. Michael Holquist explores this insight in "Tsiolkovskii as a Moment in the Prehistory of the Avant-Garde," *Laboratory of Dreams*, edited by John E. Bowlt and Olga Matich (Stanford: Stanford University Press, 1996), 100–117. Quoted from a letter to Viacheslav Ivanov published in February 1914, in Khlebnikov, *Collected Works of Velemir Khlebnikov*, 69.

79. Katerina Clark, *Petersburg* (Cambridge: Harvard University Press, 1995), 47.

80. Tsiolkovskii's preface to *Issledovanie* (1926), 1–2. The English translation, "Investigation of World Spaces by Reactive Vehicles" (in Tsiolkovsky, *Selected Works*, 128–39), lacks this preface.

81. I. N. Potapenko, "Vo tem' vremen'," *Sinii zhurnal* beginning with 1, 1 January 1912, 2–4.

82. *Vestnik inostrannoi literatury* (October 1907): 247–49; and (April 1912): 42–48.

83. Valerii Briusov, 11 May 1913, in *Sobranie sochinenii*, 7 vols. (Moscow: Khudozhestvennaia literatura, 1973), 2:100–101.

84. N. N. [Koshkarev], *O proletarskoi etike* (1905; repr., Kharkov: Proletarii, 1923), 8–9, 22–23, 52–53; Nikolai Bukharin, *Historical Materialism* (1923; repr., New York: International, 1925), 105, 116, 122. 133.

85. Sergei Solomin, "Zavtra," in *Sinii zhurnal* 13 (1912): 2.

86. B. Krasnogorskii and D. Sviatskii, *Ostrova efirnogo okeana* (Petrograd: Rassvet, 1914). N. A. Rynin offered a detailed study of this craft in *Spacecraft in Science Fiction* (Jerusalem: Scientific Translations, 1971), 62–74 (originally published as *Kosmicheskie korabli v fantaziiakh romanistov* [Leningrad: Soikin, 1928]).

87. Sergei Gorodetskii, "Geoskop Kaena," *Argus* 1 (1913): 31–34; N. A. Rynin. *Kinematografiia* (Leningrad: Gosizdat, 1924), 5. Rynin was one of Russia's leading balloonists and aeronautics engineers at the time of the Russian Revolution, a friend and patron of Tsiolkovskii since 1914.

88. Friedrich Wilhelm Mader, *Die Tote Stadt* (Stuttgart: Verlagsgesellschaft, 1923); Hugo Gernsback, "Ralph 124C41+. A Romance of the Year 2660," *Modern Electrics* (March and April 1911) (republished in book form [Boston: Stratford, 1925]); Bernard Kellerman, *Der Tunnel* (Berlin: Fischer, 1913) (translated into English in 1915 and Russian in 1914 and 1923).

89. Wells, *World Set Free*, 226–27.

90. For popular novels on the conquests of the poles, see Jules Verne, *Topsy-Turvy* (New York: Ogilvie, 1890); Wladyslaw Uminski, *Balonem do Bieguna* (1894; repr., Warsaw: Gebethnera, 1930); Fritz Holten, *Das Polarschiff* (Stuttgart: Gesellschaft, 1910); and Théophile Moreux, *L'assaut du Pole Sud* (Paris: Jouve, 1927).

91. Max de Nansouty, *Actualités scientifiques* (Paris: Juven, 1901), 30–39, 186–93.

92. Hudson Maxim, "The Warfare of the Future," *Science* 28, 11 December 1908, 829.

93. Arthur Train and Robert Williams Wood, *The Man Who Rocked the Earth* (1915; repr., New York: Arno, 1975); and Train and Wood, *The Moon Maker* (1916; repr., Hamburg: Krueger, 1958), which was translated into Russian in 1925.

94. Train and Wood, *Man Who Rocked the Earth*, 117–22, 203.

95. Train and Wood, *Man Who Rocked the Earth*, 27–28, 37.

96. Train and Wood, *Man Who Rocked the Earth*, 33–34, 45, 49.

97. See his preface in Robert H. Goddard, *A Method of Reaching Extreme Altitudes*, in *Smithsonian Miscellaneous Collections* 71, no. 2 (Washington DC: Smithsonian Institution, 1919), i; and the quote from Goddard and Pendray, *Papers of Robert H. Goddard*, 1:157–58.

98. M. E. Haggerty, "Science and Democracy," *Popular Science Monthly* (September 1915): 254. For similar points, see David Kinley, "Democracy and Scholarship," *Science* 28, 16 October 1908, 497; and David Starr Jordan, "Comrades in Zeal," *Popular Science Monthly* (February 1904): 314.

4. Lyrical Cosmism of the Russian Revolution

1. I presented portions of this chapter, also centered on material about Robert Goddard from chapters 3 and 5, at the annual conference of the Society for the History of Science and Technology, Atlanta, 15 October 2003—with thanks to Asif Siddiqi for inviting me and commenting on my work in the spring of that year.

2. *Byloe* 4–5 (1918): 8, 115–24. McDougall first recognized Kibalchich's significance in *Heavens and the Earth*, 17–19.

3. See *Iunyi proletarii* 7 (April 1925): 25; and 1 (January 1926): 28–29; as well as *Vestnik vozdushnogo flota* 4 (April 1929): 39–41; *Nauka i tekhnika* 47 (1929): 5; and *Krasnaia niva* 8 (1931): 20.

4. From George Griffith, *The Angel of the Revolution* (London: Tower, 1893); *Olga Romanoff* (London: Tower, 1894); and *A Honeymoon in Space* (London: Pearson, 1901).

5. Sergei Mstislavskii, *Partiontsy* (Moscow: Sovetskaia literatura, 1933), 14, 44–46, 51, 168–75.

6. N. A. Morozov, *Terroristicheskaia bor'ba* (London: Russkaia tipografiia, 1880). I have drawn his biographical details from Morozov, *Povesti moiei zhizni*, 2 vols. (Moscow: Akademiia nauk, 1961).

7. N. A. Morozov, *Otkrovenie v grozie i burie: Istoriia vozniknoveniia Apokalipsisa* (St. Petersburg: Byloe, 1907). In 1909 he helped establish the Russian Society of Astronomy Enthusiasts (Russkoe obshchestvo liubitelei mirovedeniia, or ROLM) and its journal, *Mirovedenie* (1912–38).

8. N. A. Morozov, *Na granitse nevedomogo* (Moscow: Zveno, 1910), 1–169. "V mirovom prostranstve" was first published in *Sovremennyi mir* 1 (1908): 159–75. Quoted from "Atomy-dushi," in Morozov, *Na granitse*, 171–89. Also quoted from N. A. Morozov, *D.I. Mendeleev* (Moscow: Sytin, 1907), 103.

9. N. A. Morozov, *Zvezdnyia pesni* (Moscow: Skorpion, 1910).

10. H. G. Wells, *Russia in the Shadows* (London: Hodder & Houghton, 1920), 11, 35; T. Konstantin Oesterreich, *Occultism and Modern Science* (London: Methuen, 1923), 1–9. See *La revue universelle* (1920–23), including the writings of Charles Maurras and Jacques Maritain.

11. W. W. Campbell, "The Daily Influences of Astronomy," *Smithsonian Annual Report* (1921): 139–40, 151–52.

12. From E. I. Ignat'ev, "Komety," *Znanie dlia vsekh* 2 (1917): 3.

13. "Mirovaia revoliutsiia stala faktom," *Izvestiia* 15, 20 January 1918, 1; Andrei Bely, "Revolution and Culture," in *A Revolution of the Spirit*, edited by Bernice Glatzer Rosenthal and Martha Bohachevsky-Chomiak, translated by Marian Schwartz (New York: Fordham University Press, 1990), 273, 289.

14. N. Bukharin and E. Preobrazhensky, *The ABC of Communism* (1919; repr., Ann Arbor: University of Michigan Press, 1966), 136–37.

15. James von Geldern, *Bolshevik Festivals* (Berkeley: University of California Press, 1993), 19, 80, 129–33, 142–61, 182–98, 216.

16. See N. Akimov's illustration of "Lenin," *Krasnaia panorama* 15 (1924): 1 and front cover. Vladimir Mayakovsky, *Vladimir Ilyich Lenin* (Moscow: Progress, 1967),

129. Vasilii Kazin's untitled poem in *Krasnaia nov'* 4 (June–July 1924): 130–31; and A. V. Lunacharskii, "Lenin," *Krasnaia panorama* 3, 20 January 1928, 3. See the poster recognizing Lenin's death at "1924: Death of Lenin," Seventeen Moments of Soviet History, www.soviethistory.org/index.php (accessed 2 August 2013).

17. See A. E. Fersman, "Zavoevaniia nauk," *Nauka i tekhnika* 1 (1922): 4–8; Fersman, *Vremia* (Petrograd: Vremia, 1922), 67–71; and Fersman, *Puti k nauke budushchego* (Petrograd: Nauchno izd., 1922). These works were also published in an abbreviated Esperanto edition: A. Fersman, *La Vojo al Scienco de Estonto*, translated by S. Rublov (Leipzig: Eldona, 1928).

18. B. P. Veinberg, "K dvukhdesiatitysiacheletiiu nachala rabot po unichtozheniiu okeanov," *Sibirskaia priroda* 2 (May 1922): 3–42.

19. As quoted from N. I. Bukharin, preface, in Ia. V. Apushkin, *Konstantin Fedorovich Iuon* (Moscow: Vsekhudozhnik, 1936), 5–6, 90–94.

20. "Rasstreliannaia zemlia" (1921), in Nikolai Aseev, *Sobranie sochinenii*, 5 vols. (Moscow: Khudozhestvennaia literatura, 1964), 5:69–75.

21. N. I. Mukhanov, *Pylaiushchie bezdny* (Leningrad: Soikin, 1924), 1, 8, 139–40.

22. See the first volume, Théo Varlet and Octave Joncquel, *Les titans du ciel* (Amiens: Malfère, 1921). Other such Mars novels of the time include Constantin Redzich, *Ein Besuch auf dem Mars* (Stuttgart: Wagnersche, 1922); George Babcock, *Yezad* (New York: Cooperative, 1922); Ernst Panhans, *Der schwarzgelbe Weltbund* (Hamburg: Vera, 1924); and Lilian Leslie, *The Melody from Mars* (New York: International, 1924).

23. Mark D. Steinberg, *Proletarian Imagination* (Ithaca: Cornell University Press, 2002), 60, 71, 118–21.

24. For these images, see Z. S. Papernyi, ed., *Proletarskie poety pervykh let sovetskoi epokhi* (Leningrad: Sovetskii pisatel', 1959), 194, 197–201, 233–34, 241, 243, 292, 303, 310, 376, 378, 472; Mayakovsky, *Vladimir Ilyich Lenin*, 83, 93, 105; and M. F. Pianykh, *Russkaia poeziia revoliutsionnoi epokhi* (Leningrad: Gosped., 1979), 6–10, 30–36.

25. See the discussions in K. Chukovskii, *Uot Uitmen i ego "List'ia Travy,"* 6th ed. (Moscow: Gosizdat, 1923). For favorable reviews of Whitman's proletarian poetry, see *Vestnik zhizni* 1 (1918): 45; 2 (1918): 25; and 3–4 (1919): 67–70.

26. On Gastev's *Poeziia rabochego udara* and his debts to Whitman, see Patricia Carden, "Utopia and Anti-Utopia," *Russian Review* 46 (1987): 12.

27. A. K. Gastev, "My posiagnuli" (1913–17), and "My vmeste" (1913–17), in Papernyi, *Proletarskie poety*, 156–58, 160.

28. M. P. Gerasimov, "My pobedim" (1918), in Papernyi, *Proletarskie poety*, 197.

29. Georgii Iakubovskii, "Praktika i teoriia v tvorchestve 'Kuznitsy'," *Krasnaia nov'* 6 (1923): 337–47.

30. Mikhail Leonov, *Pionerskii teatr*, 2 vols. (Moscow: MODPiK, 1925), 2:34, 36, 60; and 1:30.

31. See Al. Leonidov, "Tekhnika proletarskikh poetov," *Zarevo zavodov* 2 (1919): 40, referring to P. Arskii's, *Pesni bor'by* (Petrograd: Proletkul't, 1919).

32. These voices included Aleksandr Bogdanov, Pavel Lebedev-Polianksi, P. S. Kogan, and Aleksandr Lunacharskii. See Robert A. Maguire, *Red Virgin Soil* (Princeton: Princeton University Press, 1968), 159, 356–58; and Steinberg, *Proletarian Imagination*, 59, 270, 281. A. Voronskii, "O gruppe pisatelei 'Kuznitsa,'" *Krasnaia nov'* 3 (May 1923): 309–12.

33. Dem'ian Bednyi, "Mezhplanetnaia revoliutsiia," *Pravda* 21, 31 January 1920, 1; Leon Trotsky, *Literature and Revolution* (1923; repr., Ann Arbor: University of Michigan Press, 1960), 210.

34. "The Word and Culture" (1921), *Osip Mandelshtam*, 53.

35. "The Nineteenth Century" (1922), in *Osip Mandelshtam*, 95.

36. Georgii Florovsky, "In the World of Quests and Wanderings" (1923), in Rosenthal and Bohachevsky-Chomiak, *Revolution of the Spirit*, 233.

37. From "Mystery-Bouffe" (1921), in *The Complete Plays of Vladimir Mayakovsky*, translated by Guy Daniels (Evanston: Northwestern University Press, 1995), 39, 53, 139.

38. From "Noch' pod Rozhdestvo" (1922–23), in V. V. Maiakovskii, *Izbrannye proizvedeniia*, 2 vols. (Moscow: Sovetskii pisatel', 1963), 1:564.

39. From "Pis'mo Pisatelia V. V. Maiakovskogo Pisateliu A. M. Gor'komu" (1926), in Maiakovskii, *Izbrannye proizvedeniia*, 2:168. See also the references to rockets in "Zovu" (1922) and "Kemp 'Nit Gedaige'" (1925) in the same collection.

40. From "Moskva—Kenigsberg" (1923), in Maiakovskii, *Izbrannye proizvedeniia*, 1:334.

41. See Brown, *Mayakovsky*, 133, 167–69, 178.

42. Viktor Shklovskii, "Pamiatnik tret'emu internationalu," *Zhizn' iskusstva* 65, 9 January 1921, 1. N. Punin, "The Monument to the Third International" (1920), in *Tatlin*, edited by Larissa Zhadova (New York: Rizzoli, 1988): 344–47.

43. I. Rakhtanov, "Letatlin," *Pioner* 9 (1932): 12. For these contexts, see William Hutchings, "Structure and Design in a Soviet Dystopia," *Journal of Modern Literature* 9, no. 1 (1981–82): 81–102; John Milner, *Vladimir Tatlin and the Russian Avant-Garde* (New Haven: Yale University Press, 1983), 179; and Norbert Lynton, *Tatlin's Tower* (New Haven: Yale University Press, 2008), 139.

44. For context, see Scott W. Palmer, "Red Stars and Rocket Ships," in *2001*, edited by John Zukowsky (New York: Abrams, 2001), 39–44. *Unovis* was short for *Proekt Utverzhdeniia Novogo Iskusstva*.

45. See M. A. Nemirovskaia, "Proizvedeniia L. M. Lisitskogo," and the *Proun-Zvezda*, in *Lazar' Markovich Lisitskii* (Moscow: Tret'iakovskaia, 1990), 20, 55; and Patricia Railing, *More about Two Squares* (Cambridge: MIT Press, 1991), 5–6, 21–40.

46. On "projectionism," see Isai G. Lezhnev, "Dve privivki," *Rossiia* 8 (1923): 16. Kazimir Malevich, *Suprematism* (Vitebsk), 15 December 1920, as translated in Larissa Zhadova, *Malevich* (London: Thames & Hudson, 1982), 284–87.

47. Aleksandra Shatskikh, "Unovis: Epicenter of a New World," in *The Great Utopia* (New York: Guggenheim Museum, 1992), 59; with Chashnik's "Supremolet (Suprematist planit)" at plates 182–84.

48. From his notebook entries, 27 July 1920, in Aleksandr Rodchenko, *Experiments for the Future*, edited by Aleksandr M. Lavrentiev and translated by Jamey Gambrell (New York: Museum of Modern Art, 2005), 107.

49. On the "cosmic city" of Krutikov (inspired by Malevich) and on Kalmykov, see Selim O. Khan-Magomedov, *Pioneers of Soviet Architecture*, edited by Catherine Cooke and translated by Alexander Lieven (New York: Rizzoli, 1987), 280–83, 309.

50. For a fine pictorial and narrative introduction to the innovations of the Russian avant-garde in its broader European and global contexts, see Germano Celant, *Architecture & Arts, 1900/2004: A Century of Creative Projects in Building, Design, Cinema, Painting, Sculpture* (New York: Rizzoli, 2004).

51. *Monthly Evening Sky Map* 15, no. 179 (November 1921): 1; *V masterskoi prirody* 2 (1922): 1–5; and *Iunyi proletarii* 4 (March 1923): 29.

52. *Popular Science Monthly* (September 1919): 74–75; and *Science and Invention* 8 (June 1920): 135, 209.

53. "On Synthetism" (1922), in Yevgeny Zamyatin, *A Soviet Heretic*, edited and translated by Mirra Ginsburg (Chicago: University of Chicago, 1970), 86.

54. The quote is from "Radiovest'" (1921), in Aseev, *Sobranie sochinenii*, 1:125–26.

55. Valerii Briusov, "Pervaia mezhplanetnaia ekspeditsiia," in *Literaturnoe nasledstvo* 85 (Moscow: Nauka, 1976), 103–13.

56. See Aleksandr Iaroslavskii, *Koren' iz ia* (Leningrad: UIK, 1926), 10–13, 34–35. He was a leader of the Petrograd faction of Biocosmists, as discussed in Michael Hagermeister, *Nikolaj Fedorov* (Munich: Sagner, 1989), 300–317.

57. See the poems "Zalog mechti," "Zvezdnyi manifest," and "Zvezdnomu bratu," in A. Iaroslavskii, *Zvezdnyi manifest* (Vladivostok: n.p., 1918), 3–6.

58. Aleksandr Iaroslavskii, *Poema anabioza* (Petrograd: Biokosmist, 1922), 12–13. From the poem "Parad zemle," in Iaroslavskii, *Koren' iz ia*, 81.

59. Material and quotes from "Nashi ubezhdeniia" and accompanying articles, in *Biokosmist* 1 (1922): 4–7.

60. Aleksandr Sviatogor, "'Doktrina otsov' i anarkhizm-biocosmizm," in *Biokosmist* 3–4 (1922): 16–20.

61. On Kravkov, see *Krasnaia nov'* 6 (1922): 271; *Krasnaia panorama* 17, no. 35 (1924): 12–13; *Novyi mir* 7 (July 1925): 119; and A. I. Kuznetsov, *N.P. Kravkov* (Moscow: Gosizdat meditsinskoi literatury, 1948). On Andreev, see Andreev, *Opyty vosstanovleniia deiatel'nosti serdtsa* (Moscow: Mysl', 1913). See also Nikolai Krementsov, "Off with Their Heads: Isolated Organs in Early Soviet Science and Fiction," *Studies in History and Philosophy of Biological and Biomedical Sciences* 40 (2009): 87–100.

62. Sviatogor, "'Doktrina otsov,'" 9–20. Krementsov, *Revolutionary Experiments*, 29–30, offers the more complete contexts.

63. Eugen Steinach, *Verjüngung durch experimentelle Neubelebung der alternden Pubertätsdrüse [Rejuvenation by Revitalizing the Aging Puberty Gland]* (Berlin: Springer, 1920).

64. Steinach's work first appeared in Russian in N. K. Koltsov, ed., *Omolozhenie* (Moscow: n.p., 1923), 124–70. For favorable reviews, see *Priroda* 1–3 (1921):

3–26; *Iunyi proletarii* 2 (January 1923): 46–51; and *Krasnaia nov'* 6 (November–December 1922): 383.

65. A. L. (Abba) and V. L. Gordin, "Pan-Anarchist Manifesto," in *The Anarchists in the Russian Revolution*, edited by Paul Avrich (Ithaca: Cornell University Press, 1973), 49–51.

66. Gordin and Gordin, "Pan-Anarchist Manifesto," 51; Br. Gordiny, "Nothing Forgotten and Nothing Learned," in Avrich, *Anarchists*, 55. See also Paul Avrich, *The Russian Anarchists* (Princeton: Princeton University Press, 1971), 177–78.

67. V. L. Gordin, *Inventism or Eurologism* (Moscow: All-Invention House, 1925). For a detailed description of the language, see Sergej Kuznecov, "Linguistica cosmica," *Histoire, epistemologie, langage* 17, no. 2 (1995): 220–27.

68. I discuss these contexts in Michael G. Smith, *Language and Power in the Creation of the USSR* (Berlin: Mouton de Gruyter, 1998), 76–80.

69. See Victor Coissac, *L'évolution des mondes* (Tours: Intègrale, 1916), 120–23; as well as both Coissac, *La réalisation du bonheur* and *La Conquête de l'espace* (Tours: Intègrale, 1916).

70. Vivian Itin, *Strana gonguri* (Kansk: Gosizdat, 1922); and *Solntse serdtsa* (Novonikolaevsk: Sibirskie Ogni, 1923), 33, 38, 70–71.

71. Itin, *Strana gonguri*, 20–21, 24.

72. Itin, *Strana gonguri*, 27.

5. The Pioneers and the Spaceflight Imperative

1. N. A. Rynin, *Vozdushnaia voina* (Petrograd: Soikin, 1917).

2. René Lorin, *L'air et la vitesse* (Paris: Librairie aéronautique, 1919), 51–54; William C. Sherman, *Air Warfare* (New York: Ronald Press, 1926), 5–10.

3. Will Irwin, *"The Next War"* (New York: Dutton, 1921), 25–26, 40–43, 107.

4. Irwin, *"Next War,"* 46–47, 57, 78, 127.

5. Giulio Douhet, *The Command of the Air*, translated by Dino Ferrari (1921; repr., Washington DC: Office of Air Force History, 1983), 15–35, 50–68.

6. Compare *Popular Science Monthly* (December 1921): 26–27; and (August 1925): 2–3; with *Smena* 13 (1924): 26–32.

7. *Tekhnika i zhizn'* 16 (1924): 6–7, 14–15.

8. N. A. Rynin, "Polety budushchego," *Ogonek* 11, 10 June 1923, 15.

9. A. Belloni, "Della migliore arma," *Rivista marittima* (October 1921): 331–49. Col. G. A. Crocco, "Sulla possibilità della navigazione extra-atmosferica," in *Atti dell'Associazione Italiana di Aerotecnica* 3, no. 4 (1923): 258–61; and Crocco, "Possibilità di superaviazione," *Atti della Reale Accademia dei Lincei* (Rendiconti delle Seduta) 3, no. 5 (March 1926): 241–47. For Soviet appreciations of Crocco, see *Vestnik vozdushnogo flota* 10 (October 1927): 36–38; and *Vestnik znaniia* 23–24 (1928): 1109.

10. Oswald Spengler, *The Decline of the West*, edited and translated by Charles Francis Atkinson, 2 vols. (New York: Knopf, 1926–28), 2:502 (originally published in German in 1918–23). See *Rivista aeronáutica* 8 (August 1926): 67–71; and 12 (December 1926): 98.

11. See the picture in *Scientific American* (July 1926): 16, later reproduced in a variety of sources: *Die Umschau* 29, no. 23, 4 June 1927, 465; 34, no. 42, 18 October 1930, 846; 36, no. 27, 2 July 1932, 531; *Modern Mechanix* (November 1928): 52–53; *New York Times*, 10 June 1928, 125; *Science and Mechanics* (November 1931): 649; and *Nauka i tekhnika* 27–28 (1931): 17.

12. Abbé Théophile Moreux, "Pourra-t-on bientôt bombarder la lune?" in *Les énigmes de la science*, 2 vols. (Paris: Doin, 1926), 2:120, 128.

13. Palmer, *Dictatorship of the Air*, 79–102. See *Aero* 3 (March 1923): 27–28; and 5 (May 1923): 75; *Ekho* 11 (1 May 1923): 26–27. On the secret Weimar-Soviet collaboration in aviation, chemical weapon, and tank technologies, see Sally Stoecker, *Forging Stalin's Army* (Boulder: Westview, 1998), 78–97.

14. N. I. Mironets, *Revoliutsionnaia poeziia oktiabria* (Kiev: Kievskii universitet, 1988), 110. The song, written by Pavel German and Yuly Khait, was renamed "Ever Higher" during the 1930s and chosen as the official anthem of the Soviet Air Force.

15. The English version is in *Mass Culture in Soviet Russia*, edited by Richard Stites and James von Geldern (Bloomington: Indiana University Press, 1995), 257.

16. From his poem "We Go" (*My idem*, 1914), cited in Mark D. Steinberg, *Proletarian Imagination* (Ithaca: Cornell University Press, 2002), 243.

17. S. A. Obradovich, "Polety ran'she i teper'" (1923), 340, and V. T. Kirillov, "Letchik" (1923), 253, both in Papernyi, *Proletarskie poety*.

18. "Shturm Neba," 7 June 1923, in Valerii Briusov, *Sobranie sochinenii*, 7 vols. (Moscow: Khudozhestvennaia literatura, 1974), 3:168.

19. Robert H. Goddard, *A Method of Reaching Extreme Altitudes*, in *Smithsonian Miscellaneous Collections* 71, no. 2 (Washington DC: Smithsonian Institution, 1919), 5.

20. Goddard, *Method of Reaching Extreme Altitudes*, 54–57.

21. For examples of Smithsonian publications along these lines, see William Jones Rhees, *List of Publications of the Smithsonian Institution, 1846–1903* (Washington DC: Smithsonian Institution, 1903).

22. Charles G. Abbot, "The Habitability of Venus, Mars, and Other Worlds," *Smithsonian Annual Report* (Washington DC: GPO, 1920), 165–71.

23. See the *New York Times*, 12 January 1920, 1; and *Monthly Evening Sky Map* 14, no. 158 (February 1920). For discussion of Goddard as media sensation, see David A. Clary, *Rocket Man* (New York: Hyperion, 2003), chap. 5; and Frank H. Winter, "The Misunderstood Professor," *Air and Space Magazine* (April–May 2008): 56–59.

24. See the excerpts from "The Last Migration," 14 January 1918, and "The Ultimate in Jet Propulsion" (1943), in Goddard and Pendray, *Papers of Robert H. Goddard*, 3:1611–12; and for Goddard's spiritualist tendencies, see 1:328 and 2:575.

25. H. Greensback, "Flying in Space," *Science and Invention* 8, no. 12 (April 1921): 1290. Quoted from the cartoon in Winter, "Misunderstood Professor," 59.

26. Georges Houard, "L'exploration scientifique de la haute atmosphère," *La science et la vie* 19, no. 54 (December 1920–January 1921): 100; and Houard, "De la terre a la lune," *Je sais tout* 174, 15 June 1920, 654–57.

27. See the essay "Les considérations sur les résultats d'un allégement indéfini des moteurs," in Robert Esnault-Pelterie, *Notice sur les travaux scientifiques de M. Robert Esnault-Pelterie* (Paris: Gauthier-Villars, 1918). The story is in Miral-Viger, *L'anneau de feu* (Paris: Hachette, 1922).

28. F. A. Tsander, *From a Scientific Heritage* (Washington DC: NASA, 1969). Tsander had been working on the topic of human spaceflight since 1908.

29. The quote is from a conversation between Tsander and Chizhevskii just a few days after Tsander's meeting with Lenin, in Chizhevskii, *Na beregu vselennoi*, 311. The conference was held between 29 December 1920 and 2 January of 1921. Iaroslav Golovanov, *Marsianin* (Moscow: Molodaia gvardiia, 1985), argues that Tsander only imagined the meeting with Lenin.

30. V. I. Lenin, "Zakliuchitel'noe slovo" (1922), in *Polnoe sobranie sochinenii*, 55 vols. (Moscow: Izd. politicheskoi literatury, 1970), 45:125.

31. Aleksandr Belenson, "Selenity i my," *Zhizn' iskusstva* 581, 13 October 1920, 1; H. G. Wells, *Russia in the Shadows* (London: Hodder & Houghton, 1920), 123.

32. "Puteshestvie na Mars," *V masterskoi prirody* 4 (1923): 76; K. L. Baev, "Puteshestvie na lunu," *Molodaia gvardiia* 4–5 (1923): 189–95. Iakov Perel'man called Goddard nothing more than a news sensation, in the correspondence from Perel'man to Tsiolkovskii, 18 September 1924, ARAN, f. 555, o. 4, d. 482, l. 29.

33. A. S. Irison, "Vozdushnyi okean," *Molodaia gvardiia* 4–5 (1923): 170–79. See also V. L. Aleksandrov, "Zavoevanie vozdukha," in *Uspekhi i dostizheniia sovremennoi nauki i tekhniki*, edited by M. Ia. Lapirov-Skoblo and A. E. Fersman (Moscow: Rabotnik prosveshcheniia, 1926), 257.

34. Cited from Chizhevskii, *Na beregu vselennoi*, 290–95; A. L. Chizhevskii, *Vsia zhizn'* (Moscow: Sovetskaia rossiia), 95–99; and the report "Biuro po izucheniiu reaktivnykh dvigatelei (1923 g.)," ARAN, f. 1703, o. 1, d. 238, ll. 1–6.

35. Hermann Oberth, *Die Rakete zu den Planetenraumen* (Munich: Oldenbourg, 1925), 18, 24, 29–31, 83–84, 92.

36. See "My Contributions to Astronautics," in Durant and James, *First Steps toward Space*, 132.

37. See *Die Umschau* 28, no. 5, 2 February 1924, 71–75; and 28, no. 8, 23 February 1924, 128; and *Zeitschrift für den Physikalischen und Chemischen Unterricht* 1 (1924): 65. These disputes were discussed in *Izvestiia* 223, 2 October 1923, 4; and 90, 18 April 1924, 7. The quote is from B. M. Lobach-Zhuchenko, *Razvitie aviatsionnykh dvigatelei* (Moscow: Voennyi vestnik, 1924), 188.

38. See *Die Himmelswelt* 9, no. 12 (December 1923): 107–12; and the early popularization of Oberth's ideas in Willy Ley, *Die Fahrt ins Weltall* (Leipzig: Hachmeister & Thal 1926).

39. See H. Lorenz's articles in *Zeitschrift der Vereines Deutsches Ingeniure* 71, no. 19, 7 May 1927, 651–54; and in *Jahrbuch der Wissenschaftlichen Gesellschaft für Luftfahrt* (1928): 53–60.

40. L. Gussalli, *Si puo gia tentare un viaggio dalla terra alla luna?* (Milan: Societa Editrice Libraria, 1923), 53 (translated by Michael L. Ciancone as Luigi Gussalli, "Is It

Now Possible to Attempt a Voyage from the Earth to the Moon?" *Quest* 4, no. 1 [1995]: 30–34). *Zeitschrift für Flugtechnik und Motorluftschiffart* 14, nos. 17–22, 21 November 1923, 162, reviewed Gusalli as the "strange work" of an "imaginative inventor."

41. S. B., "Rockets to Reach Planetary Space," *Nature*, 23 August 1925, 270.

42. See N. Rynin's articles in *Izvestiia* 237, 17 October 1923, 2; and *Ogonek* 11, 10 June 1923, 15. "Raketa k planetam," *V masterskoi prirody* 7 (1923): 61–62.

43. A. P. Modestov, "Izobretenie K. E. Tsiolkovskogo," *Izvestiia* 243, 24 October 1923, 7. See also Ia. I. Perel'man, "Polety v mirovoe prostrantsvo," *V masterkoi prirody* 3 (1924): 1–8.

44. See Perel'man's letter to Tsiolkovskii, 18 February 1926, ARAN, f. 555, o. 4, d. 482, l. 33; Rynin's proposal in ARAN, f. 928, o. 1, d. 124a; and Riumin's letters to Tsiolkovskii, 23 April 1924, 30 May 1925, and 7 February 1926, ARAN, f. 555, o. 4, d. 549, ll. 2, 6, 19.

45. Tsiolkovskii's letter to the Society for the Study of Interplanetary Travel, 30 May 1924, ARAN, r. 4, o. 14, d. 195, l. 6; Tsiolkovskii letter to Perel'man, 17 July 1924, ARAN, f. 555, o. 4, d. 20, l. 7.

46. K. E. Tsiolkovskii, *Raketa v kosmicheskoe prostranstve* (Kaluga: Gostip., 1924), with Chizhevskii's preface and the book's title as *Eine Rakete in den Kosmischen Raume*. Tsiolkovskii's picture is reproduced in Vladimir Lytkin, "Tsiolkovskii's Inspiration," *Ad Astra* (November–December 1998): 35–37. It also appeared in *Die Rakete*, 15 January 1928, 12. Tsiolkovskii's term *cosmic space* (*kosmische raum*) now became a mainstay of the new idiom of rocketry; see, e.g., *Zeitschrift für Flug und Motorluft* 2, no. 21, 28 January 1930, 47; 12, no. 21, 28 June 1930, 310; 20, no. 22, 28 October 1931, 604.

47. See the Oberth letter to Tsiolkovskii, reprinted in B. N. Vorob'ev, "K. E. Tsiolkovskii i sovetskaia vlast'," in Islent'ev, *K. E. Tsiolkovskii*, 101. Also note the sympathetic exchange of letters, in the fall of 1929, between Oberth and Tsiolkovskii in ARAN, f. 555, o. 4, d. 457, ll. 2–4. The Oberth quote is from *Die Rakete zu den Planetenraumen*, 295.

48. Mary Proctor, *Romance of the Moon* (New York: Harper, 1928), 161.

49. Max Valier, *Der Vorstoss in den Weltraumen* (Munich: Oldenbourg, 1924–27), 4 editions. See Ilse Essers, *Max Valier* (Washington DC: NASA, 1976), 81, 119.

50. The terms *raumschiff* and *raketenmaschin* are both from Valier, *Der Vorstoss*. See also Max Valier, "Einwände gegen die Möglichkeit der Weltraumfahrt," *Die Rakete*, 15 August 1927, 109.

51. See the front cover of Valier, *Der Vorstoss*, which was subtitled a "Scientific-Popular Review," and 7, 44, 52. Max Valier, *Die Raketenfahrt* (1929; repr., Munich: Oldenbourg, 1930), 6–7, 20–21. See also Otto Willi Gail, *Mit Raketenkraft ins Weltenall* (Stuttgart: Thienemanns, 1928), 33–37, 71–72, 78 (with an arrow pointing to infinity, humanity's "cosmic route," or *kosmische bahn*, for free flight by piloted rocket).

52. Quoted from Walter Hohmann, *Die Erreichbarkeit der Himmelskörper* (Munich: Oldenbourg, 1925), 63, 77, 80. On Cook and related explorers, see Andrea Wulf, *Chasing Venus* (New York: Knopf, 2012).

53. On Valier's 29 April 1927 lecture, publicizing the scientific work of Oberth and Hohmann, see G. Manigold, "Der Vorstoss in den Weltenraum," *Zeitschrift für Flug und Motorluft* 11, no. 18, 14 June 1927, 249–50.

54. For more on Von Hoefft's proposals, see Willy Ley, ed., *Die Möglichkeit der Weltraumfahrt* (Leipzig: Hachmeister & Thal, 1928), 153–76, 240–83; Werner Brügel, ed., *Männer der Rakete* (Leipzig: Hachmeister & Thal, 1933), 33–41; and Guido von Pirquet, "Kann der Mensch die Erde Verlassen?" *Reichspost* 35, no. 1 (Vienna), 1 January 1928, 18.

55. From Guido von Pirquet, "Fahrtrouten," in *Die Rakete*, 15 May 1928, 67–74, with supplements in the January 1929 issue; and his essay "Die ungangbaren Wege zur Realisierung der Weltraumschiffahrt," in Ley, *Die Möglichkeit*, 284–328. On Pirquet's life, and for fascinating pictures of his various charts, see Brügel, *Männer der Rakete*, 57–78.

56. The terms are quoted from Hermann Noordung, *Das Problem der Befahrung des Weltraums* (Berlin: Schmidt, 1928), 11, 34, 94, 96, 174, based on the translation *The Problem of Space Travel*, edited by Ernst Stuhlinger et al. (Washington DC: NASA, 1995). "Hermann Noordung" was the pen name of Herman Potočnik.

57. Quoted from Noordung, *Das Problem der Befahrung des Weltraums*, 183.

58. V. A. Semenov, "Pochetnyi professor," in *Tsiolkovskii v vospominaniiakh sovremennikov*, edited by V. S. Zotov (Tula: Priokskoe izd., 1971), 76–77. On Tsiolkovskii's 23 August lecture, devoted to his work on the all-metal dirigible (with drafts and models), see "Proekt metalliticheskogo dirizhablia Tsiolkovskogo," *Aero* 9 (1923): 178.

59. For the photograph (from the front cover of *Nauka i zhizhn'*) and picture, see N. A. Rynin, *Dreams, Legends, and Early Fantasies* (Jerusalem: Scientific Translations, 1970), 18–19. Memoirs of V. P. Kaperskii, 25 November 1963, ARAN, r. 4, o. 14, d. 197, ll. 32–46; and the letter of M. A. Rezunov to K. E. Veigelin, 30 July 1924, in d. 195, l. 13. Rynin came from Leningrad to attend joint meetings of the study group.

60. Memoirs of M. A. Rezunov, 19 February 1961, ARAN, r. 4, o. 14, d. 197, ll. 16–21.

61. Both M. A. Rezunov and M. G. Leiteizen advanced to the second course of study by the fall of 1924, but Leiteizen advanced "with issues." From the academic report of 1 October 1926, in Rossiiskii Gosudarstvennyi Voennyi Arkhiv (RGVA), f. 24699, o. 1, d. 222, l. 799. The record shows that their classmate I. T. Kleimenov, a future administrator of rocketry research, also passed. See the memoir of V. P. Kaperskii, 25 November 1963, ARAN, r. 4, o. 14, d. 197, ll. 43–46.

62. *Tekhnika i snabzhenie krasnoi armii* 159 (1924): 14–17; and *Voina i tekhnika* 234–35 (1925): 49–51.

63. The official title of the group was "Obshchestvo izucheniia mezhplanetnykh soobshchenii" (OIMS). I have translated *soobshchenii* as "travel" rather than "communications" to reflect the group's new rocket priorities.

64. Chizhevskii's personal letters to Tsiolkovskii, 15 July 1924, 24 June 1925, and 14 October 1925, ARAN, f. 555, o. 4, d. 689, ll. 11–12, 17, 18; P. A. Rymkevich, "Zavoevanie vozdukha," *Iunyi proletarii* 1 (January 1924): 38–43. For the context, see G. M. Kramarov, *Na zare kosmonavtiki* (Moscow: Znanie, 1965); *Tekhnika i zhizn'*

12 (1924): 1; and *Iskra* 8 (August 1924): 35. Siddiqi, *Red Rockets' Glare*, 74–113, also offers a full historical survey.

65. The memoir of V. P. Kaperskii, 25 November 1963, ARAN, r. 4, o. 14, d. 197, ll. 32–46; and the list of books and sources in d. 196, ll. 106–36.

66. K. L. Baev, *Mars i zhizhn' na nem* (Moscow: Novyi mir, 1924), 92–102.

67. V. Chernov's comments, 2 July 1924, ARAN, r. 4, o. 14, d. 194, ll. 1–3; the translation of Goddard, "The High Altitude Rocket," *Monthly Weather Review* 52 (February 1924): 105–6, is at d. 194, ll. 44–48; and the letter is dated 16 August 1924, at d. 195, l. 16.

68. V. I. Lenin, "Nashe vneshnee i vnutrennee polozhenie i zadachi partii" (1920), in *Polnoe sobranie sochinenii*, 55 vols. (Moscow: Izd. politicheskoi literatury, 1969), 42:30; I. V. Stalin, "Ob osnovakh Leninizma" (1924), *Sochineniia*, 13 vols. (Moscow: Gosizdat, 1947), 6:186–87.

69. Stalin, *Sochineniia*, 13:39–42 (from a speech first published in *Pravda* on 5 February 1931). I. Vinogradov, "Sovremennoe razvitie aviatekhniki i ee dostizheniia," *Vsemirnaia illiustratsiia* 3–4 (1924): 9, which discusses Goddard's expected launch to the moon on 4 July 1924. Inzh. K. Akashev, "Zhupeli aviopromyshlennosti," *Izvestiia* 91, 19 April 1924, 2.

70. A. Voronskii, "Polemicheskie zametki," *Krasnaia nov'* 3 (1924): 320.

71. N. A. Rynin, *Puteshestvie po severo-amerikanskim soedinennym shtatam* (St. Petersburg: Sobranie inzhenerov, 1906); M. Ia. Lapirov-Skoblo, "Amerika i ee tekhnika," *Nauchnoe slovo* 1 (1928): 76–110.

72. M. Ia. Lapirov-Skoblo, "Puteshestviia v mezhplanetnye prostranstva," *Pravda* 86, 15 April 1924, 6; and Lapirov-Skoblo, "O puteshestviiakh v mezhplanetnye prostranstva," *Molodaia gvardiia* 5 (1924): 75–86, 93–95, which includes several drawings of the Tsiolkovskii, Goddard, and Oberth rockets. From my own review, the next such graphic of the human-made parabola to outer space appeared in *Die Rakete*, the journal of the German Society for Space Travel, 15 September 1927, 115; then in Hermann Noordung, *Das Problem der Befahrung des Weltraums* (Berlin: Schmidt, 1928), 37; and even as late as Eric Burgess, *Rocket Propulsion* (London: Chapman, 1954), 169.

73. Kramarov, *Na zare kosmonavtiki*, 24–25. See also Kramarov's memoir of 1 February 1961, ARAN, r. 4, o. 14, d. 197, ll. 1–15; and the memoir of V. P. Kaperskii, 25 November 1963, at ll. 32–46. Lapirov-Skoblo plagiarized a number of facts and insights from F. Gregory Hartswick, "A Rocket to the Moon," *Popular Science Monthly* (April 1924): 31–32.

74. Tsander, *From a Scientific Heritage*, 41–43; and the poster in ARAN, r. 4, o. 14, d. 4, l. 32; f. 573, o. 1, d. 60, l. 8. See also the lecture summaries (1924) in ARAN, r. 4, o. 14, d. 4, ll. 31–32. Tsander published these plans in F. A. Tsander, "Perelet na drugie planety," *Tekhnika i zhizn'* 13 (1924): 15–16; and *Problema poleta pri pomoshchi reaktivnykh apparatov* (Moscow: ONTI, 1932).

75. These ideas and terms are in a variety of sources, from which I have quoted: *V masterskoi prirody* 3 (1924): 1–8; 5 (1925): 45; and 5 (1927): 10; *Iskra* 8 (August 1924):

10–13; *Vestnik znaniia* 8 (1925): 581; and *Iunyi proletarii* 7 (April 1925): 25; 1 (January 1926): 28–29; and 14 (July 1926): 19–20.

76. From "Vystrel v lunu," *Vsemirnyi sledopyt* 4 (1926): 76. This was actually Esnault-Pelterie's somersault, first published in A. Berget, "Peut-on aller aux planètes?" *Je sais tout*, 15 October 1925, 463–64.

77. F. A. Tsander's scientific plan, 15 July 1924, ARAN, f. 573, 0.3, d. 26; and the Society for the Study of Interplanetary Travel charter, 19 June–29 November 1924, ARAN, r. 4, 0. 14, d. 4, ll. 35–48. The memoir of V. I. Prianishnikov, March 1961, ARAN, r. 4, 0. 14, d. 197, ll. 22–29.

78. The memoir of V. P. Kaperskii, 25 November 1963, ARAN, r. 4, 0. 14, d. 197, ll. 43–46.

79. On Tsiolkovskii's dirigible, see air force scientific notes, 5 November 1924–30 August 1925, RGVA, f. 29, 0. 13, d. 614(1), ll. 40–42; and State Planning Commission minutes, 16 June 1925, d. 31(1), ll. 62–63. A favorable report on it is in the "Aviakhim" report, June 1925–December 1926, Gosudarstvennyi Arkhiv Rossiiskoi Federatsii (GARF), f. 9404, 0. 1, d. 23, l. 14. For accounts of opposition to Tsiolkovskii, see Chizhevskii, *Na beregu vselennoi*, 168–76, 316, 479, 566, 583, 596–99.

80. For pictures and discussions of the "rocket dirigible" and "interplanetary dirigible," see Baev, *Mars i zhizn' na nem*, 90–92; K. E. Tsiolkovskii, "Moia gordost'," *Komsomolskaia pravda* 259, 7 November 1934, 6; G. V. Averbukh, "Pioner v oblasti zavoevaniia kosmosa," *Nauka i zhizn'* 11 (1935): 54–55; and B. N. Vorob'ev, *Tsiolkovskii* (Moscow: Molodaia gvardiia, 1940), 171.

81. Communication by aviation students to Communist Party authorities (1924), Rossiisskaia Gosudarstvennaia Arkhiv Sotsial'no i Politicheskoi Istorii (RGASPI), f. 17, 0. 1, d. 9, l. 51. Vasilii Dekabr'skoi, "Il'ich," *Aerostat* ODVF 3 (March 1925): 10.

6. Rocket Spaceships as Science Fictions

1. My thanks to David Goldfrank (Georgetown University) for reading and commenting on a draft of this chapter. K. E. Tsiolkovskii, *Vne zemli*, edited by B. N. Vorob'ev (Moscow: Akademiia nauk, 1958); and Konstantin Tsiolkovsky, *Beyond the Planet Earth*, translated by Kenneth Syers (New York: Pergamon Press, 1960), 19, 24. He began the story in 1897 and finished it in 1917; and published parts of it in *Priroda i liudi*, nos. 2–11 (1918) and the whole story in 1920. See Anton Pervushin, *Kosmonavty Stalina* (Moscow: EKSMO, 2005), 248–49.

2. Lev Kassil', in Islent'ev, *K. E. Tsiolkovskii*, 170. As noted in Siddiqi, *Red Rockets' Glare*, 50, Tsiolkovskii was arrested, imprisoned, and interrogated by the Bolshevik secret police (*Cheka*) in November 1919, then released.

3. For the fuller range of discussion on this new race of beings, see "On the Moon," 37, 21, and "Dreams of Earth and Sky," 143–45, both in Tsiolkovsky, *Call of the Cosmos*. See also "Investigation of World Spaces by Reactive Vehicles (1911–1912)," in Tsiolkovsky, *Selected Works*, 83–84, 110–17, 124–25; and the correspondence with Ia. I. Perel'man, letter of 25 May 1921, ARAN, f. 555, 0. 4, d. 20, l. 28.

4. Eugene Zamiatin, *We*, translated by Gregory Zilboorg (1924; repr., New York: Dutton, 1952); Christopher Collins, *Evgenij Zamjatin* (The Hague: Mouton, 1973), 42; Kathleen Lewis and Harry Weber, "Zamyatin's *We*, the Proletarian Poets, and Bogdanov's *Red Star*," *Russian Literature Tri-Quarterly* 12 (1975): 252–78.

5. Zamiatin, *We*, 78–79, 141; Edward J. Brown, *Russian Literature since the Revolution* (Cambridge: Harvard University Press, 1982), 54.

6. Zamiatin, *We*, 162, 174. M. N. Zolotonosov, *Slovo i telo* (Moscow: Ladomir, 1999), 741, offers a similar reading.

7. Zamiatin, *We*, 79; Collins, *Evgenij Zamjatin*, 61, 64, 76.

8. Zamiatin, *We*, 85, 88, 98, 109, 127, 206.

9. Zamiatin, *We*, 184–85.

10. "Alexander Blok" (1924), in Zamyatin, *Soviet Heretic*, 205–6.

11. "Tomorrow" (1919–20), in Zamyatin, *Soviet Heretic*, 51.

12. A. Voronskii, "Literaturnye siluety," *Krasnaia nov'* 6 (November–December 1922): 318.

13. Aleksei N. Tolstoi, *Aelita* (Berlin: Ladyzhnikov, 1923); first published as "Aelita (Zakat marsa)," beginning with *Krasnaia nov'* 6 (1923) and 1–2 (1924). I have cited here from Alexei N. Tolstoy, *Aelita*, translated by Antonina W. Bouis (New York: Macmillan, 1981).

14. See V. Dynnik, "Tretii Aleksei Tolstoi," *Krasnaia nov'* 2 (February 1926): 218.

15. Tolstoy, *Aelita*, 2–3, 5–6, 24.

16. See *Krasnaia nov'* 2 (March–April 1922): 196–241; and 3 (May 1922): 182–97.

17. Quoted from Spengler, *Decline of the West*, 1:331, 380, 386.

18. Spengler, *Decline of the West*, 2:501–5.

19. Tolstoy, *Aelita*, 45, 98.

20. See Phyllis Young Forsyth, *Atlantis* (Montreal: McGill-Queen's University Press, 1980), 184–85.

21. Burroughs published eleven books in all between 1917 and 1948, read by millions. From my survey the first books of the series (up to 1922) were published in Russian translation.

22. Edgar Rice Burroughs, *A Princess of Mars* (1917; repr., New York: Penguin Books, 2007), 186; Tolstoy, *Aelita*, 88, 16, 167.

23. See Richard Lupoff, *Edgar Rice Burroughs* (New York: Ace Books, 1968), 55–59; and John Seelye, intro., Burroughs, *Princess of Mars*, xix.

24. Gustave Le Rouge's two volumes: *Le Prisonnier de la planète Mars* and *La Guerre des vampires* (Paris: Albert Méricant, 1909).

25. Tolstoy, *Aelita*, 12.

26. D. C. Wilkerson, "Is Radio Earthbound?" *Radio News* 6 (March 1925): 1629.

27. On the rumors and craze, including discussion of the Tsiolkovskii rocket, see S. Vysotskii, "Velikoe protivostoianie Marsa," *Iunyi proletarii* 6 (May 1924): 28; K. L. Baev, *Mars i zhizhn' na nem* (Moscow: Novyi mir, 1924), 90; and "Kak dat' znat' o sebe drugim miram," *Mir prikliuchenii* 2 (1925): 1.

28. Sophus Michaelis (aka August Berthel), *Himmelskibet* (Copenhagen: Gyl-

dendal, 1921) (published in Russian in 1927). I have quoted from the titles of the film version, *Himmelskibet*, directed by Holger-Madsen (1918; Copenhagen: Fotorama and UFA productions), released in the USSR as *Puteshestvie na Mars* and in the United States as *A Trip to Mars*.

29. J. H. Rosny, *Les navigateurs de l'infini* (Paris: Fayard, 1925). A translation of the novel circulated in Russia between 1927 and 1930. Rosny also wrote a sequel, *Les astronautes* (1925), which remained unpublished until 1960.

30. Cecil B. White, "The Retreat to Mars," *Amazing Stories* 2, no. 5 (August 1927): 460–68. See also Walter Vollmer, *Flug in die Sterne* (Minden: Köhler, 1929); and Peter S. Fisher, *Fantasy and Politics* (Madison: University of Wisconsin Press, 1991), 104–6.

31. "Radios to Mars," *Monthly Evening Sky Map* 23, no. 265 (January 1929): 1. The initial versions of this story were reported in the Russian magazines *Ogonek* and *Shkval* (1926).

32. Quoted from Boris Anibal's review in *Novyi mir* 10 (October 1925): 153. See Richard Stites, "Fantasy and Revolution," in Bogdanov, *Red Star*, 1, 13–15; and a short story by Sven, "Na mars," *Baraban* 2 (April 1923): 2–4, featuring two Bogdanov "Pioneers" flying to Mars and Venus.

33. Ian Christie, "Down to Earth: *Aelita* Relocated," in *Inside the Film Factory*, edited by Richard Taylor and Ian Christie (London: Routledge, 1991), 82–87.

34. The citation is from Boris Chertok, *Rakety i liudi* (Moscow: Mashinostroenie, 1994), 36. He saw the movie at the elite "Ars" cinema house on Tverskaia Boulevard in central Moscow.

35. *Aelita na zemle: Kino-roman*, no. 1 (Moscow: Proletarskii svetoch, 1924), 8; a total of eight numbered issues were planned, but only one was ever published.

36. *Mezhplanetnaia revoliutsiia*, directed by Z. Komissarenko, Iu. Merkulov, and N. Khodataev (1924; Moscow: State Film College). For more on the film and the wider context, see Cathleen S. Lewis, "The Red Stuff: A History of the Public and Material Culture of Early Human Spaceflight in the U.S.S.R." (PhD diss., George Washington University, 2008).

37. L. Kalinin, *Peregovory s marsom* (Moscow: Gublit., 1924), 28.

38. G. Arel'skii, *Povesti o marse* (Leningrad: Gosizdat, 1925). "Graal' Arel'skii" was the pseudonym of the poet Stepan S. Petrov. M. V. Volkov, "Bairo-Tun," *Vsemirnyi sledopyt* 2 (1929): 94–112.

39. Bruno Bürgel, *Der Stern von Afrika* (Berlin: Bruno Hans, 1921) (translated as Bruno H. Burgel, "The Cosmic Cloud," *Wonder Science Quarterly* 3, no. 1 [Fall 1931]: 7–75; and B. Biurgel', *Raketoi na lunu* [Moscow: Frenkel', 1925]).

40. Otto Willi Gail, *Der Schuss ins All* (Breslau: Bergstadtverl, 1925); and *Der Stern vom Mond* (Breslau: Bergstadtverl, 1926).

41. Walter Hirsch, "American Science Fiction, 1926–1950: A Content Analysis" (PhD diss., Northwestern University, 1957), 19–26, 48–53.

42. On the "Goddard rocket," see *Amazing Stories* 2, no. 5 (August 1927): 460; 3, no. 7 (October 1928): 581; 4, no. 4 (July 1929): 374; 4, no. 8 (November 1929): 677;

and in Jack Williamson and Miles J. Breuer, *The Girl from Mars* (New York: Stellar, 1929); John W. Campbell, "Solarite," *Amazing Stories* 5, no. 8 (November 1930): 706–37; and Jack Williamson, "The Lady of Light," *Amazing Stories* 7, no. 6 (September 1932). Besides many *Amazing Stories* covers, see those of *Amazing Stories Quarterly* 1, no. 2 (Spring 1928); and 4, no. 3 (Summer 1931); *Science Wonder Quarterly* (Fall 1929); and *Science and Invention* 11 (November 1930).

43. J. M. Walsh, *Vandals of the Void* (1931; repr., Westport CT: Hyperion, 1970), 90, 160; J. Lewis Burtt, "The Lemurian Documents," *Amazing Stories* 7, no. 6 (September 1932): 525–28.

44. See the script "Chast' pervaia," ARAN, r. 4, o. 14, d. 194, ll. 118–19.

45. N. I. Miur, "Shest' mesiatsev," *V masterskoi prirody* 3 (1926): 40–41; G. Arel'skii, "Podarok selenitov," *Mir prikliuchenii* 5 (1926): 1.

46. Volkov, "Bairo-Tun," 94–112.

47. M. Zoshchenko and N. Radlov, *Veselye proekty* (Leningrad: Krasnaia gazeta, 1928), 7.

48. From a Mandelshtam poem (1914–27), in *The Complete Poetry of Osip Emilevich Mandelshtam*, translated by Burton Raffel and Alla Burago (Albany: State University of New York, 1973), 66–67. The satire is in D. Pankov, "Po planetam," *Mir prikliuchenii* 5 (1928): 49–56.

49. Inzh. A. Platonov, "Lunnaia bomba," *Vsemirnyi sledopyt* 12 (1926): 3–12. The craft was launched into space by a huge land-based, super-fast revolving wheel.

50. Innokenty Zhukov, "Voyage of the Red Star Pioneer Troop to Wonderland" (1924), in Stites and von Geldern, *Mass Culture in Soviet Russia*, 90–112.

51. S. L. Grave, *Puteshestvie na lunu* (Leningrad: Priboi, 1926); Valerii Iazvitskii, *Puteshestvie na lunu i mars* (Moscow: Gosizdat, 1928).

52. The first academic interpretations in Russia were those in the journal *Uspekhi fizicheskikh nauk* (1922).

53. S. M. Tokmachev, "Sovremennaia aviatsiia," *Chelovek i priroda* 4–5 (1923): 72; Charles A. Lindbergh, *Autobiography of Values*, edited by William Jovanovich and Judith Schiff (New York: Harcourt, 1977), 259–60.

54. Quoted from the interview in Alexander Moszkowski, *Einstein the Searcher*, translated by Henry L. Brose (London: Methuen, 1921), 116–17. Twenty years later one of Einstein's popularizers made the same point, in Hans Reichenbach, *From Copernicus to Newton* (New York: Philosophical Library, 1942), 62–63.

55. Paul Langevin, "L'évolution de l'espace et du temps," *Scientia* 10 (1911): 47–51. For context, see T. E. Gnedina, *Pol' Lanzhevin* (Moscow: Nauka, 1991), 124–29.

56. Marcel Boll, "Utopies d'hier, possibilités d'aujord'hui, réalisations de demain," *La science et la vie* 30, no. 114 (December 1926): 511–13; A. E. Fersman, "Zavoevaniia nauk," *Nauka i tekhnika* 1 (1922): 6; Fersman, *Vremia* (Petrograd: Vremia, 1922), 67–71.

57. Charles Lane Poor, *Gravitation versus Relativity* (New York: Putnam, 1922), 35; A. Eddington, *Space, Time and Gravitation* (Cambridge: Cambridge University Press, 1920), 26, 65–66, 201. See also Charles Nordmann, *Einstein and the Universe*, translated by Joseph McCabe (New York: Holt, 1922), 137–44.

58. "Trip to Moon on Light Rays Prophesied by Piccard," *Monthly Evening Sky Map* 28, no. 330 (June 1934): 1; and 28, no. 333 (September 1934): 1. The Stalin story is told in Budu Svanidze, *My Uncle Joseph Stalin*, translated by Waverly Root (New York: Putnam, 1953). Douglas R. Weiner, *Models of Nature* (Pittsburgh: University of Pittsburgh Press, 2000), 234–35.

59. Quoted from "Literature, Revolution, Entropy" (1923); and from "The New Russian Prose" (1923), both in Zamyatin, *Soviet Heretic*, 111, 105.

60. G. A. Crocco, "Sulla possibilità della navigazione extra-atmosferica," *Atti dell'Associazione Italiana di Aerotecnica* 3, no. 4 (1923): 258–61.

61. Tsander, *From a Scientific Heritage*, 43 (from a 1925 report).

62. The quotes are from the titles of the film *The Einstein Theory of Relativity*, directed by Max and David Fleischer (1923; n.p.: Premier Productions); and Garrett P. Serviss, *The Einstein Theory of Relativity* (New York: Fadman, 1923), 11–20.

63. Engineer A. V. Egorov, "Poplyli v vozdukhe! Poplyvem v efire?" *Vsemirnaia illiustratsiia* 11 (July 1923): 120–22.

64. Quoted from a conversation with Albert Einstein, in a letter from A. Shershevskii to K. E. Tsiolkovskii, 25 June 1927, ARAN, f. 555, o. 4, d. 698, l. 46.

65. V. N. Muraviev, *Ovladenie vremenem* (1924; repr., Moscow: Rosspen, 1998), 3–21, 95–96. For more, see Michael Hagermeister, *Nikolaj Fedorov* (Munich: Sagner, 1989), 318–41; and Young, *Russian Cosmists*, 209–14.

66. *Wunder der Schöpfung*, directed by Hanns Walter Kornblum (1925; Berlin: Colonna Films), and was released in the United States as *In the World of the Stars* and *Our Heavenly Bodies*. I have not found evidence that the film was shown in the USSR, likely because of its biblical quotes (even though the film was critical of the Roman Catholic Church).

67. A. Iaroslavskii, *Argonavty vselennoi* (Moscow: Biokosmist, 1926), 25, 62, 83–100, 123–25, 160–66. Other such tales, in the manner of Gail's fiction, boldly addressed the mystical and spiritual, as, e.g., V. Goncharov's, *Psikho-mashina* and *Mezhplanetnyi puteshestvennik* (Moscow: Molodaia gvardiia, 1924).

7. The Origins and Ends of Life on Earth

1. Alphonse Berget, "The Appearance of Life on Worlds and the Hypothesis of Arrhenius," *Smithsonian Annual Report* (1913), 543–51; *Popular Science Monthly* (November 1922): 40–41.

2. V. I. Vernadskii, *Nachalo i vechnost' zhizni* (Petrograd: Vremia, 1922), 33–34; S. P. Kostychev, *O poiavlenii zhizni na zemle* (Berlin: Gosizdat, 1921). See also P. N. Lebedev et al., *Davlenie sveta* (Moscow: Gosizdat, 1922).

3. F. Davydov, "Mezhplanetye polety," *Ekho* 14 (1923): 27.

4. "Proiskhozhdenie vselennoi," *Iunyi proletarii* 7, 1 April 1919, 10–11; Kornei Chukovsky, *Diary: 1901–1969*, edited by Victor Erlich and translated by M. H. Heim (New Haven: Yale University Press, 2005), 62.

5. Khlebnikov, *Collected Works of Velemir Khlebnikov*, 1:438–39; A. V. Nemilov, *Kak poiavilas' na zemle zhizn'* (Leningrad: Obrazovanie, 1924), 52–53, 64–65.

6. J. W. Gregory, *The Making of the Earth* (New York: Holt, 1912), 216–42. For similar approaches, see Félix A. Le Dantec and Robert K. Duncan, *The Nature and Origin of Life* (New York: Barnes, 1906); and E. A. Schäfer, "Life: Its Nature, Origin, and Maintenance," *Smithsonian Annual Report* (1913), 505–7 (translated into Russian in *Priroda* 1 [1913]: 37–50).

7. Henry Fairfield Osborn, *The Origin and Evolution of Life* (New York: Scribner's, 1925), 23, 48–49.

8. Bogdanov, *Red Star*, 51–52; Bukharin, *Historical Materialism*, 54.

9. K. E. Tsiolkovskii, "Zarozhdenie zhizni na zemle," *V masterskoi prirody* 1 (1922): 13–16.

10. A. I. Oparin, *Proiskhozhdenie zhizni* (Moscow: Moskovskii rabochii, 1924), 36–54. See the English translation in J. D. Bernal, *The Origin of Life* (Cleveland: World, 1967), 199–234. See also P. Iu. Shmidt, *Osnovy zhizni* (Petrograd: Gosizdat, 1920), 23–32; and *Iunyi proletarii* 1 (January 1924): 32–37; and 4 (April 1924): 23–28.

11. On the radium clock, compare William K. Gregory, "How Man Was Created," *Popular Science Monthly* (June 1931): 18–19; and A. A. Borisiak, "Istoriia zemli," *Komsomolskaia pravda* 292, 18 December 1934, 5.

12. J. B. S. Haldane, "The Origin of Life," *Rationalist Annual* (1929): 3–10; reprinted in the mass trade paperback as *The Inequality of Man* (Harmondsworth: Penguin, 1932), 145–56.

13. Oparin, *Proiskhozhdenie zhizni*, 70. This prediction filtered into popular science. V. Safonov's study of Earth's origins, *Master of the Planet*, e.g., counted history by slow geological time, if punctuated by "qualitative leaps" forward, like Oparin's abiogenetic moment, or the appearance of the "thinking creature," the human being, whose destiny it was to master evolution. V. Safonov, *Pobeditel' planet* (Moscow: Molodaia gvardiia, 1933), 7.

14. I have adapted this term from Mark Adams, "Last Judgment: The Visionary Biology of J. B. S. Haldane," *Journal of the History of Biology* 33, no. 3 (Winter 2000): 457–91. Quoted from "Lodge Seeks Life's Origin," *Monthly Evening Sky Map* 17, no. 202 (October 1923). See also *Revue scientifique* 17, 12 September 1925, 577; and Louis Houllevigue, *The Evolution of the Sciences* (New York: Van Nostrand, 1910), 290.

15. See J. B. S. Haldane, *Daedalus* (New York: Dutton, 1924), 48–55; and Haldane, *Possible Worlds* (New York: Harper, 1928).

16. J. B. S. Haldane, *The Last Judgment* (New York: Harper, 1927), 1–41.

17. From "Man's Destiny" (1927), published in *Possible Worlds*, 300–305; and in *Inequality of Man*, 141–44.

18. Cited from Bernal, *Origin of Life*, xvi, 68, 172–79.

19. J. D. Bernal, *The World, the Flesh, and the Devil* (London: Kegan Paul, 1929), 10, 20–25, 34.

20. Desiderius Papp, *Creation's Doom*, translated by H. J. Stenning (New York: Appleton, 1934), 69, 112–17, 127, 247; H. J. Muller, *Out of the Night* (New York: Vanguard, 1935), 21, 61–66, 125.

21. Winston Churchill, "Fifty Years Hence," *Popular Mechanics Magazine* 57, no. 3 (March 1932): 390–97.

22. Ellsworth Huntington, *Earth and Sun* (New Haven: Yale University Press, 1923); *Popular Astronomy* 41, no. 4 (April 1933): 198–202; Harlan Stetson, *Sunspots and Their Effects* (New York: McGraw-Hill, 1937).

23. *Bulletin de l'academie de médicine* 88 (1922): 41; and *La revue scientifique* (February 1934): 103. Carlos Garcia-Mata and Felix I. Shaffner, "Solar and Economic Relationships," *Quarterly Journal of Economics* 49, no. 1 (November 1934): 1–51; Charles Nordmann, *The Kingdom of the Heavens*, translated by E. E. Fournier d'Albe (London: Unwin, 1923), 118.

24. On the power of the stimulus-response mechanisms of our internal and external biological worlds, e.g., see Daniel Beer, *Renovating Russia* (Ithaca: Cornell University Press, 2008), 158–62, 185–88.

25. A. L. Chizhevskii, *Fizicheskie factory istoricheskogo protsessa* (Kaluga: Gostip., 1924). The work was based on his dissertation at Moscow State University (1918). See V. N. Iagodinskii, *Aleksandr Leonidovich Chizhevskii* (Moscow: Nauka, 1964); and Young, *Russian Cosmists*, 165–71.

26. Stetson, *Sunspots and Their Effects*, 179.

27. S. Vysotskii, "Sviaz revoliutsii s solnechnymi piatnami," *Iunyi proletarii* 12 (August 1924): 31.

28. See the review by I. Orlov, *Pod znamenem marksizma* 8–9 (1924): 314–15. For context, see A. L. Chizhevskii, *Vsia zhizn'* (Moscow: Sovetskaia rossiia, 1974), 171–72.

29. E. Zelikovich, "Bol'shevistskie piatna na solntse," *Bor'ba mirov* 11 (1930): 52–56.

30. A. Rollier *Heliotherapy* (London: Hodder, 1923) (originally published as *L'Héliothérapie* [Paris: Payot, 1916]).

31 A. A. Bardovskii, *Da zdravstvuet solntse!* (Leningrad: Priboi, 1929).

32. The work, *Soniachnaia mashyna*, saw five different editions (in Ukrainian) between 1928 and 1930, including a Russian translation, *Solnechnaia mashina* (Moscow: Gosizdat, 1928), 228–29, from which I have cited.

33. See the chapter on "Les influences astrales," in Abbé Théophile Moreux, *Les énigmes de la science*, 2 vols. (Paris: Doin, 1926), 1:94–102; and Moreux, *Le problème solaire* (Paris: Bertaux, 1900) (published in Russia as *Solntse*, with a preface by Camille Flammarion, translated by V. L. R-ov [St. Petersburg: Novyi zhurnal, 1904]).

34. J. S. Ricard, "Sunspots in their Relation to Human Events," *Sunspot* 13, no. 3 (April 1927): 6–8; and "Review of Past Work," *Sunspot* 13, no. 12 (January 1928): 5–7.

35. V. P. de Smitt of Columbia University read the paper for Chizhevskii, who did not attend the conference (held in December 1926). See "Tchijevsky on 'Physical Factors of the Historical Process,'" *Bulletin of the American Meteorological Society* 8, no. 2 (February 1927): 26; and *Popular Science Monthly* (June 1927): 50. For the critiques, see Stetson, *Sunspots and Their Effects*, 15–18; and Pitirim Sorokin, *Contemporary Sociological Theories* (New York: Harper, 1929), 120–29.

36. See David C. Engerman, *Modernization from the Other Shore* (Cambridge: Harvard University Press, 2003).

37. Henry Adams, *The Degradation of the Democratic Dogma* (New York: Macmillan, 1920), 98, 114, 280.

38. I have drawn the insights in these last three paragraphs from Adams, *Degradation*, 214, 300–301, 282–90, and 305–9.

39. See *La science et la vie* 102 (December 1925): 558–59; 138 (December 1928): 449–51; and *Je sais tout* 300 (December 1930): 550.

40. Aleksandr Rodchenko, "Study for Cover," LEF 3 (1923): 613. See, e.g., the title page design for *Science Wonder Quarterly* 3, no. 1 (Fall 1931): 2, and others for 1930–33; and the front cover for F. Wilhelm Mader, *Wunderwelten* (Leipzig: Verlagsanstalt, 1922).

41. V. Zarzar, "Za aerofikatsiiu SSSR," *Iskry nauki* 24 (1930): 676.

42. *Chelovek i priroda* 2 (1925): 68–72; and 7–8 (1925): 127–36.

43. G. M. Kramarov, *Na zare kosmonavtiki* (Moscow: Znanie, 1965), 38–39.

44. F. Davydov, "God stikhiinykh katastrof," *Izvestiia* 267, 22 November 1924, 6.

45. Abbé Théophile Moreux, *La vie sur mars* (Paris: Doin, 1924), 10–11; V. V. Sharonov, *Planeta Mars* (Leningrad: Soikin, 1926), 37–40.

46. Edward L. Nichols, "Science and the Practical Problems of the Future," *Science* 29, 1 January 1909, 1; A. H. Gibson, *Natural Sources of Energy* (New York: Putnam, 1913), also published in a 1922 Russian translation.

47. *Popular Science Monthly* (April 1923): 32–33; *Scientific American* (September 1923): 182; and (December 1923): 384–85; and *La revue scientifique* 10, 23 May 1925, 324–33.

48. B. P. Veinberg, "Zavoevanie moshchnosti," *Vselennaia i chelovechestvo* 12 (1928): 706, whose work was widely disseminated through the 1920s and 1930s in the Soviet science press.

49. V. Glushko, "Ugrozhaet li chelovechestvu metallicheskii golod?" *Nauka i tekhnika* 37 (1926): 5–6; and Glushko, "Stantsiia vne zemli," *Nauka i tekhnika* 40 (1926): 3–4.

50. Waldemar Kaempffert, "A Rocket Auto Opens Vistas of Star Voyages," *New York Times*, 10 June 1928, 3.

51. Eduard Suess, *Das Antlitz der Erde*, 3 vols. (Vienna: Tempsky, 1883–1909), 1:1 and 4:637 (translated into French and Italian and in English as *The Face of the Earth* [Oxford: Clarendon, 1904]).

52. Vladimir I. Vernadsky, *The Biosphere*, edited by Mark A. S. McMenamin and translated by David B. Langmuir (New York: Copernicus, 1998), 58–60.

53. D. Novogrudskii, "Geokhimiia i vitalizm (O 'nauchnom mirovozrenii' akad. V. I. Vernadskii)," *Pod znamenem marksizma* 9–10 (1931): 168–203.

54. Vernadsky, *Biosphere*, 79, 122.

55. Frederick Engels, *Dialectics of Nature*, translated by J. B. S. Haldane (1940; repr., New York: International, 1960), 18. Engels's work was finished by 1883 but only published in German and Russian in 1925. A. E. Fersman, "Uspekhi geokhimii za poslednie gody," in *Uspekhi i dostizheniia sovremennoi nauki i tekhniki*, edited by M. Ia. Lapirov-Skoblo and A. E. Fersman (Moscow: Rabotnik prosveshcheniia, 1926), 49–57.

56. M. Ia. Lapirov-Skoblo, "Nauka i tekhnika v sssr za 8 let," in Lapirov-Skoblo and Fersman, *Uspekhi i dostizheniiai*, 334.

57. V. A. Kostitsyn, "Stroenie i razvitie vselennoi po dannym sovremennoi astronomii," in Lapirov-Skoblo and Fersman, *Uspekhi i dostizheniia*, 87–88.

58. K. E. Tsiolkovskii, *Monizm vselennoi* (Kaluga: Izd. avtora, 1925). See also his exchange of letters with V. V. Riumin, May–June 1925, aran, f. 555, o. 4, d. 549, ll. 4–5, 11–12; and d. 21, l. 32. These ideas about a plural and sensate universe date to his book *Nirvana* (1914).

59. Tsiolkovskii letter to Rynin, 2 May 1927, aran, r. 4, o. 14, d. 223, l. 66. Also quoted from Islent'ev, *K. E. Tsiolkovskii*, 48, 129; Michael Hagermeister, "The Conquest of Space and the Bliss of the Atoms: Konstantin Tsiolkovskii," in *Soviet Space Culture*, edited by Eva Maurer (Houndmills: Palgrave, 2012), 27–41.

60. *Popular Science Monthly* (July 1925): 24; and (October 1926): 41.

61. For context, see Susan Lederer, *Flesh and Blood* (New York: Oxford University Press, 2008).

62. Raymond Pearl, *The Biology of Death* (Boston: Lippincott, 1922), 48–49, 149, 185, 249–51; Irving Fisher, "Lengthening of Human Life in Retrospect and Prospect," *American Journal of Public Health* 17, no. 1 (January 1927): 1–14.

63. Louis I. Dublin, *The Possibility of Extending Human Life* (New York: Metropolitan Life Insurance, 1922); Hornell Hart, "The Urban Expectation of Life in 2000 AD," *Papers and Proceedings of the American Sociological Society* 20 (July 1926): 118–22.

64. See L. M. Vasilevskii, *Bor'ba so starost'iu i smert'iu v istorii* (Moscow: Gublit., 1924); and A. B. Zalkind, *Ocherki kul'tury revoliutsionnogo vremeni* (Moscow: Rabotnik prosveshcheniia, 1924).

65. A. V. Nemilov, "'Omolozhenie' sel'skokhoziastvennykh zhivotnykh," *Chelovek i priroda* 1 (1925): 23–36; Nemilov, preface, to S. Voronov, *Starost' i omolozhenie* (Moscow: Gosizdat, 1927); and his booklet *Omolozhenie domashnikh zhivotnykh* (Moscow: Gosizdat, 1928). For contexts, see Mark B. Adams, "Eugenics in Russia, 1900–1940," in *The Wellborn Science*, edited by Mark B. Adams (New York: Oxford University Press, 1990), 153–201.

66. See the pieces in *Pravda* 128, 8 June 1924, 6; 243, 24 October 1924, 8; and *Iskry nauki* 8 (1926): 30–32; and *La revue scientifique* 4, 23 February 1929, 103.

67. See *Iunyi proletarii* 20–21 (December 1924): 36–39; *Bezbozhnik* 12 (June 1927): 6; and *Pioner* 24 (1928): 16.

68. P. Iu. Shmidt's, *Anabioz* (Petrograd: Frenkel', 1923), 171, which saw wide distribution in magazine articles and three later editions all the way to 1948.

69. Note *Novyi mir* (August 1938): 185–89; *Znanie-sila* 8 (August 1950): 7–9; and Kuznetsov, *N. P. Kravkov*.

70. A. Zamkov, "Gravidan v meditsine," *Novyi mir* 8 (August 1935): 190–212; Sengoopta, *Most Secret Quintessence*, 126–31, 201–9. On Briukhonenko, who worked closely with the Science Department of the Party's Central Committee, see "Institut vtoroi zhizni," *Pravda*, 4 January 1937, 2.

71. A. A. Bogomolets, *Prodlenie zhizni* (Kiev: Akademiia nauk, 1938), published as *The Prolongation of Life*, translated by Peter V. Karpovich and Sonia Bleeker (New York: Essential Books, 1946); O. B. Lepeshinskaia, *Proiskhozhdenie kletok iz zhivogo veshchestva i rol' zhivogo veshchestva v organizme* (Moscow: Akademiia med. nauk, 1950), published as *The Origin of Cells from Living Substance* (Moscow: Foreign Languages, 1954), 21, 75; and O. B. Lepeshinskaia, *O zhizni, starosti i dolgoletii* (Moscow: Znanie, 1953).

72. See the articles on these themes in *Chelovek i priroda* 3 (1924): 193–96; 3 (1924): 197–208; and 12 (1924): 971–76; and the advertisement in *Vestnik znaniia* 19 (1928): iii. Boris Pilnyak, *The Volga Falls to the Caspian Sea*, translated by Charles Malamar (New York: Cosmopolitan, 1931), 2, 163, 181, 185, 207, 332; V. V. Valiusinskii, *Piat' bessmertnykh* (Kharkov: Proletarii, 1928), 218–19.

73. G. V. Shor, *O smerti cheloveka: Vvedenie v tanatologiiu* (Leningrad: KUVUCh, 1925), 15–16; and *Krasnaia panorama* 47, 19 November 1926, 1, 15–16, 37; A. V. Nemilov, *Chto takoe smert'?* (Moscow: Gosizdat, 1923), 4, 20, 74–75; and A. V. Nemilov, "Lozh' i pravda v vopros ob 'omolozhenii,'" *Priroda* 8 (1932): 713–26. See also *Molodaia gvardiia* 7–8 (1924): 224–39; Aleksandr Lipshits, *Otchego my umiraem*, translated by B. G. Taubman (Leningrad: Gosizdat, 1925); and Vs. Grabov, *Kak prodlit' zhizn'* (Moscow: Gosmedizdat, 1929).

74. A. N. Tolstoi, "Golubye goroda" (1925–37), *Sobranie sochinenii*, 12 vols. (Moscow: Khudozhestvennaia literatura, 1958), 4:46–88; Vladimir Maiakovskii also centered his futuristic satire "The Bedbug" (1928) on the Soviet bureaucrat Ivan Prisypkin, found frozen under anabiosis at the defunct Institute of Human Resurrection, a parasite attached. Vladimir Maiakovskii, "The Bedbug," in *The Complete Plays of Vladimir Mayakovsky*, translated by Guy Daniels (Evanston: Northwestern University Press, 1995), 168–69.

75. A. Beliaev, "Ni zhizn', ni smert'," *Vsemirnyi sledopyt'* 5 and 6 (1926): 3–15; N. S. Komarov, *Kholodnyi gorod* (Moscow: Izd. avtora, 1927), 47–48, 54–57.

76. Freidrich Freksa, *Druso* (Berlin: Reckendorf, 1931); Neil R. Jones, "The Jameson Satellite," *Amazing Stories* (July 1931): 334–43. Stories about anabiosis, rejuvenation, synthetic life, reanimation, and immortality were staples of the popular-science and science fiction media in Europe and the United States.

77. Marie Corelli, *The Young Diana* (New York: Doran, 1918), 274, 301, 320–21, 379; Sallie Hovey, *The Rehabilitation of Eve* (Chicago: Hyman-McGee, 1924), 44.

78. Noëlle Roger, *Le nouvel adam* (Paris: Michel, 1924), republished as N. Rozhe, *Griadushchii adam* (Leningrad: Gosizdat, 1926) and *The New Adam*, translated by P. O. Crowhurst (London: Paul, 1926), 137, 204, 222, 250–53.

79. Ia. Okunev, *Griadushchii mir* (Petrograd: Priboi, 1923), 70; V. D. Nikol'skii, *Cherez tysiachu let* (Leningrad: Soikin, 1927), 66 (published as a supplement to the magazine *Vestnik znaniia*); Yan Larri, *Strana schastlyvykh* (Leningrad: Leningradskoe oblastnoe izd., 1931).

80. Aldous Huxley, *Brave New World* (1932; repr., New York: Harper & Row, 1946), 18. See chaps. 1–3 and 16 in Oldos-Kheksli, "Prekrasnyi novyi mir," *Internat-*

sionalnaia literatura 8 (1935): 82–168; and the accompanying critical article, Mikh. Levidov, "Orgiia pessimizma," 170–73.

81. Lindbergh, *Autobiography of Values*, 9, 27, 64, 130.

82. For the contexts, see Clary, *Rocket Man*; and Friedman, *Immortalists*.

83. Lindbergh, *Autobiography of Values*, 6, 15–16, 38, 335, 400.

84. Lindbergh, *Autobiography of Values*, 36–39, 385–87, 398–99, 402.

85. In Russian, Assotsiatsiia Inventistov Izobretatelei, or AIIz. From Tsiolkovskii's correspondence with the association, 1925–28, in Gosudarstvennyi Politekhnicheskii Muzei (GPM), NA, fond KETS ed. khr. 19368, ll. 22–23; and the letter from A. I. Fedorov to Tsiolkovskii, n.d., ARAN, r. 4, o. 14, d. 195, ll. 10–12.

86. A comprehensive history of the exhibit (also named the "Pervaia mezhdunarodnaia vystavka po mezhplanetnym puteshestviiam"), held from April to June, is told in Anton Pervushin, *Kosmonavty Stalina* (Moscow: Iauza, 2005), 347–63.

87. I describe these scenes and models from the photographs and drawings in the collection *Albom: Pervaia mezhdunarodnaia vystavka po mezhplanetnym puteshestviiam* (Moscow: AIIz, 1927), which I viewed at the State Polytechnic Museum (Moscow). See also N. A. Rynin, *Rockets* (Jerusalem: Scientific Translations, 1970–71), 201–6.

88. Compiled from the selected memoirs of the members, in ARAN, r. 4, o. 14, d. 198, ll. 1–15; K. E. Tsiolkovskii, *Obshchechelovecheskaia azbuka, pravopisanie i iazyk* (Kaluga: Gostip., 1927), 1–10.

89. AIIz letter to Tsiolkovskii, 21 January 1927, in the correspondence file (1925–28), in GPM NA, fond KETS, ed. khr. 19368, ll. 6–7.

90. *Monthly Evening Sky Map* 21, no. 247 (July 1927); Mary Proctor, *Romance of the Moon* (New York: Harper, 1928), 167.

8. The First Foundations of Astronautics

1. Max Valier, *Die Raketenfahrt* (1929; repr., Munich: Oldenbourg, 1930), 157, 174, 193, 240.

2. These images appear on the front cover of *Die Rakete* 15 (August 1927); in Hermann Oberth, *Wege zur Raumschiffahrt* (Munich: Oldenbourg, 1929); the Sunday supplement *American Weekly*, 13 January 1929; and *Znanie-sila*, 23–24 (1932): 15.

3. *New York Times*, 29 September 1926, 6; and *Popular Science Monthly* (September 1927): 43.

4. Quoted from "Astronautics," *New York Times*, 8 March 1928, 24. See the image in the *New York Times*, 10 June 1928, 125. For more imagery of the Paris Gun's flight, with rocket trajectory upward and meteor downward, see Rudolf Nebel, *Raketenflug* (Berlin: Raketenflugverlag, 1932), 18; and Gerald Heard, *Exploring the Stratosphere* (London: Nelson, 1936): 78.

5. Michael J. Neufeld, "Weimar Culture and Futuristic Technology," *Technology and Culture* 31, no. 4 (October 1990): 725–52.

6. See the reports in *Zeitschrift für Flug und Motorluft* 12, no. 19, 28 June 1928, 271–74; and 16, no. 23, 27 August 1932, 483–86. For a review of Tiling and Schmiedl, see *Die Umschau* 35, no. 18, 2 May 1931, 351–52; and 36, no. 13, 26 March 1932, 252–55.

7. One of the best reviews of its history remains Willy Ley, "Die Versuche des 'Veriens für Raumschiffahrt,'" in *Männer der Rakete*, edited by Werner Brügel (Leipzig: Hachmeister & Thal, 1933), 119–34.

8. See, e.g., the news features in *Je sais tout* 290 (February 1930): 657; and 308 (August 1931): 291.

9. *Bulletin of the American Interplanetary Society* 8 (March–April 1931): 13. Nebel managed the Mirak flights, though the actual device was built by Klaus Riedel, under the direction of Willy Ley and Hermann Oberth. For more coverage, see the *New York Times*, 15 March 1931, 27; 16 July 1932, 4; and 7 October 1932, 2.

10. The story is told in Frederick Ordway and Mitchell Sharpe, *The Rocket Team* (New York: Crowell, 1979), 12–20; and Winter, *Prelude to the Space Age*. See also Michael J. Neufeld, "The Excluded: Hermann Oberth and Rudolf Nebel in the Third Reich," *Quest* 5, no. 4 (1996): 22–27. Becker ran the Ballistics and Munitions Branch No. 1, part of the Army Weapons Department of the Weimar Republic.

11. Note that the entry for *Kosmonautik* in the *Technologisches Wörterbuch*, edited by Alfred Schlomann (Berlin: Springer, 1932), 371, defined it as "astronautics, cosmonautics, super-aviation, navigation extra-atmospherique, astronautique."

12. "A Dictionary of Rocketry Needed," *Astronautics* 28 (March 1934): 7; G. E. Langemak, "O edinoi terminologii," in *Raketnaia tekhnika*, edited by I. T. Kleimenov et al. (Moscow: ONTI, 1936), 9–17.

13. Oberth, *Wege zur Raumschiffahrt*, 1, 22, 300, 355. I have also relied on the English translations from Hermann Oberth, *Ways to Spaceflight* (Washington DC: NASA, 1972).

14. Oberth, *Wege zu Raumschiffarht*, 110–17, 137, 161–65, 186–87, 261.

15. Oberth, *Wege zu Raumschiffarht*, 297, 377.

16. Oberth, *Wege zu Raumschiffarht*, 44, 54, 398.

17. See Walter Dornberger, *V-2*, translated by James Cleugh and Geoffrey Halliday (New York: Viking, 1954), xiv; William Sims Bainbridge, *The Spaceflight Revolution* (New York: Wiley, 1976), 31; and Wyn Wachhorst, *The Dream of Spaceflight* (New York: Basic, 2000), 29.

18. See the quotes in Brügel, *Männer der Rakete*, 7–13, 141; Willy Ley, ed., *Die Möglichkeit der Weltraumfahrt* (Leipzig: Hachmeister & Thal, 1928), 3:1–13, 14–16, 65–66; and Rudolf Nebel, *Raketenflug* (Berlin: Raketenflugverlag, 1932), 5.

19. Milton Fairman, "The Race to Explore Outer Space," *Popular Mechanics Magazine* 53, no. 3 (March 1930): 386–88. This issue offered a cover page with Oberth's massive rocket from the movie *The Woman in the Moon*.

20. Max Valier's *Der Vorstoss in den Weltraumen* (1924) was republished as *Raketenfahrt* (Munich: Oldenbourg, 1928 and 1930). Willy Ley's *Die Fahrt ins Weltall* (1926) was retooled as Ley, *Die Moglichkeit*.

21. See Johannes Winkler, "Einführung in das Raumfahrtproblem," *Die Rakete*, beginning with the 15 September 1928 issue, 141–42; and Vladimir Mandl, *Die Rakete zur Höhenforschung* (Leipzig: Hachmeister & Thal, 1934). For reviews and critiques of the major rocketry and spaceflight works, see *Zeitschrift für Flug und*

Motorluft (1926–30); *Die Himmelswelt* 3 (February 1929): 71; 11, no. 12 (November 1929): 339–41; and 5, no. 6 (May 1930): 126–34; and *Zeitschrift für angewandte Meteorologie* 46 (September 1929): 60–64.

22. A. B. Scherschevsky, *Die Rakete für Fahrt und Flug* (Berlin: Volckmann, 1929), 5–6, 27–34, 126. Aleksandr Borisovich Shershevskii was born in 1894, studied Mechanical Engineering at the St. Petersburg Higher Technical School, and relocated to Berlin in 1919. The poem is by Irma Gohl, "Weltraumschiff," *Die Rakete* (15 September 1927): 114.

23. Otto Willi Gail, *Mit Raketenkraft ins Weltenall* (Stuttgart: Thienemanns, 1928), 56, 106.

24. Willy Ley, *Grundriss einer Geschichte der Rakete* (Leipzig: Hachmeister & Thal, 1932), 9–15; and Willy Ley, "Vom ersten Raketentier," *Die Rakete* (October 1929): 21–24. Robert Lademann, "Zum Raketenproblem," *Zeitschrift für Flug und Motorluft* 8, no. 18, 28 April 1927, 177–81; and "Die Wissenschaftliche Bedeutung des Ruckstossers," *Der Luftweg* (May 1928): 103–4.

25. See A. B. Scherschevsky, "Das Problem der Reaktionsraumschiffe und Reaktionsflugzeuge," *Zeitschrift für angewandte Mathematik. und Mechanik* 7, no. 4 (August 1927): 319–21; and his assorted articles in *Der Flug, Flugsport,* and *Zeitschrift für Flug und Motorluft* (1926–28). For appreciations of Russian cosmism, see Anna Marie Didlof, "Bücherbesprechungen," *Die Rakete,* 15 May 1928, 79; and Nebel, *Raketenflug,* 7–11.

26. Alden Armagnac, "Aims Rocket at Roof of Sky," *Popular Science Monthly* (October 1929): 24. *New York Times,* 18 July 1929, 2; and 21 July 1929, 11; 7 February 1931, 17; and 1 August 1933, 7. A. A. Rodnykh, *Rakety* (Moscow: ONTI, 1934), 56. See also the "Description of Flight of July 17, 1929," in Goddard and Pendray, *Papers of Robert H. Goddard,* 2:668–73.

27. Thea von Harbou, *Frau im Mond* (Berlin: Scherl, 1929); Klaus Kreimeier, *The Ufa Story* (New York: Hill & Wang, 1996), 167.

28. See, e.g., *La science et la vie* 38, no. 159 (September 1930): 199; and the cover of *Astronautics* 39 (January 1938).

29. Oberth's letters to Tsiolkovskii, 18 September and 24 October 1929, ARAN, f. 555, o. 4, d. 457, ll. 2–4.

30. With a confirmed firing of over a minute, for a time this was considered the world's "first rocket motor." *New York Times,* 31 January 1931, 8; and *Astronautics* 32 (October 1935): 4–8. Assisting Oberth were some leading members of the Verein, including Nebel, Engel, Reidel, and the young von Braun.

31. See Hermann Oberth, *Stoff und Leben* (Remagen: Reichl, 1959), first published in booklet form in 1930; and *Katechismus der Uraniden* (Weisbaden: Ventla, 1966).

32. Hans Hörbiger and Philipp Fauth published on this theory in 1913. See Manfred Nagl, "SF, Occult Sciences, and Nazi Myths," *Science Fiction Studies* 1, no. 3 (Spring 1974): 185–97; Max Valier, *Die entwicklung unseres Sonnensystems nach den neuen Lehren der Kosmotechnik* (Berlin: Paetel, with editions in 1922, 1923, and 1930).

33. Willy Ley, *Rockets* (New York: Viking, 1944), 260–63. The theory is described in Carl von Klinckowstroem, "Die Erde eine Hohlkugel," *Die Umschau* 36, no. 34 (20 August 1932): 663–65.

34. Quoted from Otto Willi Gail, *By Rocket to the Moon* (New York: Sears, 1931), preface, v–vii, and 88–90, 127 (originally published as *Hans Hardts Mondfarht* [Stuttgart: Union, 1928]). The novel was also published in Finnish, Swedish, Dutch, French, and Hungarian and republished in German in 1935. Its value, at least for its Russian editors, was that it was based on true physics and technical accuracy. See Ia. I. Perel'man's preface in Otto Villi Gail', *Lunnyi perelet*, translated by I. Bekker (Leningrad: Krasnaia gazeta, 1930).

35. See Hans Dominck, *Das Erbe der Uraniden* (Berlin: Keil, 1928 and 1939; Berlin: Scherl, 1941 and 1943); and Dominck, *Treibstoff SR* (Berlin: Scherl, 1940 and 1943), also set in outer space.

36. Otfrid von Hanstein, *Mond-rak I* (Stuttgart: Levy Müller, 1929); also published in French, Italian, and as "Between Earth and the Moon," *Wonder Stories Quarterly* 2, no. 1 (Fall 1930): 6–136, from which I have quoted (16–21, 45, 51–52). For similar approaches to rocketry and space travel, see Erich Dolezal, *Der Ruf der Sterne* (Vienna: Krystall, 1930); and Walther Kegel, *Rakete 33* (Leipzig: Volckmar, 1934).

37. The German newspaper *Die Woche*, e.g., published science fiction (Thea Harbou's *Frau im Mond* and Hans Dominik's *Das Erbe der Uraniden*), alongside actual news reports about rocketry. Wernher von Braun, "Das Geheimnis der Flüssigkeitsrakete," *Die Umschau* 36, no. 23 (4 June 1932): 449–52.

38. *Popular Science Monthly* (August 1928): 25; and (August 1930): 25.

39. F. V. Monk and H. T. Winter, *Adventure above the Clouds* (London: Blackie, 1933), 216; "News of the Society," *Bulletin of the American Interplanetary Society* 2 (1930): 1; *New York Times*, 18 May 1930, 30.

40. "In Memoriam," in Brügel, *Männer der Rakete*, 14.

41. *Revue scientifique* 15, 14 August 1925, 459–61. See also Edmond Marcotte, *Les moteurs à explosion* (Paris: Colin, 1927).

42. See Eugen Sänger, *Raketen-flugtechnik* (Munich: Oldenbourg, 1933), 1, 62, 203; translated as *Tekhnika raketnogo poleta* (Kharkov: Nauchno-tekhnich. izd., 1936), and as *Rocket Flight Engineering* (Washington DC: NASA, 1965), which I have used for translations.

43. Sänger, *Raketen-flugtechnik*, 10, 42, 184, 195, 216.

44. See Maurice Roy, "La propulsion par réaction," *La technique aéronautique* 99, 15 January 1930; and Roy, *Recherches théoretiques sur le rendement et les conditions de réalisation des systèmes motorpropulseurs à réaction* (Paris: Dunod, 1930), translated into Russian in 1936.

45. Robert Esnault-Pelterie, *L'exploration par fusées de la très haute atmosphère et la possibilité des voyages interplanétaires* (Paris: Société astronomique, 1928); *L'Astronautique* (Paris: Lahure, 1930); and *L'Astronautique: complément* (Paris: Société des ingénieurs civils, 1935).

46. See the letters of Tsiolkovskii and Chizhevskii, 1928, ARAN, f. 555, o. 4, d. 20,

l. 31; and d. 689, ll. 45–46. For context, see G. S. Vetrov, *Rober Esno-Pel'tri* (Moscow: Nauka, 1982), 150–69.

47. *Je sais tout* 268 (April 1928): 120; and *La science et la vie* 131 (May 1928): 369–77.

48. *Je sais tout* 288 (December 1928): 526–30; and *La science et la vie* 159 (September 1930): 199–204; and 204 (June 1934): 454.

49. Alexandre Ananoff, *Les mémoires d'un astronaut* (Paris: Blanchard, 1978), 20–21; Félix Torres and Jacques Villain, *Robert Esnault-Pelterie* (Bordeaux: Confluences, 2007), 250, 232–93.

50. I have drawn these details from V. I. Prishchepa and G. P. Dronova, *Ari Shternfel'd* (Moscow: Nauka, 1987), 33–57; and M. A. Shternfel'd, "Portret uchenogo A. A. Shternfel'da," *Istoriia nauki i tekhniki* 8 (2002): 20–28.

51. L. Rolin [A. Shternfel'd], "Utopie d'hier, possibilité d'aujord'hui," *L'Humanité*, 19 August and 2 September 1930.

52. Quoted from Ananoff, *Les mémoires d'un astronaut*, 27. Shternfel'd only ever published small portions of the work—titled *Initiation à la cosmonautique*—in the *Comptes rendus de l'Académie des Sciences* 198 (1934): 333–34; and in the popular magazines *L'Aéro* (1934) and *Les Ailes* (1935).

53. I am referring to the Russian version, A. A. Shternfel'd, *Vvedenie v kosmonavtiku* (Moscow: Nauka, 1974), originally published as a book in 1937.

54. For more of the contexts, see Mike Gruntman, *From Astronautics to Cosmonautics* (North Charleston SC: Booksurge, 2007); and for the images, see Prishchepa and Dronova, *Ari Shternfel'd*, 59 and 160–61. A. A. Shternfel'd, "K zakonu perekhoda kolichestvennykh izmenenii v kachestvennye," *Voprosy filosofii* 7 (1960): 111–12, originally completed in 1954.

55. On these and other societies, see *Astronautics*, issues 3–13 (1933–43).

56. The Explosives Act of 1875 was a measure against domestic violence (with antecedents in the famous "gunpowder plot" of 1605). See "Notes and News," *Astronautics* 39 (January 1938): 16; and Winter, *Prelude to the Space Age*, 107–8.

57. *Astronautics* 30 (October–November 1934): 12.

58. Charles G. Philp, *Stratosphere and Rocket Flight* (London: Putnam, 1937), 6–14.

59. Philip E. Cleator, *Rockets through Space* (New York: Simon & Schuster, 1936). See also Monk and Winter, *Adventure above the Clouds*, 220–24.

60. Monk and Winter, *Adventure above the Clouds*, 199–212, 231.

61. *Popular Science Monthly* (August 1928): 26; and the *New York Times*, 13 October 1929, XX 4.

62. Lindbergh, *Autobiography of Values*, 15, 335–37, 341–43.

63. Lindbergh had also met with the directors of the Carnegie Institution, which offered Goddard too little money (five thousand dollars in all).

64. See *Popular Science Monthly* (February 1927); *Literary Digest*, 21 December 1929; and *Field Artillery Journal* 21, no. 6 (November–December 1931): 640.

65. On Bull and Swann, see the *New York Times*, 10 March 1931, 16; 5 June 1931, 22; and 6 June 1931, 19. See the advertisement "Pocket Ben Celebrates the 4th in a Skyrocket," *Liberty*, 4 July 1931, 3. For context, see Winter, *Prelude to the Space Age*, 99–107.

66. For the wide media coverage of Condit's rocket and photographs, see *Je sais tout* 268 (April 1928): 120; *Popular Science Monthly* (August 1928): 25–26; and *Modern Mechanix* (November 1928): 52–53.

67. Lyon was a regular feature in the *New York Times* between January and August 1931. See also *Monthly Evening Sky Map* 25, no. 296 (August 1931): 1; and *Popular Science Monthly* (August 1931): 120. For a rare article, see Darwin O. Lyon, "Die Rakete im Werden," *Die Umschau* 35, no. 20, 16 May 1931, 389–93, boldly promising human flight into high altitudes and even interplanetary space.

68. On Lyon as Goddard's equal, see *La science et la vie* 170 (August 1931): 108; and the *New York Times*, 6 September 1931, 38.

69. *Monthly Evening Sky Map* 24, no. 282 (June 1930): 2; *Bulletin of the American Interplanetary Society* 1 (June 1930): 2; *New York Herald Tribune*, 9 November 1930, 7; and *New York Times*, 13 November 1931, 21.

70. Quoted from Philp, *Stratosphere and Rocket Flight*, 88–90. For sources that covered the story as real, see *L'exportateur français* 18, no. 821 (7 December 1933): 356; and A. A. Rodnykh, *Rakety i raketnye korabli* (Leningrad: Gosmash., 1934), 80. The front page of *L'illustré: du petit journal* from 26 November 1933 (no. 2240) showed a sophisticated cement launch pad and rising rocket, though questioning if it was real.

71. See G. Edward Pendray, "Daring Men in Seven Nations Aim to Harness Giant Rockets," *Popular Science Monthly* (August 1931): 30–31; G. H. Davis [aka. G. Edward Pendray], "From Europe to New York by Rocket," *Popular Mechanics* 57, no. 3 (March 1932): 464.

72. *New York Times*, 28 January 1931, 10, alternately described the film as a "newsreel version" of the feature film and as an amusement "rocket ride" of sorts. See also *Popular Science Monthly* (April 1931): 53.

73. An abstract of the talk is in the *Bulletin of the American Interplanetary Society* 7 (February 1931): 1–5; with reviews in the *New York Times*, 24 January 1931, 3; *Monthly Evening Sky Map* 25, no. 291 (March 1931): 1; and *Modern Mechanics and Inventions* (August 1931): 78–81, from which I have quoted.

74. "Astronautics," *Time* 18, no. 24, 14 December 1931, 42. For a comprehensive history, see John Cheng, *Astounding Wonder* (Philadelphia: University of Pennsylvania Press, 2012), 251–300.

75. Compare *Astronautics* 30 (October–November 1934): 7–11; and 50 (October 1941): 11–13. On the myth of inexplicable rocket science, see Willy Ley, "Some Practical Aspects of Rocketeering," *Aviation* 35, no. 11 (November 1936): 19–20.

76. See *Astronautics* 33 (March 1936): 2; 36 (March 1937): 7–9; and *Popular Mechanics* 65, no. 5 (May 1936): 641–64.

77. "Rocketors," *New Yorker*, 23 August 1941, 13. See also Franklin M. Gates and Merritt A Williamson, "Astronautics: A New Science," *Yale Scientific Magazine* 11, no. 2 (Winter 1937): 3, 20–21.

78. Alfred Africano, "Rocket Trips into Space," *Astronautics* 40 (April 1938): 13–14. See also Alfred Africano, "The Design of a Stratosphere Rocket," *Journal of the Aeronautical Sciences* 3, no. 8 (June 1936): 287–90.

79. Frank Malina and A. M. O. Smith, "Flight Analysis of the Sounding Rocket," *Journal of the Aeronautical Sciences* 5 (March 1938): 199–202. On Parsons and the occult, see George Pendle, *Strange Angel* (Orlando: Harcourt, 2005).

80. *Bulletin of the American Interplanetary Society* 10 (June–July 1931); 17 (March 1932): 1–2.

81. For accounts of the visits, see Clary, *Rocket Man*, 178–80.

82. "The Latest on Rockets," *Monthly Evening Sky Map* 28, no. 336 (December 1934): 1; Shepard Minnehan, "Prospects of Fourth of July Rocket Trip to Moon or Mars," *Boston Sunday Post*, 3 July 1938, 1; and Charles G. Philp, "Is Rocketry Progressing?" *Discovery* (September 1937): 269–71.

83. Robert H. Goddard, *Liquid Propellant Rocket Development* (Washington DC: Smithsonian Miscellaneous Collections, 1936) (also featured in *Scientific American* [August and September 1936]); "News of Rocketry," *Astronautics* 33 (March 1936): 2. G. E. Pendray, "Rocketry's Number One Man," *Astronautics* 37 (July 1937): 3–7. For the full context, see Clary, *Rocket Man*, 198–99.

84. See the representative pieces in *Vestnik znaniia* 19 (1928): 957–58; and 5–6 (1930): 251–52; *Nauka i tekhnika* 23 (1928): 22; and 46 (1929): 1–2; and *Aviatsiia i khimiia* 10 (1928): 17; and 7 (1930): 14–15.

85. See N. A. Rynin, *Teoriia reaktivnogo dvizheniia* (Leningrad: IIPS, 1929); Rynin, *Astronavigatsiia* (Leningrad: Akademiia nauk, 1932); and Rynin, *Teoriia kosmicheskogo poleta* (Leningrad: Akademiia nauk, 1932)—all filled with translations of Goddard's, Esnault-Pelterie's, Hohmann's, and Oberth's work (among others).

86. Kondratiuk, whose real name was Aleksandr Ignat'evich Shargei, had begun this work in 1915. See his book *Zavoevanie mezhplanetnykh prostorov* (Novosibirsk: Izd. avtora, 1929), sponsored by V. P. Vetchinkin, who also wrote the introduction.

87. See the GIRD memorandum report, June 1933, in ARAN, r. 4, o. 14, d. 243, ll. 42–43. For a comprehensive survey, see Anton Pervushin, *Krasnyi kosmos* (Moscow: EKSMO, 2000), 39–49. I also thank Valentina Ponomareva (Institut istorii estestvoznaniia i tekhniki im. S. I. Vavilova) for sharing several folders of GIRD retrospectives with me.

88. A. P. Romanov and V. S. Gubarev, *Konstruktory* (Moscow: Polit. lit., 1989), 15. The impressions come from the interview of E. K. Moshchkin, 23 June 1962, ARAN, r. 4, o. 14, d. 187, ll. 4, 25. Also quoted from F. A. Tsander, *Problems of Flight by Jet Propulsion* (Jerusalem: Scientific Translations, 1964), 100.

89. A. N. Shtern, "Vvedenie v teoriiu dvigatelei priamoi reaktsii," *Zhurnal tekhnicheskoi fiziki* 3, no. 1 (1933): 187–96.

90. Materials from the GIRD Archive, ARAN, r. 4, o. 14, d. 247, ll. 8–9.

91. "Order" of the Red Army Ordinance Chief, 17 May 1933, and the official report on GIRD finances (10–15 April 1933), GARF, f. 8355, o.1, d. 374, ll. 72–76.

92. The quote is from a print in the GIRD archive, ARAN, r. 4, o. 14, d. 247, l. 27. After Tsander's death L. K. Korneev took over direction of the GIRD X engine, working closely with L. S. Dushkin and A. Ia. Poliarnyi.

9. A Race into the Stratosphere

1. Edmond Blanc, "En avion dans le stratosphère," *La science et la vie* 178 (April 1932): 265–73. On Goddard, see the *New York Times*, 14 June 1931, 29; and 27 September 1931, x x 4; the front cover and feature article in *Popular Science Monthly* (December 1931); and Robert H. Goddard, "A New Turbine Rocket Plane for the Upper Atmosphere," *Scientific American* (March 1932): 148–49.

2. Auguste Piccard, "Ballooning in the Stratosphere," *National Geographic* 63, no. 3 (March 1933): 372–73, 353–84. The European media also widely reported on Piccard.

3. Charles G. Philp, *The Conquest of the Stratosphere* (New York: Putnam, 1937), 37–68.

4. "Piccard and His Voyage into Space," *Monthly Evening Sky Map* 25, no. 295 (July 1931): 1; and "Prisoners of the Air," *Popular Mechanics* 56, no. 2 (August 1931): 177–80. The flight was preceded by much fanfare, as in "Piccard," *Die Umschau* 34, no. 42, 18 October 1930, 845–48.

5. Quoted from *Popular Science Monthly* (November 1936): 33. Compare the images in Monk and Winter, *Adventure above the Clouds*, 177; *Popular Mechanics* 58, no. 5 (November 1932): 693; *La science et la vie* 170 (August 1931): 92–93; and *Vestnik znaniia* 20 (May 1931): 1016. Hugo Gernsback's artists actually redrew Piccard's balloon as a dirigible rocket (*Everyday Science and Mechanics* [November 1931]: 649).

6. Quoted from "Why Explore the Stratosphere," *Popular Mechanics* 60, no. 4 (October 1933): 481–83. See also "Piccard's Arrival from Space," *Monthly Evening Sky Map* 25, no. 296 (August 1931): 3; and Tyrrell Krum, "How High Is Up?" *Popular Mechanics* 61, no. 2 (February 1934): 161–62.

7. *Je sais tout* 300 (December 1930): 507–8; and 312 (December 1931): 515.

8. Gerald Heard, *Exploring the Stratosphere* (London: Nelson, 1936), 29, 39, 56—paraphrasing Samuel Taylor Coleridge, *The Rime of the Ancient Mariner* (1798), the fifth stanza, the second part.

9. Quoted from N. Rynin, "Tekhnika poleta v stratosferu," *Izvestiia* 157, 9 June 1931, 4. See also *Izvestiia* 171, 23 June 1931, 3; and *Izobretatel'* 11 (1931): 6–8; and 12 (1931): 23–24.

10. Edwin Teale, "History's Biggest Show," *Popular Science Monthly* (July 1933): 23–25; *New York Times*, 4 January 1933, 21. Piccard later denied the story about the dog, in the *New York Times*, 13 January 1933, 10.

11. Albert W. Stevens, captain in the air corps, memorandum to chief of the Army Air Corps, "High Altitude Balloon Flight to 60,000 Feet or More," 27 February 1933, in the folder "Stratosphere Flight 1933–1943," file #373, R D 2576, entry P 26, Sarah Clark Collection Central Decimal Correspondence Files, Record Group 342, Records of U.S. Air Force Commands, Activities, and Organizations, National Archives, College Park M D (hereafter cited as "Stratosphere Flight 1933–1943"). See also Kevin Cook, "Space Shot 1935," *Invention and Technology* (Fall 2006): 30–36.

12. Quoted from *Monthly Evening Sky Map* 28, no. 329 (May 1934): 1; and 28, no. 330 (June 1934): 1. For imagery of a race to the stratosphere, see N. A. Rynin, *Zavoevanie stratosfery* (Moscow: Molodaia gvardiia, 1933); *Komsomolskaia pravda*

63, 15 March 1934, 4; *Popular Science Monthly* (April 1934): 45; and *Nauka i zhizn'* 8 (1935): 20–21; Chris Gainor, *To a Distant Day* (Lincoln: University of Nebraska Press, 2008), 106; and Linda Voss, "The Race to the Stratosphere," U.S. Centennial of Flight Commission, Essays, "Lighter-than-Air," http://centennialofflight.gov/essay/Lighter_than_air/race_to_strato/LTA11.htm (accessed 5 August 2013).

13. In a communication to the Politburo, Commissar of Defense K. E. Voroshilov marked the *Stratostat SSSR* flight as a real scientific achievement, worthy of further investment (December 1934), in RGVA, f. 29, o. 76, d. 95, l. 11. For context, see Iu. A. Druzhinin and D. A. Sobolev, "Polety v stratosferu v SSSR v 1930-e gg.," *Voprosy istorii estestvoznaniia i tekhniki* 4 (2006).

14. *Tsirk*, directed by Grigori Aleksandrov (1936; Moscow: Mosfilm). N. A. Rynin described the Zacchini act (in December 1927) in *Theory of Rocket Propulsion* (Washington DC: NASA, 1970–71), 31. For the metaphor, see A. Demidov's comments in P. Iudin, ed., *Pisateli VXII parts'ezdu* (Moscow: Tov. pisatelei, 1934), 65. The term *stratonauts* now entered the general media vocabulary, as in *Komsomolskaia pravda*, 15 July 1934, 4; and 18 August 1934, 3–4; and *Rabochaia Moskva*, 30 January 1935, 4.

15. The poem is in *Druzhnye rebiata* 5 (1933): 9.

16. Quoted from A. Garri and L. Kassil', *Potolok mira* (Moscow: Sovetskaia literatura, 1934): 126–30. For this imagery and terminology, see also N. A. Rynin, "Stratostat SSSR," *Iunyi proletarii* 22, 30 November 1933, 10.

17. "Happy Landing after Stratosphere Ascent," *Monthly Evening Sky Map* 28, no. 336 (December 1934): 3.

18. *Osoaviakhim* was an acronym for the *Obshchestvo sodeistviia oborone i aviatsionno-khimicheskomu stroitel'stvu SSSR*.

19. *Komsomolskaia pravda* 26, 31 January 1934, 3. "Sirius" was also the name of the seaplane that Charles Lindbergh and Anne Morrow Lindbergh flew over the northern hemisphere in 1931.

20. *Monthly Evening Sky Map* 28, no. 327 (March 1934): 1. The pamphlet *Geroi stratosfery* (Moscow: Osoaviakhim, 1935). The official investigation also discovered improper ballast and safety measures—such as no escape hatch.

21. *Komsomolskaia pravda* 27, 1 February 1934, 4.

22. See the poems in *Komsomolskaia pravda* 27, 3 February 1934, 2.

23. T. Sikorskaia and S. Bolotin, "Pesnia o stratonavtakh," *Vozhatyi* 12 (1935): 62.

24. See "World's Largest Free Balloon to Explore Stratosphere," *National Geographic* 66, no. 1 (July 1934): 107–10; and Capt. Albert W. Stevens, "Exploring the Stratosphere," *National Geographic* 66, no. 4 (October 1934): 397–434.

25. Thomas D. White, 1st Lt., Air Corps, "Report No. D-25," 12 May 1934, Moscow, USSR, received by War Department, 11 July 1934; "Report of Russian Stratosphere Balloon Flight," file #135, RD 723, entry P 27, Sarah Clark Collection R&D Project Files, Record Group 342, Records of U.S. Air Force Commands, Activities, and Organizations, National Archives, College Park MD. Albert W. Stevens also repeated this claim in his various memorandums.

26. The quotes are from Capt. Albert W. Stevens, "The Scientific Results of the World-Record Stratosphere Flight," *National Geographic* 69, no. 5 (May 1936): 698–99; and Capt. Albert W. Stevens, "Man's Farthest Aloft," *National Geographic* 69, no. 1 (January 1936): 60.

27. Quoted from and pictured in Stevens, "Exploring the Stratosphere," 410–13, 422–25.

28. Quoted from Philp, *Conquest of the Stratosphere*, 34, 91–126, 151–98. See also "A Report of the Second Stratosphere Expedition," *National Geographic* 68, no. 4 (October 1935): 535–36; Stevens, "Man's Farthest Aloft," 59–94; and Stevens, "Scientific Results of the World-Record Stratosphere Flight," 693–714.

29. On the promise of extensive private support, see A. W. Stevens, letter to Gen. H. C. Brett, chief of Material Division, Wright Field, 28 December 1933, in "Stratosphere Flight 1933–1943"; also note Brig. Gen. H. C. Brett's approval so long as there was no financial commitment by the Army Air Corps, in Albert W. Stevens, captain in the Air Corps, memorandum to chief of the Army Air Corps, "High Altitude Balloon Flight to 60,000 feet or More," 27 February 1933, in "Stratosphere Flight 1933–1943."

30. Albert W. Stevens, letter to Captain Brock, "Stratobowl," Rapid City SD, 2 November 1935; in "Stratosphere Flight 1933–1943."

31. Stevens, "Man's Farthest Aloft," 59, 71, 80.

32. Quoted from "Hubbard Medals Awarded to Stratosphere Explorers," *National Geographic* 69, no. 5 (May 1936): 712–13. Ruth Stevens's self-published book, *My Husband the First Astronaut* (1987), is in the archival collection at Brigham Young University library.

33. I have assembled these quotes from the sources cited above in *National Geographic* magazine.

34. G. Prokof'ev, "Vtoroi etap zavoevaniia stratosfery," *Pravda* (24 March 1937): 3. Among the stratostat accidents and crashes were the SSSR II (5 September 1934), the SSSR III (18 September 1937 and 16 March 1939), and the *Osoaviakhim 2* (22 June 1940). For more on failed stratostat and "sub-stratostat" flights, see *Pravda*, 31 August 1937, 3; 16 September 1937, 5; 20 September 1937, 6.

35. Red Air Force commander Ia. I. Alksnis's comments at a celebration for the "Stratostat SSSR" (17 October 1933), in GARF, f. 8355, o. 1, d. 79, ll. 5–11.

36. Foch quoted in *Popular Science Monthly* (December 1927): 26. Voroshilov quoted in *Vestnik znaniia* 13–14 (1931): 734; in *Iunyi proletarii* 3 (February 1931): 1; and in *Front nauki i tekhniki* 2 (1935): 30.

37. *Popular Science Monthly* (October 1934): 13–15; and (January 1938): 25–27. See also Igor Sikorsky, "Wings over Europe," *Scientific American* (May 1935): 229–31; and Arthur Oxley, "Death from the Sky," *Scientific American* (October 1938): 173–75.

38. Michael J. Neufeld. "The Reichswehr, the Rocket, and the Versailles Treaty," *Journal of the British Interplanetary Society* 53 (2000): 163–72.

39. Ia. I. Alksnis, "Povysim boevuiu moshch'," *Izvestiia* 53, 23 February 1930, 3.

40. Record of a meeting of the presidium of Osoaviakhim, GARF, f. 8355, o. 1, d. 78, l. 12; Pierre Vauthier, *Voennaia doktrina generala Due*, translated by A.

M. Taube (Moscow: Gosvoenizdat, 1935); Giulio Douhet, *Gospodstvo v vozdukhe*, edited by V. V. Khripin (Moscow: Gosvoenizdat, 1935).

41. The quote found its way to the popular press, as, e.g., in *Nauka i zhizn'* 8 (1935): 33; and 11 (1936): 24.

42. The study is in RGVA, f. 33988, o. 2, dela 682–88. For context, see Lennart Samuelson, *Plans for Stalin's War Machine* (New York: St. Martin's, 2000).

43. The phrase is from a report on chemical warfare (1926–27), RGVA, f. 33989, o. 1, d. 54, ll. 15–16.

44. S. P. Korolev, *Raketnyi polet v stratosfere* (Moscow: Gosvoenizdat, 1934).

45. Translations of French popular science articles (1 December 1932), RGVA, f. 33987, o. 3, d. 365, ll. 301–12; correspondence from Marshall Tukhachevskii to Commissar Lazar Kaganovich (1931), RGVA, f. 33987, o. 2, d. 349, ll. 4–6

46. "Predislovie," Robert Knauss, *Vozdushnaia voina 1936 goda* (Moscow: Gosvoenizdat, 1934), 2–7 (originally published as *Luftkrieg 1936* [Berlin: Kolk, 1932], also translated into French and English). For a review of Western science fiction books as a preview of the coming war, see *Voina i revoliutsiia* 12 (1931): 85–88.

47. N. Rymkevich, "Griadushchaia voina," *Iunyi proletarii* 2 (1924): 33–38. Sergei Grigoriev, "Troika Or-Dim-Stakh," *Vsemirnyi sledopyt* 1 (1925): 1, also set these themes to fiction.

48. These inventors receive wide coverage in the Western media. For just a few Russian responses, see *Krasnaia panorama* 18 (1924): 14–15; *Samolet* 12 (1925): 47; and *Iskra* 31 (1927): 4–6.

49. A. Tolstoi, *Giperboloid inzhenera Garina* (Moscow: Sovetskaia literatura, 1933) (originally serialized in *Krasnaia nov'* [1925–26]); Alexei Tolstoy, *The Garin Death Ray* (Moscow: Foreign Languages, 1955), 23, 118–24, 223; André Maurois, *The Next Chapter* (London: Paul, 1927), 54, 73. On particle rays as a sure weapon of the coming war, see also Hiram Percy Maxim, "The Next War in the Ether," *Popular Mechanics* (April 1936): 530–37.

50. V. Vogak, *Smert'* (Leningrad: RKKF, 1926), 1, 97; *Voina i revoliutsiia* 7 (1926): 166–67. The Newtonian critique is in *Vestnik vozdushnogo flota* 8 (1924): 72–76, and was repeated by Philp, *Stratosphere and Rocket Flight*, 91–97.

51. "Tendentsii razvitiia tvorcheskoi mysli v oblasti voennoi tekhniki" (1928–29), RGVA, f. 33989, o. 1, d. 97, ll. 32, 46–47. On the military's interest in "death rays," see also the review of experimental programs (1929–30), RGVA, f. 33989, o. 1, d. 66, ll. 17–20.

52. The report on Tesla (September 1934) is in RGVA, f. 33988, o. 3, d. 346, ll. 20–25.

53. James R. Randolph, "Can We Go to Mars?" *Scientific American* (August 1928): 140–42. Rutherford MacMechen, "Rockets, the New Monsters of Doom," *Liberty*, 19 September 1931, 16–19.

54. Gen. William Mitchell, "The Next War—What about Our National Defense?" *Liberty*, 27 June 1931, 38–40, 43. M. A. Stuart, "Heavy Artillery vs. Rockets," *Field Artillery Journal* 21, no. 6 (November and December 1931): 630, 640, repeated these exact claims and images.

55. See Robert Lademann, "Die militärische Bedeutung des Rückstossers (Raketenproblem)," *Militär-Wochenblatt* 113, no. 25 (January 1929): 991–94; as well as 114, no. 26 (11 January 1930): 1002–6; and 114, no. 38 (11 April 1930): 1490–92. Soviet publicists responded in kind. See M. Eigenson, "Kosmicheskie korabli," *Vestnik znaniia* 17–18 (1931): 886–88; N. A. Rynin, *V stratosferu!* (Leningrad: Molodaia gvardiia, 1934), 3–14; and V. Vnukov, *Mozhno li streliat' na sto kilometrov?* (Moscow: Gosvoenizdat, 1935), 50–51.

56. I. M. Maiskii's reminiscences, in *Marshal Tukhachevskii*, edited by N. I. Koritskii et al. (Moscow: Voenizdat, 1965), 229. S. Biriuzov, "Predislovie," in M. N. Tukhachevskii, *Izbrannye proizvedeniia*, 2 vols. (Moscow: Voenizdat, 1964), 1:18–23. Sally Stoecker, *Forging Stalin's Army* (Boulder: Westview, 1998), 156–58.

57. For the contexts, see Mikhail Tsypkin's ground-breaking "The Origins of Soviet Military Research and Development System, 1917–1941" (PhD diss., Harvard University, 1985), 80–83, 194–95, and all of chap. 5.

58. GDL report (1928–29), RGVA, f. 33989, o. 1, d. 96, l. 221. The quote—*reaktivnoe deiatel'nost'*—is from RGVA, f. 33989, o. 1, d. 97, ll. 16–24.

59. "'Will Be Reported to Berlin' [November 1932]," in *The Red Army and the Wermacht*, edited by Iu. L. Diakov and T. S. Bushueva (Amherst: Prometheus, 1995), 113–14.

60. Tukhachevskii's report on his German trip to Voroshilov, 14 November 1932, RGVA, f. 33988, o. 3, d. 235, ll. 45–54.

61. Quoted from the government observational report, June 1933, ARAN, r. 4, o. 14, d. 243, ll. 41–43. See also Siddiqi, *Red Rockets' Glare*, 136–40.

62. See the Directorate's report, 22 August 1933, GARF, f. 8355, o. 1, d. 374, ll. 142–43; and the "Order" of the Red Army Ordinance Chief, 17 May 1933, and the official report on GIRD finances, 10–15 April 1933, both in GARF, f. 8355, o.1, d. 374, ll. 72–76.

63. Tukhachevskii's report, "Ob organizatsii Reaktivnogo Instituta," 16 May 1932, ARAN, r. 4, o. 14, d. 243, ll. 7–9.

64. My information is drawn from the RNII report (1936), Rossiiskii Gosudarstvennyi Arkhiv Ekonomiki (RGAE), f. 8159, o. 1, d. 147; and the report of air force commander Alksnis (August 1933–March 1934), RGVA, f. 29, o. 76, d. 100, ll. 145–52.

65. Government observational report, June 1933, ARAN, r. 4, o. 14, d. 243, ll. 41–43; "Inostrannaia aviatekhnika," 20 July 1933, RGVA, f. 29, o. 76, d. 94, ll. 21–55.

66. Descriptions of the new RNII buildings, 9 April 1933, ARAN, r. 4, o. 14, d. 243, ll. 31–32.

67. G. E. Langemak and V. P. Glushko, *Rakety* (Moscow: NKTP, 1935), 1–3. M. K. Tikhonravov, *Raketnaia tekhnika* (Moscow: Glavnaia aviatsionnaia redaktsiia, 1935), was another such primer.

68. Goddard and Pendray, *Papers of Robert H. Goddard*, 3:829, 848, 864, 1128, 1331, 1349.

69. See A. B. Scherschevsky, *Die Rakete für Fahrt und Flug* (Berlin: Volckmann, 1929), 80; Salvatore De Santis, "Stralci di Astronautica," *L'ala di Italia* 11 (November 1930): 911–12; I. Fortikov, "Raketa i ee primenenie," *Znanie-sila* 23–24 (1932): 18; A. A.

Butler, ed., *Reaktivnoe dvizhenie* (Leningrad: GROL, 1935), 3. The quote is from L. K. Korneev's letter to Stalin and Voroshilov, 13 May 1937, in ARAN, r. 4, o. 14, d. 150, ll. 19–21.

70. Michael Neufeld, *The Rocket and the Reich* (Cambridge: Harvard University Press, 1996), 6–34.

71. See Stanislaus Bialkowski's *Leuchtfeuer im Mond* (1934), *Krieg im All* (1935), and *Die macht des Unsichtbaren Stern* (1936), stories that fought wars for German racial superiority (and rejuvenation)—in the stratosphere, between Earth and Mars, even with wandering planets. See also the books of Walter Heichen, K. Eduard May, Rudolf Daumann, Paul Eugen Sieg, Gerhard Naundorf, and Arthur Oprée.

72. Minutes of the Osoaviakhim Presidium, 21 March 1933, GARF, f. 8355, o. 1, d. 43, l. 131. For the contexts, see Mark Harrison, "The Market for Inventions: Experimental Aircraft Engines," in *Guns and Rubles*, edited by Mark Harrison (New Haven: Yale University Press, 2008), 220.

73. Record of the Osoaviakhim Presidium, 10 April 1933, GARF, f. 8355, o. 1, d. 71, ll. 231–39. On the importance of GIRD's propaganda work, see V. M. Komarov, "K 40-letiiu so vremeni organizatsii v GIRD-e inzhenerno-konstruktorskikh kursov po reaktivnoi tekhnike (1932 g.)," *Iz istorii aviatsii i kosmonavtiki* 14 (1972): 118–21.

74. *Vestnik vozdushnogo flota* 12 (1934): 17–19.

75. S. P. Korolev, M. K. Tikhonravov, G. E. Langemak, and V. P. Glushko openly advised AVIAVNITO, as noted in the "thematic plan" of its Stratospheric Bureau, 18 August 1934, RGVA, f. 29, o. 76, d. 100, ll. 134–37. See public mention of them in *Nauka i zhizn'* 8 (1935): 33; and *Pravda* 99, 9 April 1936, 6.

76. On the need for inventors to reach for the fantastic, even for outer space, see *Izobretatel'* 11 (1934): 26–27; and 5 (1935): 6–9, from which I have quoted; and *Front nauki i tekhniki* 2 (1935): 11–13; and *Voina i revoliutsiia* 3 (1929): 102–5.

77. *Komsomolskaia pravda*, 17 February 1934, 3; and 18 August 1934, 3–4.

78. See also the articles by K. E. Tsiolkovskii, Iu. A. Pobedonostsev, V. I. Duda kov, M. V. Machinskii, and A. N. Shtern, in S. I. Vavilov, ed., *Trudy vsesoiuznoi konferentsii po izucheniiu stratosfery* (Leningrad: Akademiia nauk, 1935).

79. The conference program (Vsesoiuznaia konferentsiia po primeneniiu reaktivnykh letatel'nykh apparatov k osvoeniiu stratosfery) is in GPM NA, fond KETS, ed., khr. 19373, ll. 2–3, 4–5. See M. K. Tikhonravov, "Primenenie raketnykh letatel'nykh apparatov dlia issledovaniia stratosfery," in Vavilov, *Trudy vsesoiuznoi konferentsii*, 839–40; his "Primenenie raket dlia issledovaniia stratosfery," in *Raketnaia tekhnika*, edited by I. T. Kleimenov et al. (Moscow: ONTI, 1936), 18, 32–33; and Tikhonravov, "Puti ispol'zovaniia luchistoi energii dlia kosmicheskogo poleta," in *Reaktivnoe dvizhenie*, edited by P. S. Dubenskii et al. (Moscow: ONTI, 1936), 109–40.

80. "Trip to Moon Is Aim of Soviet Scientists," *Monthly Evening Sky Map* 29, no. 340 (April 1935): 2. See also the mention of L. K. Korneev's work in *New York Times*, 14 July 1935, XX6.

81. See the pieces by Alfred Busemann, Maurice Roy, N. Rynin, and Giulio Costanzi in Fondazione Alessandro Volta, *Le alte velocita in aviazione. Convegno di Scienze Fisiche, Matematiche e Naturali* (30 September–6 October 1936) (Rome:

Reale Accademia d'Italia, 1936), 563–628; and Alfred Busemann, "Compressible Flow in the Thirties," *Annual Review of Fluid Mechanics* 3 (1971): 7.

82. See Crocco's remarks, and N. A. Rinin, "Propulsione a reazione," in Fondazione Alessandro Volta, *Le Alte Velocita in Aviazione*, 18–20, 628, 645–55. For similar insights (including Rynin's rocket drawings), see Giulio C. Costanzi, *Elementi di aerodinamica e di dinamica del volo* (Rome: Aeronautica, 1938), 125–26.

83. See B. V. Raushenbakh, *German Obert* (Moscow: Nauka, 1993), 48–49, 60–63; the Osoaviakhim internal memorandum, 2 March 1932, GARF, f. 8355, o. 1, d. 370, l. 4; and Tukhachevskii's memorandum, 20 February 1932, GARF, f. 8355, o. 1, d. 370, l. 18.

84. A. A. Shternfel'd, *V Vedenie v kosmonavtiku* (Moscow: Glav. aviats. lit., 1937). Shternfel'd also published several dense technical pieces for the RNII's house journal, *Raketnaia tekhnika* 4 (1937): 13–41; and 5 (1937): 156–63.

85. This episode is also highlighted (citing different sources) in Mark Harrison, "A Soviet Quasi-Market for Inventions: Jet Propulsion, 1932–1946," *Research in Economic History* 23 (2005): 29. For more about Engel, see Michael J. Neufeld, "Rolf Engel vs. the German Army," *History and Technology* 13 (1996): 53–72.

86. Rolf Engel, "Realizatsiia poleta rakety," RGVA, f. 33988, o. 3, d. 218, ll. 161–47, and the assessment of the Technical Staff, 14 March 1932, ll. 162–63.

87. See "O rabote Goddarda po konstruirovaniiu raket v 1930–1932 gg.," containing the report of Kleimenov, 14 July 1935; and Tukhachevskii's letter to Voroshilov, 23 July 1935, ARAN, r. 4, o. 14, d. 245, ll. 1–4, 5–6.

88. Quotes from *Voina i revoliutsiia* 5–6 (1932): 166–74; and *Nauka i zhizn'* 8 (1935): 31–32, the latter a plagiarism from *Popular Mechanics* 57, no. 3 (March 1932): 462. See also the translations of Western articles in RGAE, f. 7516, o. 1, d. 323, ll. 1–18. Harrison, "Soviet Quasi-Market for Inventions," 30, discusses these dragnets of the foreign press.

89. Quoted from the reports of the RNII directors, 1936, RGAE, f. 8159, o. 1, d. 147; and d. 149, l. 220.

90. Kleimenov correspondence to Voroshilov, 27 August 1934, RGVA, f. 4, o. 4s, d. 1237, ll. 4–5. On the political rivalries in the RNII, see V. F. Rakhmanin and L. E. Sternin, eds., *Odnazhdy i navsegda* (Moscow: Mashinostroenie, 1998), 402–11.

91. From Ia. Terent'ev, head of the Red Army Directorate of Military Inventions, 5 September 1934, RGVA, f. 4, o. 4s, d. 1237, ll. 6–7.

92. "Top secret" KB-7 materials, 1938, ARAN, r. 4, o. 14, d. 150, l. 87; and RGAE, f. 8162, o. 1, d. 89, l. 122. See also Rakhmanin and Sternin, *Odnazhdy i navsegda*, 412–19; and Korneev's and Poliarnyi's memoirs in ARAN, r. 4, o. 14, d. 150.

93. Quoted from A. I. Polyarnyi, "On Some Work Done in Rocket Techniques," in Durant and James, *First Steps toward Space*, 191. For more on the achievements of KB-7, see Asif Siddiqi, *Challenge to Apollo* (Washington DC: NASA, 2000), 8–9.

94. Korneev's letter, 10 June 1935, ARAN, r. 4, o. 14, d. 150, ll. 27–37, 58; and letters to Stalin, 12 April 1937, ll. 16–17; and 15 June 1937, RGVA, f. 4, o. 14, d. 1628, ll. 123–26. On Korneev's problematic claims, see Rakhmanin and Sternin, *Odnazhdy i navsegda*, 415–18.

95. Memoirs of M. N. Kireev and M. G. Vorob'ev, ARAN, r. 4, o. 14, d. 291, ll. 77–81, l. 183.

96. For these views and quotes, see Korneev's letters to Stalin and others, 1937–38, in ARAN, r. 4, o. 14, d. 150, ll. 48–70; and RGVA, f. 4, o. 14, d. 1628, ll. 123–26.

97. Mark R. Beissinger, *Scientific Management, Socialist Discipline, and Soviet Power* (Cambridge: Harvard University Press, 1988), 94; Robert Tarleton, "'Bolsheviks of Military Affairs': Stalin's High Commands" (PhD diss., University of Washington, 2000); D. A. Sobolev, "Represii v sovetskoi aviapromyshlennosti," *Voprosy istorii estestvoznanii i tekhnologii* 4 (2000): 44–58.

98. For these contexts, see Tsypkin, "Origins of Soviet Military Research," 261–62; Rakhmanin and Sternin, *Odnazhdy i navsegda*, 99–101, 419–26; Mark Harrison and Andrei Markovich, "Hierarchies and Markets," in Harrison, *Guns and Rubles*, 73–75; and Siddiqi, *Red Rockets' Glare*, 155–95. The archives corroborate these discussions in the annual report of rocket research, 1938, RGAE, f. 8162, o. 1, d. 89, l. 25; and Military-Industrial Commission report to L. M. Kaganovich, September–May 1939, GARF, f. 8418, o. 27, d. 125, l. 11.

99. Arthur Koestler, *Darkness at Noon*, translated by Daphne Hardy (1941; repr., New York: Bantam, 1981), 11. Korolev was in prison in Moscow between June 1938 and June 1939, at the Kolyma camps from June 1939 to September 1940, then on to a prison laboratory for the rest of the war.

100. Shternfel'd delivered a lecture, "Ob osobennostiakh stratosfernoi rakety," at the Moscow Planetarium in 1937. See A. A. Shternfel'd "Nauchnye problemy kosmonavtiki," *Sovetskaia nauka* 7 (1939): 123–46.

101. See A. Shternfel'd, "Paradoksy rakety," *Tekhnika molodezhi* 1 (1940); and 12 (1940); Shternfel'd's popular pieces in *Nauka i zhizn'* 11–12 (1938); 3 (1939); and 2 (1940); *Znanie-sila* 11 (1939); and Shternfel'd, "Rakety," *Bol'shaia Sovetskaia Entsiklopediia*, 65 vols. (Moscow: Sovetskaia entsiklopediia, 1941), 48:199–202.

102. Report to Voroshilov, 20 December 1938, RGVA, f. 33987, o. 3, d. 1119, ll. 9–11; and Air Force Academy critique, 17 June 1937, d. 940, ll. 35–38.

103. For context, see Harrison, *Guns and Rubles*, 216–17. On continued support for liquid fuel rocketry, see the rocket research plans for 1939–40, in RGAE, f. 8162, o. 1, d. 300, ll. 64, 80; and RGAE, f. 7515, o. 1, d. 319, ll. 1–3. The request for a research trip, made on 2 April 1940, is in RGAE, f. 8162, o. 1, d. 305, l. 30.

104. Kendall Bailes, *Technology and Society under Lenin and Stalin* (Princeton: Princeton University Press, 1978), 405.

10. Stalinism and the Genesis of Cosmonautics

1. The term is from F. A. Tsander, "Dogonim i peregonim," 26 October 1931, ARAN, f. 573, o. 1, d. 252, l. 1. G. Arel'skii, "O problemakh poezii budushchego," *Vestnik znaniia* 2 (February 1930): 54–55.

2. Aleksandr Prokof'ev, *Sobranie sochinenii*, 4 vols. (Moscow: Khudozhestvennaia literatura, 1965), 1:95, 107–8, 127–29, 188, 425.

3. A. Gurshtein, "Poet sotsializma," *Pravda*, 12 April 1937, 4. See, e.g., M. P. Gerasimov, *Zariad* (Moscow: Tovarishchestvo pisatelei, 1933). For context, see Boris Groys and Max Hollein, eds., *Dream Factory Communism* (Schirn-Frankfurt: Hatje Kantz, 2003), 107–15, 260–77.

4. Quoted from the magazine *30 dnei* 5 (1931): 79–80; see also the front cover for 10–11 (1931); and *Krasnaia panorama* 39, 23 September 1927.

5. See these images and terms in *Komsomolskaia pravda* 18, 21 January 1934, 3; and 2, 1 January 1934, 4. *Shestaia chast' mira*, directed by Dziga Vertov (1926; Moscow: Sovkino).

6. Note the alignments of the signs of the zodiac and Lenin's portrait, along with Stalin's funeral oath for Lenin in 1924, in *Nauka i zhizn'* 1 (1936), front cover to p. 3.

7. See K. F. Iuon's painting *Liudi* (1930), in Ia. V. Apushkin, *Konstantin Fedorovich Iuon* (Moscow: Vsekhudozhnik, 1936), 78–79. El Lissitzkii's sculpture (with the assistance of Georgii Krutikov) for the "Pressa" Exhibition at Cologne (1928) is in Sophie Lissitzky-Küppers, *El Lissitzky* (Greenwich: Graphic Society, 1968), plate 201.

8. Dem'ian Bednyi, "Stal'naia krepost'," *Pravda*, 29 January 1937, 6; Leonid Ravich, "Vozdukhoflotskii marsh," *Iunyi proletarii* 3 (February 1931): 15.

9. *Znanie-sila* 23–24 (December 1932). The cartoon about Alesha is in "Puteshestvie na lunu," *Kolkhoznye rebiata* 10 (1937): 36. See also A. Abramov, *Raketa* (Moscow: Molodaia gvardiia, 1931).

10. Ia. I. Perel'man, *Mezhplanetnye puteshestviia* (Moscow: ONTI, 1935). See *Komsomolskaia pravda* 81, 5 April 1934, 4; and 222, 23 September 1934, 4; M. Val'e, *Polet v mirovoe prostrantvo kak tekhnicheskaia vozmozhnost'*, edited by V. P. Vetchinkin and translated by S. A. Shorygin (Moscow: ONTI, 1936); German Noordung, *Problema puteshestviia v mirovom prostrantsve*, edited and translated by B. M. Ginzburg (Moscow: ONTI, 1935).

11. K. E. Tsiolkovskii, *Na lune*, edited by Ia. I. Perel'man (Moscow: ONTI, 1934); K. E. Tsiolkovskii, *Grezy o zemle i nebe*, edited by Ia. I. Perel'man (Moscow: ONTI, 1935). Quoted from *Pioner* 21 (1932): 6–7; and 20 (1935): 10–12.

12. A. Volkov, "K. E. Tsiolkovskii i deti," in Islent'ev, *K. E. Tsiolkovskii*, 223. Malkov's story is told in ARAN, r. 4, o. 14, d. 223, ll. 53–65. The photograph is in *Znanie-sila* 23–24 (1932): 6; and *Izobretenie* 10 (1935): 5.

13. Nik. Bobrov, *Liudi-ptitsy* (Moscow: Osoaviakhim, 1930), 6–7; and N. N. Bobrov, *Bol'shaia zhizn': Tsiolkovskii* (Moscow: Aviaavtoizdat, 1933).

14. Iu. Geko, "Spirali k solntsu," *Priroda i liudi* 2, 30 January 1931, 6–8.

15. See the cartoon drawing in *Komsomolskaia pravda* 197, 24 August 1934, 6. I. Ivanov, "Korifei tekhnicheskoi mysli," *Komsomolskaia pravda* 218, 19 September 1940, 5.

16. Paraphrased from the thirteen "Steps in Reaction Development," in K. E. Tsiolkovskii, "Trudy o kosmicheskoi rakete," in Dubenskii et al., *Reaktivnoe dvizhenie*, 11–12. Tsiolkovskii revised these "steps" from an original sixteen-step plan that he had devised in 1926.

17. Ia. I. Perel'man, *Tsiolkovskii* (Leningrad: Gostekhizdat, 1932), 8–12, 69; I. Merkulov, "Tsiolkovskii," in *Bol'shaia Sovetskaia Entsiklopediia*, 65 vols. (Moscow: OGIS, 1934), 60:734.

18. *30 dnei* 9 (1932): 53, 59; *Iunyi proletarii* 10 (May 1933): 17; and *Nauka i zhizn'* 11 (1935): 54–55.

19. B. P. Veinberg, *Solntse* (Moscow: ONTI, 1935); and Charles Abbot, *Solntse*, edited by Ia. I. Perel'man and translated by N. Ia. Bugoslavskii (Moscow: ONTI, 1936); K. E. Tsiolkovskii, *Budushchee zemli i chelovechestva* (Kaluga: Izd. avtora, 1928); and Tsiolkovskii, "Solntse i zavoevanie pustyn'," *Vestnik znaniia* 5–6 (1933): 182–83.

20. Quoted from Aleksandr Beliaev, "Tsiolkovskii," *Iunyi proletarii* 31–32 (November 1932): 7–9; and Aleksandr Beliaev, "Pamiati velikogo uchenogo-izobretatelia," *Iunyi proletarii* 23 (1935): 43–44.

21. K. E. Tsiolkovskii, *Izbrannye trudy*, vol. 1: *Tsel'nometallicheskii dirizhabl'*, edited by Ia. A. Rapoport (Moscow: ONTI, 1934); A. Beliaev, "Vozdushnyi korabl'," *Vokrug sveta*, starting with nos. 10–12 (1934).

22. See S. A. Shlykova, "K. E. Tsiolkovskii's Correspondence with the Jet Scientific-Research Institute," in *Soviet Rocketry*, edited by A. A. Blagonravov and translated by H. I. Needler (Jerusalem: Scientific Translations, 1966), 127–32.

23. A. R. Palei, "Nauchno-fantasticheskaia literatura," *Literaturnaia ucheba* 2 (1936): 119–27. A. R. Palei, *Planeta KIM* (Kharkov: Proletarii, 1930), a novel for teenage readers. KIM was an abbreviation for the *Kommunisticheskii Internatsional Molodezhi* (Communist Youth International).

24. See Aleksandr Beliaev, *Pryzhok v nechto* (Leningrad: OGIZ, 1933); and Beliaev, *Zvezda KETS* (Moscow: Detlit, 1940).

25. V. M. Vladko, *Argonavty vselennoi* (Rostov-Don: Oblizdat, 1939). For another story that detailed Tsiolkovskii's and Tsander's rockets, see Iu. Lipilin, "Polet na Mars," *Tekhnika molodezhi* 12 (1940): 174–89.

26. From the pamphlet *Vzgliad v budushchee* (Simferopol': Krymradiokomitet, 1941); Aleksei Tolstoi, *Aelita* (Moscow: Detlit, 1937), a juvenile edition with drawings by P. A. Aliakrinskii.

27. *Komsomolskaia pravda* 120, 24 May 1934, 6.

28. *Kosmicheskii reis*, directed by V. Zhuravlev (1935; Moscow: Moscow Film Studio). Several of the sketches are in K. E. Tsiolkovskii, *Works on Rocket Technology* (Washington DC: NASA, 1965), 89, 236, 377–79, 382–83. The famous pilot M. M. Gromov also consulted on the look of the rocket cabin; the astronomer K. N. Shestovskii advised on the lunar landscape.

29. A. Garri and L. Kassil', *Potolok mira* (Moscow: Sovetskaia literatura, 1934), 12–121. Also see my earlier discussion at pages 221–22.

30. All of these images are based on my readings of *Izvestiia* and *Pravda* at the time of his death and on his biographies, with special attention to Lev Kassil', "Zvezdoplavatel' i zemliaki," in Islent'ev, *K. E. Tsiolkovskii*, 160–68. See also James T. Andrews, *Red Cosmos* (College Station: Texas A&M University Press, 2009), 86, 92–94.

31. Kleimenov letter to Stalin, 2 November 1935, RGVA, f. 4, o. 14, d. 1398, l. 54. See also Korneev's letters to Stalin, 12 April 1937, ARAN, r. 4, o. 14, d. 150, ll. 16–17; and 15 June 1937, RGVA, f. 4, o. 14, d. 1628, ll. 123–26.

32. Karl Radek, *Portraits and Pamphlets* (New York: McBride, 1935), 4, 12.

33. The translation and context is in Gregory Freidin, *A Coat of Many Colors* (Berkeley: University of California Press, 1987), 252–58.

34. The quote is from "Rech' tov. Suleimana Stal'nogo," *Pravda* 99, 19 February 1936, 22. See the balloon on Stalin's seventieth birthday, in *Ogonek* 52, 25 December 1949, front cover. On Stalin and the "vertical," see Vladimir Paperny, *Architecture in the Age of Stalin* (New York: Cambridge University Press, 2002).

35. H. G. Wells, *Experiment in Autobiography* (New York: Macmillan, 1934), 685, 689–700.

36. H. G. Wells, *The Shape of Things to Come: The Ultimate Revolution*, edited by Patrick Parrinder (1933; repr., New York: Penguin, 2003), 393, 446, 508; Haldane, *Inequality of Man*, 99, 266.

37. *Things to Come*, directed by William Cameron Menzies (1936; London: Film Productions); Waldemar Kaempffert, *Science Today and Tomorrow* (New York: Viking, 1939), 246.

38. Engels, *Dialectics of Nature*, 2–9, 22–23. On these notions, see also K. L. Baev et al., *Istoriia vzgliadov na stroenie i proiskhozhdenie vselennoi* (Moscow: Gosuchebizd., 1931), 91–92, 100–102; and V. L'vov, "Nauchnoe obozrenie," *Molodaia gvardiia* (1937): 177–86.

39. Engels, *Dialectics of Nature*, 28–38. Quoted from "Lenin," *Pechat' i revoliutsiia* 1 (January–February 1924): 5; and from G. F. Aleksandrov, *Trudy I. V. Stalina o iazykoznanii i voprosy istoricheskogo materializma* (Moscow: Gosizdat, 1952), 508.

40. Engels, *Dialectics of Nature*, 51, 171, 187.

41. See Gustav A. Wetter, *Dialectical Materialism*, translated by Peter Heath (New York: Praeger, 1958), 77, 101, 140–46, 296, 329–36, 490–96; and V. I. Lenin's own devotion to "self-movement" and the "spiral," from "On the Question of Dialectics," *Collected Works*, 45 vols. (London: Lawrence & Wisehart, 1961), 38:143, 228, 233, 247, 359–63.

42. V. Evgen'ev, "Shturm vselennoi," *Vestnik znaniia*, 3 March 1934, 156–57. New books on astronomy included P. I. Pavlov, K. L. Baev, and N. N. L'vov, *Astronomiia* (Moscow: Uchpedgiz, 1934); M. S. Eigenson, *Bol'shaia vselennaia* (Moscow: Akademiia nauk, 1936); and K. L. Baev, *Kopernik* (Moscow: Ob'edinenie, 1935).

43. G. A. Gurev, *Nauka i religiia o vselennoi* (Moscow: Molodaia gvardiia, 1938), 33, 58, 80–81, 90–91.

44. Compare "U velikoi mogily," *Pravda*, 21 January 1937, 6, with N. Kruzhkov, "Planetarii," *Pravda*, 2 June 1937, 4.

45. D. Galanin, "Kak velik mir," *Iskra* 8 (August 1924): 7–10. See the placard by N. A. Morozov, "Mekhanika neba," in *Vestnik znaniia* 4 (1930), foldout supplement. See also the large color foldout in the *Boston Sunday Post*, 26 June 1932, 2.

46. The comments of G. A. Nadson and colleagues in S. I. Vavilov, ed., *Trudy vsesoiuznoi konferentsii po izucheniiu stratosfery* (Leningrad: Akademiia Nauk, 1935),

551–84. Soviet accounts remained open to Arrhenius's "seeding" theory (married to Bakhmet'ev's anabiosis) and Oparin's views, as in *Iunyi proletarii* 1 (November 1934): 43–46; and *Druzhnye rebiata* 2 (1938): 27–28.

47. V. I. Vernadskii, "Biosfera i stratosfera," in Vavilov, *Trudy vsesoiuznoi konferentsii po izucheniiu stratosfery*, 575–78; I. P. Fortikov, "Biosfera," and N. A. Rynin, "Reaktivnoe dvizhenie v prirode," both in *Priroda* 9 (1936): 27–45.

48. See *National Geographic* 69, no. 1 (January 1936): 81; and 69, no. 5 (May 1936): 697, 705–6.

49. E. M. Antoniadi, *Le planète Mars* (Paris: Hermann, 1930). Through the 1930s *Popular Astronomy* and *Popular Science* offered a series of articles arguing the full scope of the question, for and against life on Mars. See similar pieces in *Nauka i zhizn'* 4 (1937): 26; and *Vozhatyi* 2–3 (1945): 3–4.

50. A. K. Suslov, *Gavril Adrianovich Tikhov* (Leningrad: Nauka, 1980), 62, 77, 107; G. A. Tikhov, *Astrobiologiia* (Moscow: Molodaia gvardiia, 1953).

51. K. L. Baev and V. A. Shishakov, *Pravda o nebe* (Moscow: OGIZ, 1941), 58, 67; and K. L. Baev, *Obitaemy li planety?* (Moscow: Gosizdat, 1936).

52. See *Mirovedenie* 4 (1935): 261; and *Molodaia gvardiia* 7 (1937): 186.

53. Sir James Jeans, *The Stars in their Courses* (1931; repr., New York: Macmillan, 1933), 22, 123. Also quoted from the preface, in *Dvizhenie mirov* (Moscow: Gostekhizdat, 1933), 7–8; and from *Druzhnye rebiata* 3 (1936): 25–27.

54. A. I. Oparin, *Proiskhozhdenie zhizni* (Moscow-Leningrad: ONTI, 1935); and Oparin, *The Origin of Life*, translated by Sergius Morgulis (New York: Macmillan, 1938). Laurence La Fleur, "Astrobiology," *Monthly Evening Sky Map* 36, no. 426 (December 1942): 8. See also Reinhold Beutner, *Life's Beginning on Earth* (Baltimore: Williams, 1938), 89–99, for a total acceptance of Oparin's thesis.

55. *Monthly Evening Sky Map* 36, no. 422 (July–August 1942): 3; and *Popular Mechanics* 48, no. 6 (December 1927): 963. See also Bruce Barton, "The Conflict between Science and Religion," *Popular Science Monthly* (October 1927): 12; Willelm de Sitter, *Kosmos* (Cambridge: Harvard University Press, 1932); Frances Mason, ed., *The Great Design* (New York: Macmillan, 1934); and Louise E. Ballhausen, "Astronomy and Religion," *Popular Astronomy* 48, no. 8 (October 1940): 429.

56. As reported in the *Monthly Evening Sky Map* 20, no. 232 (April 1926): 2; Harlow Shapley quoted in the *New York Times*, 5 October 1930, XX4.

57. Albert Einstein, "Religion and Science," *New York Times*, 9 November 1930, SM1 (with the drawing); and from the set of essays both critiquing and praising Einstein's views, in the *New York Times*, 16 November 1930, XX3. For a similar image, see Frank Reh, "A Journey through Space," *Sky* 1 (November 1936): 8.

58. See Einstein's remarks in the *New York Times*, 17 June 1930, 3.

59. Alexandre Ananoff, *La navigation interplanétaire* (Paris: Société astronomique, 1935), 3, 9–10, 13–16, 27–30.

60. Lucien Rudaux, *Sur les autres mondes* (Paris: Larousse, 1937), 115, 216–19. For context, see Jean-Pierre Maury, *Le palais de la découverte* (Paris: Gallimard, 1994).

61. Gerald Heard, *The Ascent of Humanity* (New York: Harcourt, Brace, 1929), 21–25, 62, 156, 211.

62. Heard, *Ascent of Humanity*, 159, 214–47. See Heard, *The Third Morality* (New York: Morrow, 1937), 158–69; and *The Science Front 1936* (London: Cassell, 1937), 159–60, 207–8, 216.

63. Heard celebrated the human mind as a kind of rocket in *These Hurrying Years* (New York: Oxford University Press, 1934), 310, 349–51; and *Exploring the Stratosphere* (London: Nelson, 1936). On the rocket as bridge into the future and toward space, see also Vernon Sommerfield, *Speed, Space, and Time* (London: Nelson, 1935), 292–96.

64. Olaf Stapledon, *Starmaker* (1937; repr., Middletown CT: Wesleyan, 2004), 271. Two coming science fiction writers, Arthur C. Clarke and Stanislaw Lem, were both fans of Stapledon's work.

65. Stapledon, *Starmaker*, 18–22, 65, 78, 87, 142.

66. Stapledon, *Starmaker*, 3, 263, 267.

67. See *Popular Science Monthly* (January 1928 and October 1936 issues); and *Popular Mechanics* 57, no. 3 (March 1932): 422. Hadley Cantril, *The Invasion from Mars* (Princeton: Princeton University Press, 1940).

68. Immanuel Velikovsky, *Worlds in Collision* (New York: Doubleday, 1950). He had begun these studies in 1940 and first serialized the book in *Collier's* magazine. For the full contexts, see Michael D. Gordin, *The Pseudoscience Wars* (Chicago: University of Chicago Press, 2012).

69. David Lasser, *The Conquest of Space* (New York: Penguin, 1931), 13, 19, 67–77, 103, 115, 123–24. See also Lasser's articles in *Scientific American* (March 1931): 164–66; *Nature* 18, no. 5 (November 1931): 275–78; and *Bulletin of the American Interplanetary Society* 13 (November 1931): 6–8.

70. On these scores, see also G. Edward Pendray's pieces in *Bulletin of the American Interplanetary Society* 5 (November–December 1930): 1–4; *Sky* 1 (November 1936): 21; and G. Edward Pendray, *The Coming Age of Rocket Power* (New York: Harper, 1945): 224.

71. *Astronautics* 37 (July 1937): 16. See *Bulletin of the American Interplanetary Society* 22 (August–September 1932): 4–5; *Astronautics* 33 (March 1936): 9–13; and 34 (June 1936): 18.

72. De Witt Douglas Kilgore, *Astrofuturism* (Philadelphia: University of Pennsylvania Press, 2003), 32–41; Lilith Lorraine, *The Brain of the Planet* (New York: Stellar, 1929), 16–19. On the progressive and socialist tendencies among rocketry and science fiction fans, see Cheng, *Astounding Wonder*, 236–37.

73. "Next Big Advance in Transport Due by Rockets, Says Lindbergh," *New Haven Register*, 5 June 1937, 1; "Lindbergh Visions Travel in Rockets," *New York Times*, 6 June 1937, 30; *New York Herald Tribune*, 26 September 1935, 16. See the front cover and Peter van Dresser, "By Virtue of Circumference," *American Boy* 11 (November 1937): 5–7.

74. Quoted from "Mural on Transportation Building by Carlo Ciampaglia,"

in the folder "Texas Centennial Exposition Dallas Texas. Typescripts 1935–1937," box 2 of 13, "Project Files, Murals," Carlo Ciampaglia Papers, Archives of American Art of the Smithsonian Institution.

75. On these approximations, see Susan Buck-Morss, *Dreamworld and Catastrophe* (Cambridge MA: MIT Press, 2000).

76. Richard Stites, *Revolutionary Dreams* (New York: Oxford University Press, 1989), 8–9, 243–44, 249.

77. Darko Suvin, *Metamorphoses of Science Fiction* (New Haven: Yale University Press, 1979), 28. Czesław Miłosz, *The Captive Mind*, translated by Jane Zielonko (New York: Vintage, 1981), 200 (originally published in France in 1953).

78. These quotes are both from advertisements in *Popular Science Monthly* (January 1931 and November 1930). On America's obsession with speed, see Enda Duffy, *The Speed Handbook* (Durham: Duke University Press, 2008).

79. See *Popular Aviation* 21 (July 1937): 43–44; and *Popular Mechanics Magazine* 57, no. 4 (April 1932), supplement without page numbers.

80. On this Soviet approach, with accompanying graphs, see *Komsomolskaia pravda*, 15 September 1934, 4; *Nauka i zhizn'* 8 (1935): 28–30; 11 (1936): 24; and *Molodaia gvardiia* 5 (1939): 144–60.

81. See the map in *Pravda* 190, 12 July 1937, 2.

82. These stories are told in Lowell Thomas and Lowell Thomas Jr., *Famous First Flights That Changed History* (Guilford CT: Lyons, 2004), 236–54; Palmer, *Dictatorship of the Air*, 235–37; and Chkalov's reminiscences in *Istoricheskii arkhiv* 2 (2004): 3–20.

83. V. Endrzhievskii, ed., *Kryl'ia sovetov* (Moscow: Iskusstvo, 1939), 12–14 (and the companion poems, 21–29, 37, 44, 110); and *Pravda*, 18 August 1937, 2.

84. Endrzhievskii, *Kryl'ia sovetov*, 69–75; and the issues of *Pravda*, 12 July 1937, 1–2; 22 July 1937, 2; and 28 July 1937, 4.

85. Boris Chertok, *Rockets and People*, translated by Asif Siddiqi (Washington DC: NASA, 2005), 124.

86. See Viktor Gusev, "Letiat nashi letchiki," *Pravda*, 25 June 1937, 3; Georgii Baidukov's story (and cartoon by K. Rotov) "Cherez dva poliusa," *Pravda*, 18 August 1937, 4.

87. See the story by L. Los', "Cherez dva poliusa," *Komsomol'skaia pravda*, 19 August 1939, 4. Stratosphere and transglobal flights were favorites in science fiction in these years: Grigorii Adamov, "V stratosphere," *Druzhnye rebiata* 11 (November 1938): 30–31; and Sergei Beliaev, *Istrebitel 2z* (Moscow: Detlit, 1939), 75. Quoted from Semen Kirsanov, "Poputchiki solntsa," in Endrzhievskii, *Kryl'ia sovetov*, 60–63.

88. My descriptions of the fair are drawn from several sources: *Official Guide Book of the New York World's Fair 1939* (New York: Exposition, 1939); Helen Harrison, ed., *Dawn of a New Day* (New York: New York University Press, 1980); and Larry Zim, Mel Lerner, and Herbert Rolfes, eds., *The World of Tomorrow* (New York: Harper & Row, 1988).

89. Edmund Gilligan, "The Report of a Subway Explorer," *Sun* (New York), 29 April 1939, sec. 2, 1.

90. See the models for Leonidov's Lenin Institute (1927) and *Columbus Monument* (1929) in Selim O. Khan-Magomedov, *Pioneers of Soviet Architecture*, edited by Catherine Cooke and translated by Alexander Lieven (New York: Rizzoli, 1987), 220–21, 233–34, 554.

91. See Zim, Lerner, and Rolfes, *World of Tomorrow*, 37, 52. The sketch is in Harrison, *Dawn of a New Day*, 79.

92. *Official Guide Book of the New York World's Fair 1939*, 45. Anthony Swift, "The Soviet World of Tomorrow at the New York World's Fair," *Russian Review* 57 (July 1998): 377–78.

93. For representative articles, note *Popular Mechanics* 59, no. 5 (May 1933): 657–59; 64, no. 2 (August 1935): 203; 82, no. 2 (August 1944): 18. Norman Bel Geddes, *Horizons* (Boston: Little, Brown, 1932), 291.

94. On cars, see *Scientific American* (June 1927): 386; (March 1930): 185–87; and *Popular Mechanics* 72, no. 3 (September 1939): 348. See also Jeffrey L. Meikle, *Twentieth Century Limited* (Philadelphia: Temple University Press, 1979), 176–77.

95. See J. M. Walsh, *Vandals of the Void* (1931; repr., Westport CT: Hyperion, 1970); Bob Olsen, "Captain Brink of the Space Marines," *Amazing Stories* 7, no. 8 (November 1932): 722; and J. Schlossel, "The Second Swarm," *Amazing Stories Quarterly* 1, no. 2 (Spring 1928): 266.

96. On the February of 1940 outing to Philadelphia, see Goddard and Pendray, *Papers of Robert H. Goddard*, 3:1350.

97. Originally named the "Missouri Rockets" (founded in St. Louis in 1925), their name was changed to the "Rockettes" in 1932.

98. "Rocket Cars," *Popular Science Monthly* (June 1933): 31; "The Editorial Viewpoint," *Aircraft Engineering* 79 (September 1935): 212.

99. *Official Guide Book of the New York World's Fair 1939*, 200. Quoted from *Astronautics* 43 (August 1939): 1, 16. For favorable reviews of the fair, highlighting Loewy's Rocketport, see *La science et la vie* 55, no. 264 (June 1939): 418–31; and *Novyi mir* (December 1939): 110–11.

100. The ticket for the ride is in the Technical Reference Files, folder #OR-600000-22, "Rocket Vehicles, Articles, 1930s," at the National Air and Space Museum Library, Washington DC; *Official Guide Book of the New York World's Fair 1939*, 67–68.

101. Pseudoman (Edwin Fitch Northrup), *Zero to Eighty* (Princeton: Scientific Publishing, 1937), 99, 178–79, 249.

102. N. A. Rynin, *Russkii izobretatel' i uchenyi K. E. Tsiolkovskii* (Leningrad: Profintern, 1931); Ia. I. Perel'man, *Tsiolkovskii* (Moscow-Leningrad: ONTI, 1937); B. Vorob'ev, *Tsiolkovskii* (Moscow: Molodaia gvardiia, 1940).

103. Vorob'ev, *Tsiolkovskii*, 168–69. Vorob'ev remained a prominent Tsiolkovskii scholar into the "Sputnik era."

Conclusion

Epigraph: From the poem (circa 1934) in P. Antokol'skii, *Sobranie sochinenii*, 4 vols. (Moscow: Khudozhestvennaia literatura, 1971), 1:380.

1. Leonard Engel, "Secret Rocket Weapons Blast Tanks and Planes," *Popular Science* (July 1943): 50–54.

2. Dornberger, *V-2*, 3, 8–12, 16–17.

3. Michael Neufeld, *The Rocket and the Reich* (Cambridge: Harvard University Press, 1996), 275.

4. Dornberger, *V-2*, 16–17.

5. Dornberger, *V-2*, 104; Neufeld, *Rocket and the Reich*, 192.

6. Thomas Pynchon, *Gravity's Rainbow* (New York: Penguin, 1973), 48, 674.

7. Mark Harrison, "A Soviet Quasi-Market for Inventions: Jet Propulsion, 1932–1946," *Research in Economic History* 23 (2005): 17. For the precise Soviet expenditures, see Siddiqi, *Red Rockets' Glare*, 167–68. Goddard's rockets saw no application in the war; instead, he eased into a small corner of the immense military-industrial complex, building "jet-assisted takeoff devices" for patrol planes, hardly one of the more glamorous research and development missions of the war.

8. On how Soviet "previous accumulation" in jet and rocket technologies—although scattered by the Terror, shortages, and war—were quickly reconfigured after the V-2, e.g., see Mark Harrison, "New Postwar Branches (1): Rocketry," in *The Soviet Defence-Industry Complex from Stalin to Khrushchev*, edited by J. Barber and M. Harrison (Basingstoke: Macmillan, 2000), 147.

9. These stories are told in Ordway and Sharpe, *Rocket Team*, 254–362; and Neufeld, *Rocket and the Reich*, 267–79.

10. The influence of the V-2 upon the first Soviet ballistic missiles is compelling. Compare Igor Afanasyev, "The Legacy of the V-2," *Journal of Slavic Military Studies* 11, no. 4 (December 1998): 164–74; and Olaf Przybilski, "The Germans and the Development of Rocket Engines in the USSR," *Journal of the British Interplanetary Society* 55 (2002): 404–27.

11. Compare S. I. Vavilov, *Isaak N'iuton* (Moscow: Akademii nauk, 1943), 204–5; with J. W. N. Sullivan, *Isaac Newton, 1642–1727* (New York: Macmillan, 1938), 266–69.

12. Mark Mills, Howard S. Seifert, and Martin Summerfield, "Physics of Rockets," *American Journal of Physics* 15, no. 3 (May–June 1947): 260. See also J. M. J. Kooy and J. W. H. Uytenbogaart, *Ballistics of the Future* (New York: McGraw-Hill, 1946); and George P. Sutton's classic *Rocket Propulsion Elements* (New York: Wiley, 1949).

13. Willy Ley and Chesley Bonestall, *The Conquest of Space* (New York: Viking, 1949), 20–26; Willy Ley, "Station in Space," *Collier's*, 22 March 1952, 30–31; Werner von Braun, "Prelude to Space Travel," in *Across the Space Frontier*, edited by Joseph Kaplan et al. (New York: Viking, 1952), 16–18; "Extra-Atmospheric War," *Time*, 2 September 1946, 52.

14. Chertok, *Rockets and People*, 334. M. K. Tikohnravov had actually admitted this much earlier, that the complex work of designing a workable, reliable, constant-

exhaust, properly cooled, liquid fuel rocket engine was at its "beginnings" ("Opyt-nye kharakteristiki raketnogo dvigatelia," *Raketnaia tekhnika* 7 [1938]: 129–73).

15. C. S. Lewis, *Perelandra* (1943; repr., New York: Scribners, 1972), 70–80, 112–13. See also the companion books, *Out of the Silent Planet* (1938) and *That Hideous Strength* (1945). Andrey Platonov, *Happy Moscow*, translated by Robert and Elizabeth Chandler (London: Harvil, 2001), 40, 95, 82–84.

16. G. Edward Pendray, "The Reaction Engine," *Popular Science Monthly* (May 1945): 70–74; and Pendray, *Coming Age of Rocket Power*. R. I. Farnsworth, *Rockets* (Glen Ellyn IL: Rocket Society, 1945), 5–21. Sutton, *Rocket Propulsion Elements*, 24–25, also recognized Kibalchich's and Tsiolkovskii's preeminence.

17. F. Zwicky, "Morphological Astronomy," *Observatory* 68, no. 845 (August 1948): 121–43.

18. Ley, *Rockets*; Herbert S. Zim, *Rockets and Jets* (New York: Harcourt, 1945), 310; Arthur C. Clarke, *Interplanetary Flight* (London: Bowling Green, 1950); and Clarke's more popular *The Exploration of Space* (New York: Harper, 1951). Heinlein was one of the writers for the screenplay of *Destination Moon*, directed by Irving Pichel (1950; Los Angeles: General Service Studios), from which I have quoted.

19. Murray Robinson, "Planet Parenthood," *Collier's*, 5 January 1952, 31, 63–64.

20. Hannibal Coons, "The Moon Maiden," *Collier's*, 10 November 1951; and Kurt Vonnegut Jr., "Thanasphere," *Collier's*, 2 September 1950, 19, 60–62.

21. See *Collier's*, 22 March 1952, 23; and 11 October 1952, 74.

22. Braun, "Prelude to Space Travel," 16, 22; and Ley, "Station in Space," 30–31. For context, see De Witt Douglas Kilgore, *Astrofuturism* (Philadelphia: University of Pennsylvania Press, 2003), 54–57.

23. The decree, "On the Questions of Reaction Weaponry," signed by Iosif Stalin, 13 May 1946, is in Iu. P. Semenov, ed., *Raketno-kosmicheskaia korporatsiia "Energiia"* (Korolev: Energiia, 1996), 12.

24. A. E. Fersman, ed., *Rasskazy o nauke i ee tvortsakh* (Moscow: Detlit, 1946), 249; and V. Bolkhovitinov, ed., *Rasskazy o russkom pervenstve* (Moscow: Molo-daia gvardiia, 1950), 99, 128, 204–6, 221, 249–52, 265. See also Inzh. M. Arlazarov, "Pioner zvezdoplavaniia," *Vozhatyi* 9 (1945): 8–9. For more on these usages and contexts, see Gruntman, *From Astronautics to Cosmonautics*; and Nikolai Krementsov, *Stalinist Science* (Princeton: Princeton University Press, 1997), 179–80, 223–24, 290. On the American obsession with its "greats" and "firsts," see *Popular Mechanics* 41, no. 6 (June 1924): 812.

25. From A. A. Kosmodem'ianskii, "Plan meropriiatii," 1947, RGASPI, f. 17, o. 125, d. 545, ll. 115–16. A host of books followed this directive: S. M. Iliashenko, *Bystree zvuka* (Moscow: Tekhniko literatury, 1947); K. A. Gil'zin, *Raketnye dvigateli* (Moscow: Gosizdoboron., 1950); B. V. Liapunov, *Problema mezhplanetnikh puteshestvii* (Moscow: DOSAV, 1951); N. G. Chernyshev, *Problema mezhplanetnykh soobshchenii* (Moscow: Znanie, 1953); and A. A. Kosmodem'ianskii, *Znamenityi deiatel' nauki* (Moscow: Voenizdat, 1954).

26. See *Znanie-sila* 8 (August 1948): 4–9; and 4 (April 1950): 7–8. For the wider

historical contexts, see Paul R. Josephson, "'Projects of the Century' in Soviet History," *Technology and Culture* 36, no. 3 (July 1995): 519–59.

27. Viktor Saparin, *Novaia planeta* (Moscow: Molodaia gvardiia, 1950), 6–12, 16. For another such story promoting the rocket, see Sergei Beliaev, *Desiataia planeta* (Moscow: Detgiz, 1945).

28. Vasilii Zakharchenko, *Puteshestvie v zavtra* (Moscow-Leningrad: Detlit, 1952).

29. B. Liapunov, *Otkrytie mira* (Moscow: Molodaia gvardiia, 1954), 125–27, 137, 155.

30. On these scores, see G. Gurev, "Krainosti vo vselennoi," *Znanie-sila* 11 (November 1948): 17–20; and Gurev, "Net granits poznaniia," *Znanie-sila* 7 (July 1949): 8–12.

31. See A. P. Kazantsev, "Vzryv," *Vokrug sveta* 1 (1946): 43; and B. Liapunov, "Iz glubiny vselennoi," *Znanie-sila* 10 (October 1950): 4–7, with front cover as well. Quoted from I. Yefremov, "Stellar Ships," in *Stories* (Moscow: Foreign Languages, 1954), 256–60 (originally serialized as I. A. Efremov, "Zvezdnye korabli," *Znanie-sila*, starting with 7–10 [July–October 1947]). A. A. Shternfel'd proved Kazantsev wrong, calculating that it was impossible for a Martian landing at that time, given celestial mechanics and rocket flight. See V. I. Prishchepa and G. P. Dronova, *Ari Shternfel'd*, edited by B. V. Raushenbakh (Moscow: Nauka, 1987), 93–94.

32. Ia. I. Perel'man, "Planeta mars i usloviia zhizni na nei," preface to Gerbert Uells, *Bor'ba mirov* (Moscow: Narkompros, 1945); R. S. Richardson and Glenn C. Moore, "What You Would Find on Mars," *Popular Mechanics* 72, no. 2 (August 1939): 218.

33. See L. A. Syrkin, *Bor'ba za dolgoletie* (Moscow: Ministerstvo zdravokhraneniia, 1946), 4–5, 20; Z. G. Frenkel', *Udlinenie zhizni i deiatel'naia starost'* (Moscow: Akad. meditsinskikh nauk, 1949); and A. V. Nagornyi, *Starenie i prodlenie zhizni* (Moscow: Sovetskaia nauka, 1950).

34. Georgii Gurevich, "Chelovek-raketa," *Znanie-sila* 10–11 (October–November 1946): 18–25; and 12 (December 1946): 14–22; B. Vorob'ev, "K. E. Tsiolkovskii," *Znanie-sila* 12 (December 1946): 25–29.

35. Quoted from K. L. Baev and V. A. Shishkov, *Nachatki mirovedeniia* (Moscow: OGIZ, 1945), 91–92. See also G. Gurev, "Skazka o gibeli zemli," *Znanie-sila* 12 (December 1950): 17.

36. *Pervye na lune*, directed by Aleksei Fedorchenko (2005; Sverdlovsk: Sverdlovsk Film Studio); Alexander I. Solzhenitsyn, *The First Circle*, translated by Thomas P. Whitney (New York: Bantam, 1969), 366, set in the late Stalin years.

37. See the subtitles of the story and the preface by Frederick Ordway, in Aleksandr Beliayev, *The Struggle in Space*, translated by Albert Parry (Washington DC: Arfor, 1965), v–vii.

38. Compare *Science and Invention* (February 1924): 962, 977, to *Tekhnika i zhizn'* 12 (1924): back cover. The Russian versions, with new English translations, are in the folder "USSR General, 1900–1939, Part 1 file" (record #14789), NASA Headquarters Archive, Washington DC.

39. Eugene Emme's letter "Request for Translation of Classic Soviet Encyclopedia by Rynin on Interplanetary Travel," 24 March 1970, in his biography file (record #585) at NASA Headquarters Archive, Washington DC.

40. Tom Wolfe, *The Right Stuff* (1979; repr., New York: Bantam, 2001), 28, 43, 55, 90, 97, 186, 215, 237.

41. McDougall, *Heavens and the Earth*.

42. See David Grinspoon, *Lonely Planets* (New York: HarperCollins, 2003), 224–27; Marina Benjamin, *Rocket Dreams* (New York: Free Press, 2003), 123; and quoted from Greg Klerkx, *Lost in Space* (New York: Vintage, 2005), 181, 353.

43. William Townsend and Roger Launius quoted in "March 16 Marks 75th Anniversary of First Liquid-Fueled Rocket Launch," *NASA News*, 12 March 2001; Neil Armstrong, "Goddard, Governance, and Geophysics," at the panel on the "Apollo 11 Moon Mission," Smithsonian National Air and Space Museum, 19 July 2009, aired on the C-SPAN Cable Network.

44. Theodore von Karman and Lee Edson, *The Wind and Beyond* (Boston: Little, Brown, 1967), 240–42. Frank Malina, "On the GALCIT Rocket Research Project, 1936–1938," in Durant and James, *First Steps toward Space*, 118, repeated the claim; as did J. D. Hunley, "The Legacies of Robert H. Goddard and Hermann J. Oberth," *Journal of the British Interplanetary Society* 49 (1996): 43–48; and B. V. Raushenbakh, *German Obert* (Moscow: Nauka, 1993), 5, 131.

45. V. I. Prishchepa, "5 Oktiabria–90 let so dnia rozhdeniia R.Kh. Goddarda," *Iz istorii aviatsii i kosmonavtiki* 14 (1972): 86–89; A. A. Blagonravov, ed., *Pionery raketnoi tekhniki* (Moscow: Nauka, 1977); I. N. Bubnov, *Robert Goddard* (Moscow: Nauka, 1978); V. N. Sokol'skii, "Raboty R. Kh. Goddarda," *Issledovaniia po istorii i teorii razvitiia aviatsionnoi i raketno-kosmicheskoi nauki i tekhniki* 3 (1984): 148–72.

46. See the images in A. E. Snopkov, ed., *Kosmos budet nash* (Moscow: Kultura, 2009); and *Nauka i zhizn'* 1 (1961): 34. Arthur C. Clarke, *2001: A Space Odyssey* (1968; repr., New York: ROC, 2005), 30–31, 179–80, 196, 230–33.

47. Carl Sagan, *Cosmos* (New York: Random House, 1980), 241. Compare Sagan's plaque designs with the picture in Willy Ley, "How Will You Talk to the Martians?" *Mechanix Illustrated* (December 1947): 88. My thanks to Melinda S. Zook (Purdue University) for seeing this comparison and for offering many valuable insights upon reading (and rereading) my book manuscript.

Selected Bibliography

Internet Sites

Several Internet sites have been valuable as archives of historical texts and information:

Anatoly Zak's "Russian Space Web," www.russianspaceweb.com/.

Mark Wade's "Encyclopedia Astronautica," www.astronautix.com/index.html.

Sergei Khlynin's "Epizody Kosmonavtiki," http://epizodsspace.no-ip.org/.

Archives

The abbreviations stand for: fond/collection (f.); opis'/group (o.); razriad/category (r.); delo/file (d.); and list/page (l.).

MOSCOW

ARAN. Arkhiv Rossiiskoi Akademii Nauk / Archive of the Russian Academy of Sciences
   ARAN f. 555, K. E. Tsiolkovskii
   ARAN f. 573, F. A. Tsander
   ARAN f. 928, N. A. Rynin
   ARAN f. 1703, A. L. Chizhevskii
   ARAN r. 4, "Raketnaia tekhnika"
Razriad (r.) 4, formerly known as "Dokumental'nykh materialov postoiannogo khraneniia po istorii raketnoi tekhniki v SSSR za 1932–1966 gg.," includes files, interviews, and reminiscences meant to celebrate (not document) USSR spaceflight achievements. I have cited these sources with care.
I thank the archivists at ARAN for their special help in locating files and identifying and procuring several of my figures.

GARF. Gosudarstvennyi Arkhiv Rossiiskoi Federatsii / State Archive of the Russian Federation

GARF f. P-7752, Vsesiouznye Otraslevye Obshchestva Izobretatelei i Ratsion-
alizatorov, 1930–38

GARF f. P-8355, Obshchestvo Sodeistviia Oborone, Aviatsionnomu i Khimi-
cheskomu Stroitel'stvu SSSR (Osoaviakhim), 1927–48

GARF f. P-9404, Obshchestvo Druzei Aviatsionnoi i Khimicheskoi Oborony i
Promyshlennosti SSSR (Aviakhim), 1925–27

GPM. Gosudarstvennyi Politekhnicheskii Muzei / State Polytechnic Museum
GPM NA, fond KETS, ed. khr. 19354, 19368, 19373, K. E. Tsiolkovskii
I would like to thank Iurii Vasilievich Biriukov and Maia Arievna Shternfel'd
of the State Polytechnic Museum for their valuable research help.

RGAE. Rossiiskii Gosudarstvennyi Arkhiv Ekonomiki / Russian State Econom-
ics Archive
RGAE f. 7515, Narodnyi Komissariat Oboronnoi Promyshlennosti SSSR (1936–39)
RGAE f. 7516, Narodnyi Komissariat Boepripasov SSSR
RGAE f. 8159, Narodnyi Komissariat Tiazheloi Promyshlennosti
RGAE f. 8162, Glavnoe Upravlenie po Proizvodstvu Korpusov Boepripasov
Portions of fond 8162 (as, e.g., o. 1, d. 62, on the work of KB-7 in 1938–39) were
closed in 2008–9.

RGASPI. Rossiisskaia Gosudarstvennaia Arkhiv Sotsial'no i Politicheskoi Istorii /
Russian State Archive of Social and Political History
RGASPI f. 17, Tsentral'nyi Komitet KPSS
RGASPI f. 386, Mekhlis, L. Z.

RGVA. Rossiiskii Gosudarstvennyi Voennyi Arkhiv / Russian State Military Archive
RGVA f. 4, Narodnyi Komissariat Oborony SSSR
RGVA f. 29, Glavnoe Upravlenie Voenno-Vozdushnogo Flota
RGVA f. 24699, Voenno-Vozdushnaia Akademiia im. Zhukovskogo
RGVA f. 33987, f. 33988, and f. 33989, Revoliutsionnyi voennyi sovet SSSR
Several important RGVA sources dealing with the RNII and KB-7 were closed
in 2008–9, including RGVA f. 33987, o. 3, dela 601, 831, 196; RGVA f. 33988,
o. 3s, dela 187, 202, 204, 205, 228–33, 248, 295, 303, 318, 360; and all of RGVA
f. 34272 (Otdel Izobretatel'stva).

WASHINGTON DC

Archives of American Art of the Smithsonian Institution
Carlo Ciampaglia Papers

National Aeronautics and Space Administration (NASA) Headquarters (History
Office and Archive)
I used the archive's extensive media, biographical, and topical folders, including the copies of Soviet papers presented at the symposia of the International Academy of Astronautics in the 1960s and 1970s.

National Air and Space Museum (NASM) Branch Library and Archives Division
    of the Smithsonian Institution
    Record Unit 7090, Robert Hutchings Goddard Papers
    Technical Reference Files, books, and journals
    Wright Field Technical Documents Library, 1915–55

National Archive Records Administration
    Record Group 18, Records of the Army Air Forces, 1917–38
    Record Group 342, Records of U.S. Air Force Commands, Activities, and
        Organizations
    Record Group 407, Records of the Adjutant General's Office, Central Files, 1923–39

The Interlibrary Loan office at Purdue University libraries was also invaluable in providing me with many of the books and periodicals cited in this study. I am grateful for the help.

Index

aviation (*cont.*)

and Soviet holiday, 168, 272; and Soviet
institutions, 250, 261, 280, 298; and spaceflight, 77–86; and weaponry, 134–37, 271,
277, 289–91, 376n13

Aviation All-Union Scientific-Engineering
Technical Society (aviavNITO), 280

Baev, K. L., 145, 301, 311, 408n38

Baidukov, Georgii, 323–24

Bailes, Kendall, 291

Bakhmet'ev, P. I., 48–51, 209, 211, 360n20,
409n46

balloon, 54, 89, 107, 137, *138*, 185, 305,
370n87, 398n5; in flight (aerostat), 40, 106;
in science fiction, 13–14, 26, 61, 97; for the
stratosphere (stratostat), 182, 253–71, *259*,
260, *267*, *270*, 281, 294, *310*

Bal'mont, Konstantin, 91–92

Bariatinskii, V., 61

Becker, Karl, 224, 392n10

Bednyi, Demian, 116, 258, 296

Beissinger, Mark, 288

Bellamy, Edward, 34

Belomor, A., 37

Bel'skii, S., 21

Bely, Andrei, 39, 106, 109

Berdiaev, Nikolai, 47, 127

Bergson, Henri, 3–4, 89, 107, 115, 117, 200

Berman, Marshall, 4

Bernal, J. D., 192–93

Besant, Annie, 63

Binder, Joseph, 324–25, *325*

biocosmism, 126–33

biology, 45, 129, 235, 301, 314; and abiogenesis, 188, 190; and evolution, 31, 42, 55;
and population growth, 207; and science
fiction, 213; as transformational science,
9, 31, 126, 130, 160, 186, 191, 306, 351

biosphere, 13, 204–5, 309–10, *310*

Birnbaum, E. K., 258

Blavatskaia, E. P., 63

Bloch, Jan, 38–39

Bobrov, N., 298

Bogdanov, Aleksandr, 31, 41–42, 86, 94, 101,
126, 174, 189, 202, 214

Bogomolets, A. A., 209–10

Bölsche, Wilhelm, 34, 44

Bolsheviks, 133, 139, 143, 153, 163, 294, 347;
and ideology, 31, 189; initiative of, 115–16,
288; and rocket, *159*, 305; Russian Revolution and, 103, 105–6, 184–87, 215; and
utopia, 155, 208–9, 258, 262, 321

Bonnier, Louis, 26

Brett, H. C., 278

Brisbane, Arthur, 32–33

British Interplanetary Society, 173, 237

Briukhonenko, S. S., 209

Briusov, Valerii, 39–40, 96, 125, 140, 196

Brown, Edward, 119

Brown-Séquard, Charles, 51

Bucke, Richard Maurice, 90, 199, 305, 312,
314–15

Buck Rogers, 264, *267*, 328, 334, 339

Bukharin, N. I. (Nikolai), 97, 111, 189, 262

Bull, Harry W., 240

Bureau for the Study of Reactive Engines,
145, 154

Bürgel, Bruno, 84, 176

Burgess, Eric, 237

Burroughs, Edgar Rice, 171, 279

Busemann, Adolf, 282

calculus, 6, 107, 207, 210, 214, 244–45, 251,
301; and Hermann Oberth, 147, 149, 224;
as an international language, 233, 337;
and I. P. Meshcherskii, 72–73, 283; and
Isaac Newton, 3, 74, 86, 169, 227; and K. E.
Tsiolkovskii, 74–75; and V. I. Lenin, 144,
157; and Walter Hohmann, 150, 281

capitalism, 42, *112*, 114, 211, 272, 299, 320,
327; and rivalry with communism, 143,
197, 202–3, 272, 307, 352

Carrell, Alexis, 206, 209, 214

catapult ramp, 221–22, 303–4, *303*, *304*, *343*,
391n2, 407n29

"catch and surpass" (*dognat' i peregnat'*), 6,
157, 248, 283, 293, 341, 349

Centennial of Flight, 352

Century of Progress, 260, 265

Century of Progress Exposition (Chicago,
1933), 256, 328

Chashnik, Il'ia, 124

Chekrygin, V. F., 45

and M. N. Tukhachevskii, 277, 284–85, 285; and rivalries, 11, 82, 146–60, 221, 225–28, 234, 241, 250–52, 282, 299, 367n45; and Roswell, 246–48, 314, *315*; in various media, 137, 170–78, 184, 193, 213, 215, 217, 238–40, 301–2, 330, 376n23, 377n32; and vision, 15, 100

Godunov, K. D., 258

Golden Gate International Exposition (San Francisco, 1939), 329

Gordin, A. L., 129–30

Gordin, V. L., 129–32, 216

Gorkii, Maksim, 39, 118, 196, 280, 296, 308

Gornostaev, A., 50–51

Gorodetskii, Sergei, 98

Gorokhov, Aleksandr, 79–80

Grave, S. L., 179

gravity, 4, 20, 23, 45, 83, 114, 117, 140, 152, 238, 248, 290; and Albert Einstein, 183–85; and aviation, 26, 95, 180; and death, 53, 79; and Isaac Newton, 2, 31, 72, 86, 158, 308; and K. E. Tsiolkovskii, 74–76, 96, 165, 304, 369n73; in media, 93, 98, 121, 127, 133, 150, 177, 202, 328, 330, 338, 349; planetary, 9, 58, 65, 81–82, 84, 89, 98, 100, 192, 205, 317, 346; and planetary assist, 151, 177, 236, 290; zero form of, 69–70, 82, 100, 124, 144, 164, 167–68, 179, 183, 193, 229, 233, 236, 302, 329, 339

Greg, Percy, 57, 172

Griffith, George, 106

Group for the Study of Reactive Propulsion (GIRD), 250–52, 276–77, 279–80, 286–87

Gruzdev, F. S., 25

Guggenheim, Daniel, 239, 245–46, 278

Guggenheim Aeronautical Laboratory of the California Institute of Technology (GALCIT), 246

Gusalli, Luigi, 147

Haeckel, Ernst, 30, 32, 206

Hagermeister, Michael, 206

Haldane, J. B. S., 191–93, 306

Halley, Edmund, 21

Halley's comet, 21, 82, 234

Harbou, Thea, 228

Harrison, Mark, 336

Hayden Planetarium, 340

Heard, Gerald, 256, 314–15

Hegel, G. W. F., 4, 22, 117

Heinlein, Robert, 339, 414n18

Heylandt, Paul, 232

Hinton, Charles, 89

Hitler, Adolf, 276, 291, 335

Hohmann, Walter, 150–51, 177, 224, 233–34, 281, 290

"Hollow Earth," 230

Houllevigue, Louis, 200

Huxley, Aldous, 213–14

Huxley, Julian, 176

Huxley, T. H., 188

Iakubovskii, Georgii, 115–16

Iaroslavskii, Aleksandr, 126, 186

Iazvitskii, Valerii, 162, 179–80

ice death, 34, 143, 186, 202–3, 316

I Know All, 21, 56, 78, *343*

immortality, 128; and flight, 9, 81, 94–97, 315, 350; philosophy of, 29, 33, 39, 45, 47–53, 89–90, 126–29, 193, 206–7, 312; science fiction and, 62–64, 208–17, 306, 338, 351

Infant'ev, P. P., 60–61, 363n52

Integral: in calculus, 107, 144, 150, 233; in science fiction and ideology, 50, 59–60, 74, 132, 165–66, 349

interplanetary communication, 9, 75, 125–26, 142, 152, 158, 298, 326; and alien life, 53–62; science fiction and, 111, 113, 301–5

Inter-Universe Grand Tours, 329–32, *331*, *332*

Irwin, Will, 135

Itin, Vivian, 132–33

Iuon, K. F. (Konstantin), 111–12, *112*, 294, 326

Jeans, James, 311–12

jet, 6, 35, 143, 213, 239, 250–51, 276–77, 280–81, 291, 329; and assisted takeoffs, 291, 413n7; and engines, 78, 232–33, 250–51, 291, 337; and military, 134–35, 154, 287, 289, 336; in science fiction, 213, 242, 340

Jordan, David Starr, 25

Jupiter, 35, 113, 151, 195, 309, 328

Kaempffert, Waldemar, 204, 306

Kalmykov, Viktor, 124

75, 111, 143, *162*, 167–76, 179, 183, 185, 210,
279, 302, 338, 340, 363n50, 403n71; travel
to, 82–83, 112–13, 150–51, 177, 250, 275, 347
Martens, L. K. (Liudvig), 145, 154
Marx, Karl, 4, 97, 115, 117, 213, 294, 307–8
Marxism, 60, 108, 188, 191, 193, 196, 205,
211, 319; and dialectical materialism, 11,
116; and historical materialism, 22, 97,
196, 202
Marxism-Leninism, 7, 307, 321
Matsievich, L. M., 78–80
Maxim, Hudson, 99
McDougall, Walter, 78, 349, 354n21
Mechnikov, Il'ia, 52–53, 96, 210, 361n28
Melies, Georges, 70–71, *71*, 365n16
Memorial Museum of Cosmonautics, 351
Mercury, 59
Meshcherskii, I. P., 72–73, 182, 283
meteor, 13, 43, 72, 112, 137, 255, 297, 329; and
rocket, 82, 106, 152, 168, 213–14, 222, 228,
230–31, 345
Meyer, Max Wilhelm, 30–32, 34, 44
Michaelis, Sophus, 172
Millikan, Clark, 246
"Mirak," 223–24, 392n9
Mitchel, Ormsby, 24–25
Mitchell, Billy, 275
Molotov, V. M., 277
Mont Blanc, 49, 60
moon, 39, 74, 90–91, 115, 124, 144, 216, 227,
266, 319, 329–30, 339–40, 350; race to, 8,
10; in science fiction, 12–14, 59, 69–71, *71*,
86, 94, 97, 100–101, 111, 176, 179–80, 186,
213, 228–30, 239, 243, 254, 274, 296, 301–2,
328, 345, 347; travel to, 1, 82–83, *85*, 137,
140–42, 147–49, 151, 154–55, 158–60, 177–
79, 183–85, 194, 210, 217, 223, 236, 241, 243,
247, 249, 282, 298–99, 317, 324, 342–45, 352
Moreux, Théophile, 70, 83, 137, 197
Morozov, N. A. (Nikolai), 107–8, 115, 139,
228, 316
Moscow Higher Technical School, 215
Moscow Planetarium, 296, 308, 405n100
Mukhanov, N. I., 112–13
Mulford, Prentice, 48
Munro, John, 75–76
Muraviev, V. N., 185

National Aeronautics and Space Adminis-
tration (NASA), 319, 348–50
National Air and Space Museum (NASM),
348
National Foundation for Scientific Research
(Belgium). See FNRS
National Geographic Society, 263, 269
Nemilov, A. V., 188, 211
Neufeld, Michael, 222
The News (*Izvestiia*), 109, 148, 203
Newton, Isaac, 45, 60, 67, 72, 74, 76, 86,
95, 107, 130, 169, 183, 274, 307–8, 337, 346;
influence of, 19–22; and orbital mountain
and canon, 84, 159; and third law of
motion, 1–3, 12, 31, 63, 136, 158, 166, 200,
274, 307, 314, 335, 336, 346
New York City World's Fair (1939), 324–27,
325, 329–31, *331*, *332*
Nietzsche, Friedrich, 4, 114
Nikolskii, V. D., 213
Noordung, Hermann, 151–52, 177, 224, 233,
297, 379n56
Nordmann, Charles, 195
North Pole, 77, 99, 322, 324
Northrup, E. F., 330

Oberth, Hermann, 5, 11, 153, 158, 160, 176,
205, 213, 215, 221, 239, 242, 250, 277–78,
283, 298–99; early writings of, 145–51;
later writings of, 223–36
OIMS. *See* Society for the Study of Interplanetary Travel (OIMS)
Okunev, Iakov, 213
Olcott, Henry Steele, 63
Oparin, Aleksandr, 189–93, 309, 312, 386n13,
409n46, 409n54
optics, 9, 26, 342
optimism: and aviation and spaceflight, 139,
147; and human progress, 25, 42, 52, 92,
207, 314; and rocketry, 247, 338; and Russian Revolution, 20, 182, 204, 301
Osborn, Henry Fairfield, 188–89
Osoaviakhim, 277, 279, 288, 399n18
Osoaviakhim 1, 261, 265–66, 269, *310*

Palace of Soviets, 303–4, *303*, *304*, 324, 327
Palei, A. R., 301
Palmer, Scott, 137

"panspermia" thesis, 43, 46, 171, 187–89
Papp, Desiderius, 193–94
parabola: in rocketry, 9, 81, 84, 101, *159*, 225, 230; in science, 3, 5, 24, 150, 190, 199–200; in various media, 36, 71, 76, 88–89, *88*, 119, *123*, *159*, 166–67, 170, *201*, 202, 210, 222, 294, *300*, 314, 322–23, 326, 330, *344*, 345, 352
paradigm of magnification, 25–26, 30, 70, 309, 314, 345, 351
Paris Gun, 136–38, *138*, 222, 275, 335, 391n4
Paris International Exhibition (1937), 313
Parsons, Jack, 5, 246
Pavlov, I. P. (Ivan), 52, 116, 196, 336
Pearl, Raymond, 207
Peenemünde, 242, 279, 291, 334–35
Pendray, G. Edward, 242–43, 245, 252, 338
People's Commissariat of Internal Affairs (NKVD), 285, 288
People's Commissariat of the Defense Industry, 287
Perel'man, Ia. I. (Iakov): and early influence, 83–86, 95, 139, 155; as Soviet publicist, 148, 153, 248, 280–81, 296, 330, 346
Perisphere and Trylon, 324–26, *325*
Piccard, Auguste, 182, 253–58, 260–61, 264, 266, *270*, 398n5
Pickering, W. H., 56
Pilniak, Boris, 210
Platonov, Andrei, 179, 338
plurality thesis, 12, 25–27, 35, 54, 63, 70, 128, 132, 164, 311
Pobedonostsev, Iu. A., 250, 252, 281, 283
Polevoi, G. A., 215–16
Poliarnyi, A. Ia., 286–87
Poor, Charles Lane, 181
Popular Science, 56, 158, 239, 243, 286, 321, 330, *331*
Potapenko, I. N., 96
Prix Internationale d'Astronautique. *See* REP-Hirsch prize for astronautics
Proctor, Mary, 149, 217
Proctor, Richard, 83
Prokof'ev, Aleksandr, 293
Prokof'ev, G. A., 258
Proletkul't, 110, 116, 165, 293
promethianism: as ideology of progress, 29, 47, 82; in imperial Russian culture, 86–97;

in Soviet ideology, 110, 175, 205, 293, 305, 341; and visions of spaceflight, 150, 177, 193, 283, 323, 330
Protozanov, Iakov, 174
Pynchon, Thomas, 336

Radek, Karl, 305
Reactive Scientific Research Institute (RNII), 277–86, *285*, 288, 290, 300, 305
Reade, William Winwood, 28–30, 199, 315
Redon, Odilon, 26
rejuvenation, 51–52, 96, 126–29, 206–15, 338, 346, 390n76, 403n71
REP-Hirsch prize for astronautics, 235, 282, 290
"Repulsor," 86, 224, 274
revolution, 1, 52, 81, 98, 101, 116, 144, 182–84, 194–96, 208, 233, 305–8, 317; in history, 7, 16, 19–24, 27–37, 96, 134, 143; and language, 216; in literature and art, 41, 64, 106–9, 113, 115, 117, 119–33, 163, 174–75, 328; and rejuvenation, 214; and rockets, 6–10, 19, 101, 106, 143, 159, 167, 199, 224–25, 253, 275, 280, 294, 317, 318, 354n21
Rezunov, M. A., 153
Ricard, J. S., 197
Richter, H. E., 43
Riumin, V. V., 81, 148, 366n41
RNII. *See* Reactive Scientific Research Institute (RNII)
Robida, Albert, 36–38
Robinson, Hugh Mansfield, 173
rocket, 1–2, 9, 19, 24, 65, 204–5, 214–17, 313, 337–39; American culture and, 327–32, 340, 345, 349; in art, 119–25, 143, *156*, *159*, *178*, *249*, *295*, *297*, *303*, *304*, *310*, *320*, *331*, *332*, *343*, *344*; first images of, *79*, *85*, *162*, *343*; and metaphor, 3–4, 7–9, 16, 43, 95, 101, 110, 118–19, 135, 193, 199–202, 228, 294, *295*, 307, *310*, 314–19, 334–35, 346, 351–52; and pioneers, 11, 67–69, 72–78, 80–84, 98, 101, 106, 140–51, 221–52, 280–86, 290; in poetry, 1, 79, 118, 162, 227; race for, 5–12, 217, 221, 226–28, 231, 238–39, 248, 253–56, *285*, 330, 335–40; and relativity, 180–84; in science fiction, 12, 14, 35, 70, 74–75, 86, 106, 126, 163–80, 186,

192–94, 197, 210–14, 228, 230–31, 323–24;
and solid fuel, 221–22, 232–33, 237–46,
276–77, 286, 336; Stalinism and, 296–306,
341–45, *343, 344*; as weapon, 7, 134–38,
272–79, 284–91, *285*
"rocket problem," 226
rocket science, 6, 10–11, 19, 73, 157, 200, 217,
244–45, 289–90, 301, 313, 328, 337, 341,
349, 352; origins of, 75–77, 101, 140–42,
173, 184, 224–28, 235–38, 276–78; as a
term, 3, 243–44, 283, 337–39, 378n46
Rodchenko, Aleksandr, 124
Rodnykh, A. A. (Aleksandr), 228
Roger, Noelle, 212
Rollier, Auguste, 197
Rosny, J. H., 35, 173, 235
Roy, Maurice, 233
Rudaux, Lucien, 313
Russian Revolution, 9–11, 22–23, 27, 57, 77,
157, 174, 180, 184, 195, 314–16; first (1905),
39, *40*, 41, 77, 90; second (October 1917),
6, 68, 101, 105–33, *112, 120, 122, 123*, 163–64,
167, 169, 184–89, 221, 294, 330, 338, 347
Rynin, N. A. (Nikolai): early writings of,
98, 134, 158; later writings of, 248, 280–81,
283, 330, 348–49; as Soviet publicist, 105–
6, 136, 148, 206, 317

Sagan, Carl, 350, 352, 416n47
Sänger, Eugen, 233, 248, 282
Saturn, 35, 110, 124, 151, 164
Scheerbart, Paul, 89–90, 358n50, 368n62
Schmiedl, Fritz, 223
Science Review, 73, 76
Scientific American, 53, 56, 137, *138*, 222, 255,
271, 286
Semenov, Vladimir, 37
Serviss, Garrett, 36
Sharonov, V. V., 203
Sheldon, H. H., 243
Shershevskii, A. B. (Aleksandr), 224, 226–
29, 283, 289, 393n22
Shmidt. P. Iu., 51–52
shooting star, 66, 100, *123, 156, 300*
Shor, G. V., 210–11
Shtamer, Frederick, 222
Shtern, A. N., 251

Shternfel'd, A. A. (Ari), 235–36, 245, 283,
290, 395n52
Smith, A. M. O., 246
Smith, Hélène, 58
Smithsonian Institution, 141–42, 147, 247–
48, 278, 299, *320*
socialist realism, 293, 306, 317, 329, 339
Society for Space Travel (Verein), 223–31,
238, 243, 252, 284
Society for the Study of Interplanetary
Travel (OIMS), 152–62, *156*, 177, 203, 215,
227, 250, 288
Society of Inventors, 279, 298
Society to Assist the Defense and Aviation-
Chemical Industries of the USSR. *See*
Osoaviakhim
Sologub, Fedor, 93–94
Solomin, Sergei, 97
Solzhenitsyn, Alexander, 347–48
spectroscope, 9, 12, 20, 28, 44
Spencer, Herbert, 28, 117
Spengler, Oswald, 136–37, 169–70, 225
spiral, 76, 83; in architecture, 26, 90, 119,
120, 247, *315*, 324, 326; in biology, 309, 313;
dialectical materialism and, 307–8, 314,
408n41; historical progress and, 12, 29, 39,
63, 108, 167, 190, 211; spaceflight and, 94,
166–67, 177, 236, 299
spiritualism, 47, 63, 216, 350
Sputnik, 6–8, 10, 251, 254, 269, 281, 324, 341,
349, 351; and early uses of the term, 65,
213, 342
Stalin, I. V. (Iosif), 168, 183, 198, 210, 256,
261, 263, 306–7, 317, 319, 330, 338, 346–48,
352; and Americanism, 157, 339, 345, 349;
and astronomy, 23–24; aviation and,
281, 322; in competition with the United
States, 157, 248, 321, 341; and cosmonautics, 293–96, 301–6, 321, 333, 342;
evolutionary theory and, 32, 182, 345; and
purges, 286–92; and rockets, 279, 336, *344*;
Walt Whitman and, 91, 305
Stapledon, Olaf, 315–16, 351
State Polytechnic Museum, 95, 152, 158,161,
290
Stechkin, B. M., 153
Steinach, Eugen, 129, 208–10

Stetson, Harlan, 198
Stevens, Albert W., 257, *260*, 263, *267*, 268–71, *270*
Stewart, John Q., 241–42
Strakhov, N. N. (Nikolai), 26–27
stratosphere, 182, 237, 248, 294, 296, 303–4, 309–10, 329; as destination, 137–40, *138*, 145, 205, 222, 255, *310*, 323; and military, 271–87; race to, *249*, 252–72, *253*, *259*, *260*, *265*, *267*, *270*, *285*, *310*, *315*; and rocket pioneers, 151, 223, 225, 229, 233, 253; and scientific conferences, 281–83, 309–10
stratostat. *See* balloon
Stratostat SSSR, 257–61, *259*, *260*, *265*
Stratostat SSSR Encore (bis), *265*, 266
Suess, Edward, 204
sunspots, 194–97
super-artillery, 136, 271
super-aviation, 136, 248, 256, 271, 392n11
suprematism, 87, *88*, *122*, *123*, *124*, *295*
Supremus No. 56, *88*, 294, *295*
Sviatogor, 127–30
Swift, Anthony, 326
Symbolism, 39, 89, 96, 108, 114, 133, 167, 293
Symonds, John Addington, 92, 305

Tatlin, Vladimir, 119–21, *120*
Tesla, Nikola, 54, 60, 274
Texas Centennial Exposition (Dallas, 1936), 318, *320*
thermodynamics, 33–34, 43, 81, 95, 166, 199
Things to Come, 306
Thompson, William, 33, 43
Tikhonravov, M. K., 250, 252, 280–83, 318
Tiling, Reinhold, 222, 232, *249*
Tolstoi, A. N. (Aleksei), 167–72, 174, 183, 196, 211, 216, 274, 302, 344
Tolstoi, Leo, 19–20, 47
Tower of Babel, 56, 119, *120*, 314
Train, Arthur, 100–101, 143, 174
Trotskii, Leon, 6, 116, 139, 288
The Truth (Pravda), 153, 155, 209, 280, 293, 305
Tsander, F. A., 144–45, 159–61, 183, 216, 250–51, 278, 287, 293, 318
Tsien, Hsue-Shen, 246
Tsiolkovskii, K. E. (Konstantin), 113, 144–45, 160–61, 189, 193–96, 199–200, 224–29,

233–35, *300*, *303*, 311, 313, 329, 352; and all-metal dirigible, 68, 161, 300, 304; aviation and, 80, 298; and philosophy, 206, 215–16, 349–50; as pioneer, 11, 47, 67–68, 95–96, 140–42, 147–50, 153–55, 182–83, 248, 256, 258, 281–83, 292, 318, 367n43, 367n47, 378n46; and rocket dirigible, 80–81, 83–84, *85*, *94*, *156*, 161, *162*, 186, 275, 296, *297*; and rocket equation, 72–77; and science fiction, 69–70, 86, 93–94, 99–100, 163–69, 172, 175, 177, 179–80, 210–13, 301–2, *303*; self-image of, 67–68, 364n4; Stalinism and, 296–308, 323, 330–33, 341–47
Tukhachevskii, M. N. (Mikhail), 275–77, 284–91, *285*
Tunguska meteor, 345

Uminski, Wladislaw, 55
Urania, 26
U.S. Army Air Corps, 257, 263–64, 266, 268, 278
Uspenskii, P. D., 89

Valier, Max, 5, 149–51, 215–16, 224, 226, 230, 232, 234, 239, 248, 255, 297, 303; and cata-pult ramp, 221–22, 303, *304*, 391n2, 407n29
Valiusinskii, V. V., 210
Veigelin, K. E., 78, 83
Veinberg, B. P., 111, 203
Velikovsky, Immanuel, 316–17
Venus, 25, 126, 187, 192, 236, 240, 254, 317; in science fiction, 59, 63–64, 75–76, 97–98, 301, 338, 342, 383n32; travel to, 82–83, 150–51, 183, 236
Verein fur Raumschiffart. See Society for Space Travel (Verein)
Vernadskii, V. I., 47, 187, 204–6, 309
Verne, Jules, 12–13, 15, 34, 71, 83, 99, 163, 244, 319, 329
vertical ascent, 74, 137, 200, 225, 250, 352
Vertov, Dziga, 294
Vetchinkin, V. P., 153, 281
Victor (Pobeditel'), 186
vitalism, 30, 33, 51–52, 205, 206
Vladko, Vladimir, 301
Volkov, M. V., 175, 177
Volta Conference on High Altitude Velocity in Aviation (1935), 282